THE TRA
IBN JUBAYR

THE TRAVELS OF
IBN JUBAYR

Being the chronicle of a mediaeval Spanish Moor concerning his
journey to the Egypt of Saladin, the holy cities of Arabia, Baghdad
the City of the Caliphs, the Latin Kingdom of Jerusalem, and the
Norman Kingdom of Sicily.

Translated from the original Arabic

By

R. J. C. BROADHURST

With an Introduction and Notes

First published in London 1952
First published by Goodword Books 2001
© Goodword Books 2001

Distributed by
GOODWORD BOOKS
1, Nizamuddin West Market,
New Delhi 110 013
Tel. 462 5454, 461 1128
Fax 469 7333, 464 7980
e-mail: skhan@vsnl.com
website: http://www.alrisala.org

Printed in India

To

SIR JOHN TRESIDER SHEPPARD, PROVOST,

and to the Fellows

of King's College, Cambridge,

in gratitude and esteem

Preface

THE undertaking of this work was prompted by Mr. Arthur Hibbert, Fellow of King's College, Cambridge, whose interests, ranging far beyond the confines of his field of mediaeval studies, first led me to the study of Ibn Jubayr, and whose enthusiasm encouraged me to attempt this translation. But this is only one of my many debts to that College and to its Provost, Sir John Sheppard, without whose broad and enlightened sympathies I should never have shared of its privileges. I am honoured that he and the Fellows should condescend to accept the dedication of this book.

To Professor A. J. Arberry, the Sir Thomas Adams's Professor of Arabic at the University of Cambridge, I owe the deepest gratitude, not only for teaching me most of what I know of Oriental scholarship, but for guidance and help in this particular work. In the midst of his monumental labours he was always ready, indeed eager, to give me of his massive erudition. I must also record my indebtedness to Professor A. W. Lawrence of Cambridge University and Professor H. A. R. Gibb of Oxford University for valuable advice and encouragement, and my thanks to Mr. A. J. Scholfield, Mr. J. Pearson, and Mr. S. Naish of the Cambridge University Library, to Mr. S. C. Sutton of the India Office Library, and to Dr. J. Leveen of the British Museum, for the liberal library facilities and personal help they gave me. Mr. A. S. Nashar of Alexandria University allowed me to draw on his ever surprising familiarity with the literature and history of the Arabs, and Mr. Muhammad Salim of Nablus, Palestine, and Mr. Robert Serjeant of London University illumined many obscurities. Mr. Steven Runciman brought his learning to a reading of my notes on Crusader Syria and saved me from serious error. To my wife I owe the undisturbed ease and abstraction I needed for my task. And I would be failing in gratitude if I did not attest my obligation to my publisher, Mr. Jonathan Cape, whose interest in things Arabian, extending from the works of Doughty and Lawrence to that of King Abdulla, has now embraced my humbler contribution.

As for the Arabs themselves, who have given me the keenest pleasures and interests of my life, I can only hope that I have helped to unveil some portion of their long and fabulous history.

R. J. C. BROADHURST.

BELVEDERE,
BALLYAUGHLIS,
Co. DOWN,
NORTHERN IRELAND.
December, 1951.

Contents

	PAGE
Preface	7
Itinerary	11
Introduction	15
The Chronicle, divided into Monthly Records of Events and Places Visited, as shown in the Itinerary . .	23
Notes	367
Glossary of Technical and Arabic Words . . .	391
Index of Persons	401
Index of Places	415
Western Forms of Names Occurring in the Text .	429

Maps

Showing the Itinerary of Ibn Jubayr

Western Half . . . . . . *facing p.*	25
Eastern Half	31

The Itinerary

PAGE

4th of February–27th of March, 1183 . . . 25
Granada, Jaen, Alcaudete, Cabra, Ecija, Osuna, Jeliver, Arcos, Casma, Tarifa, Alcazar, Ceuta, off the Spanish coast, by the islands of Iviza, Majorca, and Minorca to Cape St. Mark in Sardinia. Thence past Sicily and Crete to Alexandria.

28th of March–25th of April, 1183 31
Alexandria, Damanhur, Sa, Birmah, Tandatah, Subk, Malij, Qalyub, Munyah, Dajwah, Cairo, Misr.

26th of April–25th of May, 1183 50
Askun, Munyat ibn al-Khasib, Ansina, Jabal al-Maqlah, Manfalut, Usyut, Abu Tij, Ikhmim, Manshat al-Sudan, al-Bunyanah, Dashnah, Dandarah, Qina, Qift, Qus.

26th of May–23rd of June, 1183 59
al-Hajir, Qila' al-Diya', Mahatt al-Laqitah, al-'Abdayn, Dinqash, Shaghib, Amtan, Mujaj.

24th of June–23rd of July, 1183 63
al-'Ushara', al-Khubayb, 'Aydhab, the Red Sea, the island 'Ayqat al-Sufun.

24th of July–21st of August, 1183 . . . 69
Ubhur, Jiddah, al-Qurayn, Mecca.

22nd of August–20th of September, 1183 . . . 77
Mecca.

21st of September–19th of October, 1183 . . . 122
Mecca.

20th of October–18th of November, 1183 . . . 127
Mecca.

19th of November–17th of December, 1183 . . 140
Mecca.

18th of December, 1183–16th of January, 1184 . . 145
Mecca.

17th of January–14th of February, 1184 . . . 158
Mecca.

15th of February–15th of March, 1184 . . . 166
Mecca.

16th of March–13th of April, 1184 172
Mecca, al-Zahir, Batn Marr, 'Usfan, Khulays, Wadi
al-Samk, Badr.

14th of April–13th of May, 1184 196
al-Safra', Dhat al-'Alam (al-Rawha'), Shi'b 'Ali,
Turban, al-Bayda, al-'Aqiq, Dhu 'l-Hulayfah,
Medina, Wadi 'l-'Arus, al-'Usaylah, Nuqrah, al-
Qarura, al-Hajir, Samirah, Jabal al-Mahruq, Wadi
'l-Kurush, Fayd, al-Ajfur, Zarud, al-Tha'labiyah,
Birkat al-Marjum, al-Shuquq, al-Tananir, Zubalah,
al-Haythamayn, 'Aqabat al-Shaytan, Waqisah, Lawzah, al-Qar'a', Manarat al-Qurun, al-'Udhayb, al-
Ruhbah, al-Qadisiyah, al-Najaf, al-Kufah, al-Hillah,
the Euphrates.

14th of May–11th of June, 1184 223
al-Qantarah (Hisn al-Bashir), Zariran, al-Mada'in
(near the palace of Chosroes), Sarsar, Baghdad,
al-Harba, al-Ma'shuq, Samarra, Takrit, al-Judaydah,
al-'Aqr, al-Qayyarah, al-'Uqaybah, Mosul, 'Ain al-
Rasad, al-Muwaylihah, Judal.

12th of June–11th of July, 1184 248
Nasibin (Nisibis), Dunaysar, Tell al-'Uqab, al-Jisr,
Ra's al-'Ain, Burj Hawa, Harran, Tell 'Abdah,
al-Bayda, Qal'at-Najm, Manbij, Buza'ah, Aleppo,
Qinnasrin, Tell Tajir, Baqidin, Tamanni, Hamah,
Hims (Emessa), al-Mash'ar, al-Qarah, al-Nabk,
Khan al-Sultan, Thaniyyat al-'Uqab, al-Qusayr,
Damascus.

12th of July–9th of August, 1184 271
Damascus.

10th of August–8th of September, 1184 . . . 295
Damascus.

9th of September–7th of October, 1184 . . . 313
Damascus, Darayyah, Bayt Jann, Banyas, al-
Masiyah, al-Astil, Tibnin, Acre, al-Zib, Iskanda-
runah (Iscandelion), Sur (Tyre), Acre.

8th of October–6th of November, 1184 . . . 326
Acre, at sea on the Mediterranean.

7th of November–5th of December, 1184 . . . 329
On the Mediterranean, the Greek Archipelago, off
the coast of Crete, within sight of Sicily.

6th of December, 1184–4th of January, 1185 . . 335
Off the Calabrian coast of Italy, in the Straits of
Messina, Messina, Cefalu, Termini, Qasr Sa'd
(Castel Solanto), Palermo, Alcamo, Hisn al-
Hammah, Trapani.

5th of January–2nd of February, 1185 . . . 353
Trapani.

3rd of February–4th of March, 1185 . . . 357
Trapani.

5th of March–3rd of April, 1185 361
Trapani, the island of Favignana, south of Sardinia,
the island of Galita.

4th of April–3rd of May, 1185 364
The island of Iviza, Denia, Cartagena, Murcia,
Lebrilla, Lorca, al-Mansurah, Caniles di Baza,
Guadix, Granada.

Introduction

ONE day in the year A.D. 1182, the Moorish Governor of Granada, then the wealthiest and most splendid city of Spain, summoned his secretary to discharge some business. The incumbent of this post was Abu 'l-Husayn Muhammad ibn Ahmad ibn Jubayr, who, born in 1145 to a good family in Valencia,* had by his learning and character attained this office of trust. On arrival before his master, he had been offered a cup of wine, but the continent clerk, a sincere Muslim who emulated the temperance of his prophet, had pleaded that never before had his lips touched strong drink. The unregenerate prince, wishful of repairing this strange neglect, and with tones and gestures that allowed of no dispute, had thereupon cried: 'Seven cups, by Allah, shalt thou drink'; and the trembling scholar, his apprehensions of the wrath to come obscured by present terrors, had been fain to swallow the forbidden draughts. Yet no sooner had he done so than the prince was seized with sudden pity, and in remorse had seven times filled the cup with golden dinars and poured them into the bosom of his servant's gown.

The good man, who long had cherished the wish to discharge the duty of the pilgrimage to Mecca, at once determined to expiate his godless act by devoting the money to this end. So, seeking and obtaining his master's leave, he took up the pilgrim staff and, on the 3rd of February, 1183, accompanied by Abu Ja'far Ahmad ibn Hassan, a physician of Granada,

* He was descended from 'Abd al-Salam ibn Jubayr who, coming from the tribe of Kinanah near Mecca, had entered Spain with the army sent in A.D. 740 by the Caliph of Damascus under the general Balj ibn Bishr al-Qushayri to quell the Berber insurrection in his Spanish provinces. At the time of our diarist, the Berber dynasty of the Almohades had established themselves as the independent rulers of Muslim Spain, and it was one of their princes, Abu Sa'id 'Uthman ibn 'Abd al-Mu'min, who was his master and the Governor of Granada.

departed on his way. And in this chronicle, which he recorded daily, or at least frequently and while his impressions were still fresh, we may read of the strange events and places, and the notable people and customs, that he observed upon the mediaeval eastern scene before, on the 25th of April, 1185, he returned to his native Spain.

Embarking on a Genoese ship, he came to Egypt where, recounting his impressions of the ancient wonders that are but now unfolding their meaning, he pondered the splendid edifices and the salutary reforms prescribed by the munificence and the piety of Saladin, the rising champion of the East. He ascended the Nile, and describes the great temples of the Pharaohs now in ruin, at which 'the beholder might conceive that all time spent on their adornment would be too short'. From the Nile he journeyed in a camel caravan to the Red Sea, there to embark in a fragile craft for the Hejaz and, being delivered from the perils both of the waterless desert and a reef-set sea, arrive at the Holy Cities of Arabia. With precise and reverent detail he describes the Great Mosque of Mecca and its holy of holies, the Ka'bah, and then unfolds the unchanging pilgrim rites that, then and to-day, Muslims from all quarters of the earth must seek, if they have the means, at least once in a life-time to discharge.

The pilgrim then moved north to visit the tomb of the prophet Muhammad in Medina, which done, he turned eastward and, joining the long and motley caravan of pilgrims returning to Iraq and Turkestan, the sister of the caravan from Damascus described to us in the deathless pages of Doughty, he portrays its slow and ordered march across the deserts of Arabia to Baghdad, the City of the Caliphs, where lingered still the glories of Harun al-Rashid. He sees the reigning caliph, Nasir, 'the lustre of whose reign consists only in pages and negro eunuchs' and who, seeking to throw off the yoke of the fierce and illiberal Turk, once mercenaries and now masters, most foolishly invoked the aid of Jengis Khan; for the heathen hordes of Tartary, riding fleet horses and drawing strange bows, were soon to extinguish his dynasty, massacre the citizens, and, breaking the splendid irrigatory canals our traveller admires, reduce a fruitful countryside to a horrid waste.

The armed company of some Turkish princesses gave him protection for his passage along the Euphrates and through such ancient cities as Mosul and Nineveh until, coming to northern Syria, he descended through Aleppo to Damascus. This jewel of the East he depicts as it was a hundred years before the invasion of the Mongols, and the Great or Umayyad Mosque that is still to-day one of its glories he describes as it was before the pillage of Timurlane.

Weary now for home, our pilgrim set forth for Acre in the Crusader kingdom of Jerusalem that he might there take ship to Spain. And here we come upon the strange anomaly of those days. At a time when the kingdom is at war with the Muslims and when our diarist has even witnessed, as he left Damascus, the triumphant return of the army of Saladin, laden with booty and leading many Christian prisoners, he yet can journey to this Christian stronghold in a caravan of Muslim merchants.

This Latin kingdom, founded some eighty years before by the warriors of the First Crusade, had endured only because it was united amidst the discord and dissension of the Saracens. To the north, the contending Arab princes and Seljuk dynasts, being orthodox Sunni Muslims, acknowledged as Commander of the Faithful the elected Caliph of Baghdad. But to the south, Egypt and its large provinces was ruled by the Fatimids, who as Shi'ites believed the caliphate to be a God-given office inherent in their family as descendants of 'Ali, the husband of the prophet Muhammad's daughter Fatimah, from whom they took their name.

It was the role and achievement of Saladin to unite Islam. As lieutenant of the Seljuk prince Nur al-Din ibn Zengi, who had combined the Muslim states of Syria, he had gone south and removed the heretic caliph of Egypt. On the death of Nur al-Din he had taken his suzerain's possessions; and from the Caliph of Baghdad he had condescended to ask, and the puppet

B

Caliph had been flattered to grant, a patent of rule for Egypt and Syria and their dependent provinces. The eastern Muslim world was now one; the Frankish kingdom was enveloped, and its death-knell had sounded.

If the opponents of the Cross were at last united, all within the Christian realm was anarchy and alarm. King Baldwin IV was a dying leper, and as with the Greek princes before Troy, there was treachery and strife among the chiefs. Into their midst the pilgrim was allowed to ride without let or hap; and from the critical viewpoint of a scholarly Muslim we may observe afresh the customs and manners of the champions of the Cross.

At Acre he embarked with fifty other Muslims on a Genoese ship sailing west with two thousand Christian pilgrims from Jerusalem, and after much tribulation and peril on the sea was shipwrecked upon the shores of Sicily. And here he must have perished but for the timely arrival of the island's ruler, King William II, fourth of a line of brilliant pirates, the famous house of Hauteville which, driven by the old Norse wanderlust from their father's petty seigneury in Normandy, had won a kingdom under a blue sky.

From the Arabs they had taken Sicily, and the author records with pride the persisting art of the Arab craftsmen and husbandmen. High officers of the court, highly favoured ladies, and privileged eunuchs discovered to him their secret cleaving to the faith of Islam; and he studied the court, cities, and customs of this fabulous kingdom, where, without laying aside their dauntless valour and virile energy, the Normans, with their quick brilliance, love of magnificence, and receptive genius for acquiring what was polished and polite of the civilisations their long lances had subdued, took all, and more than all, the Eastern refinements that they found and brought to a full fruition a glorious blend of Arab-Norman art and culture. 'Amongst the orange groves of Palermo the descendant of the Vikings sat upon his throne, robed in the dalmatic of the apostolic legate and the imperial costume of Byzantium, his ministers part Greek, part English, his army composed as to half of Moors, his fleet officered by Greeks, himself a Latin Christian, but, in that balmy climate of the south, ruling in half-Byzantine, half-oriental state, with a harem and eunuchs.'* At Sicily our traveller took ship for home, whither he came without further mishap, and with a heart full of gratitude for the beneficence of Almighty God.

Throughout his journey indeed, he walked with God, and his constant supplications to his Maker when in distress and danger, and his just and ready praise and thanks for His mercies and blessings, keep us ever mindful that he is a man of piety in a community that is above all a religious community. For to its faith, Islam (Arabic, 'Submission' to the will of God), it owed its beginning and existence, its laws, social system, and code of values; and to Islam it owed its common language, Arabic, the language of the Koran. In this, the sacred scripture of Islam, communicated as Muslims believe by the Creator to His prophet Muhammad, the power, unity, and goodness of God are pronounced. Five duties are laid on all believers: (i) the profession of faith, 'There is no God but God'; (ii) the performance of divine worship five times a day; (iii) the fast between sunset and sunrise throughout the month of Ramadan; (iv) the payment of legal alms; and (v) the pilgrimage to Mecca, birthplace of Muhammad and the holy city of Islam. And all these duties we watch our pilgrim discharge.

To all his story, with its abundance of detail and interest, he brings a perspicacity and soundness of judgement, a precision and vividness of descriptive power (as in his picture of mediaeval sea-travel and the terrors of shipwreck), that may, perhaps, be expected in a scholar and writer of his repute; but in his balanced comments on Crusader Syria and Norman Sicily, despite the perfunctory malisons that by convention he must pronounce upon the Christian enemy, I can discern a moderation most rare in that fanatic age. And his portraits of these Christian outposts, otherwise mostly known to us from strongly

* H. A. L. Fisher, A History of Europe, p. 190.

biased Western and clerical sources, are for this reason most revealing and instructive.

We may further judge his merit and integrity by the comments of the historian Lisan al-Din ibn al-Khatib (A.D. 1313–74), who, in his *Kitab al-Ihatah fi akhbar Ghranata* ['Story of Granada'] describes him as a man 'clear in doctrine, and an illustrious poet distinguished above all others, sound in reason, generous-spirited, and of noble character and exemplary conduct. He was a man of remarkable goodness, and his piety confirms the truth of his works. . . . His correspondence with contemporary scholars reveals his merits and excellence, his superiority in poetry, his originality in rhymed prose, and his ease and elegance in free prose. His reputation was immense, his good deeds many, and his fame widespread; and the incomparable story of his journey is everywhere related. God's mercy upon him.'

The high literary reputation that Ibn Jubayr achieved among the Arabs was partly due to his poetical works, two of the best of those preserved being one composed on his first approach to Medina, and another addressed to Saladin concerning the vexatious imposts levied on pilgrims to Mecca on landing in Egypt, but in the main it was based on this chronicle which he published soon after his return to Spain.

The style of this chronicle, as indicated by Lisan al-Din, is, for the most, of an easy and elegant free prose to which the Arabic tongue so happily lends itself. For the benefit of scholars, historians, and students of Arabic it has been my purpose to give as literal a translation as possible, abiding faithfully by the words, arrangement, and even imagery of the author. But it is beyond the resources of our tongue to reproduce the enchanting rhythm of the frequent pieces of rhymed prose, the play upon words, assonances, and paronomasia of the Arabic, and here the translator must fail his author and, to his keen regret, his readers.

The text I have used is that edited by W. Wright in 1852 and revised by M. J. de Goeje in 1907, from a manuscript preserved in the University of Leyden. The emendations of these scholars, and their fillings of lacunae in the text by relevant extracts and quotations from other Arab authors, I have accepted almost in toto but have not indicated in my notes, since they are not wanted by the general reader and to scholars are accessible in Wright's edition, where also will be found, in the Preface, details concerning the MS. and the method by which it was edited. By a happy chance, a reprint of this edition, for some time unobtainable, has just been published by the Gibb Memorial Trust, and it is my hope that not only will the advanced student of Arabic find the study of my rendering a profitable and rewarding exercise, but that the beginner will be spurred by it to still greater efforts to read the author in his native tongue.

The excellent, so far as I can judge, Italian translation by Schiaparelli has saved me much drudgery of research for geographical, chronological, and other equivalents, and his notes, which I everywhere acknowledge, I have found most useful. And if, when checking with it those froward passages that had caused me much turning of lexicons, I sometimes found him nodding, I also often found therein a pleasant confirmation and, I gratefully confess, at times a guiding beam. This tribute I cannot extend to the Frenchman M. Amari's work (*Journal asiatique*, 1845–6), where, dealing only with the Sicilian journey, he yet is all too often errant. The few sentences translated by Burton for relevant passages in his *Pilgrimage to al-Madinah and Meccah* I found to be uniformly inexact.

The notes, I fear, are copious and sometimes long, and this is due to the need for providing both such annotations of a technical character that scholars will require and those directed to the polite layman; for it is my hope that this work, apart from academic value, will be some contribution towards the quickening and development of the already growing interest and sympathy of my countrymen in the resurgent Arab and Islamic world.

In transliteration I have followed the orthodox system, save that printers' difficulties have dictated the dropping of diacritical points and macrons, and that with some well-known names I have adopted a latitudinarian practice. My short explanatory or corrective comments in the body of the text are placed between rectangular brackets. Parenthesis signs are used to denote those words which, although not specifically mentioned by the author, are nevertheless needed to complete the meaning, or to secure the balance or euphony that otherwise would be wanting in an English sentence. Where there are lacunae in the text, and the missing words have not been supplied from other Arab writers, a row of asterisks implies the omission. Dashes are employed to isolate the many pious ejaculations which might tire some readers, but whose exclusion would not only destroy my aim of faithfully rendering each word the traveller has recorded, but would also, to my thinking, rob the book of some of its special ethos. A glossary explains the Arabic or technical words that, in the translation, are usually indicated in italics.

Nothing now remains but to make an end and come to my account with all my imperfections on my head. For I cannot but be sensible that, despite my pains and labour, since industry must supply the want of parts, my work is full of infelicities and shortcomings. To try to render with exactness the spirit, style, and import of this Moor, and yet retain the freshness of original composition, has stretched me to the full. And if I cannot dissemble my satisfaction at ending my task, neither can I conceal my sadness in parting from a gentle companion with whom, from the rustic seclusion of an Irish study, I have travelled again under Eastern skies and listened once more to the voices of Arabs in prayer and disputation.

And so I stand aside and, begging you piece out our imperfections with your thoughts, commend him to your hearing.

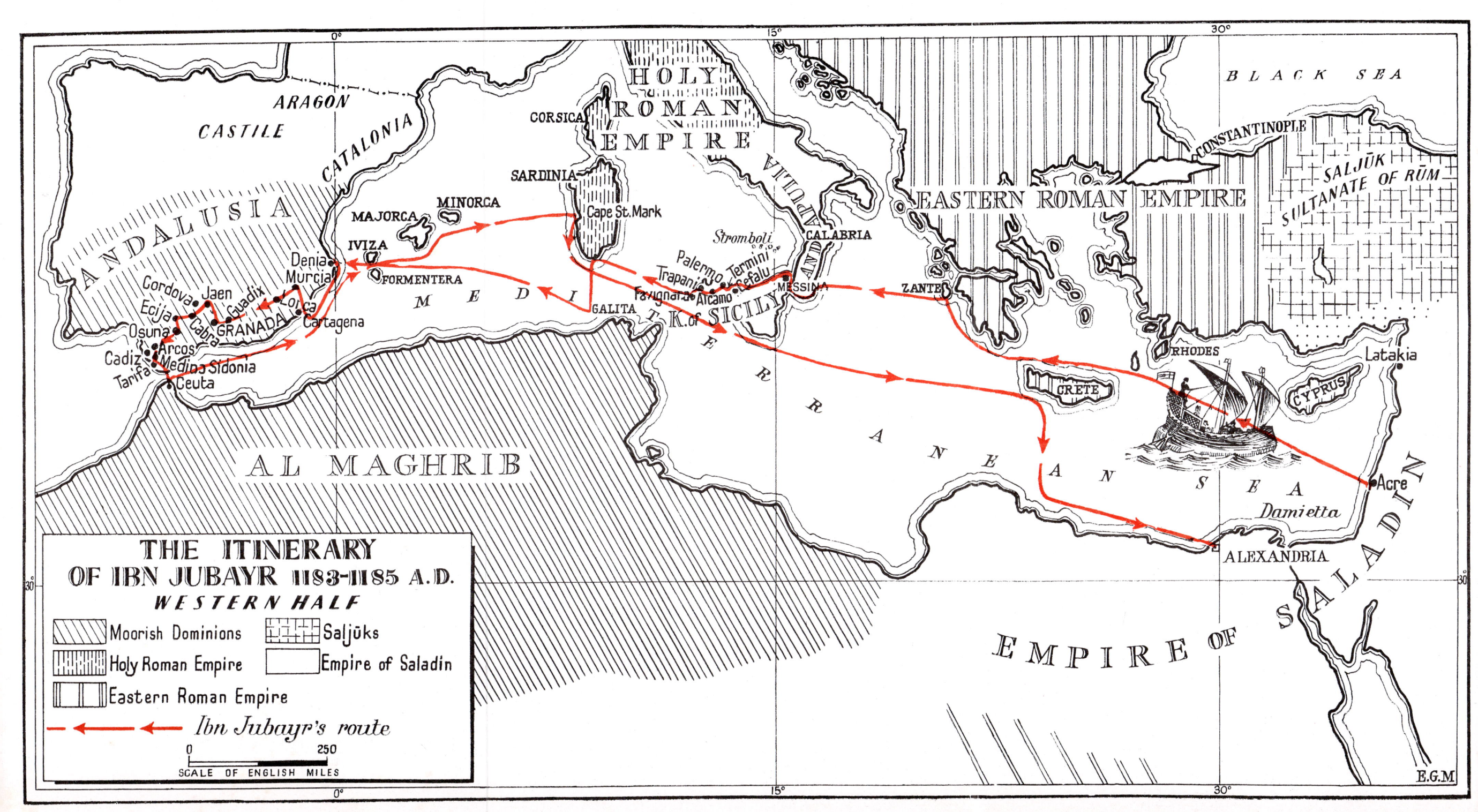

BLACK SEA

CASTILE

ARAGON

CATALONIA

CORSICA

HOLY
ROMAN
EMPIRE

SARDINIA

Cape St.Mark

CONSTANTINOPLE

EASTERN ROMAN EMPIRE

SALJŪK
SULTANATE OF RŪM

ANDALUSIA

MAJORCA

MINORCA

IVIZA

Denia
Murcia

FORMENTERA

Cordova   Jaen
Ecija   Cabra   Guadix
Osuna   GRANADA   Lorca
Arcos   Cartagena
Cadiz   Medina Sidonia
Tarifa   Ceuta

MEDI

Stromboli

Palermo   Termini
Trapani   Cefalu
Favignana   Alcamo

Messina

CALABRIA

APULIA

GALITA

K. of SICILY

ZANTE

RHODES

Latakia

CRETE

CYPRUS

AL MAGHRIB

MEDITERRANEAN SEA

Acre

Damietta

ALEXANDRIA

EMPIRE OF   SALADIN

THE ITINERARY
OF IBN JUBAYR 1183-1185 A.D.
WESTERN HALF

Moorish Dominions   Saljūks
Holy Roman Empire   Empire of Saladin
Eastern Roman Empire

Ibn Jubayr's route

0   250

SCALE OF ENGLISH MILES

E.G.M

THE TRAVELS OF IBN JUBAYR

In the name of God, The Merciful, the Compassionate;
bless and preserve our Lord Muhammad, His Kindred,
and his Companions

An Account of the Events that Befell upon Certain Journeys

The writing of this chronicle was begun on Friday
the 30th of the month of Shawwal, 578 (A.H.)[1]
[25th of February, 1183] at sea, opposite Jabal Shulayr
[Sierra Nevada]

may God with His favour grant us safety

[8th of Shawwal to the end of the month of Dhu
'l-Qa'dah 578=4th of February to the 27th of March,
1183.]

AHMAD IBN HASSAN and Muhammad ibn Jubayr left
Granada – may God preserve it – on their pilgrimage to
the blessed Hejaz – may God give easement and help and reveal
His beneficent works – at the first hour of Thursday[2] the 8th
of Shawwal 578 (A.H.), which fell, according to the foreigners
[i.e. non-Arabs] on the 3rd of February (1183).

We passed through Jayyan [Jaen] that we might despatch
some business, and left it at the first hour of Monday the 19th
of the month of Shawwal, being the 14th of February. Our
first stage from there was to the fortress of al-Qabdhaq[3] [Alcau-
dete]. Thence we moved to the fortress of Qabrah [Cabra],
to the city of Istijah [Ecija], to the fortress of Ushunah [Osuna],
to Shallabar [Jeliver], to the fortress of Arkush [Arcos], to the
burgh known as the Burgh of Qashmah[4] [Casma] which is
a burgh belonging to Madinat Ibn al-Salim [Medina Sidonia],
and then to the island of Tarif [Tarifa] which we reached on
Monday the 26th of the month (of Shawwal). At midday on
Tuesday the (twenty) second (of February) God granted us

an easy crossing of the sea to Qasr Masmudah [Alcazar].
Praise be to God.

On the morning of Wednesday the 28th of the month, we
removed to Sabtah [Ceuta] where we found a Rumi[5] Genoese
ship about to sail to al-Iskandariyah [Alexandria] by the power
of Great and Glorious God, and with His help we embarked;
and at midday on Thursday the 29th of the month, or the 24th
of February, we set sail with the power and help of God Most
High. There is no God but He.

Our course lay along the Andalusian coast, but this we left
on Thursday the 6th of Dhu 'l-Qa'dah [3rd of March] when
we were opposite Daniyah [Denia]. The morning of Friday
the 7th of the month we were off the island of Yabisah [Iviza],
on Saturday the island of Majorca, and on Sunday we were
off Minorca. From Ceuta to Minorca is eight *majari*; a *majra*
being one hundred miles.[6] We left the coast of this island, and
early on the night of Tuesday the 11th of the month, being
the 8th of March, the coast of the island of Sardinia all at once
appeared before us about a mile or less away. Between the
islands of Sardinia and Minorca lie about four hundred miles.
It had been a crossing remarkable for its speed.

That night there fell upon us from shoreward a mighty
storm with a wind which God Most High released at the time
we met the land, but from which He preserved and delivered
us. Praise be to Him for that. On the morning of Tuesday
a tempest rose and the sea raged, so that we remained hover-
ing off the coast of Sardinia until Wednesday. As we lay in
this parlous plight, with all directions locked by the storm and
being unable to distinguish the east from the west, God revealed
to us a Rumi ship approaching. When it was beside us, we
asked whither it was going and were told that it was bound
for the island of Sicily and had come from Cartagena in the
province of Murcia. Without our knowledge, we had been
sailing before this ship on its course; and thereupon we took
to following in its wake. God is the Disposer of all things,
there is no God but He.

There then rose before us a promontory of Sardinia, but we drew away and approached afresh so that we arrived at another promontory off that coast, called Qusmarkah[7] [Cape St. Mark at the north of the Gulf of Oristano], an anchorage well-known to mariners. There, at noon on Wednesday, we anchored, together with the other ship. In this place there are the remains of an ancient building which was described to us as once having been a Jewish habitation. We sailed thence at midday on Sunday the 16th of the month. During our stay in the harbour, we had renewed our supplies of water, wood, and victuals. A Muslim who knew the Rumi tongue had gone down with a party of Rum to the nearest inhabited parts, and we learnt that he had seen a group of Muslim prisoners, about eighty between men and women, being sold in the market. The enemy – may God destroy them – had just returned with them from the sea-coasts of Muslim countries. May God's mercy overtake them. On Friday, the third day after we had anchored there, the lord of the island came to the harbour with a group of cavaliers. The leading Rum in the ship went down and met him, staying long with him before they left and he departed to his dwelling.

We left the other ship at its moorings, some of her people being absent in the town, when a favourable wind arose on the night of Tuesday the 18th of Dhu 'l-Qa'dah, the 15th of March; and in the last quarter of the night, we parted from the coast of Sardinia. It has a long coast, and we had sailed beside it for about two hundred miles. The complete circuit of the island, as we were told, is more than five hundred miles. God smoothed our way and delivered us from its seas; for they are the most perilous of the journey and at most times cannot be traversed. For this may God be praised.

Early on the night of Wednesday the wind blew with violence upon us, throwing the sea into turmoil and bringing rain and driving it with such force that it was like a shower of arrows. The affair became serious and our distress increased. Waves like mountains came upon us from every side. Thus we passed the night, filled with despair, but hoping yet for relief in the morning to lighten something of what had fallen on us. But day came, it was Wednesday the 19th of Dhu 'l-Qa'dah, with increasing dread and anguish. The sea raged more, the horizon blackened, and the wind and rain rose to a tumult so that the sails of the ship could not withstand it and recourse was had to the small sails. The wind caught one of these and tore it, and broke the spar to which the sails are fixed and which they call the *qariyah* [from the Gr. Χεραια, 'a mast']. Despair then overcame our spirits and the hands of the Muslims were raised in supplication to Great and Glorious God. We remained in this state all that day, and only when night had fallen did there come some abatement, so that we moved throughout it with great speed under bare masts, and came that day opposite the island of Sicily.

We spent that night, the night of Thursday, wavering between hope and despair, but with the break of day, God spread His mercy so that the clouds dispersed, the wind abated, the sun shone and the sea was calmed. Men rejoiced, conviviality returned, and despair departed. Praise be to God who showed us the greatness of His power and restored us with His gracious mercy and bounteous compassion. Praise in requital for His grace and favour.

On that morning of Thursday the coast of Sicily appeared to us. We had already passed the greater part of it, and but little remained. Rumi sea-captains who were present, and Muslims who had gone through journeys and storms at sea, all agreed that they had never in their lives seen such a tempest. The description of it diminishes the reality.

Between the coasts of Sardinia and Sicily lie about four hundred miles. We moved along the coast of Sicily for more than two hundred miles, and then went back and forth beside it, for the wind had fallen. On the afternoon of Friday the 21st of the month, we sailed from the place where we had anchored, and early that night we parted from the land. By Saturday morning we were far distant from it. There then appeared to us the mountain which has the volcano. It is a huge mountain, rising into the skies and clothed in snow. We were told that in fine weather it can be seen across the sea for more than a hundred miles.

We now took to the main sea. The nearest land we hoped to meet was the island of Aqritish [Crete]. It is a Rumi island, owing allegiance to the ruler of Constantinople, and between it and Sicily lie seven hundred miles. God by His grace is the Guarantor of help and easement. The length of this island of Crete is about three hundred miles. On the night of Tuesday the 25th of the month (of Dhu 'l-Qa'dah), the 22nd of March, according to reckoning we were moving along its coast, but we could not see it. In the morning we parted from it, aiming for our destination. Between this island and Alexandria lie six hundred miles or thereabouts. And on the morning of Wednesday the 26th there appeared the mainland connected with Alexandria, and which is known as Barr al-Gharb[8] [Land of the West]. We sailed along it to a place called, we were told, Jaza'ir al-Hamam [The Islands of the Doves].[9] We were also told that between this place and Alexandria lie about four hundred miles. We sailed on with this coast to our right.

On the morning of Saturday the 29th of the month, God gave us the good news of our safety with the appearance of the lighthouse of Alexandria some twenty miles away. Praise be to God for that; praise due for the abundance of His favour and generous works. At the end of the fifth hour of that day we anchored in the harbour of the town, and then went down to the shore. To God we shall call for help, by His grace, in what remains (of our journey). Thirty days we had been at sea, and we had gone ashore on the 31st, for we had embarked on Thursday the 29th of Shawwal and disembarked on Saturday the 29th of Dhu 'l-Qa'dah, the 26th of March. Praise be to God for the help and easement He bestowed. And Him, exalted is He, we petition to complete His benefactions in bringing us to our longed-for aim, and speedily restoring us, happily and in health, to our native land. He indeed is the Benefactor. There is no God but He.

For lodging we stayed at an inn[10] known as the Inn of the Coppersmiths near to the soap-works.

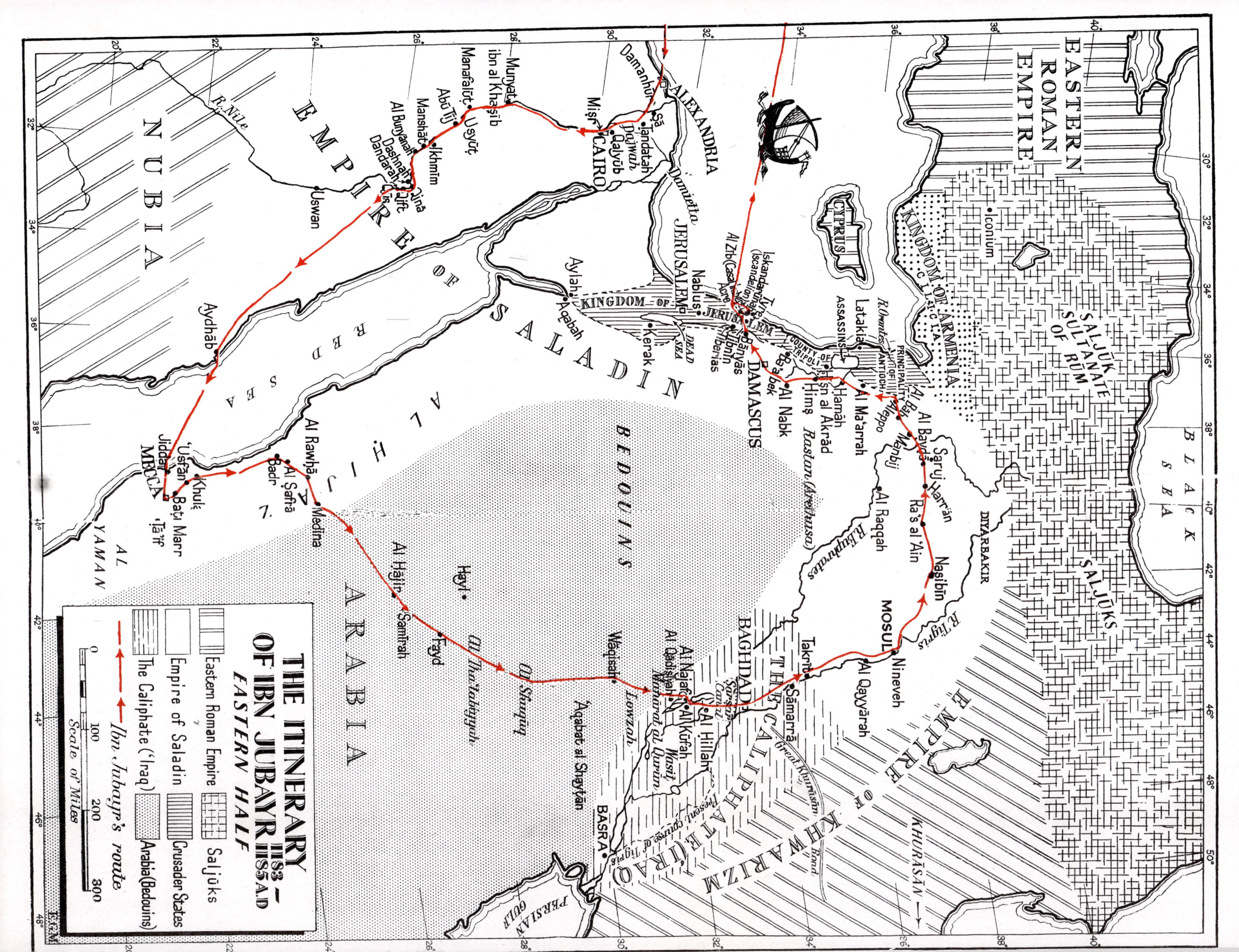

THE ITINERARY
OF IBN JUBAYR 1183—
1185 A.D.
EASTERN HALF

Scale of Miles
0
100
200
300

Ibn Jubayr's route

The Caliphate ('Iraq)
Empire of Saladin
Eastern Roman Empire

Eastern Roman Empire
Saljūks
Crusader States
Arabia (Bedouins)

EASTERN
ROMAN
EMPIRE

NUBIA

EMPIRE

R. Nile

Damanhūr
Sā
Tandatah
Dajwah
Qalyūb
CAIRO
Misr

ALEXANDRIA

Damietta

Munyat
ibn al Khaṣīb
Manafalūṭ
Abū Tīj
Manshāt
Usyūṭ
Al Bunyanah
Dashnah
Qūṣ
Dandarah
Qina
Khmim
Qifṭ

Uswan

Aydhāb

RED SEA

EMPIRE OF SALADIN

AL ḤIJĀZ

Aylah
Aqabah
Kerak

DEAD SEA

JERUSALEM
Nablus
Acre
Tiberias
KINGDOM OF JERUSALEM

Tyre
Iskandarūnah
(Scandelion)
Al Zīb (Casal-
Imbert)
Banyās

DAMASCUS
Al Nabk
Baalbek

COUNTY OF TRIPOLI

Latakia
ASSASSINS
Ḥiṣn al Akrād
Ḥamāh
Rastan (Arethusa)
Ḥimṣ

PRINCIPALITY OF ANTIOCH

Al Ma'arrah
Aleppo

R. Orontes

Manbij
Al Bāb
Al Bayḍ

Saruj
Ra's al 'Ain
Ḥarrān

Al Raqqah

MOSUL
Nineveh
Al Qayyārah

Nasībīn

DIYARBAKIR

R. Tigris

R. Euphrates

KINGDOM OF ARMENIA
c. 1151 c.

CYPRUS

SALJŪK
SULTANATE
OF RŪM

Iconium

BLACK
SEA

SALJŪKS

MECCA
Jiddah
'Usfān
Baṭn Marr
Khulaiṣ
Badr
Al Ṣafrā
'Ṭā'if

Al Rawhā
Medina

AL
YAMAN

ARABIA

BEDOUIN'S

Al Hājir
Samīrah
Hajī
Fayd

Al Tha'labīyah
Al Shuqūq

Waqiṣah
Aqabat al Shayṭān

BAGHDAD

Al Najaf
Al Qādisiyah
Al Ḥillah
Al Kūfah
Waṣiṭ
Mashārī' al Qurnaḥ

Takrīt
Sāmarrā
Great Khurāsān
Road

THE CALIPHATE ('IRAQ)

EMPIRE OF KHWĀRIZM

KHURĀSĀN

BASRA

Present course of Tigris

PERSIAN GULF

F.C.M.

The Month of Dhu 'l-Hijjah of the Same Year

[28th of March–25th of April, 1183]

THE first day of the month was a Sunday and the day after our arrival in Alexandria. The day of our landing, one of the first things we saw was the coming on board of the agents of the Sultan to record all that had been brought in the ship. All the Muslims in it were brought forward one by one, and their names and descriptions, together with the names of their countries, recorded. Each was questioned as to what merchandise or money he had, that he might pay zakat,[11] without any enquiry as to what portion of it had been in their possession for a complete year and what had not. Most of them were on their way to discharge a religious duty and had nothing but the (bare) provisions for the journey. But they were compelled to pay the zakat without being questioned as to what had been possessed by them for the complete year and what had not.

Ahmad ibn Hassan of our number was called down to be questioned as to the news of the west [i.e. from Spain and North Africa] and as to the ship's cargo. Under watch he was in turn conducted first to the Sultan, then to the Qadi, then to the officials of the Customs, and then to a group of the Sultan's suite, and after being questioned concerning everything, and his statements recorded, he was released.

The Muslims were then ordered to take their belongings, and what remained of their provisions, to the shore, where there were attendants responsible for them and for carrying to the Customs all that they had brought ashore. There they were called one by one, and the possessions of each were produced. The Customs was packed to choking. All their goods, great and small, were searched and confusedly thrown together, while hands were thrust into their waistbands in search of what might be within. The owners were then put to oath whether they had aught else not discovered. During all this, because of the confusion of hands and the excessive throng, many possessions disappeared. After this scene of abasement and shame, for which we pray God to recompense us amply, they [the pilgrims] were allowed to go.

There is no doubt that this is one of the matters concealed from the great Sultan known as Salah al-Din [Saladin]. If he heard of it, from what is related of his justice and leanings to pity, he would end it. But God is sufficient to the Faithful in this unhappy case, and (in the life to come) they will pay the *zakat* with the happiest heart. In the lands of this man [Saladin], we found nothing bad that merits mention save this affair, which was provoked by the officials of the Customs.

A note on some of the features and antiquities of Alexandria

First there is the fine situation of the city, and the spaciousness of its buildings. We have never seen a town with broader streets, or higher structures, or one more ancient and beautiful. Its markets also are magnificent. A remarkable thing about the construction of the city is that the buildings below the ground are like those above it and are even finer and stronger, because the waters of the Nile wind underground beneath the houses and alleyways. The wells are connected, and flow into each other. We observed many marble columns and slabs of height, amplitude, and splendour such as cannot be imagined. You will find in some of its avenues columns that climb up to and choke the skies, and whose purpose and the reason for whose erection none can tell. It was related to us that in ancient times they supported a building reserved for philosophers and the chief men of the day. God knows best, but they seem to be for the purpose of astronomical observations.

One of the greatest wonders that we saw in this city was the lighthouse which Great and Glorious God had erected by the hands of those who were forced to such labour as 'a sign to those who take warning from examining the fate of others' [Koran XV, 75] and as a guide to voyagers, for without it they could not find the true course to Alexandria. It can be seen for more than seventy miles, and is of great antiquity. It is most strongly built in all directions and competes with the skies in height. Description of it falls short, the eyes fail to comprehend it, and words are inadequate, so vast is the spectacle.

We measured one of its four sides and found it to be more then fifty arms' lengths. It is said that in height it is more than one hundred and fifty *qamah* [one *qamah*=a man's height]. Its interior is an awe-inspiring sight in its amplitude, with stairways and entrances and numerous apartments, so that he who penetrates and wanders through its passages may be lost. In short, words fail to give a conception of it. May God not let it cease to be an affirmation of Islam and (for that creed) preserve it. At its summit is a mosque having the qualities of blessedness, for men are blessed by praying therein. On Thursday the 5th of Dhu 'l-Hijjah, we went up to this blessed mosque and prayed in it. We saw such marvels of construction as cannot faithfully be described.

Amongst the glories of this city, and owing in truth to the Sultan, are the colleges[12] and hostels erected there for students and pious men from other lands. There each may find lodging where he might retreat, and a tutor to teach him the branch of learning he desires, and an allowance to cover all his needs. The care of the Sultan for these strangers from afar extends to the assigning of baths in which they may cleanse themselves when they need, to the setting up of a hospital for the treatment of those of them who are sick, and to the appointment of doctors to attend to them. At their disposal are servants charged with ministering to them in the manner prescribed both as regards treatment and sustenance. Persons have also been appointed to it who may visit those of the strangers who are too modest to come to the hospital, and who can thus describe their condition to the doctors, who would then be answerable for their cure. One of the Sultan's most generous acts was the allotting of two loaves daily for each of the Moorish *ibna' al-sabil* [sons of the road],[13] whatever their number; and for the daily distribution he appointed a person he trusted. Every day two thousand loaves or more, according to the lesser or greater number (of beneficiaries), were regularly distributed. (To meet this) there was his own personal *awqaf* [charitable endowments], apart from what he allotted for the purpose from the *zakat al-'ain* [*zakat* on gold and silver]. He was insistent with those in charge of this that when the fixed sums were inadequate, they should draw upon his private purse.

As for his people in this city, they live in the height of ease and comfort. No tax is exacted from them and no revenues accrue to the Sultan himself in this city save the *awqaf*, which are tied and devoted by his order to these purposes, and the tribute of the Jews and Christians. Of the revenues of the *zakat al-'ain* in particular, he receives but three eighths, the other five eighths being for the object described. The Sultan who established these praiseworthy laws and prescribed these generous – although not wholly applied – decrees is Salah al-Din [Saladin] Abu 'l-Muzaffar Yusuf ibn Ayyub. May God bless him with His peace and succour.

One of the strangest things that befell the strangers was that some persons who sought to draw near to the Sultan with advice had declared that the greater number of them received a ration of bread which they did not need as means of sustenance, since they would not have come save with provisions enough. This counsel almost had its effect. But one day, when the Sultan had gone out from the city to make an inspection, he met a group of men who had been cast up from the desert adjoining Tripoli and who were disfigured by hunger and thirst. He asked them about their journey, and enquired what they had with them, and they answered that they were on their way to the Sacred House of God [The Ka'abah in Mecca].

They had come overland (they said) and had suffered the tribulations of the desert. Saladin replied, 'Even if these men, after enduring the pathless desert and sustaining the hardships they encountered, had arrived bringing each his own weight in gold and silver, they should still partake of and not be denied the usage we have adopted for them. I marvel at those who traduce such as these, and who seek to gain our favour by trying to prevent what, in faithfulness to Great and Glorious God, we feel to be our duty.' The memorable acts of the Sultan, his efforts for justice, and his stands in defence of Islamic lands are too numerous to count.

Another of the remarkable features of this city is that people are as active in their affairs at night as they are by day. It has more mosques than any other city if Islam, so much so that men's estimates of their number vary. Some count more, some less, the former reckoning up to twelve thousand, the latter a smaller figure without being precise, although some say eight thousand. There are others who give different figures, but in short they are most numerous, there being four or five in one place and sometimes they even adjoin each other. Each has its own imam with a stipend from the Sultan, and some of them receive monthly five Egyptian dinars which is ten mu'mini;[14] others receive more and some less. This is but one of the great merits of the Sultan amongst others it would take too long to describe, and one of the benefactions too many to count.

We left Alexandria by the grace and help of God Most High on the morning of Sunday the 8th of Dhu 'l-Hijjah, the 3rd of April. Our first stage was to a place called Daman-hur, a walled town in a large plain which extends from Alexandria to Misr. This plain [the delta] is wholly cultivated, and is covered by the Nile when in flood. Right and left are innumerable villages. The next day, Monday, we crossed the Nile at a place called Sa in a ferry boat, and came to a place called Birmah. It is a large village, with a market and all

conveniences. Early on the morning of Tuesday, which was the
Festival of the Sacrifice[15] of the year 578, we shared in the
prayers in a place called Tandatah, a large and populous village, where we observed a vast concourse being addressed by
the preacher in an eloquent and comprehensive discourse. Our
way then took us to a place named Subk, where we passed the
night. That day we had passed a pleasant place called Malij.
All along the road were continuous cultivations and orderly
villages.

Early on Wednesday morning we removed, and came to
the best village we had yet passed through. It is called Qalyub,
and is six miles from Cairo, with fine bazaars and a large congregational mosque, superbly built. After that came Munyah,
also a fine place, and from there we moved to Cairo, the
Sultan's magnificent and extensive city. From there we passed
to Misr [old Cairo] the protected of God, and entered it, following the afternoon prayers, on Wednesday the 11th of Dhu
'l-Hijjah, the 6th of April. May God accord us good fortune
in this city, and complete on our behalf His beneficent works
by bringing us to our longed-for end, and in His power and
strength, depriving us not of help and easement. Verily whatever He wishes He can accomplish.

At daybreak on Wednesday we crossed the other branch of
the Nile, also by ferry boat, at a place called Dajwah. At Misr,
we lodged at the inn of Abu 'l-Thana' in the Lane of the
Lamps beside the mosque of 'Amr ibn al-'As, God's blessings
upon him. Our room was a large one at the door of the inn.

A note on Misr[16] and Cairo and some of their wonderful
monuments

We shall begin by mentioning the monuments and blessed
shrines, which for their beneficence are preserved by Great
and Glorious God. Of such is the great tomb in Cairo in which
is kept the head of Husayn, the son of 'Ali ibn Abi Talib,[17]
may God hold them in favour. It is in a silver casket and over
it has been built a mausoleum so superb as to be beyond

description and beyond the powers of the mind to comprehend. It is covered with various kinds of brocades, and surrounded by white candles that are like large columns; smaller ones are placed, for the most part, in candlesticks of pure silver and of gilt. Silver lamps are hung from it and its whole upper part is encircled with golden spheres like apples, skilfully executed to resemble a garden and holding our eyes in spell by its beauty. There too are various kinds of marble tessellated with coloured mosaics of rare and exquisite workmanship such as one cannot imagine nor come near to describing. The entrance to this garden [mausoleum] is by a mosque like to it in grace and elegance, with walls that are all marble in the style we have just described. To the right and left of the mausoleum are two chambers of exactly the same style and both leading into it. A brocade covering of exquisite workmanship is hung over all.

A strange thing we noticed as we entered this blessed mosque was a stone set in the wall which faces him who enters. It is very black and shining, reflecting the image of a man like a new-polished Indian mirror.

We observed men kissing the blessed tomb, surrounding it, throwing themselves upon it, smoothing with their hands the Kiswah [covering] that was over it, moving round it in a surging throng, calling out invocations, weeping and entreating Glorious God to bless the hallowed dust, and' offering up humble supplications such as would melt the heart and split the hardest flint. A solemn thing it was, and an awe-inspiring sight; God granted that we should share in the blessings of that venerable shrine. This is but a flash, a fragment of its description, only indicating what lies beyond; for it does not behove the wise man to apply himself to its description, since he must find himself incapable and incompetent. To be short, I do not believe that in all existence there is a more superb work or more exquisite and wonderful building. May God in His grace and favour sanctify the noble bones that are within it.

The night of that day we passed in the cemetery known as

al-Qarafah. This also is one of the wonders of the world for the tombs it contains of prophets – God's benedictions upon them – of the kindred of Muhammad – May God hold them in His favour – of his Companions, of the followers[18] of the Companions, of learned men and ascetics, and of saintly men renowned for their miracles and of wonderful report. We shall describe only those we saw ourselves.

There was the tomb of the son of the prophet Salih; that of Rubil ibn Ya'qub ibn Ishaq ibn Ibrahim [Abraham], Khalil al-Rahman [the Friend of God][19] – the blessings of God upon them all; that of Asiyah, wife of Far'aun – may God hold her in His favour; the tombs of the kindred of Muhammad – may God hold them in His favour – being fourteen men and five women. Over each of these is a splendid edifice, all being exquisite monuments of wondrous construction. For their care, persons have been appointed who live in them and receive a monthly stipend. It is indeed a sight to marvel at.

A note on the tombs of the kindred of Muhammad
May God hold them in His favour

The tomb of 'Ali ibn al-Husayn ibn 'Ali – may God hold him in His favour; that of the two sons of Ja'far ibn Muhammad al-Sadiq – may God hold them in His favour; that of al-Qasim ibn Muhammad ibn Ja'far al-Sadiq ibn Muhammad ibn 'Ali Zayn al-'Abidin aforementioned – may God hold them in His favour; the tombs of his sons al-Hasan and al-Husayn – may God hold them in His favour; the tomb of his son 'Abdullah ibn al-Qasim – may God hold him in His favour; that of his son Yahya ibn al-Qasim and that of 'Ali ibn 'Abdullah ibn al-Qasim – may God hold them in His favour; that of his brother 'Isa ibn 'Abdullah – may God hold him in His favour; that of Yahya ibn al-Hasan ibn Zayd ibn al-Hasan – may God hold them in His favour; that of Muhammad ibn 'Abdullah ibn Muhammad al-Baqir ibn 'Ali Zayn al-'Abidin ibn al-Husayn ibn 'Ali – may God hold them in His favour; that of

Ja'far ibn Muhammad of the stem of 'Ali ibn al-Husayn – may God hold them in His favour. We were told that he was the stepson of al-Malik – may God hold him in His favour.

The tombs of the Sharifat[20] [noble ladies] of the House of 'Ali

May God hold them in His favour

The tomb of the noble lady Umm Kulthum, daughter of al-Qasim ibn Muhammad ibn Ja'far – may God hold them in His favour; that of the noble lady Zaynab, daughter of Yahya ibn Zayd ibn 'Ali ibn al-Husayn ibn 'Ali – may God hold them in His favour; that of Umm Kulthum, daughter of Muhammad ibn Ja'far al-Sadiq – may God hold them in His favour; that of the noble lady Umm 'Abdullah ibn al-Qasim ibn Mohammad – may God hold them in His favour. This describes only the tombs of those noble 'Aluwiyah [descendants of 'Ali] that our eyes fell upon, but there are more. It was told to us that among them is the honoured tomb of Miriam, daughter of 'Ali ibn Abi Talib – may God hold him in His favour – and although this is famous, we did not see it.

The names of the occupants of these venerable tombs we discovered from the records engraved over them and the unbroken oral traditions which confirm them, but God best knows. Over each of these is a splendid edifice, all being most exquisite monuments of wondrous construction. For their care, persons have been appointed who live in them and receive a monthly stipend. It is indeed a sight to marvel on.

A note on the tombs of some of the Companions of the Prophet – may God bless and preserve them – in al-Qarafah and the tombs of the followers of the Companions, imams, learned men, ascetics and saintly men illustrious for their miracles – may God hold them all in His favour

The writer must be absolved from judging the truth of all this, for he did but copy the names he found inscribed upon the epitaphs, but, in short, their credibility prevails – if it pleases Great and Glorious God.

The Tomb of Mu'adh ibn Jabal – may God hold him in His favour; that of 'Uqbah ibn 'Amir al-Juhani the standard bearer of the Prophet – may God bless and preserve him; that of the possessor of the mantle of the Prophet – may God bless and preserve him; that of Abu 'l-Hasan, the jeweller of the Prophet of God – may God bless and preserve him; that of Sariyat al-Jabal – may God hold him in His favour; that of Muhammad son of Abu Bakr the Faithful – may God hold them both in His favour; the tomb of his sons – may God hold them in His favour; that of Ahmad son of Abu Bakr the Faithful – may God hold him in His favour; that of Asma' daughter of Abu Bakr the Faithful – may God hold them both in His favour; that of the son of Zubayr ibn al-'Awwam; that of 'Abdullah son of Hudhafah al-Sahmi, Companion of the Prophet – may God bless and preserve them; that of ibn Halimah the foster-brother of the Prophet of God – may God bless and preserve them.

The tombs of the imams, learned men, and ascetics
May God hold them all in His favour

The tomb of the Shafi'i imam – may God hold him in His favour – a shrine superb in beauty and size. Over against it was built a school the like of which has not been made in this country, there being nothing more spacious or more finely built. He who walks around it will conceive it to be itself a separate town. Beside it is a bath and other conveniences, and building continues to this day. The measureless expenditure on it is controlled by the sheik, imam, ascetic, and man of learning called Najm al-Din al-Khabushani. The Sultan of these lands, Saladin, bounteously pays all for this purpose saying: 'Be lavish in splendour and elegance; ours it will be to provide all.' Glory to Him who made him Salah Dinihi ['the well

being of his religion'] like his name. We visited this man
Khabushani, to be blessed by his prayers, for we had heard
of him in Andalusia. We came upon him at his mosque in
Cairo in the closet in which he lives inside the mosque; and
a narrow closet it is. He prayed for us and we departed. Of all
the men of Egypt, we saw none like him.

There is also the tomb of al-Muzani, the friend of the Shafi'i
imam – may God hold him in His favour; of Ashab the friend
of Malik – may God hold him in His favour; of 'Abd al-
Rahman ibn al-Qasim, the friend of Malik – may God hold
them both in His favour; of Asbagh, the friend of Malik – may
God hold them both in His favour; of the qadi 'Abd al-Wahhab
– may God hold him in His favour; of 'Abdullah ibn 'Abd
al-Hakam and Muhammad ibn 'Abdullah ibn 'Abd al-Hakam
– may God hold them in His favour; of the learned jurisprudent, preacher, and ascetic Abu 'l-Hasan al-Dinawari – may
God hold him in His favour; of Bunan al-'Abid [the pious] –
may God hold him in His favour; of the pious, godly, and
ascetic man known as Sahib al-Ibriq [He of the Ewer], whose
story is so wondrous for its miracles; of Abu Muslim al-
Khawlani – may God hold him in His favour; of the pious
lady known as al-'Ayna' – may God hold her in His favour; of
Rudhabari – may God hold him in His favour; of Muhammad
ibn Mas'ud ibn Muhammad ibn Harun al-Rashid, known as
al-Sabti [the Ceutan] – may God hold him in His favour; of
the pious Muqbil, the Ethiopian – may God hold him in His
favour; of Dhu 'l-Nun ibn Ibrahim, the Egyptian – may God
hold him in His favour; of the qadi al-Anbari, where lies
the Speaker who, when placed in his niche, was heard to say,
'O Lord cause me to alight a blessed lighting, and Thou art
the best cause to alight' [Koran XXIII, 29] – may God hold
him in His favour; of the bride of whom is recorded the miracle
at the time of her first unveiling before her husband: nothing
stranger than it has ever been heard; of the silent one who is
said never to have spoken forty years; of al-'Asafiri; of 'Abd
al-'Aziz ibn Ahmad ibn 'Ali ibn al-Hasan al-Khawarizmi; of

the jurisprudent and excellent preacher al-Jawhari and opposite
him those tombs of his companions – may God hold them in
His favour. The tomb of Shuqran, sheik of Dhu 'l-Nun the
Egyptian; of the pious al-Aqta‘ al-Maghrabi; of the Koran
reader Warsh, and of Shayban al-Ra‘i. But the venerable
shrines in the place are more than can properly be recorded
and numbered, and we have but mentioned those we were
able to see.

South of al-Qarafah is a plain known as the place of the
martyrs' tombs. There lie those who were martyred with
Sariyah – may God hold them in His favour; this plain appears
to the eye to be covered with mounds like the mounds of
graves that have no monuments over them.

Al-Qarafah is remarkable for being all built with mosques
and inhabited shrines in which lodge strangers, learned men,
the good and the poor. The subsidy for each place comes
monthly from the Sultan; and likewise is it for the theological
colleges [mudaris] in Misr and Cairo. We were assured that
the cost of all this exceeds two thousand Egyptian dinars,
or four thousand mu‘mini, a month. It was told us that the
mosque of ‘Amr ibn al-‘As has a daily income of about
thirty Egyptian dinars, which is spent on benefits connected
with it and the stipends of its officials, custodians, imams, and
readers.

Amongst the things we saw in Cairo, were four congregational mosques[21] superbly built and of beautiful design, as well
as many other mosques. In one of these congregational mosques
one day the preacher delivered the khutbah according to the
(orthodox) Sunni practice and included in it invocations for
the Companions of the Prophet – may God hold them in
His favour, for the followers of the Companions and others,
for the ‘Mothers of the Faithful’[22] wives of the Prophet – may
God bless and preserve them, and for his two noble uncles
Hamzah and al-‘Abbas – may God hold them in His favour.
He discoursed so sweetly and gave so moving a sermon as to
humble the hardest heart and cause the tearless eye to flow.

He came to the *khutbah* dressed in black according to the
'Abbaside usage.[23] His costume was a black *burdah* topped by
a *taylasan*[24] of fine black cloth which in the Maghrib we call
ihram, and a black turban, and he was girded with a sword.
When he had ascended the pulpit, at the first step, he struck it
with the end of his scabbard a blow which those present heard
as it were a call to silence. He did it again when halfway up,
and a third time at the end of his climb. He then saluted the
congregation right and left, standing between two black banners, white-checkered, that were planted at the top of the
pulpit. His invocations on that day were to the 'Abbaside Imam,
Abu al-'Abbas Ahmad al-Nasir li din Ilah ibn al-imam Abu
Muhammad al-Hasan al-Mustadi' billah ibn al-Imam Abu 'l-
Muzaffar Yusuf al-Mustanjid billah, and then to the reviver of
his dynasty,[25] Abu 'l-Muzaffar Yusuf ibn Ayyub Salah al-Din
[Saladin], and then to the Sultan's brother and heir to the
throne, Abu Bakr Sayf al-Din [Safadin].

We also looked upon the building of the citadel, an
impregnable fortress adjoining Cairo which the Sultan thinks
to take as his residence, extending its walls until it enfolds the
two cities of Misr and Cairo. The forced labourers on this construction, and those executing all the skilled services and vast
preparations such as sawing the marble, cutting the huge stones,
and digging the fosse that girdles the walls noted above – a
fosse hollowed out with pick-axes from the rock to be a
wonder amongst wonders of which trace may remain – were
the foreign Rumi prisoners whose numbers were beyond computation. There was no cause for any but them to labour on
this construction. The Sultan has constructions in progress in
other places and on these too the foreigners are engaged so
that those of the Muslims who might have been used in this
public work are relieved of it all, no work of that nature falling
on any of them.

Another of the things we saw, doing honour to the Sultan,
was the *maristan* [hospital] in the city of Cairo. It is a palace,
goodly for its beauty and spaciousness. This benefaction he

made so that he might deserve a heavenly reward, and to acquire merit. He appointed as intendant a man of science with whom he placed a store of drugs and whom he empowered to use the potions and apply them in their various forms. In the rooms of this palace were placed beds, fully appointed, for lying patients. At the disposal of the intendant are servants whose duty it is, morning and evening, to examine the conditions of the sick, and to bring them the food and potions that befit them.

Facing this establishment is another specially for women, and they also have persons to attend them. A third which adjoins them, a large place, has rooms with iron windows, and it has been taken as a place of confinement for the insane. They also have persons who daily examine their condition and give them what is fitting for them. All these matters the Sultan oversees, examining and questioning, and demanding the greatest care and attention to them. In Misr there is another hospital of precisely the same model.

Between Misr and Cairo is the great mosque which takes its name from Abu 'l-'Abbas Ahmad ibn Tulun. It is one of the old congregational mosques, of elegant architecture, and of large proportions. The Sultan made it a retreat for the strangers from the Maghrib [Western part of Barbary and Spain], where they might live and receive lectures; and for their support he granted a monthly allowance. A curious thing, told us by one of their prominent men, was that the Sultan had entrusted to them their own management, and allows no other hand over them. They themselves produce their own leader, whose orders they obey and to whom they appeal in sudden contingency. They live in peace and satisfaction, devoted exclusively to the worship of their Lord, and finding, in the favour of the Sultan, the greatest help to the good on whose path they are set.

There is no congregational or ordinary mosque, no mausoleum built over a grave, nor hospital, nor theological college, where the bounty of the Sultan does not extend to all who seek shelter or live in them. He is helped in this by grants from the public treasury.

Amongst the beneficent acts that proclaim his care for all the affairs of the Muslims was his ordering the building of a school which he assigned to those preachers of the Book of Great and Glorious God who teach exclusively the children of the poor and orphans. For their needs he grants an adequate allowance.

Another of the Sultan's benefactions, and a monument of enduring usefulness to Muslims, are the bridges he has begun to construct seven miles west of Misr at the end of a causeway that begins at high-Nile beside Misr. This causeway is like a mountain stretched along the ground, over which it runs for a distance of six miles until it reaches the aforesaid bridges. These have about forty arches of the biggest type used in bridges, and reach the desert which extends from them to Alexandria. It is one of the most excellent measures taken by a prudent king in readiness against any sudden onslaught by an enemy coming through the breach of Alexandria at the time of the Nile's overflow, when the countryside js in flood and the passage of soldiers thereby prevented. He prepared this as a passage-way for any time it may be needed. May God by His favour avert from the lands of the Muslims all apprehension and danger. To the Egyptians, the construction of these bridges is a warning of a coming event, for they see in it an augury that the Almohades[26] will conquer it and the eastern regions. But God is the Knower of His hidden affairs. There is no God but He.

Near to these new bridges are the ancient pyramids, of miraculous construction and wonderful to look upon, four-sided, like huge pavilions rearing into the skies; two in particular choke the firmament. The length of one of them from one angle to another is three hundred and sixty-six paces. They have been built with immense hewn rocks, arranged above each other in an awesome fashion and wonderfully joined having nothing between them that (like cement) would serve to bind them. Their tips seem to the eye to be pointed, but it

may be that the ascent to them is possible with danger and
difficulty, and that their pointed tops may be found to be broad
and level. If men sought to tear them down they must fail.
There is dispute concerning them, some saying that they are
the tombs of 'Ad and his sons; others have different views.
To be short, none but Great and Glorious God can know
their story.

One of the two large pyramids has a door, up to which
one climbs a *qamah* or more from the ground, and through
which entry is made to a large chamber about fifty spans wide
and about the same in length. Inside that chamber is a long
hollow block of marble resembling what is commonly called
al bilah [the pillar], and which is said to be a tomb. God best
knows the truth of this. Below the large pyramid is another
which from one angle to another measures one hundred and
forty paces. Below this smaller pyramid are five smaller ones,
three contiguous and two nearby and connected.

Near to these pyramids at about a bow-shot's distance, is
a strange figure of stone [the Sphinx] rising up like a minaret
in the form of a man of fearsome aspect. Its face is to the pyramids and it has its back to the qiblah where the Nile falls and
(is called) Abu 'l-Ahwal [the Father of Dread].*

In the city of Misr is a congregational mosque named after
'Amr ibn al-'As – may God hold him in His favour – who
has also another mosque in Alexandria which is the Friday
place of worship for the Malikites [a sect of the orthodox
Sunni Muslims]. In Misr too are the remains of the destruction
caused by the fire that occurred during the revolution at the
time of the break-up of the 'Ubaydin [Fatimid] dynasty in the
year 564 [1169]. Most of the city has been restored, and buildings now adjoin each other without intermission. It is a large
city, and the ancient relics to be seen in and about it attest
the size of its former boundaries.

* Ibn Jubayr is uncharacteristically careless in his description of the pyramids.
For example there are six not five smaller pyramids, and the Sphinx faces the
Nile not the pyramids.

On the west bank of the Nile, which runs between the two (cities), is a large and important burgh with fine buildings called al-Jizah [Gizeh]. Every Sunday it holds a large market where many congregate. Between it and Misr is an island [Roda] with fine houses and commanding belvederes, which is a resort for entertainment and diversion. Between this island and Misr is a canal from the Nile [the Grand Canal of Cairo, now a street], which lies along its length about a mile and has no outlet. On this island is a congregational mosque in which the *khutbah* is delivered.

Beside this mosque is the Nilometer, which measures the Nile's increase at the time of its yearly flooding. The beginning is expected in the month of June, the maximum in August, and the ending in the beginning of October. This measuring instrument is a white octagonal column of marble set in a place which confines the water as it flows into it. It is divided into twenty-two cubits [a cubit=a little over 20 inches], subdivided into twenty-four parts called 'fingers'. If the flood with them reaches the point where the water submerges it nineteen cubits, that, according to their thinking, would be the limit for giving a good year, but the submersion is often deep throughout the flood. The medium they consider to be seventeen cubits, which they deem to be better than the excess described above.

The Sultan is entitled to a land-tax in Egypt when the over-flow is sixteen cubits and above. On this, he who daily watches for the increase gives the good news. The increase on the graduations of cubits, as described, is notified daily until the full level is reached. If it should be less than sixteen cubits, the Sultan will that year receive no tribute and no land-tax.[27]

We were told that in Gizeh is the tomb of Ka'b al-Ahbar – may God hold him in His favour. On the highest point of Gizeh are marble stones from which crocodiles have been shaped, and it is said that because of them no crocodiles appear on the banks of the Nile three miles above or below them. God best knows the truth of this.

Another of the generous deeds of this Sultan close to God

Most High, and of the memorials he has left in happy remembrance of him both in religion and in the world, was his annulling of the customs duty imposed as a tax on pilgrims during the 'Ubaydin [Fatimid] dynasty. The pilgrims had suffered distress from its harsh exactment and were much wasted by it, and felt wronged by this humbling and crushing device. At times there came some who had with them no more than the bare cost of the journey, or had not even this provision, but they were compelled to pay the fixed tax, which was seven and a half Egyptian dinars, or fifteen mu'mini dinars, a head. Those who could not suffered the most painful punishment at 'Aydhab, which city is like its name without the 'y'. [Dropping the 'y' in 'Aydhab gives 'adhab, meaning 'punishment'.] Among the various inflictions devised was hanging by the testicles, or such foul acts. May God protect us from the abuse of His decrees.

At Jiddah there were similar tortures and worse for him who had not paid the dues at 'Aydhab, and whose name had arrived without bearing a mark as having paid. But this Sultan abolished the accursed impost, and to fill its place, provided foods and other things, allotting to this purpose the tribute of a certain place and making certain that it all arrived in the Hejaz, since the dues in question had been taken in the name of provisions for Mecca and Medina – may God render them prosperous. Thus did he make a most happy reform, lightening the way of the pilgrim, who had been abandoned, with no one to whom he could turn. God, at the hands of this just Sultan, was sufficient to deliver the Muslims from grievous case and a most painful state. Thanks should follow to him from all who believe that the pilgrimage to the sacred mosque (in Mecca) is one of the five fundamental pillars of Islam; until (his name) shall be spread throughout all lands; and in all countries and all regions prayers should be offered up for him. God who rewards all who do good, and whose power is great, will not fail to reward one who wrought so worthily.

Such was the impost in the lands of Egypt, besides the other taxes on everything bought and sold, great or small, to the point of paying tax for drinking the Nile water, and other things besides. This infamous exaction the Sultan abolished, and spread justice and enlarged security. Indeed, such is his justice, and the safety he has brought to his high-roads that men in his lands can go about their affairs by night and from its darkness apprehend no awe that should deter them. Such were the affairs of men that we saw in Misr and Alexandria as described above.

The Month of Muharram of the Year 579

[26th of April – 25th of May, 1183]

May God let us know His grace and favour

THE new moon rose on the night of Tuesday the 26th of April while we were in Cairo. May God prosper us in our aims. On the morning of Sunday the 6th of Muharram we left Misr and ascended the Nile towards upper Egypt, making for Qus. May God, by His favour, grant us His habitual succour and generous relief. The day on which, with the help of Great and Glorious God, we sailed, fell on the first day of May. Villages and large cities followed continuously along the banks of the Nile, as we shall presently relate.

One of these villages is Askun, which lies on the eastern bank of the Nile and to the left of him who ascends it. It is said that here was born Moses the Interlocutor[28] – the blessings of God on our Prophet and on him – and here, as it is said, his mother cast him upon the waters of the Nile. On the day of our sailing, and that following, we observed, to the west of the Nile and on our right, the ancient city of Joseph the Truthful – God bless and preserve him – where is the prison in which he was confined [Gen. xxxix. 20], which is now being demolished and its stones removed to the citadel being built at Cairo; a strong and impregnable fortress. In this city are the store-houses in which Joseph – may God bless and preserve him – stored the food [Gen. xli. 35]. They are hollow, it is said. From there we moved to a place called Munyat ibn al-Khasib, a large town on the bank of the Nile, to the right of him who ascends it, with markets, baths, and all the conveniences of a town. We passed it on the night of Sunday the 13th of Muharram, the eighth day after our sailing from Cairo, for the wind had fallen and we had been fain to stop on our way. Now were we to describe every place we happened upon on the banks of the Nile, right and left; our book would be cramped by it. We therefore intend to include only the larger and more famous places.

Near to Munyat and to our left we came upon the blessed mosque dedicated to Abraham the friend of the All-Merciful – God's blessings upon him and upon our Prophet. This mosque is celebrated and known for the benedictions it brings on those who visit it. In its court are said to be the foot-prints of the beast ridden by al-Khalil [the friend (of God)] – may God bless and preserve him. Beyond that, to the left, is a place called Ansina, a spacious and handsome village with ancient monuments. In past times it was (already) an ancient city, having ancient walls. Saladin destroyed them and imposed on all ships descending the Nile the task of carrying one stone to Cairo. They have now all been moved.

On the morning of Monday the 14th of Muharram, the ninth day after our sailing from Misr, we passed a mountain called Jabal al-Maqlah, on the eastern bank of the Nile, to our left. This mountain is halfway to Qus from Misr being thirteen post-stages [*barid*] from both.

What must be mentioned for its remarkableness is that, starting from the district of Misr, there lies along the east bank of the Nile, to the left of him who ascends, a continuous and ancient wall, some of which has been destroyed and some of which remains, which continues along that bank to Uswan at the end of Sa'id [Upper Egypt]. Between Uswan and Qus are eight post-stages. The stories concerning this wall are varied and contradictory, but to be short, it is a wonderful thing and its secret is known only to Great and Glorious God. It is known as The Wall of the old Woman. She has a story, and I think is the sorceress mentioned in the book *al-Masalik wa 'l-Mamalik*[30] [*Routes and Countries*] who reigned here for a time.

A note to repair an oversight

When we landed at Alexandria in the month mentioned [Dhu 'l-Qa'dah], the first thing we saw was a large concourse of people come forth to gaze upon Rumi prisoners being brought to the town on camels, facing the tails and surrounded by timbal and horn. We asked of their story, and were told a case that would rend the heart in compassion and pity. A number of Syrian Christians had assembled and built ships in that part of their land which is nearest to the Sea of al-Qulzum [Red Sea], and had then moved their various parts on camels belonging to neighbouring Arabs at a price they had agreed upon with them. On arrival at the shores of the Sea, they had nailed their ships together, completed their construction, set them in order, and launched them into the sea.

They had then sailed forth to harass (Muslim) pilgrims.[31] Coming to the Sea of al-Na'am,[32] they there burnt some sixteen ships, and then went on to 'Aydhab where they caught a ship coming with pilgrims from Jiddah. On the land they seized a large caravan journeying from Qus to 'Aydhab and killed all in it, leaving none alive. They captured two ships bringing merchandise from the Yemen, and burnt many foods prepared on the beaches as provisions for Mecca and Medina – God exalt them. Many infamous acts they committed, such as are unheard of in Islam, for no Rumi had ever before come to that place. The worst, which shocks the ears for its impiousness and profanity, was their aim to enter the City of the Prophet – may God bless and preserve him – and remove him from the sacred tomb.

This intent they spread abroad, and let report of it run on their tongues. But God brought punishment upon them for their audacity, and for embarking on that which Providence has forbidden. They were no more than a day's journey from Medina, when God repelled their hostile purpose with ships prepared in Misr and Alexandria, and in which were the chamberlain known as Lu'lu' [Husam al-Din Lu'lu'] and some valorous Moorish sailors. They pursued the enemy who had been near to escape, and seized them all. It was one of the signs of All-Powerful God's solicitude. They had overtaken them after a long time, for there had been more than a month and

a half or thereabouts between them. The enemy were killed
or taken prisoner. The prisoners were distributed amongst
various countries to be put to death in them, and some were
sent to Mecca and Medina. God, with His beneficent works,
is sufficient to Islam and the Muslims in this grave tide. Praise
be to God, Lord of the Universe.

The account is resumed

Amongst the places we passed in Upper Egypt after Jabal
al-Maqlah which, as we have already related, was halfway from
Misr to Qus, was a place called Manfalut, near to the west
bank of the Nile, to the right of him who ascends it. It has
markets and all that is needed of commodities, which are of
the highest quality and without rival in Upper Egypt. Its
wheat is taken to Misr for its goodness and the heaviness of its
grain. Indeed it has become renowned because of this, and
merchants ascend the Nile in ships to fetch this wheat.

After Manfalut comes the city of Usyut [Lycopolis], a famous
city of Upper Egypt about three miles distant from the west
bank of the Nile. It has a pleasing aspect, and is surrounded
by gardens of the date-palm. Its walls are old. Below it is a
place called Abu Tij [Abotis], a town on the west bank of
the Nile having markets and all the conveniences of a town.
Then comes the city of Ikhmim [Chemmis or Panapolis],
another of the famous cities of Upper Egypt, to the east of
the Nile and on its bank. It is of ancient foundation and a long-
standing site. Here is the mosque of Dhu 'l-Nun the Egyptian,
and that of Daud [David], one of the saints famed for good
works and continence. They are both mosques impressed with
the character of blessedness, and we entered them, to be blessed
by praying in them, on Saturday the 19th of Muharram. In
this city are monuments and constructions built by the Copts
and churches attended till to-day by the Christian Copt clients.
The most remarkable of the temples of the world talked of
for their wonder is the great temple east of the city and below

its walls.[33] Its length is two hundred and twenty cubits, and its breadth one hundred and sixty. The people of these parts know it as *birba*, and thus too are known all their temples and ancient constructions. This great temple is supported by forty columns, beside its walls, the circumference of each column being fifty spans and the distance between them thirty spans. Their capitals are of great size and perfection, cut in an unwonted fashion and angulated in ornate style as if done by turners. The whole is embellished with many colours, lapis lazuli and others. The columns are carved in low relief from top to bottom. Over the capital of each column and stretching to its neighbour is a great slab of carved stone, the biggest of which we measured and found to be fifty-six spans in length, ten in width, and eight in depth.

The ceiling of this temple is wholly formed of slabs of stone so wonderfully joined as to seem to be one single piece; and over it all are disposed rare paintings and uncommon colours, so that the beholder conceives the roof to be of carved wood. Each slab has a different painting. Some are adorned with comely pictures of birds with outstretched wings making the beholder believe they are about to fly away; others are embellished with images of men, very beautiful to look upon and of elegant form, each image having a distinctive shape, for example holding a statuette or a weapon, or a bird, or a chalice, or making sign to another with the hand, together with other forms it would take too long to describe and which words are not adequate to express.

Within and without this great temple, both in its upper and its lower parts, are pictures all of varied form and description. Some are of dreadful, inhuman forms that terrify the beholder and fill him with wonder and amazement. There was hardly the space of an awl or needle-hole which did not have an image or engraving or some hieroglyphic writing that is not understood. This remarkable decoration which can be wrought from hard stone where it cannot be worked in soft wood, covers the whole of this vast and splendid temple, in wonder at which the beholder might conceive that all time spent in its adornment, embellishment, and beautifying would be too short. Glory to the Creator of wondrous things. There is no God but He.

In the heights of the temple is the ceiling, spread with the great slabs of stone in the fashion we have described. The ceiling is of great height, so that the fancy is bewildered and the mind perplexed in thinking how the stones were raised and set in place.

Within the temple are chambers, chapels, entries and exits, ascents and stairs, conduits and passages, where groups of men could be lost, and never find each other except by high calls. Its walls are eighteen spans in width, and all its stones are finely joined in the manner we have described. In a word, this temple has a sublime grandeur, and its sight is one of the wonders of the world, beyond description or defining, although we have given an indication, with a fragment of its description, that will tell something of it. God embraces all knowledge of it, and knows its meaning. The reader of this book should not think our account of it is magnified, for any relater, be he a Quss or a Sahban,[34] would find himself deficient and inadequate. God embraces all knowledge. There is no God but He.

In the towns of this Upper Egypt passed on their way by pilgrims and travellers, such as Ikhmim, Qus, and Munyat ibn al-Khasib, the stopping of travellers' ships and their search and examination, the plunging of hands into the clothing of the merchants in search of what dirhams and dinars they might have under their arm-pits or in their bosoms, is abominable to hear, and hateful to relate. All was done by way of collecting zakat, without following the principle of possession for a complete year, or observing whether the goods reached the taxable level [two hundred dirhams in value in the case of merchandise], as we related in the description in this book of Alexandria. They sometimes made them give oath as to what they had and whether they had anything else (not seen), bringing forth God's Holy Book for them to swear upon. Amongst these tax-receivers the pilgrims stand in shame and abasement, being reminded of the days in the customs (at Alexandria). This state of things, there is no doubt, Saladin has no knowledge of. Did he but know, he would end it, even as he decreed the end of graver things, and fight them as a religious duty, for such it would be in view of their oppression, their exaction of painful duties, and their unjust conduct to strangers devoted to Great and Glorious God who go forth from their native land to the sanctuary of his Haram. Such a step, God willing, would lead to the payment of the *zakat* in very good face by the owners of merchandise, provided of course that a year of possession had passed, and would prevent the interference with strangers cut off from their homes, and to whom the *zakat* should be given and not taken away. And it would protect the honour of the just Sultan, whose justice fills the land and whose fame has spread through many countries, and injure not the repute of one to whom God has given good repute, nor shame the report of one to whom He has given good report.

One of the most infamous things we saw was a group of insolent exactors, carrying in their hands long, pointed prods with handles, going aboard the ships to examine what was in them. There was no bundle or sack into which they did not drive those accursed staves in case there should be in the baggage, which held nothing but provisions, some unseen goods or money. This is the most shamefully affecting of the odious happenings. God has forbidden spying [Koran XLIX, 12: 'Do not spy, nor let some of you backbite others']. What then of the exposure of that which requires a decent veiling, its owner not wishing it be gazed upon, from modesty or because it is precious to him, not from cupidity, but for some need. May God punish these oppressors at the hand of the just Sultan and if He wills, favour His success.

Amongst the places that we passed after Ikhmim was one called Manshat al-Sudan [ancient Ptolemais Hermiu] on the west bank of the Nile. It is a populous village and is said to once have been a large city. In front of this village, between it and the Nile, has been erected a high embankment of stones, like a town-wall, against which the Nile laps but does not, in its flood and rising, overtop. The village is thus safe from the river's intrusion. Below it is a place known as al-Bulyanah, a pleasant village with many palm trees on the western bank of the Nile, and distant from Qus four post-stages. Then comes a place called Dashnah on the east bank; a walled city with all the conveniences of a city. Between it and Qus are two post-stages.

We came next to a place on the west bank of the Nile and close to it, called Dandarah [Tentyras], a city of Upper Egypt. It has many palm-trees, has a pleasant aspect, and is famed for its fresh dates. We were told that it has a great temple, known to the people of these parts as *birba* as we explained in our description of Ikhmim and its temple. It is reported that the temple of Dandarah is even more magnificent and larger too than that.

From there we moved to the city of Qina [Caenepolis], also a town of Upper Egypt, white, fair to look upon, and having splendid buildings. Amongst its praiseworthy qualities is the modesty of its women, who keep to their houses so that a woman is never seen in the street in any circumstance. The stories concerning them verify this; and the women of Dashnah mentioned above are like them in it. Qina is on the east bank of the Nile, and about one post-stage from Qus. Below it is Qift [Koptos], a city to the east of the Nile, and three miles from its bank. It is one of the aforementioned towns of Upper Egypt, handsome, with clean buildings, and of finished construction.

Then, on Thursday the 24th of Muharram, the 19th of May, came our arrival at Qus [Apollinopolis]. We had been on the Nile eighteen days, and we entered Qus on the nineteenth. This is a city of fine markets, and of ample amenities, and it has many beings in it because of the comings and goings of pilgrims and of merchants from India, the Yemen, and Ethiopia. It is a place which all may come upon, a place of alighting for the traveller, a gathering place for companies of wayfarers, and a meeting-place for pilgrims from the Maghrib, from Misr, from Alexandria and from adjoining lands. From here they go into the desert of 'Aydhab, and here they return on their way back from the Hajj. We lodged at an inn called ibn al-'Ajami in Munyah, a large suburb outside the city and facing door of this inn.

The Month of Safar (579)

[26th of May–23rd of June, 1183]

May God accord us His grace and favour

THE new moon of this month rose on the night of Wednesday, the 25th of May, while we were yet in Qus and wishful of setting forth to 'Aydhab[35] – may God in His grace and favour, help us in our aims. On Monday the 13th of the month, which was the 6th of June, we took out all our baggage, provisions, and the rest, to al-Mabraz, a place in the direction of the *qiblah* and near to the city. It is a large space surrounded by palm-trees where the baggage of the pilgrims and merchants is collected and loaded. From here they set forth on their journey, and here is weighed that which the camel-masters must know the weight of. And so, when the evening prayers were over, we departed thence, and came to a waterpoint called al-Hajir where we passed the night. The day of Tuesday we tarried there because of the absence of some of the camel-masters at their houses which were nigh at hand. That night, the night of Wednesday, the 15th of the month (of Safar), while we were still in Hajir, the moon suffered a full eclipse, which began at the beginning of the night, and continued for a part of it. On the morning of Wednesday we set forth, and took our mid-day rest at a place called Qila' al-Diya'. The night we spent in a place called Mahatt al-Laqitah. This had all been through the desert in which there was no sign of cultivation.

Early on Thursday we halted at a watering place called al-'Abdayn [The Two Slaves]. It is related that they died of thirst before they could reach it. The place was named after them, and here is their tomb. God's mercy upon them. We drew water for three days and left with the dawn on Friday the 17th of the month. We journeyed on through the desert encamping in it whenever night darkened upon us, while the caravans of 'Aydhab and Qus came and went so that the desert was animated and safe. On Monday the 20th of the month we alighted at a watering place called Dinqash, a spring to which come animals and men of a number which none but Great and Glorious God can count.

Across this desert no one will journey save on camel, by reason of their endurance of thirst. The best and most comfortable camel litters used on them are the *shaqadif*, and the best of these are those made in the Yemen for, like the travelling *ashakin* [seats] they are covered with leather and are roomy. Two of them are bound together by stout ropes and put across the camel. They have supports at each corner, and on these rests a canopy. The traveller and his companion in counterpoise will thus be veiled from the blaze of the midday heat and may sit reclining and at ease beneath its covering. With his companion he may partake of what he needs of food and the like, or read, when he wishes, the Koran or a book; and whoso deems it lawful to play chess may, if he wish, play his companion, for diversion and to relieve the spirit. To be short, it eases the hardship of travel. Most travellers ride their camels on top of their baggage and so painfully endure the rigours of the burning heat.

At this spring of Dinqash, because of the press around the water, there arose a quarrel between some of the Arab camel-masters from Yemen – they were 'Bali, a sub-tribe of the Quda'ah, who held the contract for providing transport on the road to 'Aydhab – and some Ghuzz [a local Turkish tribe]. This all but became a riot, but God prevented it.

The way to 'Aydhab from Qus is by two roads. One is that known as the road of the Two Slaves, and is the one we followed and the more direct. The other is by Uswan,[36] a village on the banks of the Nile. The confluence of these two roads is near to the spring of Dinqash. They have another meeting place at a waterpoint called Shaghib, one day ahead of the spring of Dinqash.

At eventide on Monday, we provisioned ourselves with

water for a day and a night and removed to water in a place called Shaghib, reaching it early on the morning of Wednesday the 22nd of Safar. This water comes from a hole dug in the ground and flows bountifully at little depth, but is brackish. After providing ourselves with water for three days, we moved on from it at dawn on Thursday, towards water at a place called Amtan. We left the water-track at a place called ★ ★ ★ ★, to our left, with no more than a day's journey between it and Shaghib, but the road is difficult for camels. In the early forenoon of Sunday the 26th of Safar we dismounted at Amtan. And on this day I completed my learning by heart the Book of Great and Glorious God. Praise and thanks to Him for helping us in this.

The water of Amtan is in a spring which God has blessed in particular, for its water is the best and sweetest of the way. Water buckets beyond counting will be found there, and there will water the many caravans that descend upon it, with the camels so far gone in thirst that were they brought to a river they would exhaust it and dry it up. We wished to count the caravans that came and went upon this road but could not (for their number), especially those from 'Aydhab bearing the merchandise of India that came through the Yemen to 'Aydhab. The greater part of this was the loads of pepper, so numerous as to seem to our fancy to equal in quantity only the dust. A curious circumstance that we observed in this desert is that you will discover loads of pepper, cinnamon, and the like thrown unguarded by the side of the road.[37] They are left on the road like this through the sickness of the camels that bear them, or for some other reason, and remain thus in their place until their owners remove them, secure from all risk despite the number of men of all kinds who pass beside them.

We left Amtan on the morning of Monday, following the Sunday described, and at midday alighted by the water of a place called Mujaj nigh to the road. We took from it four days' water to bring us to al-'Ushara', a day distant from 'Aydhab. From this station of Mujaj the road leads through al-Wadah, a sandy and toilsome stretch that reaches to the shores of the Jiddah sea. Through this stretch the march continues, if God wills, to 'Aydhab, and lies in a wide plain over which the eyes, right and left, can range.

At midday on Thursday the 28th of the month, we departed from Mujaj and took our way to al-Wadah.

The Month of Rabi' al-Awwal (579)

[24th of June–23rd of July, 1183]

May God let us know His favour

THE new moon of this month rose on the night of Friday, the 24th of the month of June, when we were at the end of al-Wadah and about three stages from 'Aydhab; and on the morning of Friday we halted at the waters of 'Ushara', two stages from 'Aydhab. In this place are many *ushar* plants [*Asclepias gigantea*], which are like the *utrujj* [*Citrus cedra*],[38] but have no spines. The water of this place is not especially sweet; it is in an uncased well, and we found that the sand had fallen into it and covered the water. The camel-masters sought to dig it that they might bring forth water, but failed, so that the caravan remained without it. We marched that night, the night of Saturday the 2nd of the month, and after sunrise we encamped at the waters of al-Khubayb, within sight of 'Aydhab. Here both the caravans and the people of the country take water, which suffices for them all, for the well is large, like a huge cistern.

On the evening of Saturday, we entered 'Aydhab, a city on the shores of the Jiddah sea. It has no walls and most of its houses are booths of reeds. It has now, however, some houses, newly-built, of plaster. It is one of the most frequented ports of the world, because of the ships of India and the Yemen that sail to and from it, as well as the pilgrim ships that come and go. It is in the desert, with no vegetation and nothing to eat save what is brought to it. Yet its people, by reason of the pilgrims, enjoy many benefits, especially at the time of their passing through, since for each load of victuals that the pilgrims bring, they receive a fixed food tax, light in comparison with the former customs duties which, as we said, have been raised by Saladin. A further advantage they gain from the pilgrims is in the hiring of their *jilab*: ships which bring them much profit in conveying the pilgrims to Jiddah and returning them when dispersing after the discharge of their pious duty. There are no people of easy circumstances in 'Aydhab but have a *jilabah* or two which bring them an ample livelihood. Glory to God who apportions sustenance to all in divers forms. There is no God but He.

We took lodging there in a house named after Munih, one of its Ethiopian leading men who had become established there with houses, spring-encampments, and *jilab*.

In the sea of 'Aydhab and near to the city are some islands where there are pearl-fisheries. The season for diving is the time at which we write these words, which is the foreign month of June, and the month which follows, and they extract precious pearls of great value. The divers go out to these islands in small boats [*zawariq*] and stay in them some days and then return with what God has meted out to each according to his lot. The catch is not deep, and they bring it out in double sea-shells (whose flesh is) like a kind of fish resembling somewhat the sea-turtle. When they are split, the insides of the two valves show as silver shells. They are then opened and inside them is found the core of the pearl covered by the fleshy part of the sea-shell, and these they gather according to their fortune. Glory be to God who so determines. There is no God but He. But they (live) in a country which has no (produce) fresh or dry, and live therein the lives of beasts. Glory to Him who makes dear a country to its people, but indeed these folk are closer to wild beasts than they are to men.

The journey from Jiddah to 'Aydhab is most calamitous for pilgrims, save those few of them whom Great and Glorious God preserves, for the wind takes most of them to anchorages on the desert far to the south of 'Aydhab. There the Bujat, a type of Sudanese living in the mountains, come down to them and hire them their camels, and lead them through a waterless track. Often the greater number of them perish from thirst, and the Bujat seize the money and other things that they have left behind. Not seldom pilgrims will stray on foot through the wayless desert and, being lost, die of thirst. Those who survive and reach 'Aydhab are like men quickened from the shroud. While we were there we saw some who had come in this manner, and in their ghastly shape and changed form was 'a portent for those who observed carefully' [Koran XV, 75]. Most of the deaths of the pilgrims took place at these anchorages; some were helped by the wind to the port of 'Aydhab but they were few.

The *jilab* that ply on this Pharaonic sea are sewn together, no nails at all being used on them. They are sewn with cord made from *qinbar*, which is the fibre of the coconut and which the makers thrash until it takes the form of thread, which then they twist into a cord with which they sew the ships. These they then caulk with shavings of the wood of palm-trees. When they have finished making a *jilabah* in this fashion, they smear it with grease, or castor oil, or the oil of the *qirsh* [shark], which is best. This *qirsh* is a huge fish which swallows drowning men. Their purpose in greasing the boat is to soften and supple it against the many reefs that are met with in that sea, and because of which nailed ships do not sail through it. The wood for these parts is brought from India and the Yemen, as is the coconut fibre. A singular feature of these *jilab* is that their sails are woven from the leaves of the muql tree [Theban palm or Bdellium, a kind of gum-tree], and their parts are conformably weak and unsound in structure. Glory to God who contrives them in this fashion and who entrusts men to them. There is no God but He.

The people of 'Aydhab use the pilgrims most wrongfully. They load the *jilab* with them until they sit one on top of the other so that they are like chickens crammed in a coop. To this they are prompted by avarice, wanting the hire. The owner of the craft will exact its full cost from the pilgrims for a single journey, caring not what the sea may do with it after that, saying, 'Ours to produce the ships: the pilgrims' to protect their lives.' This is a common saying amongst them.

E

This is the country of Islam most deserving a *hisbah*,[39] and the scourge employed should be the sword. The best for him who can is not to see it, and to take his way by Syria to 'Iraq and join there with the Emir of the Baghdad pilgrimage. If this is impossible for him when going to Mecca, he should then, at the dispersion of the pilgrimage, go with that Emir al-Hajj to Baghdad and thence to Acre. Thence, as he pleases, he may go to Alexandria, or Sicily, or elsewhere. He may even find a Rumi ship sailing to Ceuta or another Muslim land. And should he find this circling road to be too long, it will be easy in comparison with what he would meet with at 'Aydhab and places like it.

The people of 'Aydhab belong to a tribe of Sudanese called al-Bujat. Their Sultan is one of their kind, and lives with them in the mountains near the city. He will, on occasion, come to meet with the Wali [Governor] of the Ghuzz there, in order to display his obedience. He is appointed the Wali's deputy in the country and all the revenues, save for a small part, go to him. This race from the Sudan is more astray from the (right) path, and have less reason, than the animals. They have no religion save the formal words professing the unity of God, which they utter to display that they are Muslims. But behind that are corrupt beliefs and practices that cannot be condoned and are unlawful. Their men and women go naked abroad, wearing nothing but the rag which covers their genitals, and most not even this. In a word, they are a breed of no regard and it is no sin to pour maledictions upon them.

On Monday the 25th of Rabi' al-Awwal, the 18th of July, we embarked on a *jilabah* to cross to Jiddah. We waited that day at anchor because of the stillness of the wind and the absence of the nawati [Gr. ναμται, 'sailors']. But with the morning of Tuesday, we sailed with the favour of Great and Glorious God and in the hope of His gracious aid. Our stay in 'Aydhab, not including the Monday now mentioned, had been three and twenty days, of which God, Great and Glorious is He, will hold count for us because of our adversities and ill-

condition and for the ravages on our health from want of proper
food. It is enough for you of a place where everything is
imported, even water; and this (because of its bitterness) is less
agreeable than thirst. We had lived between air that melts the
body and water that turns the stomach from appetite for food.
He did no injustice to this town who sang,

'Brackish of water and flaming of air.'

A sojourn in it is the greatest snare on the road to the Ancient
House [the Ka'bah] – may God magnify it in esteem and
veneration, and enlarge the (heavenly) reward of the pilgrims
for what they have endured, more especially in that accursed
town. Men tell stories of its abominations, even saying that
Solomon the son of David – on our Prophet and on him be
peace – took it as a prison for the 'ifrit [afrite or demon, mentioned in the Koran XXVII, 39]. May God relieve the pilgrims
of it by furnishing the straight road to the Sacred House, which
is from Misr by 'Aqabah of Ailah [Elim] to holy Medina.
This is the shortest road, with the sea to the right and the
venerable Jabal Tur (Mount Sinai) to the left. But the Franks
have near to it a garrisoned castle which prevents men from
passing it – may God by His favour grant victory to His faith
and glorify His word.

Our passage over the sea on Tuesday the 26th of Rabi'
al-Awwal, and the Wednesday following it, was long-lasting
because the wind was light. But at the end of the vespers of
the night of Thursday, when we had been rejoicing in the sight
of the birds from the Hejaz coast circling in the air, the lightning
flashed from the direction of that land, which was to the east.
Then rose a storm which darkened the skies and at last covered
them. The tempest raged and drove the ship from off its course
and backwards. The fury of the wind continued, and the darkness thickened and filled the air so that we knew not which
way lay our course. Then a few stars appeared and gave us
some guidance. The sail was lowered to the bottom of the
daqal,[40] which is the mast, and we passed that night in a storm

which drove us to despair, seeing one of the famous storms of
the Pharaonic sea. Then with the morn God brought us relief
in our destitution ＊ ＊ ＊ ＊ the wind fell, the clouds dispersed,
and the skies cleared; and in the distance the lands of the Hejaz
appeared before us. We could see only its mountains east of
Jiddah, and the *rubban* of the ship, that is the captain, said that
between those mountains which we saw and the coast of Jiddah
lay two days' travel. May God by His power and favour help
us in every difficulty and aid us in every strait.

That day, Thursday, we sailed along under a good light
breeze and at eventide anchored at a small island in that sea,
near to the coast. We had met many reefs which had broken
the water and made it laugh, and we entered their windings
with care and caution. The *rubban* was shrewd in his art, and
skilled, and God delivered us from the reefs so that we anchored
at this island. Here we disembarked and passed the night of
Friday the 29th of Rabi' al-Awwal. The morning was calm,
but the wind blew from a direction unsuitable to us, so we
remained there all that Friday.

On Saturday the 30th a slight wind rose, and we sailed
quietly in a calm sea that seemed to the beholder to be a dish
of blue crystal. Thus we moved along, praying for the beneficent works of Great and Glorious God. The name of this island
is 'Ayqat al-Sufun [the Obstacle of Ships], but Great and
Glorious God preserved us from the evil auguries of its unhappy
name. Praise and thanks to Him for that.

The Month of Rabi' al-Akhir (579)

May God let us know His favour

THE new moon of this month rose on the night of Saturday, while we yet were at the aforementioned island, but its crescent was not revealed to our eyes because of the storm. The following night it was seen large and high in the sky, so we confirmed its rising on the night of Saturday 23rd of July.[41] At eventide on Sunday the second we anchored at a harbourage called Ubhur, a day's distance from Jiddah. The position of this harbour is most uncommon, since a channel of the sea penetrates the land, which encompasses it on both sides, and ships can find therein a safe and tranquil anchorage. At dawn on Monday, we sailed from this place, by the favour of God Most High, under a light breeze – God is the disposer of all things. There is no Lord but He.

When night fell we anchored near Jiddah, which was within sight. The wind raged on the morning of the Tuesday that followed, and stopped our entering the port. The entry into it is difficult to achieve because of the many reefs and the windings. We observed the art of these captains and the mariners in the handling of their ships through the reefs. It was truly marvellous. They would enter the narrow channels and manage their way through them as a cavalier manages a horse that is light on the bridle and tractable. They came through in a wonderful manner that cannot be described. At midday of Tuesday the 4th of Rabi' al-Akhir, being the 26th of July, we arrived at Jiddah, praising Great and Glorious God and thanking Him for our safety and our deliverance from the tempest we had faced those eight days of our voyage on the sea. From their divers perils God in His goodness and favour had preserved us. There had been the sudden crises of the sea, the perversity of the wind, the many reefs encountered, and the emergencies that arose from the imperfections of the sailing gear which time and again became entangled and broke when sails were raised or lowered or an anchor raised. At times the bottom of the *jilabah* would run against a reef when passing through them, and we would listen to a rumbling that called us to abandon hope. Many times we died and lived again – praise be to God who, in His power and glory, bestowed on us His care, ensuring our protection and sufficiency; praise fitting His kindness, and in solicitation of His continuing favour. There is no God but He.

We lodged, in Jiddah, in the house of the governor Ali, who ruled it in the name of the above mentioned[42] Emir of Mecca. We were in one of those upper apartments built of palm-leaves at the top of their houses. They go out from them on to the roof to spend the night. On landing at Jiddah, happy in the safety which Great and Glorious God had granted us, we earnestly beseeched Him that our return should not be by this accursed sea unless some necessity arose preventing our going by other ways – God in His power acts with beneficence in all that He decrees and disposes.

This Jiddah is a village on the coast we have mentioned. Most of its houses are of reeds, but it has inns built of stone and mud, on the top of which are reed structures serving as upper chambers, and having roofs where at night rest can be had from the ravages of the heat. In this village are ancient remains which show that it is old. Traces of the walls that encompassed it remain to this day. In it is a place having an ancient and lofty dome, which is said to have been the lodging place of Eve, the mother of mankind – God's blessing upon her – when on her way to Mecca. This edifice was erected to illustrate its blessedness and excellence. God best knows concerning it. The city has a blessed mosque attributed to 'Umar ibn al-Khattab – may God hold him in His favour – and another with two pillars of ebony wood, also attributed to him – may God hold him in His favour – although some attribute it to Harun al-Rashid – may God have mercy on him.

Most of the inhabitants of this town and the surrounding desert and mountain are Sharifs, 'Aliites, Hasanites, Husaynites and Ja'farites – may God hold in His favour their noble ancestors. They lead a life so wretched as to break the hardest stone in compassion. They employ themselves in all manner of trades, such as hiring camels should they possess any, and selling milk or water and other things like dates which they might find, or wood they might collect. Sometimes their women, the Sharifahs themselves, would share in this work. Glory to the Determiner in what He decrees. Beyond a peradventure they are of a house to which God is pleased to give the life to come and not this world; and He has made us amongst those who it is proper should love the family of the Prophet, from whom He has removed impurity and whom He has cleansed.

Outside the city are ancient constructions which attest the antiquity of its foundation. It is said that it was a Persian city. It has cisterns hewn from the hard rock, connected with each other and beyond count for their number. They are both within and without the town, and men say that there are three hundred and sixty outside the town, and the same within. We indeed saw a great number, such as could not be counted. But in truth the things of wonder are many. Glory to Him whose knowledge encompasses them all.

The greater number of the people of these Hejaz and other lands are sectaries and schismatics who have no religion, and who have separated in various doctrines.[43] They treat the pilgrims in a manner in which they do not treat the Christians and Jews under tribute, seizing most of the provisions they have collected, robbing them and finding cause to divest them of all they have. The pilgrim in their lands does not cease to pay dues and provide foods until God helps him to return to his native land. Indeed, but for what God has done to mend the affairs of Muslims in these parts by means of Saladin, they would suffer the most grievous oppression, with no remission of its rigours. For Saladin lifted from the pilgrim the customs duty, and in its stead provided money and victuals with orders that they should be sent to Mukthir, Emir of Mecca. But when this consignment allotted to them was somewhat delayed, this Emir returned to intimidating the pilgrims and made show to imprison them for the dues.

In this regard, it happened that when we arrived at Jiddah the matter was under discussion with Mukthir, this Emir, and we had been arrested. His order came that the pilgrims should guarantee each other (for payment) and might then enter the Haram [Holy Mosque] of God. Should the money and victuals due for him from Saladin arrive it would be well; otherwise he would not forego his dues from the pilgrims. Such was his speech, as if God's Haram were an heirloom in his hand and lawfully his to let to the pilgrims. Glory to God who alters and changes laws.

That which Saladin had substituted for the pilgrim's customs dues was two thousand dinars and two thousand and two *irdabb* of wheat, which is about eight hundred *qafiz* in our Seville measure, and this was exclusive of the land-rents granted to them by this ordinance in Upper Egypt and in the Yemen. And but for the absence of this just Sultan, Saladin, at the wars against the Franks in Syria, these actions of the Emir against the pilgrims would never have occurred.

The lands of God [i.e. Islamic lands] that most deserve to be purified by the sword, and cleansed of their sins and impurities by blood shed in holy war are these Hejaz lands, for what they are about in loosening the ties of Islam, and dispossessing the pilgrims of their property and shedding their blood. Those of the Andalusian jurisprudents who believe that the pilgrims should be absolved from this religion obligation believe rightly for that reason, and for the way, unpleasing to Great and Glorious God, in which the pilgrims are used. The traveller by this way faces danger and oppression. Far otherwise has God decreed the sharing in that place of His indulgence. How can it be that the House of God should now be in the hands of people who use it as an unlawful source of livelihood, making it a means of illicitly claiming and seizing property, and detaining the pilgrims on its account, thus bringing them to humbleness and abject poverty. May God soon correct and purify this place by relieving the Muslims of these destructive schismatics with the swords of the Almohades, the defenders of the Faith, God's confederates, possessing righteousness and truth, the protectors of the Haram of Great and Glorious God, the abstainers from what is unlawful, the zealous raisers of His name, the proclaimers of His message and the upholders of His creed. Truly He can do as He wishes. He is the best of Protectors, the best of Helpers.

Let it be absolutely certain and beyond doubt established that there is no Islam save in the Maghrib lands. There they follow the clear path that has no separation and the like, such as there are in these eastern lands of sects and heretical groups and schisms, save those of them whom Great and Glorious God has preserved from this. There is no justice, right, or religion in His sight except with the Almohades – may God render them powerful. They are the last just imams of this time, all the other Kings of the day follow another path, taking tithes from the Muslim merchants as if they were of the community of the dhimmah, seizing their goods by every trick and pretext, and following a course of oppression the like of which, oh my God, has never been heard of. All of them, that is, except this just Sultan, Saladin, whom we have mentioned for his conduct and virtues. If he but had a helper in the cause of righteousness * * * * of what I desire. May Great and Glorious God mend the affairs of the Muslims with His beneficent attention and kind works.

A singular circumstance that we observed in the matter of the propagation of the Mu'min Almohade faith and the spreading of its word in these lands, and the inclination of its people to their dominance, is that most, indeed all their peoples, hint at it covertly and even quite plainly. They relate this to certain omens which fell to the notice of some of them and gave warning of coming events which they saw in the result to be true. Amongst the omens leading to this is the following. Between the mosque of ibn Tulum and Cairo are two old and closely-built towers. On one is a statue facing the west, while on the other there had been a statue looking to the east. They used to relate that if one of them should fall, it would give warning of conquest by the people in whose direction it faced over the lands of Egypt, and others besides. By a strange conjuncture, the falling of the statue facing the east was followed by the victory of the Ghuzz [the Seljuk Turks under Saladin] over the 'Ubaydin [Fatimid] power and their conquest of the terri-tories of Misr and other lands. They now expect the fall of the statue facing west and the fulfilment of their hopes of being governed by the people of the west [the Almohade rulers of Spain]. Please God it may be so. There remains nothing but the happy prospect of an Almohade conquest of these lands, and attentively they watch for it one auspicious morning, being certain of it, and expecting it as they expect the (last) hour, the fulfilment of the promise of which no one feels doubt.

In this regard, we learnt in Alexandria and Misr and other places, both directly and by hearsay, of a strange circumstance which indicated that this dear event is truly decreed by God and that the claims concerning it are true. For it was told us that some jurisprudents and leaders of these countries have pre-pared an embellished discourse to be delivered before our lord the Prince of the Faithful – may God exalt his state – and that he expects that day as he expects the Day of Resurrection and composedly awaits it with the patience which is (proper to) our faith. May Great and Glorious God unfold His word and exalt His claim. As He wishes, so He disposes.

At eventide on Tuesday the 11th of the month, being the 2nd of August, we left Jiddah, after the pilgrims had guaranteed each other (for payment), and their names had been recorded in a register kept by the governor of the city, 'Ali ibn Muwaffaq in accordance with an order from his lord, the ruler of Mecca, Mukthir ibn 'Isa, mentioned above. This man Mukthir is of the stock of al-Hasan ibn 'Ali – may God hold him in His

favour – but he is of those who act unrighteously, and not like
his noble forebears – may God have them in His favour.

We passed on our way that night until we arrived at al-
Qurayn, with the rising of the sun. This place is a staging post
for pilgrims and a place of their encampment. There they put
on the *ihram*,[44] and there they rest throughout the day of their
arrival. If they remove in the evening and travel all night, they
will come in the morning to the Haram al-Sharif – may God
increase its honour and sublimeness. The returning pilgrims
rest there too, and from it they pass on by night to Jiddah. In
this place is a well of sweet spring water, and by reason of it
the pilgrims do not need to supply themselves with water save
for the night on which they travel to it. Throughout the daylight hours of Wednesday we stayed resting at al-Qurayn, but
when evening had come, we left it in the pilgrim garb to perform the *'Umrah* [Lesser Pilgrimage],[45] and marched throughout the night. With the dawn, we came near to the Haram,
and descended as the light was about to spread.

We entered Mecca – God protect it – at the first hour of
Thursday the 13th of Rabi', being the 4th of August, by the
'Umrah Gate. As we marched that night, the full moon had
thrown its rays upon the earth, the night had lifted its veil,
voices struck the ears with the *Talbiyat*[46] ['Here am I, O God,
here am I'], from all sides, and tongues were loud in invocation, humbly beseeching God to grant them their requests,
sometimes redoubling their *Talbiyat*, and sometimes imploring
with prayers. Oh night most happy, the bride of all the nights
of life, the virgin of the maidens of time.

And so, at the time and on the day we have mentioned, we
came to God's venerable Haram, the place of sojourn of
Abraham the Friend (of God), and found the Ka'bah, the
Sacred House, the unveiled bride[47] conducted (like a bride to
her groom) to the supreme felicity of heaven, encompassed by
the deputations [pilgrims] of the All-Merciful. We performed
the *tawaf*[48] of the new arrival, and then prayed at the revered
Maqam.[49] We clung to the covering of the Ka'bah near the

Multazam, which is between the Black Stone and the door, and is a place where prayers are answered. We entered the dome of Zamzam and drank of its waters which is 'to the purpose for which it is drunk',[50] as said the Prophet – may God bless and preserve him – and then performed the sa'i[51] between al-Safa and al-Marwah. After this we shaved and entered a state of halal.[52] Praise be to God for generously including us in the pilgrimage to Him and for making us to be of those on whose behalf the prayers of Abraham reach. Sufficient He is for us and the best Manager. We took lodging in Mecca at a house called al-Halal near to the Haram and the Bab al-Suddah, one of its gates, in a room having many domestic conveniences and overlooking the Haram and the sacred Ka'bah.

The Month of Jumada 'l-Ula (579)

[22nd of August–20th of September, 1183]
May God let us know His favour

THE new moon rose on the night of Monday the 22nd of August, when we had been in Mecca – may God Most High exalt it – eighteen days. The new moon of this month was the most auspicious our eyes had seen in all that had passed of our life. It rose after we had already entered the seat of the venerable enclosure, the sacred Haram of God, the dome in which is the maqam of Abraham, the place from whence the Prophet's mission (was sent out), and the alighting place of the faithful spirit Gabriel with inspiration and revelation. May God with His power and strength inspire us to thanks for His favour and make us sensible of that amount of privilege He has made our portion, finally accepting us (into Paradise) and rewarding us with the accustomed generosity of His beneficent works, and giving us of His gracious help and support. There is no God but He.

A description of the Sacred Mosque and the Ancient House
May God bless and exalt it

The venerable House has four corners and is almost square. The chief of the Banu Shayba who are the custodians of the House, one Muhammad ibn Isma'il ibn 'Abd al-Rahman ibn ✶ ✶ ✶ ✶ of the stock of 'Uthman ibn Talhah ibn Shaybah ibn Talhah ibn 'Abd al-Dar, the Companion of the Prophet – may God bless and preserve him – and the incumbent of the chamberlainship of the House, informed me that its height, on the side which faces the Bab [Gate] al-Safa and which extends from the Black Stone to the Rukn al-Yamani [Yemen

Corner], is twenty-nine cubits. The remaining sides are twenty-eight cubits because of the slope of the roof towards the water-spout.

The principal corner is the one containing the Black Stone. There the circumambulation begins, the circumambulator drawing back (a little) from it so that all of his body might pass by it, the blessed House being on his left. The first thing that is met after that is the 'Iraq corner, which faces the north, then the Syrian corner which faces west, then the Yemen corner which faces south, and then back to the Black corner which faces east. That completes one *shaut* [single course]. The door of the blessed House is on the side between the 'Iraq corner and the Black Stone corner, and is close to the Stone at a distance of barely ten spans. That part of the side of the House which is between them is called the Multazam: a place where prayers are answered.

The venerable door is raised above the ground eleven and a half spans. It is of silver gilt and of exquisite workmanship and beautiful design, holding the eyes for its excellence and in emotion for the awe God has clothed His House in. After the same fashion are the two posts, and the upper lintel over which is a slab of pure gold about two spans long. The door has two large silver staples on which is hung the lock. It faces to the east, and is eight spans wide and thirteen high. The thickness of the wall in which it turns is five spans. The inside of the blessed House is overlaid with variegated marbles, and the walls are all variegated marbles. (The ceiling) is sustained by three teak pillars of great height, four paces apart, and punctuating the length of the House, and down its middle. One of these columns, the first, faces the centre of the side enclosed by the two Yemen corners, and is three paces distant from it. The third column, the last, faces the side enclosed by the 'Iraq and Syrian corners.

The whole circuit of the upper half of the House is plated with silver, thickly gilt, which the beholder would imagine, from its thickness, to be a sheet of gold. It encompasses the four sides and covers the upper half of the walls. The ceiling of the House is covered by a veil of coloured silk.

The outside of the Ka'bah, on all its four sides, is clothed in coverings of green silk with cotton warps; and on their upper parts is a band of red silk on which is written the verse, 'Verily the first House founded for mankind was that at Bakkah [Mecca]' [Koran III, 96]. The name of the Imam al-Nasir li Din Ilah, in depth three cubits, encircles it all. On these coverings there has been shaped remarkable designs resembling handsome pulpits, and inscriptions entertaining the name of God Most High and calling blessings on Nasir, the aforementioned 'Abbaside (Caliph) who had ordered its instalment. With all this, there was no clash of colour. The number of covers on all four sides is thirty-four, there being eighteen on the two long sides, and sixteen on the two short sides.

The Ka'bah has five windows of 'Iraq glass, richly stained. One of them is in the middle of the ceiling, and at each corner is a window, one of which is not seen because it is beneath the vaulted passage described later. Between the pillars (hang) thirteen vessels, of silver save one that is gold.

The first thing which he who enters at the door will find to his left is the corner outside which is the Black Stone. Here are two chests containing Korans. Above them in the corner are two small silver doors like windows set in the angle of the corner, and more than a man's stature from the ground. In the angle which follows, the Yemen, it is the same, but the doors have been torn out and only the wood to which they were attached remains. In the Syrian corner it is the same and the small doors remain. It is the same in the 'Iraq corner, which is to the right of him who enters. In the 'Iraq corner is a door called the Bab al-Rahmah [Door of Mercy, usually called the Door of Repentance, Bab al-Taubah] from which ascent is made to the roof of the blessed House. It leads to a vaulted passage connecting with the roof of the House and having in it a stairway and, at its beginning, the vault containing the venerable maqam [the standing-stone of Abraham; see

Note 49]. Because of this passage the Ancient House has five corners. The height of both its sides is two statures and it encloses the 'Iraq corner with the halves of each of those two sides. Two-thirds of the circuit of this passage is dressed with pieces of coloured silk, as if it had been previously wrapped in them and then set in place.

This venerable maqam that is inside the passage is the maqam of Abraham – God's blessings on our Prophet and on him – and is a stone covered with silver. Its height is three spans, its width two and its upper part is larger than the lower. If it is not frivolous to draw the comparison it is like a large potter's oven, its middle being narrower than its top or bottom. We gazed upon it and were blessed by touching and kissing it. The water of Zamzam was poured for us into the imprints of the two blessed feet [of Abraham who stood on this stone when he built the Ka'bah], and we drank it – may God profit us by it. The traces of both feet are visible, as are the traces of the honoured and blessed big toes. Glory to God who softened the stone beneath the tread so that it left its trace as no trace of foot is left in the soft sand. Glory to God who made it a manifest sign. The contemplation of this maqam and the venerable House is an awful sight which distracts the senses in amazement, and ravishes the heart and mind. You will see only reverent gazes, flowing tears, eyes dissolved in weeping, and tongues in humble entreaty to Great and Glorious God.

Between the venerable door and the 'Iraq corner is a basin twelve spans long, five and a half spans wide, and about one in depth. It runs from opposite the door post, on the side of the 'Iraq corner, towards that corner, and is the mark of the place of the maqam at the time of Abraham – on whom be (eternal) happiness – until the Prophet – may God bless and preserve him – moved it to the place where now it is a musalla [place of worship]. The basin remained as a conduit for the water of the House when it is washed. It is a blessed spot [called al-Ma'jan] and is said to be one of the pools of Paradise, with men crowding to pray at it. Its bottom is spread with soft white sand.

The place of the venerated Maqam, behind which prayers are said, faces the space between the blessed door and the 'Iraq corner, well towards the side of the door. Over it is a wooden dome, a man's stature or more high, angulated and sharp-edged [i.e. pyramidal], of excellent modelling, and having four spans from one angle to another. It was erected on the place where once was the maqam [standing-stone], and around it is a stone projection built on the edge like an oblong basin about a span deep, five paces long, and three paces wide. The maqam was put into the place we have described in the blessed House as a measure of safety. Between the maqam and the side of the House opposite it lie seventeen paces, a pace being three spans. The place of the Maqam also has a dome made of steel and placed beside the dome of Zamzam. During the months of the pilgrimage, when many men have assembled and those from 'Iraq and Khurasan have arrived, the wooden dome is removed and the steel dome put in its place that it might better support the press of men.

From the corner containing the Black Stone to the 'Iraq corner is scarcely fifty-four spans. From the Black Stone to the ground is six spans, so that the tall man must bend to it and the short man raise himself (to kiss it). From the 'Iraq corner to the Syrian corner is scarcely forty-eight spans, and that is through the inside of the Hijr [an adjacent enclosure]; but around it from the one corner to the other is forty paces or almost one hundred and twenty spans. The *tawaf* [circum-ambulator] moves outside. (The distance from) the Syrian corner to the Yemen corner is the same as that from the Black corner to the 'Iraq corner for they are opposite sides. From the Yemen to the Black is the same, inside the Hijr, as from the 'Iraq to the Syrian for they are opposite sides.

The place of circumambulation is paved with wide stones like marble [they are in fact of fine polished granite] and very beautiful, some black, some brown and some white. They are

F

joined to each other, and reach nine paces from the House save in the part facing the Maqam where they reach out to embrace it. The remainder of the Haram, including the colonnades, is wholly spread with white sand. The place of circumambulation for the women is at the edge of the paved stones.

Between the 'Iraq corner and the beginning of the wall of the Hijr is the entrance to the Hijr; it is four paces wide, that is six cubits exactly, for we measured it by hand. This place is not enclosed in the Hijr, and is that part of the House which the Quraysh left,[53] and is, as true tradition has it, six cubits. Opposite this entrance, at the Syrian corner, is another of the same size. Between that part of the wall of the House which is under the Mizab [waterspout] and the wall of the Hijr opposite, following the straight line which cuts through the middle of the aforementioned Hijr, lie forty spans. The distance from entrance to entrance is sixteen paces, which is forty-eight spans. This place, I mean the surroundings of the wall (of the Ka'bah, under the Mizab), is all tessellated marble, wonderfully joined * * * * with bands of gilded copper worked into its surface like a chess-board, being interlaced with each other and with shapes of mihrabs. When the sun strikes them, such light and brightness shine from them that the beholder conceives them to be gold, dazzling the eyes with their rays. The height of the marble wall of this Hijr is five and a half spans and its width four and a half. Inside the Hijr is a wide paving, round which the Hijr bends as it were in two-thirds of a circle. It is laid with tessellated marble, cut in discs the size of the palm of the hand, of a dinar and more minute than that, and joined with remarkable precision. It is composed with wonderful art, is of singular perfection, beautifully inlaid and checkered, and is superbly set and laid. The beholder will see bendings, inlays, mosaics of tiles, chess-board forms and the like, of various forms and attributes, such as will fix his gaze for their beauty. Or let his looks roam from the carpet of flowers of many colours to the mihrabs over which bend arches of marble, and in which are these forms we have described and the arts we have mentioned.

Beside it are two slabs of marble adjacent to the wall of the Hijr opposite the Mizab, on which art has worked such delicate leaves, branches, and trees as could not be done by skilled hands cutting with scissors from paper. It is a remarkable sight. The one who decreed that they should be worked in this fashion is the Imam of the East, Abu 'l-'Abbas Ahmad al-Nasir ibn al-Mustadi' billah Abu Muhammad al-Hasan ibn al-Mustanjid billah Abu 'l-Muzaffar Yusif al-'Abbasi – may God hold him in His favour. Facing the waterspout, in the middle of the Hijr and the centre of the marble wall, is a marble slab of most excellent chiselling with a cornice round it bearing an inscription in striking black in which is written, '(This is) among the things ordered to be done by the servant and Caliph of God Abu 'l-'Abbas Ahmad al-Nasir li dini Ilah, Prince of the Faithful, in the year 576 [1180]'.

The Mizab is on the top of the wall which overlooks the Hijr. It is of gilded copper and projects four cubits over the Hijr, its breadth being a span. This place under the waterspout is also considered as being a place where, by the favour of God Most High, prayers are answered. The Yemen corner is the same. The wall connecting this place with the Syrian corner is called al-Mustajar [The Place of Refuge]. Underneath the waterspout, and in the court of the Hijr near to the wall of the blessed House, is the tomb of Isma'il [Ishmael] – may God bless and preserve him. Its mark is a slab of green marble, almost oblong and in the form of a mihrab. Beside it is a round green slab of marble, and both [they are *verde antico*] are remarkable to look upon. There are spots on them both which turns them from their colour to something of yellow so that they are like a mosaic of colours, and I compare them to the spots that are left in the crucible after the gold has been melted in it. Beside this tomb, and on the side towards the 'Iraq corner, is the tomb of his mother Hajar [Hagar] – may God hold her in His favour – its mark being a green stone a span and a half wide. Men are

blessed by praying in these two places in the Hijr, and men
are right to do so, for they are part of the Ancient House and
shelter the two holy and venerated bodies. May God cast His
light upon them and advantage with their blessings all who
pray over them. Seven spans lie between the two holy tombs.
The dome of the Well of Zamzam is opposite the Black
Corner, and lies twenty-four paces from it. The Maqam, which
we have already mentioned and behind which prayers are said,
is to the right of this dome, from the corner of which to the
other is ten paces. The inside of the dome is paved with pure
white marble. The orifice of the blessed well is in the centre
of the dome deviating towards the wall which faces the
venerated House. Its depth is eleven statures of a man as we
measured it, and the depth of the water is seven statures, as it
is said. The door of this dome faces east, and the door of the
dome of 'Abbas and that of the Jewish dome face north. The
angle of that side of the dome named after the Jews,[54] which
faces the Ancient House, reaches the left corner of the back
wall of the 'Abbaside corner which faces east. Between them lies
that amount of deviation. Beside the dome of the Well of
Zamzam and behind it stands the qabbat al-Sharab [the dome
of drinking], which was erected by 'Abbas – may God hold
him in His favour. Beside this 'Abbaside dome, obliquely to
it, is the dome named after the Jews. These two domes are
used as storerooms for pious endowments made to the blessed
House, such as Korans, books, candlesticks, and the like. The
'Abbaside dome is still called al-Sharabiyyah because it was a
place of drinking for the pilgrims; and there, until to-day, the
water of Zamzam is put therein to cool in earthenware jars
and brought forth at eventide for the pilgrims to drink. These
jars are called dawraq and have one handle only. The orifice
of the Well of Zamzam is of marble stones so well joined,
with lead poured into the interstices, that time will not ravage
them. The inside of the orifice is similar, and round it are lead
props attached to it to reinforce the strength of the binding
and the lead overlay. These props number thirty-two, and their

tops protrude to hold the brim of the well round the whole of the orifice. The circumference of the orifice is forty spans, its depth four spans and a half, and its thickness a span and a half. Round the inside of the dome runs a trough of width one span, and depth about two spans and raised five spans from the ground, and it is filled with water for the ritual ablutions. Around it runs a stone block on which men mount to perform the ablutions.

The blessed Black Stone is enchased in the corner facing east. The depth to which it penetrates it is not known, but it is said to extend two cubits into the wall. Its breadth is two-thirds of a span, its length one span and a finger joint. It has four pieces, joined together, and it is said that it was the Qarmata[55] [Carmathians] – may God curse them – who broke it. Its edges have been braced with a sheet of silver whose white shines brightly against the black sheen and polished brilliance of the Stone, presenting the observer a striking spectacle which will hold his looks. The Stone, when kissed, has a softness and moistness which so enchants the mouth that he who puts his lips to it would wish them never to be removed. This is one of the special favours of Divine Providence, and it is enough that the Prophet – may God bless and preserve him – declare to be a covenant of God on earth. May God profit us by the kissing and touching of it. By His favour may all who yearn fervently for it be brought to it. In the sound piece of the stone, to the right of him who presents himself to kiss it, is a small white spot that shines and appears like a mole on the blessed surface. Concerning this white mole, there is a tradition that he who looks upon it clears his vision, and when kissing it one should direct one's lips as closely as one can to the place of the mole.

The sacred Mosque is encompassed by colonnades in three (horizontal) ranges on three rows of marble columns so arranged as to make it like a single colonnade. Its measurement in length is four hundred cubits, its width three hundred, and its area is exactly forty-eight *maraja'* [sing. *maraj'*, a measure

of area amongst the western Arabs equalling fifty square cubits].
The area between the colonnades is great, but at the time of
the Prophet – may God bless and preserve him – it was small
and the dome of Zamzam was outside it. Facing the Syrian
corner, wedged in the ground, is the capital of a column which
at first was the limit of the Haram. Between this capital and
the Syrian corner are twenty-two paces. The Ka'bah is in the
centre (of the Haram) and its four sides run directly to the
east, south, north and west. The number of the marble columns,
which myself I counted, is four hundred and seventy-one,
excluding the stuccoed column that is in the Dar al-Nadwah
(House of Counsel), which was added to the Haram. This is
within the colonnade which runs from the west to the north
and is faced by the Maqam and the 'Iraq corner. It has a large
court and is entered from the colonnade. Against the whole
length of this colonnade are benches under vaulted arches where
sit the copyists, the readers of the Koran, and some who ply
the tailor's trade.

The Haram enfolds rings of students sitting around their
teachers, and learned men. Along the wall of the colonnade
facing it are also benches under arches in the same fashion. This
is the colonnade which runs from the south to the east. In the
other colonnades, the benches against the walls have no arches
over them. The buildings now in the Haram are at the height
of perfection. At the Bab Ibrahim [Abraham's Gate] is another
entrance from the colonnade which runs from the west to the
south and has also stuccoed columns. I found in the writing of
Abu Ja'far ibn ['Ali] al-Fanaki al-Qurtubi, the jurisprudent and
traditionalist, that the number of columns was four hundred
and eighty; for I had not counted those outside the Safa Gate.

Of the enlarging of the Sacred Haram and the adornment of
its buildings by the Mahdi Muhammad ibn Abi Ja'far al-Mansur
al-'Abbasi there is noble evidence. On the side running from
west to north high on the wall of the cloister I found written,
'The servant of God Muhammad al-Mahdi, Prince of the Faithful – may God have him in His care – ordered the enlargement

of the Sacred Mosque for the pilgrims to God's House and for those upon the 'umrah. In the year 167 [A.D. 783].'

The Haram has seven minarets. Four are at each corner, another is at the Dar al-Nadwah, and another at the Safa Gate indicates the Gate and is the smallest of them, no one being able to climb up to it for its narrowness. The seventh stands at the Abraham Gate which we shall mention later.

The Safa Gate faces the Black corner in the colonnade which runs from the south to the east. In the middle of the colonnade which is opposite the door are two columns facing the aforementioned corner and bearing this engraved inscription: 'The Servant of God Muhammad al-Mahdi, Prince of the Faithful – may God have him in His favour – ordered the erection of these two columns to indicate the path of the Messenger of God [Muhammad] – may God bless and preserve him – to al-Safa, that the pilgrims to the House of God and those that dwell therein might follow him. (Done) by the hand of Yaqtin ibn Musa and Ibrahim ibn Salih in the year 167 [A.D. 783].'

On the door of the holy Ka'bah is engraved in gold, with graceful characters long and thick, that hold the eyes for their form and beauty, this writing: 'This is amongst those things erected by order of the servant and Caliph of God, the Imam Abu 'Abdullah Muhammad al-Muqtafi li Amri Ilah, Prince of the Faithful. May God bless him and the Imams his righteous ancestors, perpetuating for him the prophetic inheritance and making it an enduring word for his prosperity until the Day of Resurrection. In the year 550 [A.D. 1155].' In this wise (was it written) on the faces of the two door-leaves. These two noble door-leaves are enclosed by a thick band of silver gilt, excellently carved, which rises to the blessed lintel, passes over it and then goes round the sides of the two door-leaves. Between them, when they are closed together, is a sort of broad strip of silver gilt which runs the length of the doors and is attached to the door-leaf which is to the left of him who enters the House.

The Kiswah [lit. 'robe', covering] of the sacred Ka'bah is of green silk as we have said. There are thirty-four pieces: nine on the side between the Yemen and Syrian corners, nine also on the opposite side between the Black corner and the 'Iraq corner, and eight on both the side between the 'Iraq and Syrian corners and on that between the Yemen and the Black. Together they come to appear as one single cover comprehending the four sides. The lower part of the Ka'bah is surrounded by a projecting border built of stucco, more than a span in depth and two spans or a little more in width, inside which is wood, not discernible. Into this are driven iron pegs which have at their ends iron rings that are visible. Through these is inserted a rope of hemp, thick and strongly made, which encircles the four sides, and which is sewn with strong, twisted, cotton, thread to a girdle, like that of the *sirwal* [the Arab cotton bloomers], fixed to the hems of the covers. At the juncture of the covers at the four corners, they are sewn together for more than a man's stature, and above that they are brought together by iron hooks engaged in each other. At the top, round the sides of the terrace, runs another projecting border to which the upper parts of the covers are attached with iron rings, after the fashion described. Thus the blessed *Kiswah* is sewn top and bottom, and firmly buttoned, being never removed save at its renewal year by year. Glory to God who perpetuates its honour until the Day of Resurrection. There is no God but He.

The door of the sacred Ka'bah is opened every Monday and Friday, except in the month of Rajab, when it is opened every day. It is opened at the first rising of the sun. The custodians of the House, the Shayba advance, seeking to forestall each other in moving a big stairway that resembles a large pulpit. It has nine long steps, and wooden supports that reach the ground and have attached to them four large wheels, plated with iron as against their contact with the ground, on which the ladder moves until it reaches the Sacred House. The highest step reaches the blessed threshold of the door. The chief of the Shayba, a mature man of handsome mien and aspect, then ascends it, carrying the key of the blessed lock. With him is a custodian holding up a black veil that is (hung) before the door and under which his arms sag[56] while the aforesaid chief of the Shayba opens the door. When he has opened the lock, he kisses the threshold, enters the House alone, closes the door behind him and stays there the time of two rak'ah. The other Shayba then enter and also close the door and perform the rak'ah. The door is then opened and men compete to enter. While the venerated door is being opened, the people stand before it with lowered looks and hands outstretched in humble supplication to God. When it is opened they cry, 'Allahu Akbar' [God is Great], raising a clamour and calling in a loud voice, 'Ah, my God, open to us the gates of Your mercy and pardon, Most Merciful of the Merciful.' They then 'enter in peace, secure' [Koran XV, 46].

In the wall facing the entrant, which is that running from the Yemen corner to the Syrian, are five marble panels set lengthways as if they were doors. They come down to a distance of five spans from the ground, and each one of them is about a man's stature in height. Three of them are red, and two green, and all have white tessellations so that I have never seen a more beautiful sight. They are as if speckled. A red one adjoins the Yemen corner, and next to it at a distance of five spans is a green. At the place opposite this, falling back from it three cubits, is the musalli [praying place] of the Prophet – may God bless and preserve him – and men crowd to pray at it and be blessed. They are all sited in this manner, there being between each panel and the other the distance we have stated. Between each pair is a marble slab of pure and unstained whiteness on which Great and Glorious God had fashioned, at its first creation, remarkable designs, inclining to blue, of trees and branches, and another beside it with the same designs exactly, as if they were parts (of the same stone); and if one were placed over the other each design would correspond with its opposite. Beyond a peradventure each slab is the half of the other, and when the cut was made they divided to make these designs and each was placed beside its sister. The space between a green and a red panel is that of two slabs, their combined width being five spans, according to the number mentioned above. The designs on these slabs vary in shape, and each slab lies beside its sister. The sides of these marble slabs are braced by cornices, two fingers wide, of marble tessellated with spotted greens and reds, and speckled whites, that are like wands worked on a lathe, such as to stagger the imagination. In this wall there are six spaces with white marble. In the wall, which is to the left of him who enters, which is from the Black corner to the Yemen, there are four marble panels, two green and two red. Between them are five [two spaces must therefore be on the flanks] spaces with white marble, and all in the fashion described. In the wall to the right of the entrant, which is that from the Black corner to the 'Iraq, there are three panels, two red and one green, interspersed with three spaces of white marble. This is the wall that runs to the corner containing the Bab al-Rahmah [the Door of Mercy or to-day the Bab al-Taubah] which is three spans wide and seven spans high. That side-piece of this door which is to your right as you face it is of green marble and two-thirds of a span wide. In the wall from the Syrian to the 'Iraq corner are three panels of marble, two red and one green, connected by three spaces of white marble in the manner described. These slabs of marble are crowned with two fasciae, one over the other, each being two spans wide, and of gold with an inscription in lapis-lazuli of fine hand. These fasciae reach the gold engraving on the upper half of the wall. The side on the right of the entrant has one fascia. In these double fasciae some parts (of the inscription) have been effaced.

In each of the four corners, towards the ground, are two small tablets of green marble which enclose the corner (on both sides). Similarly, both of the two (small) silver doors which, in the form of windows, are found in each corner, are enclosed by small side-pieces of green marble the size of the openings. At the beginning of all the walls described comes a red marble panel and at the end also comes a red, while the green are distributed between them after the manner related, save on the wall to the left of the entrant, for there the first marble you find, beside the Black corner, is green; then comes a red, and so on until the end of the arrangement we have explained.

Beside the noble Maqam is the preacher's pulpit [*minbar*] which also is on four wheels in the mode we have explained. When, on Fridays, the time of prayer approaches, it is brought to the side of the Ka'bah that faces the Maqam, which is that which runs between the Black and the 'Iraq corners, and is propped against it. The khatib [preacher] comes through the Gate of the Prophet – may God bless and preserve him – which is opposite the Maqam and in the colonnade which runs from east to north. He wears a black dress, worked with gold, a black turban similarly worked, and a *taylasan* of fine linen. All this is the livery of the Caliph, which he sends to the preachers of his land. With lofty gait, calm and stately, he slowly paces between two black banners held by two muezzins of his tribe. Before him goes another of his people bearing a red staff, turned on a lathe, and having tied to its top a cord of twisted skin, long and thin, with a small thong at its tip. He cracks it in the air with so loud a report that it is heard both within the Haram and without, like a warning of the arrival of the preacher. He does not cease to crack it until they are near the pulpit. They call (this whip) the *farqa'ah*.

Coming to the pulpit, the khatib turns aside to the Black Stone, kisses it, and prays before it. Then he goes to the pulpit, led by the Zamzam muezzin, who is the chief of the muezzins of the noble Haram and also dressed in black clothes. He bears on his shoulder a sword which he holds in his hand without girding it. The muezzin girds the khatib with the sword as he ascends the first step, which then, with the ferrule of his scabbard, he strikes a blow which all present can hear. He strikes it again on the second step and on the third. When he reaches the top step, he strikes the fourth blow, and stands facing the Ka'bah praying in low tones. Then he turns to right and left and says, 'Peace upon you, and the mercy and blessings of God.' The congregation returns the salutation ['Upon you be peace'] and he then sits. The muezzins place themselves in front of him

and call the adthan in one voice. When they have finished,
the khatib delivers the address, reminding, exhorting, inspiring,
and waxing eloquent. He then sits down in the conventional
sitting of the preacher and strikes with the sword a fifth time.
He then delivers the second (part of) the Khutbah multiplying
prayers for Muhammad – may God bless and preserve him –
and for his family, begging God's favour for his Companions
and naming in particular the four Caliphs – may God have
them all in His favour – praying for the two uncles of the
Prophet – may God bless and preserve them – Hamzah and
'Abbas, and for al-Hasan and al-Husayn, uniting to all (the
words): 'May God hold them in His favour.' He then prayed
for the Mothers of the Faithful wives of the Prophet – may God
bless and preserve them – and begged God's favour for Fatimah
the Fair and for Khadijah the Great in this language. He then
prayed for the 'Abbaside Caliph Abu 'l-'Abbas Ahmad al-Nasir,
then for the Emir of Mecca, Mukthir ibn 'Isa ibn Fulaytah ibn
Qasim ibn Muhammad ibn Ja'far ibn Abi Hashim al-Hasani,
then for Salah al-Din [Saladin] Abu 'l-Muzaffar Yusif ibn
Ayyub and his heir and brother Abu Bakr ibn Ayyub. At the
mention in the prayers of Saladin, from all sides tongues
quivered (in emotion) as they cried 'Amen' to that.

> 'If God to His servant one day gives love,
> He gives it him in love of all mankind.'

And right it is they should, for the goodly care and kind
attention he has lavished on them, and for his raising of the
customs tax from off them.

We learnt at this time that a letter had come from him to
the Emir Mukthir, the most important chapter of which was
the commendation regarding the care of the pilgrims, with the
insistence on beneficence and kindness being shown towards
them, and the raising of the hand which bore upon them, and
the giving of orders to this effect to the servants, the men of the
following, and the officers of the army. 'We and you,' said
the Sultan, 'are charged with the well-being of the pilgrims.

Reflect upon this noble task and generous aim. The benefits
of God are two-fold for him who benefits His servants, and
His bounteous care reaches him who exerts his care for them.'
Great and Glorious God is the guarantor for the reward of
those who do good. For He directs all these things. There is
no Lord but Him.

During the khutbah, the two black banners are planted on
the first step of the minbar, and held by two muezzins. At the
side of the entrance to the minbar are two rings in which the
banners are placed. When the khatib has ended the prayers, he
leaves with the banners on his right and left and before him the
farqa'ah, after the manner in which he entered. This is at once
the signal of the departure of the preacher and the end of the
prayers, and the minbar is returned to its place beside the Maqam.

On the night on which the new moon of this month of
Jumada 'l-Ula rose, the Emir of Mecca, the aforesaid Mukthir,
came early in the morning, as the rising of the sun, to the
noble Haram. Around him were his leading men, and Koran
readers went before him. He entered by the Gate of the Prophet
– may God bless and preserve him – with his Negroes, those
that are known as *harrabah* [spearmen], who, spear in hand,
whirled in front of him. His aspect was modest, calm, and
dignified, and his mien that of his noble ancestors – may God
bless and preserve them. He wore a white dress, was girded
with a short sword, and for a turban had a *kurziyyah* of fine
white wool. When he had come close to the noble Maqam,
he stopped. A linen carpet was spread for him and he prayed
two *rak'ahs*. He then advanced to the Black Stone and kissed
it and then began the *tawaf*. On the dome of Zamzam had
climbed a youth who was the brother of the Zamzam muezzin,
he who is the first muezzin in making the calls and whom the
others imitate and follow. When the Emir had completed one
shaut [circuit] and was approaching the Stone, the youth, who
was dressed in his finest cloths and wore a turban, raised his
voice in prayer from the top of the dome, opening with
these words: 'Grant this day, oh God, to our Lord the Emir

everlasting happiness and all-embracing favour.' This he followed with good wishes for the month, and a gifted discourse in rhymed prose full of invocations and eulogies, and then, concluding with three or four verses of poetry in praise of the Emir and his noble ancestors and the excellence of the Prophecy, came to silence.

When the Emir was under the shade of the Yemen corner on his way to the Stone, the youth began another prayer of the same kind, adding other verses of exactly the same purport, which seemed to have been taken from an ode of praise to him. So it continued for seven circuits and until it was over. The Koran readers were in front of the Emir throughout his *tawaf*. The order and splendour of this scene, the beauty of the voice of that muezzin, notwithstanding his youth, for he was about eleven years old or thereabout, the eloquence of the discourse he made in prose and verse, the high voices of the readers of the Book of Great and Glorious God, all these things together move and affect the spirit, draw tears from the eyes, and bring to the memory the family of the Prophet from whom God has removed all impurity and whom He has cleansed. When the Emir had finished the *tawaf*, he prayed two *rak'ahs* at the Multazam, then prayed a *rak'ah* behind the Maqam and departed with his retinue around him; and it is his custom not to appear again in the Haram save at the time of the new moon.

The Ancient House is built of large blocks of dark granite, compactly set together and joined by a strongly binding cement, so that the days cannot change them nor time destroy. An odd feature of it is that a piece which split from the Yemen corner was nailed in its place with silver nails, which are to be seen, and it became better than it was.

One of the wondrous things about the Ancient House is that it rises in the middle of the Haram like, if it is not irreverent to make the comparison,[57] a lofty tower. The pigeons in the Haram cannot be counted for their number, and their safety is a matter for proverbs. In no case will a pigeon come down to the roof of the Ancient House or alight upon it in any circumstance. You will see a pigeon flying over all the Haram, and when it approaches the House turning from it right or left. All other birds are the same. I read in *The Notes on Mecca* that no bird will alight upon the House save when struck by illness, in which case either will it die upon the instant or straightway be cured. Glory to Him who has made the House worthy of honour and deference.

Another remarkable fact is that when the noble door (of the House) is opened on the set days we have mentioned, and the Haram is choked with people, all will enter the House and yet, by the power of Great and Glorious God, it will not be too small for them. There will not be one place (of prayer) but everyone has prayed in it. When they have gone forth from it, men will meet each other and ask whether they had been in the House that day and all will answer, 'I entered and I prayed in such a place and in such another,' and all will have prayed there. To God indeed are palpable wonders and miraculous proofs. May He be glorified and exalted. One of the marvels of the care of God – Blessed and Exalted is He – is never, for any hour of the day or time of night, is there not someone performing a *tawaf*; and never will you find a man who says that he saw the House without there being someone circumambulating it. Glory to Him who honoured it and made it grand, perpetuating its nobility until the Day of Resurrection.

Over the colonnades of the Haram is a roof which encompasses with them all four sides. It is embattled throughout with large and angulated merlons, each side of the merlon having three angles which themselves are like small merlons. The lowest angle touches the angle of the adjoining merlon. Underneath each juncture is a round hole, a span in circumference, which penetrates it and allows the air to pass through. The rays of the sun and the moon strike through these holes and then they appear like round moons. Around the four sides the merlons continue as if (first) it was built in one piece and then the interruptions and angles made. The result is a form that is a remarkable sight. In the centre of all four sides (of the Haram) is a stuccoed frieze, chiselled and having apertures, that passes between the merlons and which I estimate to be about thirty spans long. Each frieze faces one side of the holy Ka'bah which surmounts the merlons like a crown.

The minarets also have singular forms, for the (lower) half is angulated at the four sides, by means of finely sculptured stones, remarkably set, and surrounded by a wooden lattice of rare workmanship. Above the lattice there rises into the air a spire that seems as the work of a turner, wholly dressed with baked bricks fitting the one into the other with an art that draws the gaze for its beauty. At the top of this spire is a globe also encircled by a wooden lattice of exactly the same pattern as the other. All these minarets have a distinct form, not one resembling the other; but all are of the type described, the lower half being angulated, and the upper columned.

In the upper half of the Zamzam Dome, of the 'Abbaside Dome which is called the 'Place of Drinking', and of the dome which sits obliquely to its left and is called The Jewish Dome, there is wonderful ornamental wood carving in which the artificer displayed much elegance, and at their summits are wooden balustrades of lattice-work with delicate perforations and apertures. Inside the lattice of the Zamzam Dome is a terrace in whose middle is a kind of minaret ball and on which the Zamzam muezzin makes his call to prayers. From this ball rises a slender stuccoed column with at its tip an iron vessel which in the solemn month of Ramadan they use as a lamp. On that side of the dome which faces the Ancient House are chains on which hang crystal lamps that are lit each night; and on the side to the right, which faces north, it is the same. On all its sides are three balustrades set up like doors and sustained by small glass columns than which no more beautiful work could be seen. Some were twisted like bracelets, especially on the side of the dome facing the Black Stone where the work on the column reaches the height of perfection. Round each column are three or four fillets, and below, between each fillet * * * * in which there are artistic works that are wonderful to look upon. Some of the columns are twisted like a bracelet.

The side of the dome facing the Black Stone has a marble bench running round it. On this men sit pondering the nobility of that place, for it is the most noble of the world, and described as partaking of the nobility of places in the world to come. For the Black Stone is before you, the venerated door and the House face you, the Maqam is to your right, the Safa Gate to your left, and the well of Zamzam is behind your back. Let this be sufficient to you.

Attached to each of these balustrades are bars of iron interlaced with each other as if they were other balustrades. One of the corners of the wooden lattice enclosing the 'Abbaside Dome touches one of the corners of the lattice of the Jewish Dome, and whoever may be on the roof of this can cross to the roof of the other over the two corners. Inside this dome are ornamental stucco works of great beauty.

The Haram has four Sunnite [orthodox] imams, and a fifth for the sect called the Zaydis. The nobles among the inhabitants of this town follow the Zaydi rites. In the call to prayer they add, 'Come to the best of works' after the muezzin's words, 'Come to Salvation.' They are blaspheming Rafidites, and God in the life to come will take them to account and give them their deserts.[58] On Fridays they do not attend congregational prayers but repeat the midday prayers four times, and at sunset pray after the other imams have ended. The first of the Sunni imams is the Shafi'i – God's mercy upon him – and we have mentioned him first for he is the surrogate of the 'Abbaside Caliph. He is the first to offer prayer, which he does behind the Maqam of Abraham – may God bless and preserve him and our noble Prophet. But at the evening prayers, all four imams pray together concurrently because of the shortness of time. The Shafi'i muezzin begins with the *iqamah* [requiring the congregation to stand in line and introducing the prayers], and then the muezzins of the other imams follow. Sometimes into these prayers there enters an oversight or inadvertence by the

G

worshippers, and then from all sides comes the cry, 'God is Great.' At times a Maliki will recite the *rak'ah* of the Shafi'i or of the Hanafi, or salute an imam that is not his. You will observe every ear listening to the voice of its imam or muezzin, fearing an oversight, yet still many occur. Then comes the Maliki – God's mercy upon him – who prays opposite the Yemen corner. He has a stone mihrab resembling the mihrabs placed on the high road.[59] The Hanafi – God's mercy upon him – follows, and he prays opposite the waterspout and under a hatim made for him. He is the most splendid of the imams, having more candles and such like, for the whole of the Persian Empire is of his rite and his congregation is very large. He comes last, for the Hanbali – God's mercy upon him – prays with the Maliki at one time. His place of prayer is opposite the side between the Black Stone and the Yemen corner. The noon and afternoon prayers he recites near to the Hanafis in the colonnade which runs from west to north; and the Hanafi recites them in the colonnade running from west to south facing his mihrab, for he has no hatim. The Shafi'i has a richly embellished hatim opposite the Maqam. The description of the hatim is as follows: Two wooden boards are joined by rungs like a ladder, and facing them are two more wooden boards in the same style. This wooden arrangement is set on two pedestals of stucco that do not rise high, and another piece of wood is nailed high across them. From this suspend iron hooks on which glass lanterns are hung. Sometimes a latticed balustrade is attached to the upper transverse for its whole length. Between the two pedestals of stucco that hold the wooden arrangement the Hanafi imam has a mihrab in which he prays. The Hanbali has a hatim without decoration, near the Hanafi hatim, and ascribed to Ramasht, a Persian of substance of whose liberality some bounteous records stand in the Haram. God's mercy upon him.

Facing the Hijr is a hatim, also undecorated, ascribed to the vizier al-Muqaddam, (as he is known) in this vague form of utterance. All these places are included in the circuit of the

Ancient House. A short distance from the House are torches that are kindled in iron vessels fitted on wooden poles driven (into the ground), thus illuminating the whole of the noble Haram. Candles are set in front of the imams in their mihrabs. The Maliki has fewer candles than the rest and is the poorest, for his rite is uncommon in these parts. The bulk of the people are of the Shafi'i rite, to which also belong the learned men and jurisprudents of the land. But this is not so in Alexandria, where most of the people are Malikis, and where lives the jurisprudent ibn 'Awf, a venerable man of learning and the best among the Malikite imams.

At the end of the sunset prayers the Zamzam muezzin stands on the roof of the Zamzam Dome, to which ascent is made by a wooden stairway on the side facing the Safa Gate and raises his voice in invocation for the 'Abbaside Imam [Caliph], Ahmad al-Nasir li din Ilah, then for the Emir Mukthir, then for Salah al-Din [Saladin] Emir of Syria and of all the provinces of Egypt and of the Yemen, famed for his good deeds and having noble virtues. When in the prayers they come to his mention, those performing the tawaf raise their voices in 'Amen' with tongues fortified by sincere hearts and true intentions, and trembling (with emotion), so that hearts melt with feeling at the fine praise which God has bestowed on this just Sultan, and at the love of mankind which He has planted in him; and the worshippers of God in his land are witness of this. The muezzin follows this with a prayer for the Emirs of the Yemen, vice-regents of Saladin, and then for all Muslims, pilgrims, and travellers. He then descends. Thus is his constant practice.

In the 'Abbaside Dome is a store containing a large and capacious chest that holds the Koran of one of the four Caliphs who were Companions of the Messenger of God – may God bless and preserve him. It is written in the hand of Zayd ibn Thabit – may God hold him in His favour – and was copied in the eighteenth year after the death of the Messenger of God – may God bless and preserve him. It lacks many pages. Two wooden boards, covered with leather, bind it, and the clasps are of brass; the pages are big and comprehend much script. We inspected it and were blessed in kissing it and stroking our cheeks with it. May God advantage us for our purpose in this. The custodian of this dome, whose task it was to show it to us, told us that when the people of Mecca are smitten by a drought, or suffer a rising of prices, they take out this Koran and, opening the door of the venerated House, place it on the blessed threshold with the venerated maqam, the maqam of the Friend (of God) Abraham – may God bless both the Prophet and him. With bared heads they gather round, humbly beseeching and entreating God by the venerated Koran and the sublime maqam, and leaving not their place until the mercy of God, Great and Glorious is He, has overtaken them. God indeed is good to His servants. There is no God but He.

Beside the Haram are many houses whose doors open upon it – let it suffice for you so noble a vicinage – such as the house of Zubaydah, that of the qadi, one called al-'Ajalah, and others. Around the Haram too are many houses with belvederes and with roofs from which one can go over on to that of the Haram, and on which their inhabitants pass the night and cool their water on top of the merlons. They look upon the Ancient House in continuous worship, and are gifted, by the grace and favour of God, with the vicinage of His Holy House.

In the hand of the jurisprudent, the ascetic and godly Abu Ja'far al-Fanaki of Cordova we found it recorded that the measurements of the Sacred Mosque, both in length and in breadth, are those I have already given. The length of the Mosque of the Prophet [in Medina] – may God bless and preserve him – is three hundred cubits, and the breadth two hundred. The number of its columns is three hundred and its minarets three. Its area is twenty-four Maghribi maraja', which is fifty square cubits. The length of the mosque of Jerusalem – may God restore it to the Muslims – is seven hundred and eighty cubits, and its breadth four hundred and fifty. It has four hundred and fourteen columns, five hundred lamps, fifty doors and an area of one hundred and forty and two-fifths maraja'.

A note on the Gates of the noble Haram

May God sanctify it

The Haram has nineteen gates, most of which have several openings as we shall presently, God willing, describe. Bab [Gate] al-Safa with five doors and anciently described as the Gate of the Banu Makhzum; Bab al-Khalaqiyyin [the Old Clothes Men], also called Bab Jiyad the lesser,[60] which has two doors and is new; Bab al-'Abbas – may God hold him in His favour – with three doors; Bab 'Ali – may God hold him in His favour – with three doors; Bab al-Nabi [the Prophet] – may God bless and preserve him – with two doors; a small Bab, beside the Bab Banu Shayba, and without name; Bab Banu Shayba, with three doors and also called the Bab Banu 'Abd al-Shams, and being the Gate by which the Caliph enters; Bab al-Nadwah [of Counsel], consisting of three gates, two in the Dar al-Nadwah [House of Counsel] in line with each other, and a third in the west corner of the Dar; by including this separate gate, the number of gates in the Haram is twenty; a small Bab beside the Bab Banu Shayba like a wicket-gate and having no name, but said to be called Bab al-Ribat [Asylum] because through it entrance is made to the Sufi Ribat; a small Bab in the Dar al-'Ajalah which is new; Bab al-Suddah,[61] single; Bab al-'Umrah, single; Bab al-Hazwarah, with two doors; Bab Ibrahim – may God bless and preserve him – single; a Bab also ascribed to Hazwarah, with two doors; Bab Jiyad the greater, with two doors; Bab Jiyad the greater also having two doors;[62] a Bab called Jiyad also having two doors. There are some who ascribe two of the four Jiyad Gates to flour-millers. Stories vary, but we have done our best to give the names that are closest to authenticity. God is our recourse: there is no Lord but He.

The Bab Ibrahim – may God bless and preserve him – is in a large and spacious square in which also is the house of the jurisprudent al-Miknasi – may God have mercy on his soul – who was the Maliki imam of the Haram. There too is a room which acts as a store for the books endowed in piety to the Malikis in the Haram. This square adjoins the colonnade running from west to south, and is outside it. Beside the Bab (Ibrahim), to the right of the entrant, is a minaret unlike those we have mentioned. It has a stuccoed lattice of oblong shape like mihrabs and surrounded by ornamental carving of remarkable workmanship. By the Gate is a great dome, prominent in height, in which it approaches the minaret. Within are notable works of stucco, and ornamental lattices, of which description fails. Without are pieces of stucco like round pedestals set one over the other. The ball on the minaret rests on stucco supports, with apertures between each one. Outside the Bab Ibrahim is a well named after him – on whom be (eternal) happiness.

We began (the enumeration of these Gates) with the Bab al-Safa because it is the biggest, and because it is from this gate that one goes forth to perform the *sa'i* [the running seven times between Mounts Safa and Marwah]. Every pilgrim who comes to Mecca – may God exalt it – on the 'umrah [lesser pilgrimage] should preferably enter by the Bab Banu Shayba, then perform the seven circuits, and finally leave by the Bab al-Safa making his way between the two columns that the Mahdi – God's mercy on his soul – had ordered should be erected to show, as we have already remarked, the way that the Messenger of God had taken to al-Safa. Forty-six paces lie between these two columns and the Yemen corner, and from them to the Bab al-Safa is thirty paces. From Bab al-Safa to al-Safa is seventy-six paces. The Safa has three high arches and fourteen steps, the top one being wide like a stone bench. It is surrounded by houses and is seventeen paces wide. Between al-Safa and the green mil lie what we shall mention. The mil is a green column, dyed that colour, at the angle of the minaret that is at the eastern corner of the Haram, on the upper part of the torrent bed leading to al-Marwah, and to the left of him who is performing the sa'i and (does the ritual running) towards it. From this mil he will run, in doing the sa'i, to

two green mils, both being green columns after the style men-
tioned. One of them is beside Bab 'Ali, in the wall of the
Haram and to the left of him who leaves the Gate; the other
faces it, in the wall of a house that adjoins the house of the
Emir Mukthir. At the top of both these columns, like a crown,
is set a tablet on which I found inscribed in gold characters:
'Al-Safa and al-Marwah are surely among the signs of God',
continuing the verse [Koran II, 158], and then following with:
'The servant of God and His Caliph Abu Muhammad al-
Mustadi bi Amri Ilah, Prince of the Faithful – may God glorify
his conquest – ordered the erection of this mil in the year 573
[A.D. 1177].'

Between al-Safa and the first (and single) mil are ninety-
three paces; and from this mil to the two mils is seventy-five
paces, which is the distance of the running, for coming and for
going, from the mil to the two mils, and from the two mils
to the mil. From the two mils to al-Marwah is three hundred
and twenty-five paces, and so the total number of paces of
him who does the sa'i from al-Safa to al-Marwah is four
hundred and ninety-three.

Al-Marwah has five steps, and is a large single arch of the
same width as al-Safa: seventeen paces. Between al-Safa and
al-Marwah lies the course of the torrent which to-day is a
market full of all the fruits and other things like grain and the
various kinds of foodstuffs. Those who are doing the sa'i can
hardly free themselves from the great crowd. The vendors'
stalls are right and left, the town having no organised market
save this, with the exception of those for the cloth and the
perfume merchants. These are at the Bab Banu Shayba, below
the market just mentioned, and so close to it as almost to touch it.

Over the noble Haram is Jabal [Mount] Abi Qubays, to the
east and facing the Black Stone corner. At its summit is a
blessed asylum for the needy, with a mosque, having a roof
which overlooks the Good City [Mecca]. From there is seen
its beauty, and the fairness and range of the Haram, and the
grace of the Holy Ka'bah rising in its midst. I read in Notes

on Mecca by Abu 'l-Walid al-Azraqi that it was the first mountain made by God, Great and Glorious is He, and that on it
was deposited the Black Stone at the time of the Flood. The
Quraysh called it al-Amiri [The Trustworthy] because it transmitted the stone to Abraham – may God bless and preserve
him. On it is the tomb of Adam – God's blessings upon him. It is
one on the two great mountains of Mecca, the other being the
mountain contiguous with the mountain Qu'ayqi'an in the west.

We climbed Jabal Abu Qubays and prayed in its blessed
mosque. On it too is the place where stood the Prophet – may
God bless and preserve him – when for him the moon clave
by the power of Great and Glorious God. Let this virtue and
blessedness suffice you. Virtue is in the hand of God, who gives
it to whom He wills, even to His inanimate creatures. There
is no God but He. At the top of the mountain are the remains
of a lofty stucco building which the Emir of the land, 'Isa,
the father of Mukthir, had taken as a stronghold, but which
the Emir of the 'Iraq pilgrimage, because of a dispute with
him, destroyed and left in ruins.

Outside the Bab al-Safa, and facing one of the two columns
in the Haram which we have mentioned (p. 87) as having
been erected to indicate the way the Prophet – may God bless
and preserve him – took to al-Safa, is a column on which I
found inscribed: 'The servant of God, Muhammad al-Mahdi,
Prince of the Faithful – may God Most High have him in His
care – in the year 167 [A.D. 783] ordered the extension of the
Sacred Mosque on the side of the Bab al-Safa in order that
the Ka'bah might be in the centre of the Mosque.' This inscription shows that the Holy Ka'bah is in the centre of the Mosque.
It was indeed thought that there had been a deviation towards
the Bab al-Safa, and we tested its blessed sides by measurement
and found the case to be true and in accordance with the content of the inscription on the column. Under this inscription
and at the base of the column is another saying, 'The servant
of God, (Muhammad) al-Mahdi, Prince of the Faithful – may
God have him in His care – ordered the widening of the middle

gate which is between these two columns and is the road of the
Messenger of God – may God bless and preserve him – to al-
Safa.' At the top of the column which stands beside it there is
also an engraving which says: 'The servant of God, Muhammad
al-Mahdi, Prince of the Faithful – may God have him in His
care – ordered the restoration of the river-bed to the course it
held in the time of his father Abraham [his father by descent
through Ishmael] – may God bless and preserve him – and its
enlargement in the space around the Sacred Mosque, for the
convenience of the pilgrims to God's House and of those upon
the 'umrah.' Below this is written what also is written on the
first column concerning the widening of the middle gate.

The valley in question is that named after Abraham – may
God bless and preserve him – and its course was (once) by the
Bab al-Safa, but then the torrent took a different way and came
by the course between al-Safa and al-Marwah and entered the
Haram so that, at the time of the flooding from the rains, men
had to swim the *tawaf* of the Ka'bah. So al-Mahdi – God's
mercy on him – ordered the raising of a dam in the higher part
of the city, called Ra's al-Radm [the Peak of the Debris]; and
when the torrent comes, it turns from the dam to its (former)
course, passing the Bab Ibrahim to the place called al-Masfalah
[the Lower Part], and leaving the town. Thus no water runs
through the town except at the fall of large and continuous
rains. This is the valley to which the Prophet –, may God bless
and preserve him – refers in the Koran [XIV, 37] when God –
may He be blessed and exalted – declares Abraham as saying,
'Our Lord! Surely I have settled part of my posterity in an
uncultivable valley.' Glory to God who preserves to Himself
signs palpable.

A note on Mecca – may God Most High exalt it – and
its noble monuments and honourable history

Mecca is a city set by Great and Glorious God amongst the
mountains that enclose it. It is in the bosom of a holy valley,

large and long, filled with creatures so many that only Great
and Glorious God can count them. It has three gates, the first
being the Bab al-Ma'la [The Upper] from which one goes forth
to the blessed cemetery which is in the place called al-Hajun.
To the left of him who passes by it is a mountain, with at its
top a mountain pass having a sign like a tower where one comes
out to the road of the 'Umrah [The Lesser Pilgrimage]. This
pass is known as Kada', and it is to it that Hassan refers when
he says in his poem:

'(*The horses*) *raise the dust, and Kada' is their meeting-place.*'

The Prophet – may God bless and preserve him – on the day
of his taking (of Mecca) said, 'Enter at the place of which
Hassan speaks,' and they entered by that pass.

The place called Hajun is the one referred to by al-Harith
ibn Mudad the Jurhumite when he says:

'As if between al-Hajun and al-Safa there is no living soul,
and in Mecca no talk o' nights. Ah but we were its people,
and we rendered null the vicissitudes of the night and the
distressful misfortunes.'

In the cemetery (at Hajun) are the burial places of many of
the Companions of the Prophet, of the followers of the Companions, and of saints and men of piety, whose blessed shrines
have perished, and whose names have gone from the people
of the town. Here is the place in which al-Hajjaj ibn Yusif –
may God requite him – crucified the body of 'Abdullah the
son of al-Zubayr – may God have them both in His favour.
At this place to this day are the clear remains of a tall building
which was destroyed by the people of al-Ta'if in vexation at
the repeated curses (which it evoked from the pilgrim visitors)
of their fellow townsman Hajjaj. To your right, as you face
the cemetery, is a mosque in a gully between two hills. It is
said to be the mosque in which the jinn [genii] acknowledged
the Prophet – may God bless and preserve him – and so gained
honour and distinction. At this Gate [al-Ma'la] starts the road
to Ta'if and to 'Iraq as well as the ascent to 'Arafat. God grant

that we may be among those who succeed in standing on it. This Gate lies between the east and the north, inclining to the east. Then the Bab al-Masfal [The Lower]. It is on the south side and from it goes the road to the Yemen. Through it entered Khalid ibn al-Walid – may God hold him in His favour – the day of the taking of Mecca (by Muhammad). Then comes the Bab al-Zahir, also called Bab al-'Umrah. It is on the west, and from it goes the road to the City [Medina] of the Messenger – May God bless and preserve him – and to Syria and to Jiddah. From it one passes to al-Tan'im, the first (ritual) place of meeting on the lesser pilgrimage. To come to it from the Haram one leaves by the Bab al-'Umrah (in the Haram) and so this (town) Gate bears the same name.

Al-Tan'im is a parasang away from Mecca on a fine broad road with wells of sweet water called al-Shubaykah. As you leave the city, at the distance of a mile, you will find a mosque beside which is a stone placed on the road like a bench, and overtopping it and leaning against it is another stone with an inscription whose characters have become effaced. It is reported that it is the place where the Prophet – may God bless and preserve him – sat and rested when he returned from the lesser pilgrimage. Men win blessings by kissing it and smoothing their cheeks against it, as indeed they should in duty, and they lean against it that their bodies might receive blessings by its contact. After this place, at the distance of a bow-shot, you will find, on the side of the road and to the left of him going towards the 'umrah, two tombs piled high with heaps of large stones. It is said that they are the tombs of Abu Lahab and his wife.[63] God's curses on them. From old times on, men have not ceased the custom of stoning them, until now they are covered by two large mountains.

From here, after a mile, you come to al-Zahir, which is built on both sides of the road and has houses and gardens. All are the property of a Meccan. Places for bathing and drinking have been made for those performing the 'umrah. At the side of the road is a long bench on which is a row of (drinking) mugs,

and there are tubs or qasari [Gr. γαστρα], filled with water
for the ritual ablutions. The place has a well of sweet water
from which they fill the bathing places mentioned above. The
pilgrim will find a great convenience for washing, ritual ablutions, and drinking; and its founder is on the prosperous road
to reward and recompense (from God). Many others who seek
to acquire merit for the life to come help him in what he is
about. It is said that he obtains from it much advantage.

On the sides of the road at this part are four mountains, two
on this side and two on that, on which are cairns of stone. We
were told that they are the blessed mountains on which Abraham
– on whom be (eternal) happiness – placed pieces of birds and
then called to them, according to the declaration of Great and
Glorious God that Abraham had asked Him to show him how
He gave life to the dead [Koran II, 260]. Round those four
mountains are others, and some say that the mountains on which
Abraham put the birds were seven of these. God best knows.

When you have passed al-Zahir, you go by a valley known
as Dhu Tawa, in which it is said that the Prophet – may God
bless and preserve him – descended when he came into Mecca,
and that ('Abdullah) the sun of 'Umar – may God hold them
both in His favour – was bathing there at the time and thereupon entered (with him). Round al-Zahir are some wells
called al-Shubaykah, and it has a mosque said to be that of
Abraham – on whom be (eternal) happiness. Ponder the blessedness of this road, the many miracles attached to it, and the
holy relics that surround it.

You cross the valley and make towards a narrow pass from
which you go forth to come upon the signs put up as a par-
tition between the *haram* [sacred territory of Mecca] and the
hill [country unbound by the sacred prohibitions on carrying
arms, molesting game, fighting, etc.]. All that is within them
and on the side of Mecca is *haram*, and all beyond them *hill*.
They are like towers, big and small, placed in a row the one
close to the other. They begin at the top of the mountain which
stands on the right of the road of him who goes towards the

'umrah, cross the road, and so to the summit of the mountain on his left. Here is the miqat [appointed place] of the pilgrims on the 'umrah, with mosques built of stone where they pray, and here the pilgrims put on the ihram [pilgrim garb]. The mosque of 'A'ishah – may God hold her in His favour – is beyond these signs, at a distance of two bow-shots, and the Malikis go out to it and there assume the ihram. But the Shafi'is assume it at the mosques around the signs. In front of the mosque of 'A'ishah – may God hold her in His favour – is another dedicated to 'Ali ibn Abi Talib – may God hold him in His favour.

A noteworthy thing shown us at the aforementioned Bab Banu Shayba, was a threshold of large stones, long like a bench and set before the three entrances of the Gate. We were told that they were idols worshipped by the Quraysh in the days of ignorance [before Islam], the greatest of them being Hubal. (Now) prostrate they lie upon their faces, trampled on by men and treated with the contempt of their slippers, unable to help themselves much less their worshippers. Glory to Him who is alone in His Oneness. There is no God but He. The truth concerning these stones is that on the day of the taking of Mecca, the Prophet – may God bless and preserve Him – directed that the idols be broken and burnt, and that those shown to us are not authentic. These at the door are merely transported stones and are likened to the idols only because of their size.

Amongst the famous mountains of Mecca, after Jabal Abu Qubays is Jabal Hira'. It is to the east, about a parasang distant, overlooking Mina, and its peak reaches high into the skies. This is the blessed mountain to which the Prophet – may God bless and preserve him – would often repair to worship, and beneath it he shook (in emotion). The Prophet – may God bless and preserve him – had said to it, 'Be calm, Hira', none shall go over you save a prophet, a faithful one, and a martyr', and indeed there were with him (at the time) Abu Bakr [surnamed 'The Faithful'] and 'Umar [murdered by a Persian] –

may God hold them in His favour. According to another account (the Prophet said), 'Be firm. None shall go over you save a prophet, a faithful one and two martyrs', and that 'Uthman [slain by rebels] was also with them. The first verse of the Koran was revealed to the Prophet – may God hold him in His favour – on this mountain which runs from west to north. Behind its northern edge is the cemetery of Hajun that we have already mentioned.

Mecca is walled only on the side of al-Ma'la where there is a way into the city, on the side of al-Masfal where also there is an entrance, and of Bab al-'Umrah. On the other sides there are mountains, so for walls there is no need. The Walls of Mecca are now destroyed, but traces remain and the Gates stand.

A note on some of the illustrious shrines of Mecca and its holy relics

Mecca – may God exalt it – is all a noble shrine. Honour enough for it is God's especially placing in it the August House, and the prayers that anciently the Friend (of God) Abraham made for it [Koran II, 126]. It is the Haram [sacred precinct] of God, and His place of security. Enough that it is the place of origin of the Prophet – may God bless and preserve him – whom God distinguished with honour and liberality, sending with him the verses of the Koran and wise invocations. It is the source of inspiration and revelation, and the first place where the spirit of the faithful Jibril [Gabriel] descended. It was the resort of the prophets of God and his noble apostles, and also the birthplace of many of his Quraysh Companions, the emigrants whom God made as lamps of religion and as stars for those upon the right path.

Amongst the shrines that we observed was the chamber of the prophetic inspiration in the house of Khadijah, the mother of the Faithful – may God hold her in His favour – where the Prophet – may God bless and preserve him – first went in to his wife. In the same house also is a small chamber in which was born Fatimah the virgin – may God hold her in His favour – and here were born the two Lords of the youth which peoples heaven, al-Hasan and al-Husayn – may God have them both in His favour. These holy places, which are locked and guarded, were built in a manner fitting to them. Also amongst its noble shrines is the birthplace of the Prophet – may God bless and preserve him – and the undefiled ground that was the first earth to touch his immaculate body and over which has been built a mosque that never was seen more finely built, being for the most of inlaid gold. The holy place where the Prophet – may God bless and preserve him – came forth in the blessed and happy hour of his nativity, a nativity ordained by God in compassion for all the people, is girt with silver. What earth to be honoured by God in making it the place of the coming forth of the purest of bodies, the birthplace of the best among men! May God bless and preserve him, his stock, his family, and his noble Companions. This blessed place is opened, and all men enter it to be blessed, on every Monday of the month of Rabi' al-Awwal; for on that day and in that month was born the Prophet – may God bless and preserve him. All the holy places mentioned are opened on that day, which is always a famous one in Mecca.

Another of its noble shrines is the House of the Khayzuran, where the Prophet – may God bless and preserve him – worshipped God in secret with the noble group of pioneers for Islam, some of his Companions – may God hold them in His favour – until God spread Islam from it by the hand of al-Faruq [The Distinguisher between True and False] (the Caliph) 'Umar ibn al-Khattab – may God hold him in His favour. This meritorious attribute shall be enough. Another shrine is the house of Abu Bakr the Faithful – may God be pleased with him – which is now the Emir's mint.[64] Opposite it is a wall containing a blessed stone which brings benedictions on those who touch it. It is said that it saluted the Prophet – may God bless and preserve him – whenever he passed it, and there is a story that one day he – may God bless and preserve him – came to

the house of Abu Bakr – may God hold him in His favour –
and called him. But he was not there, and Great and Glorious
God gave voice to this stone which said, 'Oh Messenger of
God, he is not here.' This was one of the wondrous miracles
done for the Prophet – may God bless and preserve him.

Another holy place is the dome between al-Safa and al-
Marwah attributed to 'Umar ibn al-Khattab – may God hold
him in His favour – in whose centre is a well, and where it is
affirmed he – may God hold him in His favour – sat in judgement. But the truth of this dome is that it was the dome of
his grandson, 'Umar ibn 'Abd al-'Aziz – may God hold him
in His favour – and beside it is the house from which this takes
its name and where he sat in judgement during the days in
which he governed Mecca. So were we told by one of our
reliable sheiks. Men say that the well was anciently there, but
now there is none for we went into the place. We found it
paved and of elegant work.

Near to the house where we lodged, was the house of Ja'far
ibn 'Abi Talib – may God hold him in His favour – of the Two
Wings.[65] On the side of al-Masfal, which is the far part of the
town, is a mosque attributed to Abu Bakr the Faithful – may
God hold him in His favour – and girt with a lovely garden
having palm-trees, pomegranate and jujube trees, and we saw
there hinna' trees [*Lawsonia inermis*]. In front of the mosque
is a small house with a mihrab which, it is related, was a hiding-
place for Abu Bakr – may God hold him in His favour – from
the idolators who sought for him. Near the house of Khadijah
– may God hold her in His favour – and in the same by-street
as her honoured house, is a bench with a support to which
men repair to pray and to smooth its sides, for it is a place
where sat the Prophet – may God bless and preserve him.

Among the mountains which have honoured relics and august
shrines is the mountain called Abu Thawr, which is on the
Yemen side of Mecca, a parasang or more away. In it is the
cave in which the Prophet – may God bless and preserve him
– took refuge with his Companion, the Faithful One [Abu

Bakr] – may God hold him in His favour – as described by God Most High in His Glorious Book [Koran IX, 40]. I read in the work, *Notes on Mecca*, by Abu 'l-Walid al-Azraqi, that the mountain called to the Prophet – may God bless and preserve him – saying, 'To me, oh Muhammad, to me, oh Muhammad, for I have given sanctuary to a prophet before you.' On this mountain Great and Glorious God worked especially for His prophet palpable miracles. In one of these the Prophet – may God bless and preserve him – entered with his Companion [Abu Bakr], a cleft in the rock two-thirds of a span wide and a cubit deep. When they were at peace inside it, God ordained that a spider should make its home over it, and that a bird should build its nest and have its eggs therein. The idolators arrived, led by a tracker who followed the footprints on the road and stopped them at the cleft, and said, 'Here the footprints end. Your friend either ascended from here to the skies, or was swallowed by the earth.' They looked upon the spider spinning its web across the face of the cleft, and the bird hatching its eggs, and saying, 'No one has entered here,' they departed. Said the Faithful One – may God hold him in His favour – 'Oh Messenger of God, had they got in to us through the mouth of the cave what should we have done' and the Apostle of God – may God bless and preserve him – replied, 'Had they got in to us, we should have gone forth from there,' and with his blessed hand he pointed to the other side of the cave. In it there had been no cleft, but on the instant, and by the power of Great and Glorious God, there opened a door in its face. Glory to God who can discharge that which He wishes.

Most men make several visits to this blessed cave, avoiding entry by the door which Great and Glorious God had made and seeking to enter through the cleft by which entry was made by the Prophet – may God bless and preserve him – that they might be blessed thereby. He who attempts this lies down upon the ground and lays his cheek beside the cleft. He first puts in his head and hands and then manipulates the entrance of the rest of his body. Some there are who can do this from the slenderness of their bodies; others get their bodies in the middle of the cleft and there are gripped. They seek to go in or to come out and cannot. Ensnared, they suffer distress and wretchedness until, from behind, they undergo a violent pull. Wise men avoid it for this reason, and more particularly for another and humiliating reason, which is that the generality of men believe that he who cannot fit it, and who is caught by it and cannot escape, is not a child of lawful wedlock. This story has so run upon their tongues that it has become with them an absolute truth of which there is no doubt. He, therefore, who is caught and fails to get through, must reckon with bearing this shameful and mortifying thought, in addition to what his body is suffering from the constriction of that narrow place, from which because of pain he looks on death, cut short of breath and afflicted by suffering. Some men quote the proverb, 'None but a *thaur* [ox, i.e. fool] would go up Jebel Abu Thawr.'

Near to this cave on the same mountain, is a prop standing out from the mountain, set in the form of a raised arm and measuring half a man's height. At its top there extends what is like a hand coming out from the arm by the power of Great and Glorious God to be a sort of spreading pavilion under which about twenty men can shade. It is called the Dome of Gabriel – may God bless and preserve him.

One of the things that deserve to be confirmed and recorded for the blessings and favour of seeing and observing it is that on Friday the 19th of Jumada 'l-Ula (579), which was the 9th of September [1183] God raised from the sea a cloud which moved towards Damascus and rained heavily like an abundant fountain, according to the words of the Messenger of God – may God bless and preserve him [ibn al-Athir, *Nihayah*, iii, p. 151]. It came at the ending of the afternoon's prayers and with the evening of the same day, raining copiously. Men hastened to the Hijr and stood beneath the blessed water-spout, stripping off their clothes and meeting the water that flowed from it with their heads, their hands, and their mouths. They pressed round it in a throng, raising a great clamour, each one coveting for his body a share of the divine mercy. Their prayers went up, the tears of the contrite flowed, and you could hear nothing but the swell of voices in prayer and the sobs of the weeping. The women stood without the Hijr, watching with weeping eyes and humble hearts, wishing they could go to that spot. Some pilgrims listful of performing a meritorious act, and moved as well to pity, drenched their clothes in the blessed water and, going out to the women, wrung them into the hands of some of them. They took it and drank it and laved it over their faces and bodies.

This blessed cloud lasted until the evening and men continued to flock that they might catch the water from the spout with their hands, their faces, and their mouths, and sometimes raised vessels that it might fall therein. It was an auspicious evening, and our souls conceived that they had gained the mercy pledged by His favour and bounty. It was auspicious too for the conjuncture of blessed circumstances. One was that it was the evening of Friday, a day above all others excellent and on which we may hope that our prayers will be accepted by God Most High, according to what has come to us from true tradition. Another was that the gates of the skies opened at the falling of the rain. Again, men were standing under the Mizab [water-spout] which is one of the places where prayers are answered, and their bodies were cleansed by His mercy falling from His sky on to the roof of His Ancient House, which corresponds with His House in the heavens. Let this be enough of generous combinations and noble arrangement. God granted that we should be amongst those who were cleansed with this water from the impurities of their sins, and specially endowed with favour, by the mercy of God Most High. The mercy of God, Glorious is He, is wide, and encompasses His erring servants, for He is the Forgiving, the Compassionate.

It is related that the imam Abu Hamid al-Ghazali prayed to God Most High while he was in the noble Haram, making some requests. These were in part granted by Great and Glorious God, and in part denied. Of those denied was the falling of rain during his stay in Mecca, for he wished to lave himself with it under the Mizab, and pray to Great and Glorious God at His noble House in the hour at which the gates of the sky opened upon it. This was refused him, while all his other prayers were answered. So praise and thanks to Him for what He has bestowed upon us. May it be that one of His good servants on the pilgrimage to His noble House will in particular be shown by God His special favour, and that all we transgressors shall be included in his intercessions. May God advantage us of the mediations of the sincere among His servants, and leave us not among those destitute of them. He is the great Benefactor.

A note on the favours and blessings which God Most High has bestowed exclusively on Mecca

This blessed town and its peoples have from ancient times profited from the prayers of the friend of God, Abraham, for Great and Glorious God speaking for His friend – may God bless and preserve him – has said, 'Therefore incline the hearts of men to yearn towards them [i.e. the seed of Abraham living in Mecca] and provide them with fruits; haply they may be thankful' [Koran XIV, 37] and Himself has declared: 'Have we not established for them a safe sanctuary [the sacred and protected territory of Mecca] to which products of all kinds shall be brought' [Koran XXVIII, 57]. The proof of this in Mecca is manifest, and will continue to the Day of Resurrection, for the hearts of men yearn towards it from far countries and distant regions. The road to it is a place of encounter for those, coming and going, to whom the blessed claims (of Islam) have reached. From all parts produce is brought to it, and it is the most prosperous of countries in its fruits, useful requisites, commodities, and commerce. And although there is no commerce save in the pilgrim period, nevertheless, since people gather in it from east and west, there will be sold in one day,

apart from those that follow, precious objects such as pearls,
sapphires, and other stones, various kinds of perfume such as
musk, camphor, amber and aloes, Indian drugs and other articles
brought from India and Ethiopia, the products of the industries
of 'Iraq and the Yemen, as well as the merchandise of Khurasan,
the goods of the Maghrib, and other wares such as it is impossible to enumerate or correctly assess. Even if they were spread
over all lands, brisk markets could be set up with them and all
would be filled with the useful effects of commerce. All this
is within the eight days that follow the pilgrimage, and exclusive
of what might suddenly arrive throughout the year from the
Yemen and other countries. Not on the face of the world are
there any goods or products but that some of them are in Mecca
at this meeting of the pilgrims. This blessing is clear to all, and
one of the miracles that God has worked in particular for
this city.

Concerning the foods, fruits, and other good things, we had
thought that Spain was especially favoured above all other
regions. So it was until we came to this blessed land and found
it overflowing with good things, and fruits such as figs, grapes,
pomegranates, quince, peaches, lemons, walnuts, palm-fruit,
water-melons, cucumbers, and all the vegetables like egg-plant,
pumpkin, carrot, cauliflower and other aromatic and sweet-
smelling plants. Most of these vegetables, like the egg-plant,
cucumber, and water-melon are hardly ever cut off throughout the year. This is one of the most remarkable of those things
we observed and which it would be too long to enumerate
and describe. All these various kinds of vegetable and fruit had
an excellence of taste greater than those of other lands, and
our surprise at that lasts long.

The choicest of the fruits we tried were the water-melon and
the quince. All its fruits are good, but the water-melon has a
particular and exceptional merit in that its odour is the most
fragrant of smells and the best. When someone approaches you
with one, you find the fragrant odour coming first to you so
that from the enjoyment of its sweetness you almost abstain

from eating it; and when you taste it, it seems to you like
sugar-candy or purest honey. It may be that the reader of these
words will think that in this description there is some hyper-
bole. No, in the name of God it is more than I described, and
above what I said. Mecca has a honey better than that (called)
al-mahdi and which has become a proverb; they call it *al-mas'udi*.
The various kinds of milk are of the highest excellence, and
all butter made from it you can scarce distinguish from honey
for its goodness and sweetness.

A people from the Yemen called al-Saru bring to Mecca a
kind of raisin, the black and the red, of surpassing quality; and
with them they bring many almonds. Then there is the sugar-
cane in plenty, brought from where they bring the vegetables
we have already mentioned. It has an ample stock of imported
sugar and all the good things and best of commodities. Praise
be to God. As to confectionery, they make all kinds of unusual
forms of it, with honey and thickened sugar in many shapes,
including imitations of all the fruits, fresh and dry. In the three
months of Rajab, Sha'ban, and Ramadan, the ground is spread
with these foods between al-Safa and al-Marwah, and no one
has seen a more perfect sight either in Egypt or anywhere else.
From them are shaped human and fruit-like forms displayed
on pedestals like brides on nuptial thrones, ornamentally disposed in their coloured variety and appearing like beautiful
flowers, which fix our looks and ask the dirham and the dinar
to abdicate (their supremacy of brilliance). As for the meat in
Mecca, it is wonderful. The statement falls from all who move
across the horizons and traverse the regions of the earth, that
it is the best meat they have ever eaten in it. This, though God
knows best, cannot come save from the goodness of its pas-
tures. And it is despite the excess of fat, such that were it meat
of another land reaching such a degree of fat a man would
spit it from his mouth, rejecting it and casting it aside. But
here the opposite is the case, the fatter it is, the more appetising
and acceptable it is, and you will find it so tasty and tender
that it will melt in the mouth before you bite it, and for its

lightness be speedily digested by the stomach. I do not look at this save as one of the rare attributes and blessings of the protected land whose welfare has, beyond a peradventure, been assured, and the tale of which is less than the reality. May God with His power and glory, provide sustenance for those (who have come to it from) yearning for His sacred town, and longing for the august sight and the venerable rites.

The fruits are brought to Mecca from al-Ta'if, which is three days from it, going gently and easily, and from the villages around it. The nearest of these places is called Udum, which is a day's journey or less from Mecca and, lying in the valley of Ta'if, comprises many villages. Also there is Batn Marr, which is a day or less away, and Nakhlah the same distance, and the valleys near the town like 'Ayn Sulayman and others. To Mecca God brought from the Maghrib men skilled in tillage and husbandry who created in it gardens and sown lands, and they are one of the reasons for the fertility of these lands. All this is from the bounty of Great and Glorious God and by reason of His generous care for His noble Haram and protected town. One of the most remarkable fruits we found and enjoyed eating, and whose merits, particularly as we had never before met them, we began to extol, were the fresh dates, which with them take the place of (our) green figs. They are plucked and eaten off the tree, and are so good and so delicious that one cannot weary of eating them. The time of their maturity is a great occasion with these people, who go out to them as if going forth to a country property, or like the people of the Maghrib leaving for their farms at the time of the ripening of the fig and vine. When this is over, and the maturing is complete, they are spread upon the ground for time enough for them to dry a little. They then are heaped on each other in baskets and jars, and laid up in store.

Amongst the good works and general favours of God on our behalf, was that on arriving at this honoured city we found that all the settled pilgrims there, those who had come before or whose stay there had been long, spoke as a matter of wonder at its freedom from the thieves who (once) had robbed the pilgrims, snatching what was in their hands, and being a plague in the noble Haram. No one could neglect his belongings the twinkling of an eye or they would be taken from his hand or girdle with amazing cunning and astonishing smoothness, for there was not one of them but was light of hand. But this year, save in a few cases, God gave protection against their ill-doing, and the Emir of the land showed severity towards them, wherefore their evil ceased.

In this year were combined mildness of weather, a mitigation of the customary heat of the summer, and an abatement of the fierceness of the *samum* [the notorious hot wind]. We passed the nights on the roof of the place where we stayed, and sometimes the cold of the night air would fall on us, and we would need a blanket to protect us from it; this was a strange thing for Mecca. The pilgrims also spoke of the many goods in Mecca this year, and the mildness of their prices, which was contrary to their earlier experience. The price of wheat was one mu'mini dinar for four *sa*', which is two *awbahs* [one *awbah*=5 bushels] in the weight system of Egypt and its provinces. Two *awbahs* are equal to two and a half qadahs of the Maghrib measure. This price in a land that has no farms, and no source of sustenance for its people save the provisions imported to it, is one in which the aid and favour of God is manifest. It is the more so in view of the many pilgrims settled there this year, and the succession of men coming into it. I was told by more than one of the pilgrims who had been settled there long years that never had they seen there such a concourse, nor had they ever heard of such. May God, by His favour, grant to this multitude His compassion and safe-keeping. The pilgrims did not cease, the one after the other, to describe the conditions of this year and to compare them with preceding years. They even declared that the blessed water of Zamzam had become more palatable, and that before it had not been of this purity. A singular feature of this water is that when you drink it on its issuing forth from the bottom of the

well you find it, to the sense of taste, like milk coming from
the udders of a camel. In this miracle of God Most High is
evidence of His care and blessing that needs no description.
'It serves the purpose for which it is drunk' [see note 50], as
said the Prophet – may God bless and preserve him. 'God, with
His grace and favour, granted that all who thirst for it should
drink therefrom'. One of the tried effects of this blessed water
is that if perchance a man should feel a touch of sickness or
languor of the limbs, either from many circumambulations (of
the Ka'bah) or from the performance on foot of the lesser
pilgrimage or for other reasons causing fatigue, and pours this
water on his body, he will on the instant find relief and be
enlivened and that which afflicts him will pass away.

The Month of Jumada 'l-Akhirah (579)

[21st of September–19th of October, 1183]
May God show us His grace and favour

THE new moon of this month rose on the night of Wednesday the 21st of September, according to the foreigners, while we were still in the Holy Haram – may God increase its grandeur and honour. On the morrow of that night the Emir Mukthir came (to the Haram) with his followers and attendants in the manner we described in the month of Jumada 'l-Ula and with the same procedure. The Zamzam muezzin sang his praises and prayed for him on the dome of the Zamzam well, raising his voice in invocation and commendation as the Emir made each circuit (of the Ka'bah). The Koran readers walked before him until he had finished the *tawaf*, and was on his way to depart. At the beginning of each month of the year, all the peoples of these eastern parts follow a pleasing practice. They shake hands, congratulate each other, pray for God's forgiveness the one on behalf of the other, and pray for each other; and so they always do at the festivals. This happy custom instils into the spirit a renewed sincerity and invokes the mercy of Great and Glorious God, with the Faithful shaking each others' hands and the blessings of the prayers they have made for each other. The Muslim communion is under the mercy of God, and its prayers have a place with Him.

This blessed city has two baths; one named after the jurisprudent al-Mayanishi, one of the lecturing sheiks in the venerable Haram, and the other which is the larger, named after Jamal al-Din who, like his name, was indeed the splendour of religion. In Mecca and Medina – may God exalt them – there are to be seen his – may God's mercy rest upon his soul – noble monuments, his praiseworthy works, and the strongly made cisterns done in God's name, such as no one before him had ever done, not even the greatest of the Caliphs, much less the Viziers. He – may God's mercy rest upon his soul – had been vizier to the Lord of Mosul and long had prosecuted these high designs, embracing all things useful to the Muslims both in the Haram of God Most High, and in that of His Messenger – may God bless and preserve him. For fifteen years and more he ceased not to give lavishly and beyond count of his substance, building in Mecca quarters dedicated to charitable and pious ends, inalienably and in perpetuity, making reservoirs, placing on the high roads wells where rainwater could collect, and restoring the remains of buildings in the two noble Harams. One of the noblest of his actions was the bringing of water to Mount 'Arafat; and he engaged the Bedouin tribe of Banu Shu'bah, who lived in those regions from which the water was brought, that on payment to them of a large allowance, they should not cut the water from the pilgrims. But when he died – may God's mercy rest upon his soul – they returned to their culpable practice of cutting it. Among his generous acts and achievements was the placing of the City [Medina] of the Apostle – may God bless and preserve him – under the shelter of two strong walls, on which he spent immeasurable wealth. But among the most wonderful of the works in which God Most High helped him to success was his restoring of all the doors of the Haram, and the door of the Ka'bah which he covered with silver gilt and which is the one there now and the one we have already described [p. 78]. He clothed the blessed lintel in a sheet of pure gold, which also we have described. The old door he took, and directed that from it should be made a coffin for him to be buried in. When his death drew nigh, he enjoined that he should be put into that blessed coffin and sent in it on the pilgrimage, he being dead. He was taken to 'Arafat, and at a certain distance from it the coffin was uncovered, and when the pilgrims performed the ifadah [the ritual 'return' from Mina] they made it with him. All the rites were observed for him, including the tawaf of the ifadah. He – may God's mercy rest upon his soul – had never

in his lifetime done the pilgrimage. After this he was carried
to the City [Medina] of the Prophet – may God bless and preserve him – where were the noble monuments of his which
we have mentioned, and where the Sharifs almost carried him
on their heads. A mausoleum was built for him beside that of
the Chosen One – may God bless and preserve him – and in it
was opened a window looking on the holy mausoleum of the
Prophet. This was conceded him, despite the extreme reluct-
ance in making such privileges, in token of his bounteous deeds,
and in that mausoleum he was buried. God made him happy
with that noble vicinage, granting him in particular a sepulchre
in that holy and illustrious earth. In truth God does not fail
to reward those who do good. We shall mention the date of
his death when, if Great and Glorious God so wills, we come
to the date inscribed on his tomb. God is He who can confer
easement, there is no Lord but He. This man – may God's
mercy rest upon his soul – has to his name splendid monuments
and glorious acts which have not been excelled by the most
munificent, or the most eminent of the bountiful of former
times. They are beyond count and exceed all praise, and
throughout the length of time shall be accompanied by the
voices of men in prayer.

Let it be enough to tell you that his care extended to the
repair of all the roads of the Muslims in eastern parts, from
'Iraq to Syria and to the Hejaz, as we have said, and that he
dug wells, built cisterns, founded hostelries in the deserts with
orders that they be furnished as a place of rest for the sons of
the road [poor travellers] and indeed for all travellers, built
inns in the cities between 'Iraq and Syria, and appointed them
for the lodging of those poor sons of the road who could not
pay the account, assigning to these inns and hostelries a staff
who should administer to their needs. This he ordained in perpetuity, and these noble requests remain until this day, so that
travellers upon the way speak handsomely of this man, and
the horizons are filled with his praises. During his lifetime in
Mosul, as we were told by more than one of those pilgrim

merchants deserving of credence who witnessed it, he maintained a large and generous board which was open daily to all strangers that they might take their fill of food and drink; and under his shade the poor sons of the road who came and went found wholesome sustenance. So it continued through his life – may God's mercy rest upon his soul. His monuments are enduring, and his fame is ever renewed upon the tongues of men. Praised and happy he died; and for the happy, an honoured remembrance means continuous life or a second period of existence. God will ensure the reward of those who do good to His servants. He is the most generous of the generous, and the most certain of guarantors.

Amongst the things prohibited in this noble Haram – may God exalt and honour it – is (private) disbursement on it, and no rich man may restore a building or build a *hatim* or anything else connected with the blessed Haram for the purpose of gaining a heavenly reward. If it were lawful to do so, the wealthy who wished to spend on acts of piety would make its walls of gold and its floors of amber, but this they may not do. When one of the great men of the world seeks to restore any of its monuments or any of its noble remains, he must gain permission of the Caliph, and if it is something that may be engraved or inscribed upon, the name of the Caliph will be traced on it with a statement that it was done at his command. Of the name of the benefactor, no mention will be made. Furthermore, a large portion of the bequest must inevitably go to the Emir of the country, and this sometimes is equal to the whole of the original gift, so that the expense must be doubled for the owner that the object might be achieved.

One of the strangest things happened to a shrewd foreigner, a man of wealth and property, who came to the venerated Haram in the time of the grandfather of the present emir, Mukthir, and saw the orifice of the well of Zamzam and its dome to be not of a fashion that pleased him. He met with the Emir and said to him, 'I wish to undertake the careful reconstruction of the orifice of the Well of Zamzam and its brick casing, and to restore the dome, bringing them to the highest possible limit (of perfection) and lavishing upon them the bulk of my fortune. One condition I lay upon you, and on your observance of it depends the attainment of the purpose. It is that you appoint on your behalf a man holding your confidence who shall record the amounts spent in this matter. Then, when the building is completed and, the expenditure being over, the reckoning is made, a like sum shall be paid to you in requital of the consent you gave me.' Filled with greed, the Emir exulted, for he knew that according to the description given him, the cost would reach thousands of dinars. He gave his approval, and attached to the man a registrar who should record all expenses, great and small. And so the man began his work, applying himself with the greatest assiduity, and exhausting all efforts to obtain by his work the favour of Great and Glorious God and 'to lend Him a goodly loan' [i.e. one without interest: Koran II, 245, and LVII, 11]. The registrar recorded everything in his books and the Emir supervised what he wrote, expecting to take with wide-stretched hands that handsome sum. At last the construction was completed and brought to the style we described earlier in our account of the Well of Zamzam and its dome. When nothing remained but to present the account to the author of the scheme and demand of him the sum agreed upon, he left the place and entered into the past tense. He rode throughout the night, and with the morning the Emir 'began to wring his hands' [Koran XVIII, 42] and beat his breast, but since the building was placed in the Haram of God Most High, he could do nothing to change or remove it. The man gained his reward, and at his death God undertook his care, granting him a fair sanctuary. 'Whatsoever you spend (for good), He replaceth it. He is the best of Providers' [Koran XXXIV, 39]. The story of this man with the Emir men continued to tell one another for its strangeness and wonder, and all who drink of the blessed water offer prayers on his behalf.

The Month of Rajab the Unique (579)

[20th of October–18th of November, 1183]
May God let us know His favour

THE new moon of the month rose on the night of Thursday the 20th of October, according to the testimony of a great number of mujawir [settled] pilgrims and Sharifs of Mecca, who declared that they had seen it on the road of the 'umrah, and from Jabal Qu'ayqi'an, and from Jabal Abu Qubays, and who recorded their testimony before the Emir and the qadi.[66] No one had seen it from the sacred mosque. This blessed month is held by the people of Mecca to be a solemn time of meeting of the pilgrims, and is their greatest festival. They have not ceased to observe it in times both ancient and modern, each generation inheriting it from the one before, uninterruptedly from the days of ignorance [i.e. before Muhammad]. They then called it *munsil al-asinnah*, because it was one of the sacred months during which fighting was unlawful. It is the month of God (called) al-Asamm, 'The Deaf', according to the tradition concerning the Apostle of God – may God bless and preserve him. The 'umrah of Rajab is the equivalent of the 'Standing' on 'Arafat, for they throng to it in multitudes, the like of which has not been heard of. The people of adjacent countries flock to it, so great a number assembling that none could count them but Great and Glorious God. Those who have not witnessed this occasion in Mecca have not seen a sight that asks to be recorded for its strangeness and wonder.

In this regard we observed something it is impossible to describe, concerning the night on which the new moon rises, and the morning that follows. Preparations are made for this days before, and we observed something of it that we shall briefly describe. On the afternoon of Wednesday at whose

eventide the new moon was expected, we saw the streets and
by-ways of Mecca to be filled with *hawdaj* [dome-shaped camel
howdahs] bound to the camels and covered with various silk
drapings, and other trappings of fine linen, according to the
circumstances and affluence of their owners, all of whom gave
to it all the care and attention that was in their power. They
set forth to Tan'im, the (ritual) place of assembly for those
going on the *'umrah*, the *hawdaj* flowing through the valleys
and mountain tracks of Mecca. The camels beneath them were
adorned with all kinds of ornaments, and set forth to the sacred
places without guidance in collars of silk and other materials
that were comely to look upon. Sometimes the drapings on
the *hawdaj* fell so low as to draw their hems along the ground.
The most remarkable of these *hawdaj* that we noticed were
that of the Sharifah Jumanah, daughter of Fulaytah and aunt
of the Emir Mukthir, which drew a long train over the ground,
and those of the harem of the Emir and the harem of his principal officers, as well as other *hawdaj* whose number we cannot
record because of the impossibility of counting them. On the
backs of the camels these *hawdaj* appeared as raised pavilions,
and the beholder would conceive them to be an encampment
with its pitched tents of every lively colour. There was no one
of the people of Mecca and the *mujawir* [settled pilgrims] who
that Thursday night did not go forth on the *'umrah*, and we
were among those who went, being earnestly desirous of
acquiring the blessings of that solemn night.

We ourselves were hardly able to reach the Mosque of
'A'ishah, because of the press of men and the blocking of the
narrow parts of the way by the *hawdaj*. Fires were lit throughout the road on both its sides, and lighted torches preceded
the camels carrying the *hawdaj* of the secluded ladies of Mecca
to whom we have referred. When we had done the *'umrah*,
fulfilled the *tawaf*, and come to the sa'i between al-Safa and
al-Marwah, a part of the night had passed, and we saw the
course to be wholly lit with fires and lanterns and thronged
with men and women performing the ritual in their *hawdaj*.

We could not get through save between the *hawdaj* and the legs of the camels, because of the press and the collidings of the *hawdaj* the one with the other. We witnessed the most remarkable night of the nights of this world, and he who has not seen it has not seen a thing wonderful to talk of, than which there is nothing more marvellous to remind him of the gathering at the day of resurrection, so great is the multitude of people, dressed in pilgrim garb, crying 'Labbayka' [Here am I, O Lord] [see note 46] and invoking and beseeching Great and Glorious God. The venerated mountains that flanked the road answered them with their echoes until the ears were deafened; and at awe of that sight tears flowed and hearts melted in emotion.

That night the Sacred Mosque was filled with brightly shining lamps. When the seeing of the new moon had been proven before the Emir, he ordered the beating of tymbals and drums and the sounding of trumpets as a sign that it was the night of the festival. When the morning of that night of Thursday came, he set forth on the *'umrah* with a vast concourse the like of which has never been heard of. The people of Mecca collected round him to the last person, and went forth according to their ranks, tribe by tribe, quarter by quarter, bristling with weapons, on horse and on foot, assembling in numbers too numerous to count. He who beheld them would marvel at their exceeding number, and if they had come from many lands it yet would be a wonder. How then when they were from one city! It is the proof of proofs of the blessedness of that city.

They set forth in admirable order; the cavaliers left on their horses and playing with their weapons, while the foot leaped upon each other vying in skill-at-arms. They carried spears, swords, and targes, and appeared to pierce with the spear, strike with the sword, and defend with the targe with which they protected themselves, revealing all manner of marvels in their skilful contests. They hurled their spears into the air, and hastened after them to catch them in their hands, although at times the course of the weapons brought them on to their heads, they being in such a press that they had no chance to manœuvre. Some on occasions threw their swords into the air and caught them by the hilt as if they had never left their hands. (This continued) until the Emir came forth with solemn step, surrounded by his officers, and led by his sons who were near to being young men, and by waving banners and tymbal and drum. An air of calmness lay upon him. The mountains, roads, and paths were filled with the *mujawir* who had come to view the scene. The Emir came to the place of assembly, performed his mission, and then began his return. The two troops of horsemen were disposed before him, playing and making merry, while the footmen wheeled around in the manner described. A party of Bedouin rode well-bred camels free from blemish; a finer sight could not be seen. The riders of these camels raced with the horsemen before the Emir, raising their voices in invocations and praise for him, until they came to the Sacred Mosque. There he circumambulated the Ka'bah, led by the Koran reciters, while the Zamzam muezzin warbled on the terrace of the Zamzam Dome raising his voice in wishing him joy of the feast, lauding him, and praying for him according to the custom.

When the Emir had finished the circumambulation, he prayed at the Multazam, and then went to the maqam and prayed behind it. It had been brought out from the Ka'bah for him and placed inside the wooden dome behind which prayers are said. When he had ended his prayers, the dome was raised for him from off the maqam, which he kissed and touched. The dome was then replaced and he began to leave by Bab al-Safa towards the *mas'a* [place of the ritual course], the people crowding before him. He performed the *sa'i* on horseback, with his officers around him and his foot spearmen before him. When he had done the *sa'i*, swords were drawn before him and he was encompassed by his followers, and in this imposing state, followed by the multitude, he returned to his dwelling. All that day the *mas'a* billowed with men and women performing the ritual course (between al-Safa and al-Marwah).

On the second day, which was Friday, the road was nigh as crowded as on the day before, with horsemen and pedestrians, and men and women. The women who walked in the hope of a heavenly reward were many, and they competed with the men on that blessed way. May God, by His favour, hear the prayers of them all. During all this, the men met and shook hands, offering prayers and praying for God's forgiveness each on behalf of the other, while the women did likewise. All wore their finest clothing, adorning themselves after the fashion of the people of the land on their days of festival. As for the population of the Safe City [Mecca], this meeting of the pilgrims is the festival for which they make (great) preparation, and assemble in large numbers, contending in magnificence and indulging in much ceremony. There is much activity in the markets at this time, and sales are brisk; foreseeing this, they make provision for it months before.

Amongst the benevolent acts of Great and Glorious God towards them at this time, and revealing the bounteous care that He – may He be exalted – bestows on His Safe Haram (is the following). A Yemenite tribe called al-Saru, who people an impregnable mountain in the Yemen called Sarat – connected it might be with Sarat al-rijal [noble men], as I was told by a jurisprudent from the Yemen named Ibn Abi 'l-Sayf, the people deriving this name from the land they live in – and who are divided in sub-tribes like the Bajilah and others, prepare themselves to arrive at this Blessed City ten days before the festival combining the aims of performing the lesser pilgrimage, and of provisioning the land with various kinds of foods such as wheat and other grains, and even kidney-beans and lesser-esteemed products, and bringing to it butter, honey, raisins, and almonds, their stock comprising wheat, condiments, and fruits. They arrive in thousands, men and camels, laden with the goods we have described, and bringing an abundance of viands to the people of the City and to the pilgrims who have settled there, so that they are well nourished and sustained. Prices are lowered, and commodities are everywhere to be found, and the people take from them what will last them for a year and until the next provisioning. But for this provisioning the population of Mecca would lead a miserable life.

A curious fact concerning these victuallers is that they do not sell any of the things we have mentioned for dinars or dirhams, but exchange them for cloths, 'abat and shimal [kinds of cloaks]. The Meccans prepare these for them, together with women's veils and strong quilts, and similar things such as are worn by the Bedouin, and thus they buy and sell from them. It is related that when these Saru remain in their own country and do not bring provisions, they are afflicted with a drought and death visits their flocks and herds, but when they come with them their land produces a bountiful harvest, and blessings are shed on their substance. So when the time for departure draws nigh and there has been some carelessness in preparation, the women collect and drive them from their houses. All this is from the goodness of God Most High for the protection of the Safe City [Mecca].

The country of the Saru, as was told to us, is fertile and extensive, abounding in figs and vines, and having broad cultivations and rich crops. They are firmly persuaded that their prosperity is wholly due to these provisions that they bring, and in this too they enjoy a profitable commerce with Great and Glorious God. These people are pure Arab, and eloquent of speech. They are brusque and robust, and have not been nourished by the comforts of city life, nor have they been polished by the urban manner. The religious laws do not direct them in their affairs, and you will find among them no devotionary practices beyond that of good intention. When they compass the Holy Ka'bah, they throw themselves upon it as do children upon a loving mother, seeking shelter beside her. They cling to its curtains, and wherever their hands grasp them, they tear from the violence of their dragging and their throwing themselves upon them. Meanwhile their tongues give sonorous prayer, such as to break the heart and cause the hard eye to flow copious tears. You will see men standing around them, hands outstretched, saying 'Amen' to their prayers and repeating those prayers after them. Throughout the time of their stay, it is impossible to perform the *tawaf* with them, or find a way to kiss the Black Stone.

When the noble door is opened, they enter 'in salute', and you will observe that in making their entry they form a chain as if tied the one to the other. They are linked together in this fashion up to thirty or forty or even more, and the chains thus formed follow the one after the other. At times it happens that someone breaks off and falls from the blessed stairway that leads to the noble House, and all fall with him so that the looker-on will observe a spectacle that will provoke his laughter. As for their prayers, no more pleasant drollery of the Bedouin is told than of them. They face the noble House and prostrate themselves in prayer without performing a *rak'ah*,[67] and pray very rapidly. Some make one prostration, some two, three, and four, then raise their heads a little from the ground, on which their palms are spread, and turn to right and left like one in fear. They then recite the *taslim* [the closing benediction: 'The peace and mercy of God be with you'] or rise without saying it, or without assuming the attitude for the *tashahhud* [the testimony of faith: 'I testify that there is no deity but God, and I testify that Muhammad is the Messenger of God']. Sometimes they converse during this, and at times during his prostrations one will raise his head to his companion and, calling to him, lay some charge to him as he wills, and then return to his prostrations. And so they go on with their odd ways.

They wear no habit save a dirty wrapping or a skin with which they cover themselves. With all this they are a brave and vigorous people. They have a large Arab bow resembling the bow used for teasing cotton, which never leaves them on their journeys. When they set forth to visit the holy places, the Bedouin on the way who are wont to prey upon the pilgrims fear their boldness and avoid encountering them, leaving the road clear to them. The pilgrims making the visit accompany them and praise their company, for despite our description of their habits they are a people who believe sincerely in the Faith. It is said that the Prophet – may God bless and preserve him – spoke of them and praised them nobly saying, 'Teach them the ritual of the prayers, and they will teach you how to pray (from the heart).' Let it suffice that they are included in all his sayings – may God bless and preserve him – from 'The Faith is Yemenite' to those other traditions that have come down concerning the Yemen and its people. It is said that 'Abdullah ibn 'Umar – may God hold him in his favour – esteemed the time in which they made their circumambulation and sought to enter among them that he might partake of the blessings won by their prayers. Everything in their regard is indeed remarkable.

In the Hijr we saw one of their boys sitting beside a pilgrim who was teaching him the opening surah [Chapter] of the Koran, and the surah of The Unity [CXII]. The pilgrim pronounced the words, 'Say: He, Allah, is One', and the boy said, 'Allah is One.' The teacher repeated it to him and the boy replied: 'Did you not tell me to say "He, Allah, is One"? Well, I have said it.' The pilgrim was hard put to it to make him understand, and only after much difficulty hung the words on the boy's tongue. He then recited, 'In the name of God, the Beneficent, the Merciful. Praise be to God, Lord of the Universe,' and the boy answered, 'In the name of God, the Beneficent, the Merciful. And praise be to God——' The teacher repeated it to him, and added, 'Do not say, "And praise be to God," but say only, "Praise be to God."' Then said the lad, 'When I have said, "In the name of God, the Beneficent, the Merciful," I say, "And praise be to God" to give the conjunction. If I had not first said, "In the name of God," and was beginning with this part I should then say, "Praise be to God."' We marvelled at the affair of this boy, and his natural knowledge of the joining and separation of language, being without schooling. Their eloquence is most remarkable, and their prayers greatly move the soul. May God, by His favour, prosper their affairs and those of all His servants.

The 'umrah lasts throughout this month, night and day, and is celebrated both by men and women, but the general assembly takes place only on the first night (of the month), which is the night of their great festival.

The noble House is opened daily in this blessed month, but on the 29th it is reserved especially for women, and on that day they appear in Mecca in great multitudes. It is their famous day of festival, for which they make (great) preparation. On Thursday the 15th of this month we witnessed a concourse for the 'umrah that was almost equal to the first, which we spoke of at the beginning of the month, and there was not a man or woman but went forth to it. In a word, all this blessed month is attended by various forms of devotional practices such as the 'umrah and other ceremonies, and a particular attention is paid to its beginning and middle part as well as to the twenty-seventh day.

On the evening of this aforementioned Thursday, we were sitting in the venerated Hijr when suddenly we saw the Emir Mukthir appear in pilgrim garb. He had just come from the place of meeting for the 'umrah, being wishful of winning the blessings of that day, and also of discharging its rites. Behind him came his sons, also in the pilgrim garb, and some of his retinue encompassed him. At once the Zamzam muezzin hastened to the roof of the Zamzam dome and made his customary invocations, taking turns in this with his younger brother. The evening prayers were at hand at the time the Emir ended his tawaf, so he prayed behind the Shafi'ite imam, and then left to the blessed mas'a.

On Friday the 16th of the month a large pilgrim caravan of about four hundred camels left with the Sharif al-Da'udi to visit (the tomb of) the Apostle of God – may God bless and preserve him. In the preceding month of Jumada 'l-Thaniyah there had also been another visit by certain pilgrims in a smaller caravan than this. There remained to be done the visit of the month of Shawwal, and that with the pilgrims from 'Iraq after the 'standing' (on Mount 'Arafat), if it pleased Great and Glorious God. On the 19th of Sha'ban, this large caravan returned in peace and safety. Praise be to God.

On the night of Tuesday the 27th of this same month of Rajab, the people of Mecca again appeared in a vast concourse, going forth on the 'umrah in numbers not less than on the first occasion. Men and women all poured forth to it that night in the style and manner we have already described, in order that they might gain the blessings of the grace of that night, for it is one of the nights famous for grace. In its morning hour it was remarkable for the great host of people and for the splendid spectacle it presented. May God render this pleasing before His noble countenance.

This 'umrah they call the 'Umrah of the Hill [Akamah], because during it they wear the pilgrim garb as from the hill that rises before the mosque of 'A'ishah – may God hold her in His favour – about a bow-shot distant from it. It is close to the mosque dedicated to 'Ali – upon whom be eternal peace. According to them, the origin of this 'umrah of the hill was due to the fact that when 'Abdullah ibn al-Zubayr – may God hold them both in His favour – completed the rebuilding of the Ka'bah he went forth barefooted to perform the 'umrah, accompanied by the Meccans, and came to this hill, where he donned the pilgrim garb. That was on the 27th of Rajab. He made his way through the pass of al-Hajun that leads to al-Ma'la [Upper Mecca], where the Muslims entered the day they conquered Mecca, as we have already mentioned. This 'umrah became an established observance for the Meccans, on that same day and at that same hill. That day of 'Abdullah – may God hold him in His favour – is celebrated, for on it he offered sacrificial victims of a number that cannot be truly established, although I have tried to verify it, but that, in short, was very large. There is no Sharif or person of means in Mecca who does not offer victims, and for days the people of Mecca stay eating and giving to eat, deriving and granting pleasure, and thanking Great and Glorious God for the help and assistance He gave to them in the building of His Sacred House in the style it had in the time of (God's) Friend, Abraham – may God bless and preserve him. But Hajjaj – God's maledictions upon him – demolished it, and restored it to the form it had held in the time of the Quraysh who in their reconstruction had reduced the dimensions of Abraham – may God bless and preserve him. Our Prophet, Muhammad – may God bless and preserve him – left it as it was, because of the recency of their conversion from unbelief, as it is established in the tradition of 'A'ishah – may God hold her in His favour – in the *Muwatta* of Malik ibn Anas – may God hold him in His favour.

On the 29th of the month, which was a Thursday, the House was reserved for women exclusively, and they congregated from all parts. They had assembled for it some days before, as they had done for (the visit to) the venerated sanctuaries, and there was no woman in Mecca but that day went to the Sacred Mosque. When the Shayba [the hereditary guardians] arrived to open the venerated House, they made haste that they might depart to leave it free to the women, and likewise the men left clear to them the place of circumambulation and the Hijr, so that not a man remained around the blessed House. The women rushed to ascend the steps, and the Shayba could hardly get through them as they made their descent from the venerated House. They formed a chain, the one holding the other, and fell into such a state of confusion that they collapsed. Some shrieked, some wailed, and some cried, 'God is Great,' and others, 'There is no God but God.' One saw in them the same crowding that was seen at the time of the stay of the Yemenite Saru in Mecca when they ascended to the Holy House the day that it was opened, one case resembling the other. Thus they continued for the first part of the day, at their ease performing the *tawaf*, pausing in the Hijr, and dividing themselves between kissing the Black Stone and touching the corners (of the Ka'bah). It was their grandest, most splendid, and most solemn day. May God give them advantage from it, and make it pleasing before His noble countenance.

Yet on the whole, in comparison with the men, they are wretched and cheated. They see the venerated House and may not enter it, they gaze upon the blessed Stone but cannot touch it, and their lot is wholly one of staring and feeling the sadness that moves and holds them. They have nothing but the *tawaf* at a distance. This day (therefore) which is an annual event, they expect as one expects the most solemn of festivals, and for it they make many provisions and preparations. May God, by His grace and favour, advantage them for their sincere intentions and their faith.

Early next day, the Shayba began to wash the Ka'bah with the blessed water of Zamzam, for many of the women had brought their little children and sucking babes with them. They found it proper to wash it both out of respect and in order to rid it of impurities, as well as to remove what might put thoughts in the mind of him who has no self-control that would prevent him from committing an unclean act in that noble Abode and Station of exclusive holiness and sublimity. When the water poured from the Ka bah many men and women hastened to it, seeking blessedness by laving their hands and faces in it, and often collecting it in vases they had brought for the purpose. This they did all careless of the use to which the water had been put in the cleansing, although some of them did abstain, and perhaps they surveyed the spectacle as one who did not deem it lawful, or whose mind could not find it good. What do you think of the blessed water of Zamzam being poured into God's Holy House, going in waves to its blessed corners and then flowing beside al-Multazam and the (much-) kissed Black Stone? Is it not fitting that it should be met with the mouths rather than the hands, and that the face should be plunged into it rather than the feet? God forbid then that there should arise a cause to prevent anyone from that, or a doubt that might deter him. (Good) intentions are accepted by God Most High, and zeal in the magnifying of His holy places leads to His approval. He is the Rewarder of latent thoughts and hidden secrets. There is no God but He.

The Month of Sha'ban the Honoured (579)

[19th of November–17th of December, 1183]

May God let us know His favour

THE new moon of this month rose on the night of Saturday the 19th of November. Early next morning the Emir Mukthir came to perform the *tawaf* that is customary at the beginning of each month. With him were his brother, and his sons, and those of his officers, followers, and adherents who were accustomed to accompany him. It was in the manner before described, the Zamzam muezzin, according to his practice, calling in turns with his younger brother from his look-out.

At dawn on Thursday the 13th of the month, being the 1st of December, and after day had broken, the moon was eclipsed. The eclipse began while men were saying the morning prayers in the noble Haram, and the moon set while in eclipse. The maximum eclipse reached was two-thirds. God teaches us to draw true knowledge from His prodigies.

On Friday the following day, a strange circumstance occurred in the Haram. It was that there was not a boy in Mecca but did not come early to it; and congregating all in the dome of Zamzam they cried with one voice, 'Recite the *tahlil* ["There is no God but God"] and the *takbir* ["God is Great"], O servants of God,' and the people cried out the *tahlil* and the *takbir*. Sometimes one of the crowd joined with these boys and called with them. Men and women were crowding round the dome of the blessed well because they thought, rather on the affirmation of the ignorant than of the wise, that the water of Zamzam rose on the night of the middle of the month of Sha'ban. They were in doubt as to (the date of) the new moon of that month, for it was said that it had been seen on the night of Friday in the direction of the Yemen. And so they came early to the dome, forming a crowd the like of which has not been seen.

Their aim in this was to gain the grace of that blessed water
whose rise was evident. The water distributors stood on the
orifice of the well, drawing water and pouring it on the heads
of people by throwing it from a bucket. Some received it on
the face, others on the head or elsewhere, and often the water
would go far from the force of the thrust from their hands.
The men nevertheless called for more, and wept, while the
women on their side rivalled them in weeping, and competed
with them in prayers, the boys meanwhile raising a clamour
with their *tahlils* and *takbirs*. It was an overwhelming spectacle
and thrilling to hear. Because of it those performing the *tawaf*
could not complete it, nor, because of the high cries that occupied the ears and understanding, could those at prayer discharge
their orisons.

One of our number that day entered into the dome, and
from the press of the crowd suffered distress and difficulty. He
heard men crying, 'The water has risen seven cubits,' and direct-
ing himself towards one of the white-moustachioed ones who
bore some impress of intelligence and perspicacity in his features,
questioned him concerning it. 'Yes,' he replied, the tears stream-
ing down his face. 'The water has risen seven cubits, there is
no doubt of it.' 'Is your information sure?' our comrade asked,
and the man gave answer, 'Yes.' It is very strange that among
them was one who said that he had come at dawn on Friday,
and found the water to be about the stature of a man from the
brim. Oh strange and false invention! We take refuge in God
from such seducements. It was by chance that we concerned
ourselves with this affair, through the predominance of the
reports spread about it, and their continuance over many years
among the common people of Mecca.

On Friday night one of us lowered his bucket into the blessed
well until it touched the surface of the water, and made a knot
in the rope at the place where it reached the brim. We were
thus able to measure it truly. In the morning the people cried
out that the water had plainly risen, but one of us, making
his way with difficulty through the crowd, and accompanied

by one who carried the bucket, lowered the vessel into the well and found that the measurement was the same, neither more nor less. On the other hand, it is remarkable that when he returned to measure it on Saturday night, he found it had somewhat decreased because of the large amount that people had drawn from it that day. But if they had been drawing from the ocean, the loss would still have been apparent. Glory to God who especially endowed this water with the blessedness it has, and infused it with benefit. On the morning of Saturday the 15th of the month, we carefully examined this measurement in order to clear all doubt as to the truth of the matter, and found it to be as it was before. But if anyone had remarked that day that the water had not risen, he would have been thrown into the well, or been trodden under foot until he dissolved. We take refuge in God from the violence and excesses of the crowd, and their indulgement of ungoverned passions.

This blessed night, that is, the night of the middle of Sha'ban, is held in high esteem by the Meccans, because of the noble tradition that has come down to us concerning it. They contend with each other in performing pious acts such as the 'umrah, the tawaf, and prayers, both singly and in congregation, dividing into blessed divisions. On the Saturday night, which was the middle night of the month, and after the evening prayers, we observed a vast concourse in the Haram. Men began in groups to say the tarwih prayers, to recite the opening Surah of the Koran and to swear 'God, He is One' ten times for each rak'ah, until they had done fifty taslim with one hundred rak'ah. Each group had elected an imam, mats were spread, candles lit, torches kindled, and lamps lighted. The lamp of the bright, moonlit sky shed its radiance on the earth and spread its rays, its beams meeting in this noble Haram which is itself a light. Oh what a spectacle, that the imagination could not conceive or the fancy conjecture!

That night the people divided into groups. One took part in these tarawih in congregation, of which there were seven or eight, another stayed in the Hijr to pray there individually, another left on the *'umrah*, and another chose to perform the *tawaf*, most of these being Malikites. It was one of the famous nights, which it is hoped will be the choicest and the best of the propitiatory acts. May God, by His favour, grant profit from it, dispensing not with the grace and excellence of it, and bringing to this holy place of meeting all who yearn for it.

That blessed night one of us, Ahmad ibn Hassan, witnessed a remarkable circumstance; one of those strange events that are memorable among things of sensibility. It happened that he was struck by the urge to sleep in the remaining third of the night, and retired to the bench that surrounds the Dome of Zamzam, on the part that faces the Black Stone and the door of the House, and there laid himself down to sleep. Suddenly a foreign man came and sat on the bench beside his head and began to recite the Koran in a moving and gentle voice, accompanying it with deep sighs and sobs. He recited beautifully, instilling the sentiments into the soul, and infusing them with a power to move (even) the insensible. Our comrade abstained from sleeping that he might enjoy the beauty of what he heard, with all its yearning and emotion. At last the man ended his reciting and said:

'If evil deeds have taken me far from You
My honest thoughts have brought me near again,'

repeating the words in tones of harmony that would cleave stones and break the heart. On he went retelling these lines, while his tears flowed and his voice trembled and grew weak, until it came to Ahmad ibn Hassan that the man would faint. This thought had no sooner passed through his mind than on the instant the man fell swooning to the ground, and lay there like something cast aside, moving not. Ibn Hassan rose up much alarmed at the frightening thing he had seen, uncertain as to whether the man were dead or alive, so violent had been the fall, the place being raised high from the ground. Another who had been sleeping near him then got up, and both stood bewildered, being fearful of shaking the man or even of approaching him. At last a foreign woman passed and crying, 'Is it thus you leave this man, and in this state?' made speed to take a little water from the Well of Zamzam and sprinkle it on his face. The other two then approached the man and raised him. But when he saw them, he straightway concealed his face from them, for fear that his features should be impressed upon their minds, and rose without delay and betook himself towards Bab Banu Shayba. The two remained marvelling at what they had seen, and Ibn Hassan bit his fingers in regret at the opportunity he had missed of gaining the blessings of the man's prayers. For the situation had not allowed him to ask of them, and he had retained no image of him that he might seek his blessings when he should encounter him again. The assemblies of these foreigners, in sensibility, in emotionalism, in the ready ecstasies, in zealous ardour of worship, in assiduity in acts of piety and in the manifestation of grace, are truly remarkable and exalted. Grace is in God's hands, and He bestows it on whom He wishes.

At dawn on Thursday the 13th of the month, the moon was eclipsed to an extent of two-thirds, and it set in this state of eclipse at the rising of the sun. God inspires us to ponder His portents.

The Month of Ramadan the Sublime (579)

[18th of December, 1183–16th of January, 1184]
May God let us know His favour

THE new moon rose on the night of Monday the 19th of December – may God let us know His grace and justice, and grant unto us the acceptance of our prayers throughout this month. The month's fast began on Sunday for the people of Mecca, on a claim that the new moon had been observed, a claim unverified but nevertheless supported by the Emir. The signal for the fast was given by drumbeat on the Sunday night, following the rites observed by him and his sect the 'Aliites and those of their persuasion. For, as it is said, they deem the fast to fall due on a day that is doubtful [being either the last day of Sha'ban or the first of Ramadan]. God best knows concerning this.

During this blessed month there was much ceremony in the sacred Mosque, making necessary the renewal of the mats, and the increasing of the candles and firebrands and other appointments until the Haram blazed with light and shone with brightness. The imams formed separate groups in order to recite the *tarwih*. The Shafi'ites, who had precedence over the others, had set up an imam on one side of the Mosque, and the Hanbalites, the Hanafites, and the Zaydis had done the same. As for the Malikites, they had gathered round three reciters who recited in turn. In this year, the attendance of this sect was greater than usual and it possessed more candles, because a party of Malikite merchants had vied with each other, bringing to the imam of the Ka'bah a vast quantity. Two of the largest, weighing each a *qintar*, were placed in front of the *mihrab*, and round them were the lesser candles, some big some small. Thus the Malikite part of the Mosque excited wonder for its beauty and overpowered the eyes with its radiance. There was hardly

K

a recess or direction in the Mosque where there was not a reciter with a group praying behind him. The Mosque shook with the voices of reciters in every part, so that the eyes beheld a sight, and the ears heard strains that ravished the senses with emotion and fervour.

Some of the foreigners confined themselves to performing the *tawaf* and to praying in the Hijr, and did not take part in the *tarwih*, deeming that that was the best advantage they could take of their opportunity, and the noblest function they could undertake, for not in every place can be found the Venerated Corner and the Multazam. The Shafi'ite imam was the most assiduous in the *tarwih*, in that having completed the customary *tarwih*, which is ten *taslim*, he joined in a *tawaf* with one of the groups. And when he had done the sevenfold *tawaf* and the *rak'ah*, he commenced again to recite more *tarawih*, and cracked the preacher's whip, of which we have already spoken, a crack that could be heard throughout the Mosque so loud it was, and that seemed to be a signal to return to prayers. When his group had ended two *taslim* they returned to perform again seven *tawaf*. When they had finished them, the whip was cracked again and they turned once more to the *taslim*, and then again back to the *tawaf* and so on until they had done ten *taslim* and completed twenty *rak'ah*. They then recited the shaf' wa watar prayers[68] and departed.

The other imams add nothing to the customary (ritual). The imams that in turn officiate at these *tarawih* beside the Maqam are five. The first of them is the obligatory imam,[69] and the middle one is our friend the jurisprudent, the ascetic and God-fearing Abu Ja'far ibn ('Ali) al-Fanaki of Cordova, whose recitations soften the hard stones in emotion. The whip which we mentioned is used in this blessed month. It is cracked three times at the conclusion of the sunset call to prayers, and similarly at the end of the call to evening prayers. Beyond a doubt it is one of the recent innovations in this august Mosque – may God sanctify it.

The Zamzam muezzin is encharged with the duty of

announcing the daybreak meal [*sahur*]. He does it from the minaret in the east corner of the Mosque because of its nearness to the Emir's house. There he stands, at that time, calling, reminding, and urging to the meal. With him are two younger brothers who answer him and call in their turn. At the top of the minaret has been fixed a long board at whose end, crosswise like outstretched arms, is a pole supporting at its tips two small pulleys on which hang two large glass lanterns that remain alight throughout the time of the meal. When the 'first gleams of dawn draw near' [Koran II, 187], and the signal to end the meal has time and again been sounded, the muezzin lowers the two lanterns from the top of the board, and commences the call to prayer, when from all sides the muezzins take up the call. All the houses of Mecca have high roofs, and whosoever does not hear the call to the daybreak meal because of the distance of his house from the Mosque may see the two lanterns alight on the top of the minaret. When he does not see them, he knows that the period for eating has ended (and the fast resumed).

The night of Tuesday the 2nd of Ramadan, in the evening, the Emir Mukthir performed a *tawaf* of farewell and then left (Mecca) to meet the Emir Sayf al-Islam (Tughtagin or Tuldequinas) ibn Ayyub, brother of Saladin. News of his coming from Egypt had come ahead of him some time before; then came consecutive messages until at last it was confirmed that he had arrived at Yanbu' [Yenbo], and had turned aside to Medina to visit the tomb of the Apostle – may God bless and preserve him. His heavy baggage had been sent before him to Al-Safra'. As to the reason for his journey, men said that he was on his way to the Yemen because of some disputes hat had risen there, and because of a rebellion raised by its emirs. But into the minds of the Meccans entered a dreadful apprehension, and fear fell upon them. So this Emir Mukthir left to meet and greet him, and in truth to make submission to him. May God Most High acquaint the Muslims with His goodness.

In the forenoon of Wednesday the 3rd of the blessed month, we were sitting in the honoured Hijr when we heard the drums of the Emir Mukthir and the voices of the women of Mecca ululating for him. While we were listening, the Emir entered, for he had returned from meeting the Emir Sayf al-Islam. He made the *tawaf* of the *taslim* around the venerated House, while the people manifested their joy at his return and their happiness at his safety. Report had gone abroad that Sayf al-Islam had come to al-Zahir, and that his tents had been pitched there. An advanced party of his army had arrived at the Haram, and encompassed the Emir Mukthir as he performed the *tawaf*. While the people were gazing on them, they suddenly heard a great clamour and fearful shouting and there they saw the Emir Sayf al-Islam entering by the Bab Banu Shayba. The flashings of the swords before him almost obstructed the view of him. The Qadi was on his right, and the chief of the Shayba on his left. The Mosque was in great commotion, being filled with spectators and pilgrims; and the voices of men in prayer for him and for his brother Saladin rose so high as to deafen the ears and confound the understanding. From his high post the Zamzam muezzin raised his voice in prayer and praise for him; the voices of the people rose above the muezzin's; and great was the awe of the scene to look upon and hear.

As the Emir drew near to the sublime House, swords were sheathed, spirits contracted, the fine clothing was cast off, necks were depressed and their napes enhumbled, and minds were bereft of steadiness, in awe and reverence of the House of the King of Kings, the Powerful, the Mighty, the One, the Conquering, who grants possessions to whom He wishes, and takes them away from whom He wills. Praise be to Him. Great is His strength, glorious His power.

This troop of Ghuzz [Seljuk Turks] hurled itself into God's Ancient House with the impetuosity of moths at a lamp. Humility had bowed their heads [lit. 'chins'], and tears bathed their moustaches. The Qadi and the chief of the Shayba performed the *tawaf* with Sayf al-Islam, but the Emir Mukthir was overcome by the crowd, and made speed to end it, hastening to his residence. When Sayf al-Islam had ended his *tawaf*, he prayed behind the Maqam, and then entered the Zamzam Dome and drank of its waters. After this he left by the Bab al-Safa to perform the *sa'i*. He commenced to march on foot, that he might show humbleness and submission to whom humbleness is due. Swords were drawn before him, and from one end of the *mas'a* to the other the people had drawn themselves up in two ranks as they had done for the *tawaf*. He performed the *sa'i* on foot both ways, from al-Safa to al-Marwah and from al-Marwah to al-Safa. He ran between the two green mil, and then, seized by fatigue, he mounted his horse and finished the *sa'i* in the saddle.

The people had now assembled for the midday prayers, and the Emir returned to the Sacred Mosque in the same frightening and impressive manner, proudly walking between the dazzling glitter of the drawn swords. The Shayba had hastened there before him to open the door of the venerated House, for it was not a (normal) day of opening. The stairway by which one ascends to it was brought close, and the Emir mounted it. The chief of the Shayba made to open the door, when on account of the throng, the key fell from his sleeve and he stood there bewildered and afraid. The Emir stood waiting on the steps, but God gave help at once in finding the key and the noble door was opened. The Emir entered alone with the Shayba and the door was locked, while the leading men and notables of the Ghuzz remained crowding round the steps. After some delay, the door was opened to the emirs of the suite and they entered. Sayf al-Islam tarried a long time in the venerated House, and when he came forth, the door was opened to the vulgar. O what crowding and piling up! They were so arranged as to form a sort of long string of beads, being joined together in a chain. I compare it to something of the days when the Saru entered the House as already described. The Emir Sayf al-Islam then took to his horse and left to his pitched tents in the aforementioned place. This day in Mecca had been one of those that present a portentous spectacle and a wonderful sight, being a most remarkable affair. Glory to Him whose dominion has no end, and whose authority does not grow less. There is no God but He.

A group of pilgrims from Egypt and other lands had travelled with the Emir that they might take advantage of the security given on the road across open country, and they arrived safely and in good health. Praise be to God.

In the forenoon of the following Thursday we were again in the venerated Hijr when once more the sound of timbals, drums, and trumpets smote the ears, and all parts of the noble Haram shook from it. While we gazed that we might understand its meaning, the Emir Mukthir appeared before us, surrounded by his close followers, and trailing a golden mantle that was like glowing coal. On his head was a turban of fine linen, cloud-coloured but touched with gold, whose windings rose up on his head like heaped clouds. Beneath the mantle were two coats of honour, made from *Dabiqi* material and beautifully embroidered, bestowed on him by the Emir Sayf al-Islam. Dressed in these, he arrived gaily and cheerfully, and by decree of Sayf al-Islam, timbals and drums announced his coming as a mark of this prince's respect for him and to affirm his standing. Round the noble House he walked, thanking God for granting him the consideration of this Emir when once he had been throbbing with fear of him. May God by His favour fortify and prosper him.

On Friday the Emir Sayf al-Islam arrived for the prayers at the beginning of the appointed time. The venerated House was opened for him, and he entered it with the Emir Mukthir. For some time they stayed within, and when they came forth, the Ghuzz so crowded round to enter that the spectators were amazed and the point came when the stairway had to be removed. But this availed nothing, and they continued to swarm, raising themselves over each other and persisting in this until the khatib arrived. They then emerged to listen to the khutbah and the door was closed. The Emir Sayf al-Islam prayed with the Emir Mukthir in the 'Abbaside Dome, and when the prayers had ended he left by the Bab al-Safa and rode to his encampment. On Wednesday the 14th of the month this Emir left with his soldiers for the Yemen. May God by His favour grant that the Muslims in that land shall n his coming be acquainted only with good.

We have descanted upon the zeal of the settlers [mujawirin] in the noble Haram in discharging religious duties and reciting the tarawih of the blessed month (of Ramadan), and on the number of imams (officiating) in the Haram. On every odd night of the last ten nights of the month the whole of the Koran is recited. At the first night, which was the 21st of the month, a Meccan y uth recited in the presence of the Qadi and a number of sheiks. When this was over, he rose among them and preached a khutbah. The father of the youth then invited them to his house for food and sweetmeats, which he had prepared with much care. The next night, the 23rd, the reciter was one of the sons of a rich Meccan, a boy who had not reached the age of fifteen. His father had made uncommon preparations for this night, having arranged a chandelier, made of wax, with branches, set with all manner of fruits, fresh and dry, and furnished with many candles. In the middle of the Haram, towards the Bab Banu Shayba, was a sort of quadrilateral mihrab with a wooden balustrade, standing on four pedestals and having at its summit wooden shafts, from which hung lamps, and on which stood lighted lanterns and torches. Round the mihrab were driven sharp-headed nails on to which were fixed the candles that surrounded all the mihrab. The branched chandelier bearing the fruits was then lit. In all this the father of the lad had shown assiduous care.

Near to the mihrab was placed a pulpit adorned with a cloth chequered in many colours. The youthful imam arrived and said the tarawih and completed his recitation of the whole Koran, all who were in the sacred Mosque, men and women, assembling around him. In his mihrab, he could hardly be seen for the many rays of the candles that encompassed him. He then came forth from his *mihrab*, strutting proudly in his rich apparel, with the port of an imam and the calmness of youth, his eyes shaded with *kuhl* [collyrium] and his hands hennaed to the wrists. But from the press of men he could not make his way to the pulpit, so one of the guardians of that part took him in his arms and brought him to the top of the pulpit, where he settled smiling, and signed in greeting to those present. Before him sat the Koran readers, who began to recite in chorus. When they had finished a tenth part of the Koran, the (young) preacher rose and pronounced an eloquent sermon that moved most spirits, more from its mellifluous delivery than from its piously recollective or emotional qualities. In front of him, on the steps of the pulpit, was a small group of men holding candlesticks in their hands and crying aloud, 'O Lord! O Lord!' at each pause in the sermon. The readers began their reciting during these pauses, and the preacher held silence until they had done. He then returned to his sermon, freely recalling various pious memories, and referring during this to the Ancient House – may God honour it – baring his arms in pointing at it. He followed on by mentioning the Well of Zamzam and the Maqam, pointing at them with both fingers. He ended with the valediction of the blessed month, saluted repeatedly, and made invocations for the Caliph and for all the Emirs for whom it was customary to pray. He then descended, and that large assembly dissolved. They had found the preacher intelligent and talented, although his discourse had not touched the soul as had been hoped and the pious recollections that left his tongue had not gone beyond the ears. It was reported that selected persons among this assembly, such as the Qadi and others, were provided with abundant food and sweetmeat, after the fashion of such meetings. The father of the preacher that night incurred large expense on the preparations which we have described.

Then came the night of the 25th, and the reciter appointed for that evening's portion of the reading of the whole Koran was a Hanafite imam. He had brought a son of his to do it, a boy of about the age of the first preacher we mentioned.

The Hanafite imam had made great preparations on behalf of his son for this night. He produced four candle-bearing chandeliers of varying styles, some being like trees with branches laden with all kinds of fruits, fresh and dry, and some being without branches. They were arranged in line before his *hatim*, on whose summit were boards and planks covered with lamps, torches, and candles, that illuminated all the *hatim* until it shone in the air like a great crown of light. The candles were brought forward in brass candlesticks, and then was set in place the *mihrab* with the wooden balustrades, its upper part ringed with candles and itself encompassed by candlesticks that threw a halo of light around it. In front of it was placed the pulpit, which also was covered with a cloth of various colours. The massing of the people to see this lustrous spectacle was greater than at the first. The boy did his portion of the reading of the whole Koran and then moved from his *mihrab* to the pulpit, bearing himself shyly and dressed in vestments beautiful to behold. He climbed his pulpit and signed in greeting to those present, and then began his sermon, calmly and with gentleness, in language of transparent modesty. Considering his youth, it was graver and more moving than the first, his exhortations were more eloquent, and his pious recollections more profitable. The Koran readers took post in front of him after the fashion of the first occasion, and, during the pauses between the readings, began to recite the Koran. He would keep silence until they had ended the verses they had selected and then return to his sermon. Before him on the steps of the pulpit was a group of (mosque) attendants holding candlesticks in their hands, and one of them the censer which repeatedly spread the aroma of the aloe [*Aquilaria agallocha*]. When the preacher came to a break in a pious recollection or a moving entreaty, these men raised their voices crying, 'O Lord! O Lord!' three or four times, sometimes being joined in their cries by the congregation; and so it continued until he had ended his sermon. He then came down and the imam (his father) followed after him to serve the food to those personages of the place who were present, either by inviting them to his house that night, or by sending it to their homes.

Then came the night of the 27th, which was a Friday, the month having been deemed to have begun on a Sunday. It was a noble night, with its auspicious portion of the reading of the whole Koran, its full and mature dignity, and the state that make prayers acceptable to Great and Glorious God. And what state can compare to attending the reading of the Koran on the night of the 27th of Ramadan behind the venerated Maqam and in front of the sublime House? It is a night which in grace makes all others seem but mean, as does the Haram make insignificant all other places. Thought and preparation are given to this blessed night two or three days before. Beside the *hatim* of the Shafi'ite imam were planted huge wooden poles of considerable height, joined every three by stout beams and forming a continuous row that occupies almost half of the width of the Haram and reaches to the *hatim*. Long planks passed between them, extending over the beams and raised to form one storey over another until three storeys were completed. The upper storey was a long wooden platform perforated throughout with sharp-headed nails, close-set like the back of a hedgehog, on which candles were fixed. The two lower stages were of planks pierced with close-set apertures in which were placed the glasses of lamps with pipes that rose from below them and hung from the sides of these planks and poles. From all the beams hung lanterns, large and small, interspersed by a form of large brass disc, to each of which were fixed three chains which held them in the air. All these discs were pierced with apertures in which were glasses with pipes coming from below these brass discs, no pipe being bigger than another. In them the lanterns were lighted so that they seemed like a many-legged table shining forth light.

Connected with the second *hatim*, which faces the south corner of the Dome of Zamzam, was a wooden construction of the same style which reached to that corner. The firebrands which were on top of the ball (surmounting) the dome were

lit, and along the edge of its lattice, on the side facing the
venerated House, was set a row of candles. The noble Maqam
was encompassed by a construction composed of a carved
wooden balustrade, its upper part surrounded by sharp-headed
nails which, as before described, were all provided with candles.
To the right and the left of the Maqam were ranged thick
candles in candlesticks proportionate to them in size. These
candlesticks were disposed on the stools which the guardians
use for their ascent to kindle the lights. All the walls of the
venerated Hijr were covered with candles in brass candlesticks
forming a circle of radiant light. The Haram itself was surrounded by torches, and all the illuminations described were
set alight. The merlons around the Haram were filled with
Meccan boys, each of whom held a cloth soaked in olive oil
which they placed burning on the tops of the merlons. Each
group of them took one of the four sides, and competed with
the one beside it as to who should first light up its side. The
beholder conceived that the flame leapt from merlon to merlon,
for the persons of the boys were hidden behind the light that
dazzled the eyes. As they did this they cried aloud and in chorus,
'O Lord! O Lord!' and the Haram shook with their voices.
When all that we have described was set alight the brilliant
rays bade fair to blind the eyes, and not a glance could fall on
any edge or fringe where there was not a light to engage the
sense of sight from turning elsewhere. Let the imagination play
on the grandeur of what can be seen upon that blessed night,
which in its nobleness strips off the clothes of darkness and
adorns itself in the illuminations of the sky.

The Qadi advanced and said the last obligatory prayer of
the evening, rising then to begin the Surat al-Qadr,[70] which
the imams of the Haram had reached in their recitation of the
previous night. Thereupon all the other imams stayed their tell-
ings of the *tarawih* in deference to the reciting of the Koran at
the Maqam, and presented themselves to acquire blessedness
by attending it. The immaculate maqam was brought forth
from its new repository in the Ancient House, as we described

in the first mention of it in this journal, and placed in its noble place; the place used as an oratory and covered by a dome behind which men pray. The Qadi ended with two *taslim* [benedictions], and then rose, facing the Maqam and the Ancient House, to preach the sermon. But it could not be heard because of the crowd and its clamour. When he had finished, the imams resumed their *tarawih* and the congregation dispersed. Their spirits had taken wing from emotion and their eyes streamed with tears; and from the grace of that blessed night their souls took hope that from the omens God Most High would by His favour accept their prayers. They perceived that it was indeed the noble night of Qadr described in the revelation. May Great and Glorious God deprive none of the blessing of sharing in it and the grace of witnessing it. For He is Kind and Gracious. There is no God but He.

Following this night, the five imams of the Maqam of whom we have earlier spoken were assigned to the reciting of verses that they selected from various chapters of the Koran and which contained pious recollections, warnings, and good news, according to the choice of each. The order of their *tawaf*, which followed two *taslim*, remained unvarying. God is He who accepts the prayers of all.

Then came the night of the 29th. The reader of the final part of the whole Koran is one of the remaining imams who conduct the *tarawih*, and who undertake the ceremony of the khutbah that follows the reading of the Koran. The one appointed in this case was the Malikite. He came forward with a number of boards and beside his *mihrab* he planted six in the form of a *mihrab's* circle [semicircle] and rising little less than a man's stature from the ground. Over every two of these crossed a wide board; the top was ringed with candles, and the lower part with the remainder of the many candles we mentioned in our first description of the blessed month. The inside of that circle was also fringed with other candles of medium size. It was a simple spectacle, a scene without display, wholesome and quiet, and expectant of full recompense and reward proportionate to the goodly aspect of the *mihrab*. The candles, instead of being placed in candlesticks, were supported by stones. The result was remarkable for its simplicity, being removed from pride and display and within the bounds of humbleness and modesty.

All the Malikites flocked to the final part of the reading of the whole Koran, which was done in turn by the imams of the *tarawih*, who ended their prayers sharply and with speed, so that the beginning and the end almost met, so great was the haste and despatch with which they were said. One of them then rose and tied his garments between the supports as a prop and delivered his khutbah, which was composed of extracts from the khutbah of the youthful son of the Hanafite imam; and these he rendered a second time to his listeners in accents grave according to his temper. The congregation then dispersed, with tears congealing in their ducts. In a moment the candles were torn from their supports, and preying hands were let loose, there being none among that concourse who felt shame or respect. For this God Most High will give requital and reward, for He, Glory to Him, is the Generous One and the Giver.

So ended the nights of the month (of Ramadan), which for us passed tranquilly. May God grant that we shall be among those who have been cleansed of their sins during it, and be not bereft of the favour of the acceptance of our prayers, because of the blessedness of fasting beside the Ka'bah, the Sacred House. May He seal our days, and those of all within the community of sincere Muslims, by death within Islam. Instil in us the praise and thanks such benefits deserve; make them for us a treasure in the life to come, and render unto us, because of them, recompense and reward. Let us hope that by His grace and favour, He will not overlook the days on which we broke our fast with the waters of Zamzam. He is the Merciful, the Liberal. There is no Lord but He.

The Month of Shawwal (579)

[17th of January–14th of February, 1184]

May God let us know His favour

THE new moon rose on the night of Tuesday the 16th of
January. May God prosper its rising and bestow on us its
blessings. This blessed month is the first of 'the well-known
months of the pilgrimage' [Koran II, 197], and after it follow
three sacred and blessed months. The night of the rising of
this new moon was one of great assembly in the sacred Mosque
– may God increase it in honour. The pattern of lighting the
torches, chandeliers, and candles was the same as for the night
of the twenty-seventh of the Sublime month of Ramadan. The
minarets at the four sides of the Haram were illuminated, as
was the roof of the mosque on the summit of Jabal Abu Qubays.
The muezzin stayed all that night on the roof of the Dome of
Zamzam, calling out the *tahlil* ['There is no God but God'],
the *takbir* ['God is Great'], the *tasbih* ['I extol the holiness of
God'], and offering up praise. Most of the imams and the
people remained awake that night performing the *tawaf*, saying prayers, and calling the *tahlil* and the *takbir*. May God
accept the prayers of all. In truth He it is who hearkens to
prayers and guarantees hope. Glory to Him. There is no God
but He.

When morning came, and the dawn-prayers had ended, the
people donned their festival dress and hastened to take their
stations for the prayers of the Feast in the sacred Mosque. For
it was the rule to pray in the Mosque rather than in an oratory,
from a desire to profit from the nobleness of the place and the
grace of its blessedness, as well as the merit of the prayers of
the imam and those who perform them with him behind the
Maqam. First in their early arrival were the Shayba who opened
the door of the holy Ka'bah. Their chief sat on the holy threshold,

and the others entered the Ka'bah until they perceived that the Emir Mukthir had arrived. They then went down to him and met him near to the Gate of the Prophet – may God bless and preserve him. He came to the venerated House and made the sevenfold circumambulation. The people had come in great numbers for their feast, and the Haram was teeming with them; and on the dome of the Well of Zamzam the muezzin stood, according to his practice, raising his voice in praise and invocation. In this he took turns with his brother.

When the Emir had done the seven circuits, he went to the bench at the Zamzam Dome on the side facing the Black Corner, and there sat, with his sons to the right and left of him, and his viziers and suite about him. The Shayba returned to their posts in the venerated House, while the people gazed upon them with their eyes filled with emotion towards the House, and with unembittered envy of them in their connection with it and their offices as chamberlains and guardians. Glory to God who gave them the special honour of serving it. Four poets of the Emir's suite presented themselves and recited poetry the one after the other until they had done. During this, the sun had well risen and the time of the midday prayer was at hand. The Qadi, who was to deliver the sermon, advanced majestically between his two black banners, himself in black robes, and preceded by the whip which we have already mentioned, and the crack of which reverberated throughout the Haram. He came to the venerated Maqam, and the congregation rose to prayer. When it was ended, he ascended the pulpit which had been placed in the spot allotted to it every Friday, beside the wall of the venerated Ka'bah where the noble door opens, and delivered an eloquent sermon. The muezzins were seated below him on the steps of the pulpit, and when he opened each part of the sermon with *takbir* they repeated it with him, and so it continued until he had ended his sermon. The people then went up to each other to shake hands and offer greetings, begging God's pardon each on behalf of the other, and wishing each other good; glad, joyful, and happy at the favour that God had bestowed on them. They then hastened to the venerated House and entered with the 'salute' in peace, coming on in crowds, wave upon wave, and forming a sublime spectacle and a concourse that by the grace of God Most High shall gain His compassion. May God make it a treasure for them in the life to come, as, by His grace and favour, He made this noble festival the most excellent of our time. Over all this He holds sway, and these things He determines.

When the people had dispersed from their prayers and the ritual of greeting each other, they betook themselves to the visit of the cemetery in Ma'la. They did this to gain blessings, (heavenly) count being taken of the steps they take to it and of the prayers for mercy made on behalf of those of His saintly servants and others who have lain there since the first days of Islam. May God hold them all in His favour and reckon us of their number and advantage us of their love. 'For man', as said the Prophet – may God bless and preserve him – 'is with him whom God loves.'[71]

On Saturday the 19th of this month, being the 3rd of February, we ascended Mina to observe the solemn rites that are discharged there, and to inspect the lodging hired for us in readiness for our stay there if it so pleases God, on the days of the *Tashriq*.[72] We found that it filled the soul with joy and solace. It is a city of great ruins, of wide extent, and of ancient foundation, but all of it has been destroyed save for a few buildings taken as lodging places that enfold on both sides a road that in length and width is like a course for running horses. The first thing that a person on his way there finds, to his left and near to it, is the Mosque of the Blessed Covenant, referring to the first covenant in Islam; that which was concluded by 'Abbas – may God hold him in His favour – on behalf of the Prophet – may God bless and preserve him – with the Ansar [Auxiliaries of Madinah], as is well-known. From there he goes to the Cairn [*jamrah*] of al-'Aqabah, which is the beginning of Mina when coming from Mecca and to the left. It is on the side of the road, and is an elevated spot because of the piled-up stones that have been cast, and but for the miracles of God manifest in it, it would have seemed to have been a large mountain, so great has been the collection (of stones) over the successive ages and through long centuries. But in it Great and Glorious God has one of His hidden and venerated secrets. There is no God but He.

On the cairn is a blessed mosque, and a sign has been raised on it similar to those in the Haram that we have described. One who is casting stones, facing Mecca – may God honour it – has this cairn to his right. At this place he will throw seven stones on the Day of Sacrifice after sunrise. He will then slaughter (his victim) and shave his head. The place of shaving is round the Cairn, and that of slaughter anywhere on Mina, for as said the Prophet – may God bless and preserve him – 'Mina is all a place of slaughter.' From then on, everything is permitted to the pilgrim save women and scent (which he may not indulge in) until he has done the ritual course of the return to Mecca (al-ifadah).

After this Cairn of al-'Aqabah comes the Centre Cairn [Jamrat al-Wasta] on which also a sign has been erected. Between these two cairns lie a bow-shot. After this comes the First Cairn [al-Jumrah al-Ula], which is the same distance from it as the other. At the sun's decline on the second day of the Sacrifice seven stones are thrown on the First Cairn, and the same number on both the Centre Cairn and the Cairn of al-'Aqabah; a total of twenty-one stones. On the third day of the Sacrifice, at the same time, a similar arrangement is followed, giving forty-two stones in two days. These, with the seven thrown at al-'Aqabah at sunrise on the Day of Sacrifice, as we mentioned, and which released the pilgrims from the abstinence from prohibited things save women and scent, bring the number up to forty-nine stones. Following this, and after that day, the pilgrims disperse to Mecca. In these times, dispense is made with the twenty-one stones that were thrown on a fourth day according to the same system. This is because of

L

the haste of the pilgrims who fear the Bedouin tribe of Shu'-biyyah and other dreaded trials, that cause the traditions of the Sunni to be infringed. To-day the practice is carried out with forty-nine stones, but in the past there were seventy. God accepts the goodwill of His servants.[73]

The first thing that he who leaves 'Arafat for Mina will meet is the First Cairn, then the Centre Cairn, and then the Cairn of al-'Aqabah. On the Day of Sacrifice the Cairn of al-'Aqabah comes singly and alone, with seven stones as has already been mentioned. No other cairn shares (a stoning) that day. In the two days that follow they adopt the system we have described with the help of Great and Glorious God.

After the First Cairn, and deviating a little from the road, is found the place of sacrifice of the Sacrificed One [Ishmael] – may God bless and preserve him – where 'he was ransomed by the sacrifice of a great victim' [Koran XXXVII, 107]. On the blessed spot has been built a mosque which stands near the foot of Mount Thabir. At the place of sacrifice, and fixed in a wall built there, is a stone bearing the impressions of small feet said to be the footprints of the Sacrificed One – may God bless and preserve him – left there as he writhed. By the power of Great and Glorious God the stone, in pity and sympathy, softened to receive them, and men touch and kiss it that they might be blessed thereby.

From there, one passes to the blessed mosque of al-Khayf [the Declivity], which is at the end of Mina as you go, that is to say the end of that part of it which contains structures. As for the ancient ruins, they extend a very long way off, in front of the mosque. This blessed mosque is of very wide extent, like the biggest possible cathedral mosque. The minaret rises in the middle of the court, and to the south it has four rows of arcades covered by a single roof. This is one of the mosques that are celebrated for their blessedness and the nobleness of their site. It is enough that according to the venerable tradition it is the immaculate place of burial of many prophets – God's blessings upon them. Fast by this mosque, and to the right of

the passer-by on this road, is a large stone resting on the side
of the mountain, standing high off the ground, and giving
shade to whoever may be under it. The story has it that the
Prophet – may God bless and preserve him – sat beneath its
shade, and that his revered head pressed against it whereupon
it softened to his touch and received an impression the size of
his head's circumference. Men hasten to put their heads in that
place, to obtain blessings and protection from the spot touched
by his revered head, that by the power of Great and Glorious
God the fires (of hell) should not touch them. When we had
finished our visit to this venerated shrine, we took our departure, rejoicing at the favour that God had granted to us of
knowing it, and came to Mecca near midday. Praise be to God
for what He has bestowed (on us).

On the following Sunday, which was the 20th of Shawwal,
we climbed the sacred mountain of Hira to gain the blessings
of visiting the grotto on its summit where the Prophet – may
God bless and preserve him – dedicated himself to God. It is
the place where first the revelation descended upon him – may
God bless and preserve him, and avail us of his intercessions,
including us in the number of his followers, and granting that
we may die according to his law and in his love. This by His
grace and favour. There is no Lord but He.

After sunrise on Tuesday the 22nd of the month, being the
6th of February, all the people assembled before the exalted
Ka'bah to pray for rain. The Qadi, who had summoned them,
had urged them to a fast of three days before it. And so they
assembled on this fourth day, having consecrated their aims
to Great and Glorious God. Early came the Shayba and opened
the venerated door of the Ancient House. Then the Qadi,
clothed in white, approached between his two black banners.
The maqam of the Friend (of God), Abraham – may God bless
and preserve him – was then brought forth and placed on the
threshold of the door of the venerated House, and the Koran
of 'Uthman – may God hold him in His favour – was taken
from its cupboard and opened beside the immaculate maqam,

one board resting on it, and the other on the venerated door. All the people were then called to prayer, and the Qadi prayed with them behind the Maqam in the place used as an oratory. He prayed two *rak'ah* saying in the first, 'Glorify the name of thy Lord, the Most High' [Koran LXXXVII, 1], and in the second reciting the *surah* of al-Ghashiyah [the Overwhelming: Koran LXXXVIII].

He then ascended the pulpit, which had been set in its appointed place beside the wall of the holy Ka'bah and delivered an eloquent sermon in which he combined prayers for their forgiveness of God, exhortations, and pious recollections, moving their souls and rousing them to repentance and a return to Great and Glorious God. The eyes of men ran dry of tears and their lachrymatory ducts were exhausted of water. Their cries rose high, and loud were their sobs and chokings.

He wrapped himself in his *rida*, as likewise did the congregation, in observance of the tradition. They then dispersed, hopeful and not despairing of the mercy of Great and Glorious God. May He comfort His servants with His beneficence and bounty.

In this fashion he continued for three consecutive days to pray with the people for rain, for dryness was sore afflicting the inhabitants of the Hejaz. The drought had caused them much damage, and the aridity had destroyed their flocks, for in spring, autumn, and winter there had fallen nothing but a little raining that was inadequate and brought no relief. But Great and Glorious God is kind to His servants, punishing them not for their sins. He is the Compassionate, the Benefactor. There is no God but He.

On Thursday the 24th of Shawwal we ascended Jebel Thaur to visit the blessed grotto where the Prophet – may God bless and preserve him – took refuge with his friend the Faithful One [Abu Bakr] – may God hold him in His favour – as has come down to us on the authority of the illustrious revelation [Koran IX, 40]. Of this grotto and its description we have already spoken in this journal. We entered it by a gap that is difficult for some people to squeeze through, and acquired blessings by touching with our own bodies the place touched by the blessed body – may God sanctify it – for by it the Prophet – may God bless and preserve him – had entered the grotto. One of the Egyptians who that day climbed to it suffered a mortifying and ignominious experience for he sought to enter by this narrow way, but could not by any means. Many times he tried and failed, so that seeing him, men stopped and wept in pity and had recourse to prayers to Great and Glorious God. But this availed him nothing. There was one of them who was stouter than he, and him God helped, causing men long to wonder and reflect. After we had left that day, we learnt that during it three persons had found themselves in this derogatory state. God preserve us, in this life and in that to come, from humiliating attitudes.

This mountain is most difficult to climb, taking away the breath, and one cannot reach its summit without exhausting and fatiguing the hands. It is three miles from Mecca, and the same distance from Mount Hira'. May God, by His grace and favour, deprive us not of the blessings of this shrine. The grotto is eighteen spans long, and its width is eleven spans in the middle and two-thirds of a span at the ends. Entrance is made on to the middle. The width of the other entrance, whose ingress is wider, is five spans; for as we have already said, the grotto has two entrances.

On the following Friday the Yemenite Saru arrived in large numbers on their way to visit the tomb of the Apostle – may God bless and preserve him. According to their custom, they brought provisions to Mecca, and the people of Mecca rejoiced exceedingly at their coming, even deeming them a compensation for the lack of rain. The benefactions of God to the dwellers in His noble Haram are manifold, for He – Glory to Him – is kind to His servants. There is no God but He.

The Month of Dhu 'l-Qa'dah (579)

THE new moon of this month rose on the night of Wednesday, corresponding with the 14th of February, and the testimony of its observation was proved before the Qadi. The greater part of the people in the sacred Mosque saw nothing of it, although they stayed there watching until the end of the sunset prayers. There were among them who imagined that they observed it and who pointed towards it, but when their claim was examined the vision disappeared and their information was proved false. God best knows the truth of the matter. This blessed month is the second of the sacred months and the second of the months of the pilgrimage. May God, by His power and compassion, bring forth this new moon upon Muslims enjoying security and faith, together with His pardon and His favour.

On Monday the 13th of the month we entered the birthplace of the Prophet – may God bless and preserve him. It is (now) a superbly built mosque, and had been the house of 'Abdullah ibn 'Abd al-Muttalib, the father of the Prophet – may God bless and preserve him – of which we have already spoken. The actual spot of his nativity has the likeness of a small basin (in the floor), three spans wide, with in its centre a green marble tablet, two-thirds of a span wide and encircled by silver so that with this attached silver its width is one span. We smoothed our cheeks on this holy spot which was the place of delivery for the most illustrious child in the world, and which was touched by the purest and most noble of offspring – may God bless and preserve him, and advantage us with the blessings of visiting the place of his birth. Beside it is a *mihrab* of beautiful ornamental carvings, with a cornice worked with gold. All this has been described before (by others). This blessed spot is to the east of the Ka'bah and adjoins the side of the mountain. Overlooking it close by is Jabal Abu Qubays, and also near to it is a mosque on which is written: 'This mosque is the birthplace of 'Ali ibn Abi Talib – may God hold him in His favour – and here was nurtured the Apostle of God – may God bless and preserve him. It was the house of Abi Talib, uncle and guardian of the Prophet – may God bless and preserve him.'

On the same day I entered the house of Khadijah the Great [Muhammad's first wife] – may God hold her in His favour. Here is the chamber of prophetic inspiration, and the birthplace of Fatimah – may God hold her in His favour – which is a small chamber, somewhat oblong. The actual place of delivery has the likeness of a small basin (in the ground), with a black stone in its centre. In this same house, contiguous to the wall, were born al-Hasan and al-Husayn his sons – may God hold them in His favour. The place of the delivery of al-Hasan is beside that of al-Husayn, and over them are two stones inclining to black that seem to be signs of the blessed and noble birth sites. We smoothed our cheeks on these noble places of delivery that have been privileged by the touch of the bodies of these noble children – may God hold them in His favour. Also in this venerated house is al-Makhtaba' [the hiding place] of the Prophet – may God bless and preserve him – which is a sort of cell. In it is a seat deep in the ground like a ditch and penetrating the wall a little. From the wall projects a large stone that forms a sort of shade to the seat, and that is said to have been the stone that covered the Prophet – may God bless and preserve him – when he hid in that place. The blessings of God be upon him, and upon those unspotted ones of his family. Over each one of these places of birth is a small movable wooden dome that protects them. When a visitor comes, he puts it aside and touches the noble spot to acquire blessings from it and then replaces the dome.

On Friday the 24th of the month, the order of the Emir Mukthir for the arrest of the chief of the Shayba, Muhammad ibn Isma'il, and the raiding of his house, was executed. He was dismissed from his custodianship of the sacred House – may · God keep it inviolate – for some defects charged against him which were unbecoming in him who is entrusted with the guardianship of the Ancient House. 'Whoever shall incline therein to wrong injustly, him we shall cause to taste a painful chastisement' [Koran XXII, 25]. May God protect us by His favour from wrong judgement, and the piercings of the arrows of (false) accusation.

In the foregoing days of this month, the Yemenite Saru were arriving increasingly in many bands with provisions of food and other things, and all manner of condiments and dried fruits. They brought plenty to the city * * * *; and but for them the continuing drought and the high prices would have reduced it to distress and affliction. They were a mercy to this Safe City [Mecca]. They then set forth on the blessed visit to the sacred tomb in Taybah [Medina], the burial place of the Apostle of God – may God bless and preserve him – arriving in a brief space of time, for they covered the road from Mecca to Medina in a few days. Those pilgrims who went with them praised their company. While they were away, another party of them arrived for the pilgrimage (in Mecca) only, and having no time for the visit to Medina, they remained in Mecca. When those of them who had visited Medina returned, even wide spaces became constricted because of them.

On Monday the 27th of the month, the Ancient House was opened. The one entrusted with the opening was a cousin of the deposed Shayba and, according to report, of more exemplary character. The Saru, as was their habit, thronged to enter, but reached a state never known before, ascending in troops until the venerated door was choked with them; and to go forward or to retire they were unable. At last with the greatest difficulty they entered; and then they came forth in haste and the venerated door was too narrow for them. A group of them would go down the steps while another ascended and they would meet and become entangled with each other.

Sometimes those descending would be borne on the breasts of those coming up, and at times the climbers would be stopped by those coming down and push until, losing balance, they fell over each other. Those who watched them saw a shocking sight for some of them were hurt, although some were not. The greater part of them came down by jumping on men's heads and necks. One of the most extraordinary things we saw on that Monday was some of the Shayba going up at the time of the crowding, seeking to enter the noble House and being unable to get through. They clung to the curtains at the side of the doorposts, and then one of them seized one of the hemp ropes that hold the curtains and so rose over the heads and necks and then trampled over them and thus entered the House. He could find no other place to put his foot, such was the crowding, piling up, and massing together. The like of the host of Saru who arrived in this year had never been known in the years before. God has the power to perform miracles. There is no God but He.

On the same day, which was the 27th of the month of Dhu 'l-Qa'dah, the curtains of the holy Ka'bah were tucked up about a man's stature and a half from the walls on all four sides. They call this 'ihram' and say 'the Ka'bah is in a state of ihram'. This is the custom always throughout the months mentioned, and the Ka'bah is not opened from the time of its ihram until after the 'standing' (on Mount 'Arafat). It is as if this tucking up (of the curtains of the Ka'bah) were a signal to set forth on the (return) journey, and a warning of the drawing nigh of the time to give the awaited farewell. God grant that it be not our last farewell, and by His power and glory, vouchsafe to us a return to it, and the easing of our way.

On Friday the 24th of the month, before this day we have been speaking of, we seized the fleeting opportunity of some relief in the crowding and entered the venerated House to make our farewell. For after that it would be impossible to enter, because of the continuous thronging of men, especially of the foreigners who would arrive with the Emir of the 'Iraq pilgrimage. One sees in them such a rush and press upon it, and such a crowding inside, as to make one forget, such is their rudeness and want of manners, the Yemenite Saru. Not one of them is capable of a civility, much less anything else. May Great and Glorious God grant in His grace and bounty that this be not our final visit to His venerated House, and favour us with a return to it in happiness and good health.

On the day on which the Ka'bah assumed the state of ihram, the wooden dome was removed from its position over the sacred maqam (of Abraham) and replaced by an iron dome in readiness for these foreigners; for were it not of iron they would eat it or do worse, such is their rude fervour for His holy shrine: even throwing their persons on it. May God in His grace and favour advantage them for their (good) intentions.

On Tuesday the 28th of the month, the deposed chief of the Shayba, with display and ostentation, strode proudly between his sons to the holy Ka'bah, bearing in his hand its key which had been restored to him. He opened the venerated door and mounted with his sons to the blessed roof by means of stout hempen ropes secured to iron pegs driven into the roof and hanging down to the ground where a form of wooden chair is tied to them. In this (customarily) sits one of the Shayba guardians of the House who, by the agency of pulleys provided for that purpose, can be drawn to the roof-top and undertake the mending of the tears in the curtains caused by the wind. We enquired how this deposed Shayba could be restored to his office, the charges levelled against him being true, and we learnt that five hundred Meccan dinars had been demanded from him before he could resume it. This sum he borrowed and paid. Long we marvelled and pondered over this. We discovered also that his arrest was not from jealous care or indignation at the violation of God's Holy Places at his hands, although his function is no less in honour than the caliphate. But one circumstance resembles another. 'The unjust are friends of each other' [Koran XLV, 19]. To God we should complain of this clear corruption in even the most noble place on the earth. Sufficient is He to us. He is our best Trustee.

On Wednesday the 29th of Dhu 'l-Qa'dah, we entered the house of Al-Khayzuran, which is the place whence sprang Islam. It is beside al-Safa, and adjoining it, and to the right of him who enters it is a small chamber that was the dwelling of Bilal – may God hold him in His favour. The house is approached across a large courtyard, like that of a caravanserai, enclosed by chambers that are hired to pilgrims. This venerated house is small and found to the left of him who enters the courtyard. It has been restored by Jamal al-Din, whom we have mentioned in this journal as leaving generous tracings of himself, and who spent on it about a thousand dinars. May God advantage him for his past good deeds. To the right of him who enters the blessed house is a door by which one enters a large and splendidly built dome in which is the place where the Prophet – may God bless and preserve him – sat, and the stone against which he leant. To his right is the place of Abu Bakr the Faithful, and to the right of Abu Bakr is the place of 'Ali ibn Abi Talib together with this stone against which he leant, and which is in the wall in the form of a *mihrab*. In this house 'Umar ibn al-Khattab embraced Islam, and from it, at his hand, the faith spread, while God made it illustrious from there. May God advantage us with the blessedness of this venerated shrine and august monument, and grant that we may die in the love of those who through them have been honoured, and who all are fitted for the benedictions of God.

The Month of Dhu 'l-Hijjah (579)

[16th of March–13th of April, 1184]

May God let us know of His blessings

THE new moon of this month rose on the night of Thursday, corresponding with the 15th of March. In the watching for it the people were involved in a strange circumstance, and a remarkable fabrication; and a false utterance almost provoked the stones, not to mention else, to rebut and deny it. It happened in this wise. They were watching for the appearance of the new moon on the night of Thursday the 30th of the month. On the horizon the air had thickened and the clouds had piled up when, with the sunset, a faint glimmering of red appeared. Eagerly the people yearned for some break in the clouds that their eyes might catch a glimpse of the new moon. While they were about this, one of them cried, 'God is Great,' and the vast concourse followed him and cried, 'God is Great,' rising to behold what they could not see, and pointing at what they only imagined, such was their eagerness that the standing on Mount 'Arafat should fall on Friday. As if the pilgrimage must be tied to that precise day. They therefore forged the false testimonies; and a party of Maghrabis – may God prosper their affairs – together with some Egyptians and their chiefs went to the Qadi and testified that they had seen it. He answered them most harshly, and peremptorily rejected their evidence; and in declaring their statements spurious he put them to the greatest shame, saying, 'Wonder of wonders! Did one of you affirm that he had seen the sun under such thickly woven clouds I would not accept his affirmation. How then can I believe that you saw a new moon that is twenty-nine nights old.'[74] Amongst other things he said was: 'The Maghrabis are disordered. A hair from the eyebrow comes in sight, and with fancy's eye they deem it to be the new moon.' This Qadi,

Jamal al-Din, displayed in this matter of the false testimony firmness and prudence, so that the learned praised him and the wise thanked him. And well might they do so, for the rights of the pilgrimage are of great consequence to Muslims who come to them 'from every remote path' [Koran XXII, 27]. If complaisance were shown, zeal would be impaired and unsound thought admitted. May God by His favour raise all obscurities and their evils.

On the night of this Friday the new moon appeared during a break in the clouds, clothed in the radiance of the thirtieth night. The crowds then raised tremendous shouts and proclaimed that the 'standing' (on Mount 'Arafat) would take place on Friday, crying, 'Praise be to God who did not render vain our efforts or bring to nought our proposals,' as if it were a truth with them that if the standing did not fall upon a Friday it would not be acceptable to God, nor could God's mercy be hoped for or expected. But God is above that. On Friday they met before the Qadi and gave testimony as to the truth of its being seen, making truth to weep and falsehood to chuckle. But he put aside their evidence and said, 'Until when, O ye people, will ye persist in your ardour, and until when will ye pursue the paths of error?' and let them know that he had asked leave of the Emir Mukthir that the ascent to 'Arafat be made on the morning of Friday. They would stand on 'Arafat in the evening and on the morning of the following Saturday, and would pass the night at Muzdalifah. If the 'standing' were done on Friday, there would be no objection to their delaying the passing of the night in Muzdalifah, this being permitted by Muslim imams. If it took place on the Saturday, they would pass the night at Muzdalifah, and be favoured therein. But if they decided on Friday, the Muslims would be deceived and their rights corrupted, for the 'standing' on the Day of Tarwiyah[75] [8th of Dhu 'l-Hijjah] is not considered lawful by the imams, whereas it is by them considered lawful on the Day of Sacrifice [9th of Dhu 'l-Hijjah]. All those present thanked the Qadi for his conduct of the enquiry and prayed for him, and the laity who were there revealed their approval and departed in peace. Praise be to God for that.

This blessed month is the third of the sacred months. The first ten days are those in which the people assemble. It is the great period of the pilgrimage, the month of cries [of *labbayka*, 'Here am I, O Lord'] and of the flowing of blood [Sacrifice], and the time when from all lands and ways the deputations to God [pilgrims] do meet. It is the target of God's mercy and blessings, and (the month) in which occurs the solemn 'standing' on 'Arafat. May God by His favour and bounty, grant that we be of those who during it win benefits, and divest us of the raiment of sin and transgressions. For He is at once the All-Powerful and the Forgiving.

The Emir (of the pilgrimage) from 'Iraq awaited the clearing in men's minds of the confusion surrounding this matter, and it may be, God willing, that the truth of the matter was already clear to him.

During all these days, and in those that followed, there arrived companies of Yemenite Saru and pilgrims from divers lands, in numbers beyond count save by Him who watches the terms of their lives, and their sustenance. There is no God but He.

A manifest miracle is that this Safe City [Mecca], which lies in a valley bed that is a bow-shot or less in width, can contain this vast host; a host such that were it brought into the greatest of cities it could not be contained. This venerated city, in what concerns it of manifest miracles, namely its expansion for multitudes beyond count, is described only by the true analogy of the *ulema* [learned doctors of divinity] that its enlargement for newcomers is that of a uterus for the foetus. So it is with 'Arafat and the other great shrines in this sacred land. May God with His grace and bounty increase its sanctity, and in it grant to us His mercy.

From the beginning of this blessed month the drums of the Emir Mukthir were beaten morning and evening and at the hours of prayer, as a sign that this was the solemn period of the pilgrimage. So it continued until the day of the ascent to

'Arafat – may God accord us there the acceptance of our prayers
and the extension of His mercy.

On Monday the fourth or fifth of this month there arrived
the Emir 'Uthman ibn 'Ali, the governor of Aden, who had
left it in flight before Sayf al-Islam who was moving on the
Yemen. He had put to sea in many ships [jilab] laden with
great treasures and monies beyond computation so abundant
were they. For he had long been governor of that province,
and his acquisitions had been extensive. But while he was dis-
embarking at a place called Sr * * * * his ships were overtaken
by the fire-ships [harariq] of the Emir Sayf al-Islam and all the
heavy treasures had been seized. The lighter objects of worth
and value he carried away with him to the shore, accompanied
by a number of his men and slaves, and arrived in safety at
Mecca in a camel caravan laden with belongings and money.
Under the eyes of the people this was taken into a house that
he had earlier caused to be built, after sending before him by
night the most precious of his treasures and the money he had
to his hand, together with a party of slaves and servants. To
be short, it is impossible to describe the abundance and amplitude of his state. The part that was seized from him was the
greater, for he was described during his governorship as dealing ill with the merchants, all the profits of commerce going
to him. The treasures brought from India came wholly to his
hands, so that he acquired vast illicit profits and attained the
treasures of Qarun.[76] But the vicissitudes of time have begun
to reduce him, and he knows not how his case will be with
Saladin. This world destroys all those who love it most, and
its sons it devours. The reward of God is the best treasure, and
obedience to Him is the most noble booty. There is no God
but He.

The question of testimony as to (the sighting) of the blessed
and felicitous new moon continued to provoke anxiety until
repeated news of its being seen was received on the night of
Thursday, which corresponds with the 15th of March. Evidence of this was given by some devout and God-fearing men

of trust among the Yemenites, and others who had arrived from Medina the venerated. But the Qadi persisted in his firmness and refusal to accept (this evidence) and in his determination to defer the matter until a messenger should arrive giving news of the arrival of the Emir of the 'Iraq (Pilgrimage); for he wished to know from this envoy the views of the Emir of the pilgrimage upon the matter. And on Wednesday the 7th, the messenger arrived. The minds of the Meccans were filled with apprehension at his delay, being fearful of the rancour of the Caliph towards their Emir, Mukthir, for some reprehensible actions he had committed. The arrival of this messenger reassured and calmed their frightened souls, for he came with pleasant countenance and good grace. He gave notice that the new moon had been seen on the night of Thursday. The news passed from one to the other and was confirmed before the Qadi, thus obliging him to deliver the *khutbah* that day, in accordance with the established custom, the 7th of Dhu 'l-Hijjah after the midday prayers. In this sermon he advised the people of the rites they should observe, and told them that the morrow, being Yaum al-Tarwiyah, would be the day of their ascent to Mina, and that the 'standing' (on Mount 'Arafat) would be observed on Friday. He reminded them that the venerated tradition that comes directly from the Prophet – may God bless and preserve him – has it that a 'standing' on this day is equivalent to seventy on any other, and that the superiority of a year in which this standing (falls on a Friday) is as the superiority of Friday over all the other days (of the week).

Early on the morning of Thursday the people began their ascent to Mina, and thence passed on to 'Arafat. It is the rule that the night should be passed there, but perforce they omitted this in fear of the Banu Shu'bah, who make raids on the pilgrims on their way to 'Arafat. The Emir 'Uthman, of whom we have already spoken, displays much zeal in this matter, even waging holy war against them, for which we hope for him, if God so wills, the forgiveness of his sins. He goes forth, with all his companions bristling with weapons, to the gorge between

Muzdalifah and 'Arafat, which is the place where the road is hemmed in by two mountains from one of which, being that which is to the left of him who goes to 'Arafat, the Shu'bah descend upon the pilgrims and plunder them. The Emir raised a pavilion in this gorge between the two mountains, after one of his companions had gone before (to reconnoitre) and had climbed to the top of the mountain on his horse. The mountain is difficult of ascent, and we marvelled at his achievement, and even more so at that of his horse which was able to climb that difficult slope that * * * * could not climb. All the pilgrims felt secure in the company of this Emir who earned two rewards; one for the holy war, and one for the pilgrimage, since the safeguarding of those who came in deputation [pilgrimage] to Great and Glorious God on such a day, has the merit of the greatest holy war.

The ascent of the people continued all that day, all night, and all Friday so that there was assembled on 'Arafat a multitude whose numbers could not be counted save by Great and Glorious God. Muzdalifah lies between Mina and 'Arafat; from Mina to Muzdalifah lies the same distance as from Mecca to Mina, which is about five miles; and from Muzdalifah to 'Arafat is the same or a little more. Muzdalifah is also called al-Mash'ar al-Haram [the place of ritual ceremonies] as well as Jam [reunion], and therefore has three names. Before coming to it, about a mile away, is the Wadi [valley of] Muhassir, which it is the custom to pass through with a brisk step. It is the boundary between Muzdalifah and Mina, for it lies between them. Muzdalifah is a wide stretch of land between two mountains, and around it are the reservoirs and cisterns that were used for water in the time of Zubaydah – may God's mercy rest upon her soul. In the middle of this plain is an enclosure at whose centre is a rounded knoll on the top of which is a mosque that is approached by steps on both sides. Men crowd as they climb up to it and at the prayers inside it, the night they pass at Muzdalifah.

'Arafat also is a wide plain, and if it were men's place of

M

congregation on the Day of Resurrection it could contain them all. This broad plain is enfolded by many mountains, and at its extremity is the Jabal al-Ramah [Mount of Mercy] on and around which is the standing ground of the pilgrims. The 'Two Signs' [Al-'Alaman] come about two miles before this place, and the area stretching from the 'Two Signs' to 'Arafat is neutral [lit. 'lawful' *hill*], while that on the hither side is sacred. Near to them on the 'Arafat side, is the valley of 'Uranah, from which place the Prophet – may God bless and preserve him – has enjoined that avoidance be made by saying, ' 'Arafat is all a standing ground. But turn aside from the valley of 'Uranah.' He who 'stands' there invalidates his pilgrimage, and this should be kept in mind, for on the evening of the 'standing' the camel-masters often hurry many pilgrims, making them apprehensive of the crowding in the return from 'Arafat and taking them down by the 'Two Signs' that face them, until they come to the valley of 'Uranah or overreach it and so annul their pilgrimage. The prudent will not therefore leave his standing ground on 'Arafat until the disc of the sun has completely subsided.

The Mount of Mercy rises in the middle of the plain, apart from the other mountains. It consists wholly of separate blocks of (granite) stone and it is difficult of ascent. Jamal al-Din, whose memorable works we have already mentioned in this journal, provided on its four sides low steps that can be climbed by laden beasts, and spent great sums upon it. At its summit is a cupola that is attributed to Umm Salimah – may God hold her in His favour – but it is not certain whether this is true. In the centre of the cupola is a mosque into which men crowd to pray, and around this venerated mosque runs a terrace, broad and handsome to look upon, that overlooks the plain of 'Arafat. To the south is a wall against which are erected the *mihrabs* that the people pray in. At the foot of this sacred mountain, to the left of him who looks towards the *qiblah* [direction of Mecca], is a house of ancient construction in whose upper part is a vaulted upper chamber, attributed to Adam – may God bless and preserve him. On the left of this house, facing the *qiblah*, is the rock beside which was the standing ground of the Prophet – may God bless and preserve him – and it is on a small hill. Around the Mount of Mercy and this venerated house are water cisterns and wells. Also to the left of the house and near to it is a small mosque. Fast by the 'Two Signs', and to the left on him who faces the *qiblah*, is an ancient mosque of large proportions, of which the south wall that is named after Abraham – may God bless and preserve him – remains. The preacher delivers a sermon in it on the day of the 'standing', and then leads the combined midday and afternoon prayers. Also to the left of the 'Two Signs', when facing the *qiblah*, is the Wadi 'l-Arak [the valley of the Thorn Tree, *Salvadora persica*] which is the green thorn that stretches before the eye a long way over the plain.

The assembling of the people on 'Arafat is completed during Thursday and all the night of Friday. Near the third part of this night of Friday, the Emir of 'Iraq pilgrimage arrived and pitched his tent in the wide plain that, for him who faces *qiblah*, is contiguous with the right side of the Mount of Mercy. The *qiblah*, relative to 'Arafat, is to the west, for the sacred Ka'bah is in that direction.

Upon that Friday morning there was on 'Arafat a multitude that could have no like save that which there will be on the Day of Resurrection; but, within the will of God Most High, it was a gathering that will win reward, giving promise as it does of God's mercy and forgiveness when men assemble for the Day of Reckoning. Some truth-demanding sheiks of the *mujawir* [settled pilgrims] asserted that never had they seen on 'Arafat a more numerous concourse, and I do not believe that since the time of al-Rashid, who was the last Caliph to make the pilgrimage, there had ever been such a concourse in Islam. May God by His favour grant that it bring mercy and immunity from sin.

When, on Friday, the midday and afternoon prayers were said together, the people stood contrite and in tears, humbly beseeching the mercy of Great and Glorious God. The cries of 'God is Great' rose high, and loud were the voices of men in prayer. Never has there been seen a day of such weeping, such penitence of heart, and such bending of the neck in reverential submission and humility before God. In this fashion the pilgrims continued, with the sun burning their faces, until its orb had sunk and the time of the sunset prayers was at hand. The Emir of the Pilgrimage had arrived with a number of his soldiers clad in mail, and they stood near the rocks beside the little mosque already mentioned. The Yemenite Saru took up position in their appointed stations on Mount 'Arafat, places that, by successive inheritance from their ancestors, they had occupied since the days of the Prophet – may God bless and preserve him; and no tribe of them encroached upon the station of another. Their numbers this year were such as had never been equalled before. Likewise the Emir of 'Iraq arrived with a great host such as had never come before; and with him came foreign Emirs from Khurasan, high-born ladies called Khawatin, which in the singular is 'Khatun', and many ladies daughters of emirs, together with those from other lands in countless numbers, all of whom took up their posts.

For their return from 'Arafat, they had appointed the Malikite imam as their guide and model, for the practice of Malik – may God hold him in His favour – demands that there should be no departure from 'Arafat until the sun's disc has fallen below the horizon and the time for sunset prayers has come. Yet some of the Yemenite Saru had taken their leave before this. So when the time had come, the Malikite imam gave the sign with his hands and descended from his post. The people then pressed forward on their return with such a surge that the earth trembled and the mountains quaked. What a standing it had been, how awesome to regard and what hopes of happy reward it had brought to the soul. God grant that we may be among those on whom He there conferred His approbation and covered with His bounty. For He is bounteous, generous, compassionate, and beneficent.

The encampment of this Emir of 'Iraq was beautiful to look upon and superbly provided, with large handsome tents and erections, and wonderful pavilions and awnings, and of an aspect such that I have never seen more remarkable. The grandest camp to look upon was that of the Emir, for it was surrounded by a linen screen, like a wall to form a sort of closed-in garden or an ornamented building. Within this were the pitched pavilions, all black on a white background and dappled and variegated as if they were flowers in a garden. The faces of the four sides of the screen were wholly covered with forms of black shields painted on the white (linen) such as to startle the beholder, who might conceive them to be shields on steeds covered with embroidered horse-cloths. In these wall-like screens were tall doors, like those of lofty castles, through which one entered into vestibules and mazes, passing from them into the open ground where stood the pavilions. It is as if this Emir lives in a walled city that moves when he moves and settles when he settles. It is a piece of regal splendour, the like of which is never seen with western kings. Within the doors are the Emir's chamberlains, his servants, and his followers. So high are these doors, that a horseman might come with his banner and pass through them without inclining or stooping his head. All this erection was held firm by thick linen cords connected with pegs driven (into the ground), and the whole was arranged with remarkable constructional skill. The other Emirs who came in the company of the Emir of 'Iraq had camps of less magnificence, but they were all similar in style, with splendid pavilions of uncommon form set up like poised crowns, and such as to take long to describe and to consume many words so great was the magnificence of this encampment in equipment, furnitures, and the like. All this indicates amplitude of circumstances and a great profusion of wealth and riches.

In their journeys on camel, they are shaded by canopies, handsome to look upon and of unusual shape, that are erected over wooden litters which they call *qashawat*. These are like hollow biers, and to those men and women who ride in them are as cradles to infants, being filled with soft mattresses on which the traveller may sit in comfort as though he were in a soft and commodious bed. Opposite him, in the other half of the litter, sits in counterpoise his man or woman companion, and over them both spreads the canopy. Thus, all unconscious of the movement, they journey on, slumbering and doing as they will. When they arrive at their place of alighting, upon the instant their screens are set up if they are people of easy and luxurious means, and they enter still riding. Steps are then brought to them and they descend, passing from the shade of the litter's canopy to that of their resting place without any breath of wind o'ertaking them or being touched by any ray of sun. Enough for you of this luxuriousness. In their journeys, however long, they are put to no distress or weariness; and in the continual pitching and striking of camps, they have no fatigue to endure. Less comfortable than these were those who rode in *maharat*, which resemble the *shaqadif* already described in our account of the desert of 'Aydhab; but the *shaqadif* are larger and ampler, these being more compact and less commodious. But they also have shades as protection against the heat of the sun. As for him whose means fall short of these conveniences of travel, he must bear the fatigues of the way which are but a part of the chastisements (of God).

We return to complete our narrative concerning the return [*nafar*] from 'Arafat on the evening of the standing there. The people departed after the sun had set as we have said, and in the late evening came to Muzdalifah, where they recited the combined sunset and early night prayers according to the rule laid down by the Prophet – may God bless and preserve him. Throughout the night the Ma'shar al-Haram [Muzdalifah] was illuminated by candle-wick lamps. As for the mosque which we mentioned before, it was all light, seeming to the beholder as if all the stars of the sky shone upon it. After the same fashion was the Mount of Mercy and its mosque on the night of Friday;

for these foreigners from Khurasan, and others among the 'Iraqis, are the most zealous of men in bringing candles in great numbers that these venerated shrines might be irradiated. Because of them, the Haram had the same aspect throughout their stay. Each one of them would enter it with a candle in his hand, and most would go to the *hatim* of the Hanafite imam, for they were of that rite. One huge candle like a cypress tree we saw 'that would be a burden to a troop of mighty men' [Koran XXVIII, 76] and which was set before the Hanafite imam. That night which was the night of Saturday, men spent in al-Ma'shar al-Haram, and when they had said the morning prayer, they early left it for Mina. They stood and prayed (upon the way), for all Mu⁻dalifah is standing ground save the valley of Muhassir, where one must move speedily [*harwala*] in the direction of Mina until emerging from it. At Muzdalifah most of the pilgrims provide themselves with stones (to cast at) the cairns. This is the more favoured custom, but there are others who collect them from around the mosque of al-Khayf in Mina, and it is as they wish.

When the pilgrims arrived at Mina they made speed to throw seven stones on the Cairn of 'Aqabah and then slaughtered in sacrifice, after which it became lawful for them to do everything save (to have contact with) women and (to use) scent, (from which they must still abstain) until they have performed the *tawaf* of the *ifadah* [return to Mecca]. This cairn was stoned at the rising of the sun on the Day of Sacrifice, and most of the pilgrims then left to do the *tawaf* of the *ifadah*. Some of them stayed until the second day, and some until the third, which is the day of the descent to Mecca. The second day, following the Day of Sacrifice, at the declension of the sun, the pilgrims cast seven stones at the First Cairn, and then did the same at the Centre Cairn, stopping at both for prayers. They did the same at the Cairn of al-'Aqabah, but did not stop here, imitating in all this the actions of the Prophet – may God bless and preserve him. The Cairn of the 'Aqabah is stoned last on these two days; but on the Day of the Sacrifice it is the first and only cairn to be stoned, the others not being associated with it on that day.

The day following the Day of Sacrifice, after the casting of the stones, the khatib preached a sermon in the mosque of al-Khayf, and then conducted the combined midday and afternoon prayers. This khatib came with the 'Iraqi Emir, being delegated by the Caliph to deliver the khutbah and to discharge the duties of Qadi in Mecca as it is said. His name is Taj al-Din. It became clear that he was dull and stupid; his discourse revealed this, and his speech did not observe the rules of grammatical analysis. On the third day, the pilgrims hastened to descend to Mecca. They had completed the throwing of forty-nine stones, seven on the Day of Sacrifice at al-'Aqabah which are those that release from abstentions, twenty-one on the second day, after the declension of the sun with seven at each cairn, and the same number on the third day, returning then to Mecca. Some there were who said the afternoon prayers in the bed of the torrent, others in the sacred Mosque, and some had made haste and said the midday prayers in the torrent bed. It had anciently been the practice to stay at Mina three days after the Day of Sacrifice in order to complete the throwing of seventy stones. But in these times it is despatched in two days in accordance with the saying of God – may He be blessed and exalted – 'Whoso hasteneth (his departure) two days, it is no sin for him; and whoso delayeth, it is also no sin for him' [Koran II, 203]. This is done in fear of the Banu Shu'bah and what might be sprung on them by the Meccan robbers.

On the day of the descent, there occurred dissension and riot between the negro inhabitants of Mecca and the Turks of 'Iraq in which there were some hurts. Swords were drawn, arrow notches were put to the bow-string, and spears were thrown, while some of the goods of the merchants were plundered. Mina in those three days is one of the greatest of markets, and in it are sold wares ranging from precious jewels to the cheapest strings of beads, together with other articles and various merchandises of the world, for it is the meeting place of men from all lands. God preserved us from the evils of this disturbance, and speedily brought calm. Thus ended this successful standing upon 'Arafat, and the faithful had ended their pilgrimage. Praise be to God, Lord of the Universe.

On Saturday, which was the Day of Sacrifice, the Kiswah ['Robe' or covering] of the holy Ka'bah was conveyed on four camels from the encampment of the 'Iraqi Emir to Mecca. Before it walked the new Qadi, wearing the black vestment given him by the Caliph, preceded by banners and followed by rolling drums. A cousin of the (late) Shayba (chief), one Muhammad ibn Isma'il, went with it, for it was reported that the Caliph's decree regarding the chief's deposal from the custodianship of the House on account of some notorious actions had been executed. May God by His favour purify His venerated House at the hands of whom He wishes amongst His servants. This cousin followed a more becoming path and behaved with more exemplariness, as we have already mentioned when referring to the first deposal. The Kiswah was placed on the venerated roof of the Ka'bah, and on Tuesday the 13th of the blessed month the Shaybites were busily employed in draping it. It was of a ripe green colour, and held the eyes in spell for its beauty. In its upper part it had a broad red band (that ran around the Ka'bah), and on the side that faces the venerated Maqam, the side that has the venerated door and that is blessed, there was written on this band, after the Bismillah [the invocation 'In the name of God'] the words 'Surely the first Sanctuary appointed for mankind (was that at Bekkah [Mecca])' [Koran III, 95]. On the other sides was written the name of the Caliph with invocations in his favour. Running round the band were two reddish zones with small white roundels containing inscriptions in fine characters that included verses from the Koran as well as mentions of the Caliph. The clothing (of the Ka'bah) was completed and the venerated hems of the Kiswah were tucked up to protect them from the hands of the foreigners who pull them violently and throw themselves impetuously upon them. To the beholder the Ka'bah then presented the most comely sight, appearing as an unveiled bride in the finest green silk-brocade. May God by His favour, grant that it might be seen by all who yearn to come to it, and long to gather around it.

In these times the venerated House is opened daily for the foreigners of 'Iraq and Khurasan and for those others who arrive with the 'Iraq Emir. The throngings of these men, the way in which they hurled themselves upon the noble door, their collisions with each other, and the swimming of some over the heads of the others as if they were in a pool of water, was something that never more horrible was seen and that led to destruction of life and breaking of limbs. During all this they were unmindful of everything and never rested; rather, in an excess of emotion and animation, they hurled themselves upon that venerated House as do moths upon a lamp. The manner of the entry of the Yemenite Saru into the blessed House in the fashion we have described was staid and composed compared with that of these barbarous-tongued foreigners. Yet may God advantage them for their intentions. In that dreadful press, there perished amongst them those whose allotted term of life had come to its end. May God give pardon to them all. Sometimes a group of their women would enter the press and emerge 'with their skins burned' [Koran IV, 56], baked by the squeezings of a struggle that is inflamed by the gasps of emotion and ecstasy. May God, by His favour, advantage them all for their faith and sound intention.

On the night of Thursday the 15th of the blessed month, after the nightfall prayers ['atamah] the preaching pulpit was set before the Maqam, and it was mounted by a preacher from Khurasan, a man of handsome countenance and graceful gestures. He used both the Arabic and the Persian tongues, employing them together with a lawful magic[77] of rhetoric, an eloquence of language, and a distinction of expression. He then addressed his discourse to the Persians, using their tongue and

causing them to shake with emotion and to melt in sighs and
sobs. The following night another pulpit was placed behind
the Hanafite hatim, and, also after the nightfall prayers, it was
mounted by a white-moustachioed sheik of impressive dignity
who was outstandingly distinguished in grace and perfection.
He delivered a sermon through which he strung, word by
word, the verse of 'The Throne' [Koran II, 256], employing
all forms of exhortatory exposition, and dealing with all
branches of knowledge. Also in this he used both languages,
moving hearts to rapture, and, after overwhelming them, setting them on fire with emotion. Throughout all this he was
assailed by the arrows of interrogation, and these he met with
the shield of ready and exhaustive reply, so that minds were
ravished by him, and spirits were possessed with wonder and
admiration for him. It was as if he was by God inspired. In
this manner the preachers of these eastern lands meet their
inquisition and the copious shower of questions that fall upon
them. It is a remarkable performance that very clearly revealed
their rare qualities and expresses the enchantment of their discourse; and this not in one single branch of learning but in
many. At times men would seek to confuse and distract
them with questions, but they would give their answer
with the speed of lightning, and in the twinkling of an eye.
Superiority is in the hand of God, who grants it to whom He
wills.

In front of these preachers stood reciters intoning the Koran
with harmonies that would win over things inanimate, for in
feeling and liveliness they were as the psalms of David.[78] And
none in that assembly knew what to admire most. Verily
God gives wisdom to whom He wills. There is no God but
He. I listened to this preacher sheik, who in support of a
tradition (concerning the Prophet) quoted five ancestors
in uninterrupted succession, the one after the other, from
his father back. Each had borne a cognomen that had
indicated his position in the world of learning and his standing as a recaller of pious memories and a preacher. Our sheik

was immersed in his noble calling, where the glory was hereditary.

Throughout all the days of the festival, the sacred Mosque – may God preserve it free from imperfection and exalt it – became a great market in which were sold commodities ranging from flour to agates, and from wheat to pearls, and including many other things of merchandise. The sale of flour was done in the Dar al-Nadwah [House of Counsel], on that side of the Mosque where stands the Banu Shayba Gate. But the greater part of the market was in the colonnade that runs from west to north and in that which runs from north to east. That this is forbidden by divine law is known. 'God is the master of His affairs' [Koran XII, 21]. There is no God but He.

On the evening of Sunday the 20th of the month, corresponding with the 1st of April[79] [3rd of April], we set forth (from Mecca) to the encampment of the Emir of 'Iraq in al-Zahir, some two miles from the city. We had completed our arrangements for the hire (of transport) to Mosul, which is ten days' journey north of Baghdad. May God by His favour grant that we know prosperity and happiness (upon our way). Three days we tarried in al-Zahir, and on each of them we returned to the Ancient House that we might bid farewell again. But on the forenoon of Thursday the 22nd of the month of Dhu 'l-Hijjah we removed from our encampment, and journeyed at a sober and easy pace on account of the slowness and lagging of some of our number. We alighted in the neighbourhood of Batn Marr, some eight miles distant from the place we had left. God by His favour will guarantee our safety and protection.

Our stay in Mecca – may God sanctify it – from the day of our arrival, which was Thursday the 13th of Rabi' al-Akhir of the year 579 [4th of August, 1183], to the day on which we departed from al-Zahir which was Thursday the 22nd of Dhu 'l-Hijjah of the same year [5th of April, 1184], was in all eight and a third months which, taking count of their greater and shorter lengths, amounted to two hundred and forty-five felicitous and blessed days. May God by His favour hold them in our count as showing our regard for Him and make them acceptable according to His pleasure. Throughout this time, we were away from the sight of the venerated House (but) three days: the Day of 'Arafah, the following Day of Sacrifice, and Wednesday the 21st of Dhu 'l-Hijjah, preceding the Thursday on which we left al-Zahir. May God by His favour grant that it be not the last visit to His venerated Haram.

It was after the midday prayers on Thursday that we left al-Zahir for Batn Marr, which is a fertile valley with many palm-trees and possessing a spring whose abundant waters irrigate the land of that district. In this valley is a broad territory, containing many villages and springs, from which fruits are brought to Mecca – may God defend it. We paused there on Friday for a curious reason concerning the royal khatun, daughter of the Emir Mas'ad, Lord of Darub [Cilician Gates], of Armenia, and of the regions contiguous with Bilad al-Rum ['The land of the Greeks', though usually and here applied to the Anatolian frontier province of the Byzantine empire]. She was one of the three khatuns who had come on the pilgrimage with the Emir of the Pilgrimage, Abu 'l-Mukarim Tashtikin, an officer of the Prince of the Faithful sent each year by the Caliph, and who had discharged this function for eight years or more. This princess held the most consequence between them on account of the size of her father's dominions. The cause of our mentioning her is that on the night of Friday she had left Batn Marr, betaking herself with her personal servants and retinue to Mecca, so that on Friday she was missing from her place (in the encampment). The Emir Abu 'l-Mukarim despatched from his personal retinue men of trust who might seek knowledge from her regarding her return, and set men who should await her. She returned at nightfall on Saturday, and the arrows of conjecture flew at random concerning the cause of the departure of this much indulged princess, while conceits were adduced that might bring out her close-kept secret. Some declared that she left in remonstrance for something she disapproved of in the Emir, others that it was the promptings of a yearning to be near (the Sacred Mosque) that had inclined her to that venerated place of meeting. But none can know such hidden things save God, and however the case may be, He is enough to repair the idleness she has occasioned, and to speed the pilgrims on their way. Praise be to Him for that.

The father of this woman is, as we have said, the Emir Mas'ud. His realm is large, and wide is his sway. More than one hundred thousand horsemen, so we were assured, ride at his command, and for his son-in-law through this princess, Nur al-Din, Lord of Amid and of other lands, ride about twelve thousand cavaliers. This princess has provided many good works upon the pilgrim road, among them being public water supplies, furnishing thirty water-bearing beasts for this purpose, and a similar number for provisions. With her she brought around a hundred camels especially to bear clothing, provisions, and other things. Indeed, it would take long to describe her state. Her age is about five and twenty years. The second *khatun*, mother of Mu'izz al-Din Lord of Mosul, has as husband Babek the brother of Nur al-Din who was Lord of Syria – may God have mercy on his soul. She also has many pious works to her name. The third *khatun* is the daughter of al-Daqus [Tukush Shah] Lord of Isbahan in the land of Khurasan.[80] She also is of great consequence and impressive circumstance, and is much given to good work. And in all three is this most strange admixture of pious work and regal pride.

We removed at noon on Saturday the 24th of Dhu 'l-Hijjah, and came to rest not far from 'Usfan, moving on towards that place at midnight, and arriving there early on the morning of Sunday. It lies in a plain between mountains, and possesses spring wells named after 'Uthman – may God hold him in His favour. Here are many muql trees [Bdellium; Gr. βδελλιον, a fragrant gum],[81] and a deserted fortress of ancient construction, with lofty towers, on which time has left its prints and which, through rare inhabitation and continuing decay, has fallen into ruin. We passed some miles beyond it, and then dismounted to repose and take our midday slumber. After the midday prayer we set forward to Khulays, arriving there at eventide. This place also lies in an ample plain, and has many palm-groves and a mountain at whose summit is a towering fortress. In the plain is another fortress on which decay has left its trace. Khulays has a spring of abundant waters to which are joined underground conduits whence water is drawn through orifices as in wells. At these men renew their supplies of water, for there is little of it upon the way on account of the continuous drought. May God send rains in plenty to His country and His servants. At this place the caravan paused on the morning of Monday to water the camels and to collect a supply of water.

This assembly of 'Iraqis, together with the people from Khurasan, Mosul, and other lands who were united in the company of this Emir of the Pilgrimage, formed a multitude whose number only God Most High could count. The vast plain was teeming with them, and the far-extending desert could barely contain them. You could see the earth shake giddily because of them, and form waves through their great number. You might behold them as a sea of swollen billows; its waters the mirage, its ships the mounts, and its sails the raised canopies and palanquins. Like piled up clouds they moved along, commingling with each other, and brushing against each other's sides. Upon the wide desert plain you would observe such a throng as would fill you with fear and alarm, with the collisions of the nab'a-wood [Chadara tenax] of the litters beating against each other. He who has not witnessed this journeying of the 'Iraqis has not seen one of those wonders of time that are discussed amongst men and that beguile listeners by their strangeness. Power and strength belong to God alone. It is enough to tell you that should one who has a station in this encampment go forth on any need and leave no sign to guide him back to his location, he will go astray and, exhausted, wander crying out amongst the number of the lost. At times the situation will compel such an one to repair to the pavilion of the Emir and raise the matter to him. He will instruct one of his heralds to give out a proclamation and direct one of the public criers appointed for the purpose to take the man behind him on his camel and tour with him that clamorous camp. He will have given his name, and those of his camel-master and of the land from whence he came, to the crier, who then will raise his voice in notice of this lost one, calling out the name of the camel-master and of his country until he comes upon him and delivers the man to him. Were this not done, he never again would meet his companion, unless he met him unawares or came upon him in some chance encounter. This is one of the amazing features of this caravan, whose marvels are such that a description cannot comprehend them. Its members possess such wealth and resources as will help them to all they will need upon their way. Possessions are in the hand of God, who grants them to whomsoever He wills.

Each year, if these ladies the princesses do not themselves perform the pilgrimage, they despatch with trusted men some water-bearing camels that quench the thirst of forlorn travellers upon the pilgrim road. This they do in places where water is known to be, throughout the road, on 'Arafat, and in the sacred Mosque, each day and night. For this their reward in heaven shall be great. From God alone assistance comes. Exalted is His majesty. You will hear the crier with the water-camels announcing with loud voice the free water, and those whose store has been exhausted will hasten to him with their water-skins and ewers that they might fill them. With all his breath the crier will proclaim: 'God preserve the royal Khatun, daughter of the king of such and such a state and consequence,' and extolling him, and announcing her name and making known her good deed, and bringing the people to offer prayers for her. God will not fail to reward her good works. We have already

explained this expression 'Khatun' which with them does the
office of 'princess' or whatever is a fitting designation for a
royal lady.

Among the remarkable features of this caravan is that despite
its size and magnitude – for indeed it is a world of its own –
when, its baggage being unladen and camping site adopted,
the Emir's drum, which they call 'kus', is beaten as a signal
for departure, not a moment will pass between the saddling
and loading of the camels and their being mounted; and the
drummer will scarce have made his third beat when the beasts
will have taken their way.[82] All this comes from the careful
preparations and diligent precautions taken by the travellers.
Power and strength belong to God alone. There is no God
but He.

By night they march by lighted torches held in the hands of
footmen, and you can see no litter that is not led by one, so
that the people march between wandering stars that lighten
the darkness of the night, while the earth vies in splendour
with the stars of the sky. The appurtenances of industry, the
worldly conveniences, and the requisites of animal satisfaction,
all were present in this nothing-lacking caravan. Long it would
take to describe it, and its story cannot all be embraced.

After the midday prayers on Monday we took our way
from Khulays and marched until the late evening when we
halted to slumber a little. The drum then beat and we set forth
again, journeying forward until the sun had well risen, when
we alighted to rest until noon, it then being Tuesday. Leaving
our resting place, we trended to a valley called Wadi 'l-Samk
[The Deep Valley], a name that does not conform to reality,
and there in the late evening encamped. We tarried there the
morning of Wednesday renewing our store of water, which
in this valley lies in pools, and is sometimes dug for in the
sand. We departed thence at midday on Wednesday, and at
night moved up a stony slope, difficult of ascent, where many
camels perished. We then came down to a plain, and slept there
till the middle of the night. Over a wide and deep-extending

waste, stretching as far as the eye could see and covered with sand, we bent our way; and so broad and easy was the road that the camels marched untied. On Thursday the 29th of Dhu 'l-Hijjah, we dismounted for our midday rest two stages yet away from Badr. No sooner had noon come than we marched to a place near Badr where we descended to pass the night, departing thence before midnight and coming to Badr when the day had well risen.

Badr is a village of continuous palm-groves and has a fortress on a high hill which is approached from the bed of a valley lying between mountains. Badr has a spring with copious waters, but the place of the ancient well beside which occurred the Islamic battle which exalted the faith and abased the polytheists is to-day all palms. Behind this lie the martyrs who died upon that day. The Mount of Compassion, on which the angels descended, is on the left of him who, leaving Badr, enters into (the valley of) al-Safra', and beside it is Jabal al-Tubul [Mount of the Drums], which is like a large mound of sand. This name comes from a legend to which most Muslims are attached. They declare that every Friday the roll of drums is heard upon that hill, as if it were the remaining trace of the signal of the Prophet's victory in that place. God best knows concerning these hidden things.

The place where once stood the arbour of the Prophet – may God bless and preserve him – touches the foot of this Mount of the Drums, and the battlefield lies before it. Beside the palm-grove at the ancient well is a mosque said to be the place where the Prophet's – may God bless and preserve him – camel knelt. We were assured, on the word of one of the Bedouin living in Badr, that they hear the beat of the drums on the mountain, but he specified every Monday and Thursday for its occurrence. We marvelled greatly at his statement, and the truth of it none but God Most High can know.

One post-stage lies between Badr and al-Safra', the road to which lies in a valley between mountains with continuous palm-groves and many springs; a beautiful road in truth. In al-Safra' is a lofty fortress and close at hand are many other forts, among them two that are called respectively Hisn al-Tu'aman [Fort of the Twins] and Hisn al-Hasaniyah [Hasan's Fort], and there is a third called Hisn al-Jadid [The New Fort]. Many other strongholds there are, as well as successive villages.

The Month of Muharram in the Year 580

[14th of April–13th of May, 1184]

May God let us know its blessings, and the blessings of the year it opens,
favouring us during it with His mercy and guaranteeing us His protection

THE new moon of this month rose on the night of Saturday
as we were leaving Badr for al-Safra', and we spent the
night below its crescent in this venerated ground of Badr where
God gave victory to the Muslims and vanquished the polytheists. Praise be to God for that. We alighted at al-Safra' after
the last evening prayer, and there, until noon on Saturday the
1st of the month, we tarried that the people might renew their
provision of water and take some rest. From al-Safra' to the
venerated Medina is, within God's pleasure, three days' journey.
We left it at noon on Saturday, and prolonged our march until
the end of the last evening prayer. Our way had lain through
a valley running continuously through mountains. The night
of Sunday we rested until midnight when we again set forth
and travelled until the forenoon, alighting for our midday rest
at the well Dhat al-'Alam where it is said that 'Ali ibn Abi
Talib – may God hold him in His favour – fought with the jinn
[demons]. It is also known as al-Rawha', is fed by a spring,
and is exceeding deep, the bucket-cord scarce reaching to the
bottom. We left it after the midday prayers on Sunday and
prolonged our march until after the last evening prayer, when
we halted at Shi'b 'Ali [the Mountain Path of 'Ali] – may God
hold him in His favour. We removed thence at midnight to
Turban and then to al-Bayda', whence can be seen Medina
the venerated.

In the forenoon of Monday the 3rd of Muharram we
encamped in the valley of al-'Aqiq on whose side is the mosque
of Dhu 'l-Hulayfah where the Apostle of God – may God bless

and preserve him – assumed the *ihram* [pilgrim garb]. Medina
is five miles from this place. At Dhu 'l-Hulayfah commences
the *haram* [sacred territory] of Medina (which extends) to the
tomb of Hamzah and to Quba'. The first thing that strikes
the eye is the tall white minaret of its mosque. We left Dhu
'l-Hulayfah after the midday prayers on Monday the 16th of
April, and alighted outside Medina the Refulgent, the White
Mausoleum, the ground ennobled by Muhammad, Lord of the
Prophets – may God bless and preserve him throughout all
time.

On the evening of that day we made our entry into the
sacred Haram that we might visit the venerated and immaculate
Rawdah [Tomb]. We stood beside it in salutation and kissed
the earth on its sacred sides. We prayed in the Rawdah[83] that
is between the sacred tomb and the pulpit, and kissed[84] the
wooden supports of the old pulpit on which once stood the
Prophet – may God bless and preserve him – and the rest of
the palm-tree trunk which leant towards him – may God bless
and preserve him. This is attached to the pillar erected in front
of the little Rawdah between the tomb and the pulpit and to
your right if, standing in the Rawdah, you face the *qiblah*. We
then said the sunset prayers with the congregation.

By a happy chance we found a measure of room on this
occasion, for the people were engaged in pitching their tents
and arranging their baggage. We thus were able to achieve
our object. We had succeeded in coming to the much-praised
tomb, and in making our due salutes to the two Companions
there reclining, Al-Saddiq [The Faithful One] of Islam [Abu
Bakr], and Al-Faruq [The Distinguisher (of True from False),
'Umar], and then returned to our baggage, rejoicing and thanking God for His favour towards us. There remained no hope
or purpose of our blessed journey that we had not satisfied,
no object we had not achieved, and our thoughts were freed
to think of return to our native land. May God unite us with
those we have left behind, and complete thereby His favour
towards us. Praise be to God for the benefits He has conferred

and for the beneficent works that from the first and always He has done. He it is to whom praise and thanks are due. There is no God but He.

A description of the Mosque of the Apostle of God – may God bless and preserve him – and of his sacred and immaculate Rawdah

The blessed Mosque is oblong in shape, and is surrounded on all four sides by porticoes. In its centre is a court covered with sand and gravel. The south side has five rows of porticoes running from west to east, and the north side also has five porticoes in the same style. The east side has three porticoes and the west four. The sacred Rawdah is at the eastern extremity of the south side. It extends over two rows of porticoes on the side of the court and projects about four spans into the third. It has five angles and five sides, and its form is so wondrous that one can barely portray or describe it. Four of its sides incline away from the direction of the qiblah in an ingenious fashion, and because of this deviation from the qiblah, no one is able to face them in his prayers. The sheik, the imam, learned and pious, last of the learned doctors, and pillar of jurisprudents, Abu Ibrahim Ishaq ibn Ibrahim the Tunisian – may God hold him in His favour – told us that 'Umar ibn 'Abd al-'Aziz – may God hold him in His favour – determined this in planning the construction from a fear that men might take them as a place of prayer. From the east side, the Rawdah also covers two rows of porticos, and thus encloses six portico columns.

The length of the side facing the qiblah is twenty-four spans,[85] that of the east thirty, that between the east and north corners thirty-five, that from the north corner to the west thirty-nine, and that from the west corner to the south twenty-four. On this side is an ebony chest inlaid with sandal-wood, faced with silver and embellished with stars. It is opposite the head of the Prophet – may God bless and preserve him – and is five spans long, three wide and four high.[86] On the side between the north and the west corners is a place over which hangs a curtain that is said to be where the angel Gabriel came down. Upon him be (eternal) happiness.

The circumference of the venerated Rawdah is two hundred and seventy-two spans. It is covered with finely cut marble of splendid quality. The wainscot rises to a third (of its height) or a little less. Above this another third of the blessed walls is daubed with an unguent of musk and other perfumes to a depth of half a span, and blackened, cracked, and accumulated by the passage of time. The walls above this are composed of wooden lattice-work that reaches to the ceiling, for the top of the blessed Rawdah touches the ceiling of the Mosque. The veils (that covers the Rawdah) fall as far as the line of the marble wainscot. They are of azure colour with a check of white quadrangular and octangular figures containing roundels and encircled by white dots. They present a handsome spectacle of novel design. In the upper part runs a band tending to white. In the south wall, opposite the venerated face of the Prophet – may God bless and preserve him – is a silver nail before which men stand to give their salutations. At his feet – may God bless and preserve him – lies the head of Abu Bakr The Faithful – may God hold him in His favour – and the head of 'Umar The Distinguisher (of True from False) is nigh to the shoulders of Abu Bakr The Faithful – may God hold them both in His favour. He who makes his salutation turns his back to the *qiblah* and, looking towards the venerated face, gives his salute. He then turns right towards the face of Abu Bakr, and then towards that of 'Umar – may God hold them both in His favour.

Before this venerated wall hang about twenty silver lamps, and amongst them are two of gold. At the north of the sacred Rawdah is a marbled trough having at its southern end a kind of *mihrab*. It is said that it is the house of Fatimah – may God hold her in His favour – and also reputed to be her grave. God best knows the truth of this. To the right of the venerated Rawdah the noble pulpit stands forty-two paces away from it.

It is set in the blessed *haud* which is fourteen paces long, six wide, and a span and a half high, and wholly clothed in marble. Between it and the small Rawdah that lies between the venerated tomb and the pulpit, and which tradition declares to be one of the Rawdahs [gardens] of Paradise, lie eight paces. Into this Rawdah men throng to pray, as indeed it is meet and proper that they should. Beside it, to the south, is a pillar said to enclose a relic of the palm-tree trunk that leant towards the Prophet – may God bless and preserve him. A piece of it can be seen in the pillar and men kiss it and hasten to acquire blessings by touching it and passing their cheeks over it. At the south end of this small Rawdah is the chest (described above).

The venerated pulpit is a man's stature or more in height, five spans wide, five paces long, and has eight steps. The door is in the form of a grille four and a half spans long. It is locked, but is opened every Friday. The pulpit is covered with ebony-wood, and the seat of the Prophet – may God bless and preserve him – can be seen above, covered by an ebony board that does not touch it, but protects it from being sat upon. Men insert their hands beneath it and smooth the venerated seat to acquire blessings by touching it. At the top of the right support of the pulpit, where the preacher puts his hand when delivering the khutbah, is a hollow silver ring, resembling that which the tailor puts on his finger, but only so in shape and not in size, for this is larger and loose and encircles the support. Men say that it was the plaything of al-Hasan and al-Husayn – may God hold them in His favour – when their grandfather [Muhammad] – may God bless and preserve him – delivered the khutbah.

The venerated Mosque is one hundred and ninety-six paces long and one hundred and twenty-six wide. It has two hundred and ninety columns that are like straight props, for they reach the ceiling and have no arches bending over them. They are composed of stone hewn into a number of round, bored blocks, mortised together and with melted lead poured between each pair so that they form a straight column. They are then covered with a coat of plaster, and rubbed and polished zealously until they appear as white marble. The portico to the south, which we have mentioned as having five rows of porticoes, is enfolded by a *maqsurah* that flanks its length from west to east and in which there is a *mihrab*. The imam prays in the aforementioned little Rawdah beside the chest. Between this maqsurah and the Rawdah and the sacred tomb is a big painted reading-desk on which lies a large Koran locked in a case. It is one of the four copies [see note 120] sent by 'Uthman ibn 'Affan – may God hold him in His favour – to the several cities.

Beside the maqsurah, to the east, are two large cupboards containing books and Korans endowed as a waqf to the blessed Mosque. Hard by these cupboards, in the second (row of) porticoes and also to the east, is a trap-door fitted to the level of the ground and locked. It covers a subterranean passage, to which one descends by steps, that leads out from the Mosque to the house of Abu Bakr the Faithful – may God hold him in His favour. This is the way that 'A'ishah was wont to use. Fast by this house is that of 'Umar ibn al-Khattab, as well as that of his son 'Abdullah – may God hold them both in His favour. Beyond a peradventure this place is the passage leading to Abu Bakr's house which the Prophet – may God bless and preserve him – especially commanded should be preserved. In front of the sacred Rawdah is another large chest that holds the candles and chandeliers which every night are lit before it.

Towards the east is a wooden structure where some of the guardians of the blessed Mosque sleep. These guardians are Abyssinian eunuchs and slaves of handsome presence, elegantly clad and ornamented. The resident muezzin of the Mosque is a descendant of Bilal – may God hold him in His favour. In the north part of the court is a large pavilion, newly-built, called Qubbat al-Zayt [The Pavilion of the Oil], that acts as a store for all the appointments of the blessed Mosque and contains all that is needful for it. Beside it in the court are fifteen palm-trees. In the upper part of the mihrab that is in the south wall, inside the maqsurah, is a square yellow stone, one span square and of a bright and shining surface, that is said to be the mirror of Chosroes. God best knows. Above this in the mihrab there is a nail driven into the wall, and on it is a kind of small casket of which no one knows the origin but which men say may be the drinking-cup of Chosroes. God best knows the truth of all this.

The lower half of the south wall is cased with marble, tile on tile, of varying order and colour: a splendid marquetry. The upper half is wholly inlaid with pieces of gold called *fusayfisa* [Gr., ψηφος] in which the artist has displayed amazing skill, producing shapes of trees in divers forms, their branches laden with fruits. The whole Mosque is of this style, but the work in the south wall is more embellished. The wall looking on the court from the south side is of this manner, as also is that which does so from the north side. The west and east walls that overlook the court are wholly white and carved, and adorned with a band that contains various kinds of colours. It would take too long to portray and describe the decorations of this blessed Mosque that contains the sacred and unspotted tomb whose charge is more noble and whose resting-place is more exalted than all that adorns it.

The blessed Mosque has nineteen gates of which only four are open. On the west there are two, one called Bab al-Rahmah [Gate of Pity], and the other Bab al-Khashyah [Gate of Fear]. On the east there are also two, one called Bab Jibril [Gate of Gabriel] – upon whom be eternal happiness – and the other Bab al-Rakha' [Gate of Plenty]. Facing Bab Jibril – upon whom be eternal happiness – is the house of 'Uthman – may God hold him in His favour – in which he was martyred. Facing the venerated Rawdah on this eastern side is the tomb of Jamal al-Din of Mosul – may God have mercy on his soul – whose story and the monuments of whose generosity are celebrated, and whose memorable deeds we have already recorded. In front of the venerated Rawdah is (a window with) an iron grating opening on the Rawdah from which exudes a perfumed aroma. To the south there is a small locked gate; to the north there are four locked gates; to the west another five, also locked; and to the east yet five more locked, which with the four open gates gives a total of nineteen gates. The blessed Mosque has three minarets, one in the angle between the east and the south, and the other two in the two north corners. They are small and have the form of turrets but the first is like a minaret.

A note on the venerated tombs in Baki' al-Gharqad[87] and on the slopes of Jabal Uhud

The first of these we shall mention is the mosque of Hamzah – may God hold him in His favour. It is to the south of Mount Uhud, which stands three miles north of Medina. Over the tomb of Hamzah – may God hold him in His favour – has been built a mosque, and the tomb lies in a court north of it with the martyrs – may God hold them in His favour – beside him. The cave in which the Prophet – may God bless and preserve him – lived is alongside the martyrs at the foot of the mountain. Around the martyrs is a red sepulchre which is the one ascribed to Hamzah, and here men come to acquire blessings.

The cemetery of al-Gharquad lies to the east of Medina, and men go forth to it by the gate called Bab al-Baqi'. The first thing you meet on leaving this gate, on your left, is the tomb of Safiyyah, aunt of the Prophet – may God bless and preserve him – and mother of al-Zubayr ibn al-'Awwam – may God hold him in His favour. In front of this tomb is that of Malik ibn Anas, the Madinite iman – may God hold him in His favour. Over this is a small cupola, modestly built. In front of this is the tomb of the immaculate scion, Ibrahim, son of the Prophet – may God bless and preserve him – surmounted by a white cupola. To the right of this is the tomb of a son of 'Umar ibn al-Khattab – may God hold him in His favour – called 'Abd al-Rahman al-Awsat and commonly known as

Abu Shahmah. He it was who was scourged by his father in exactment of a divine penalty and fell sick therefrom and died. May God hold them both in His favour. Close by it is the tomb of 'Aqil ibn Abi Talib – may God hold him in His favour – and of 'Abdullah ibn Ja'far al-Tayyar – may God hold him in His favour. Alongside them is a rawdah in which lie the wives of the Prophet – may God bless and preserve him – and nigh to this is a small rawdah holding three sons of the Prophet – may God bless and preserve him. Bordering this is the rawdah of al-'Abbas ibn 'Abd al-Muttalib and al-Hasan ibn 'Ali – may God hold them in His favour – which consists of a dome rising into the air. It is near the Bab al-Baqi' mentioned above, and to the right of him who leaves by it. The head of al-Hasan is towards the feet of al-'Abbas – may God hold them in His favour – and both their tombs rise prominently from the ground. They are covered by admirably joined panels inlaid with brass plates and decorated with stars formed from nails in a remarkable fashion that is most beautiful to regard. After this style is the tomb of Ibrahim, son of the Prophet – may God bless and preserve him.

Fast by this dome of al-'Abbas is the house named after Fatimah, daughter of the Apostle – may God bless and preserve him. It is known as the House of Sorrow, and is said to be the house to which she withdrew and kept within while grieving for the death of her father the Chosen One – may God bless and preserve him. At the end of the cemetery is the tomb of the ill-used martyr 'Uthman, possessor of the Two Lights[88] – may God hold him in His favour – and over this is a small and simple cupola. Near to this is the shrine of Fatimah, daughter of Asad and mother of 'Ali – may God hold her and her sons in favour. The tombs in this cemetery are more than can be counted, for it is the burial place of the greater part of the Companions, Fugitives and Helpers[89] – may God hold them all in His favour. On the tomb of Fatimah is written: 'No tomb holds such an one as Fatimah, daughter of Asad' – may God hold her and her sons in favour.

Quba' lies about two miles to the south of Medina. It was once a large city contiguous with Medina, the venerated. The road to it goes through continuous palm-groves. Medina itself is surrounded by palms, which are most plentiful on the south and east sides, and less so on the west. The mosque founded in Quba' from sentiments of piety has been restored. It is square-shaped with straight sides and has a tall white minaret that can be seen from afar. In its midst is the 'Place of Kneeling of the She-Dromedary', that of the Prophet – may God bless and preserve him – which is surrounded by a low enclosure forming a kind of small rawdah in which men pray to acquire blessings. In the south part of the court, on a stone bench, is a species of mihrab that is the place where the Prophet – may God bless and preserve him – performed his first *rak'ah*. To the south of this are other mihrabs. The mosque has one door only, at the west, and has seven rows of porticoes through its length and the same number breadthways. South of the mosque is a hut belonging to the Banu 'l-Najjar that was the dwelling of Abu Ayyub the Ansarite. In an open space west of the mosque is a well beside whose brink stands a broad stone in the form of a trough at which men do their ritual ablutions. Adjacent to the hut of the Banu 'l-Najjar is that of 'A'ishah – may God hold her in His favour – and contiguous with that is those of 'Umar, Fatimah, and Abu Bakr – may God hold them in His favour. Beside them is the well of 'Aris into which the Prophet – may God bless and preserve him – spat, so that from being brackish its waters became sweet. It was into this well that the Prophet's ring – may God bless and preserve him – fell from the hand of 'Uthman, and the tradition concerning it is well known.[90] At the end of the village is a tall hill called 'Arafat by which one passed to Dar al-Suffah [the House of the Choice Ones, see note 124] where stayed 'Ammar and Salman with their companions called Ahl al-Suffah [The Choice Ones]. This hill is called 'Arafat because the Prophet – may God bless and preserve him – stood upon it on the Day of 'Arafah and, the land contracting for him, he gazed upon the people on Mount

'Arafat (at Mecca). The antiquities and shrines of this venerated town are numerous beyond computation.

Medina the Venerated is double-walled, with four gates, each gate facing another in the opposite wall. One of the gates is all iron, whence it is called Bab al-Hadid. Next to it is the Bab al-Shari'ah [Watering Gate], then Bab al-Qiblah which is locked, then Bab al-Baqi' already mentioned. Before you come to the walls of Medina, a bow-shot to the west, you come upon the famous ditch that the Prophet – may God bless and preserve him – made when the Confederates[91] [al-Ahzab] mustered against him. Between it and Medina, on the right of the road, is the spring named after the Prophet – may God bless and preserve him – round which is a large oblong enclosure. The source of the well is in the middle of this enclosure, which forms a sort of oblong basin. Below it are two oblong troughs the length of the basin, and between each trough and the basin a wall has been built so that the basin is itself enclosed by two walls. The basin supplies the water to the troughs, to which descent is made by means of twenty-five steps. The water of this blessed spring is enough for all the people of the earth and not only the inhabitants of Medina. Men use it for their ablutions, for drinking, and for washing their garments; but the water in the basin is not taken save for drinking that it might be kept pure and preserved. Near to it, in the direction of Medina, is the Dome of the Rock of Oil, of which it is said that oil oozed forth from it for the Prophet – may God bless and preserve him. North of this is the well of Buda'ah, beside which, to the left, is Satan's Mount where, on the day of 'Uhud, he – God curse him – cried out saying, 'Your prophet has been slain.'

On the brink of the ditch that we have mentioned is a stronghold called Hisn al-Uzzab [the Castle of the Celibates], and now in ruins. It is said that 'Umar – may God hold him in His favour – built it for the celibates of Medina. Before it, at a distance to the west, is the well of Rumah of which 'Uthman – may God hold him in His favour – bought the half for twenty thousand (dirhams). On the road to Uhud is the mosque of 'Ali – may God hold him in His favour – and those of Salman – may God hold him in His favour – and of al-Fath [Victory] where the *surah* of the Fath [The Chapter of 'The Victory', Koran XLVIII] was revealed to the Prophet – may God bless and preserve him. Medina the blessed has a third fountain of spring water,[92] inside the Bab al-Hadid, to which one descends by steps and which is near the venerated Haram. South of this Haram is the house of the Imam of the Dar al-Hijrah [Home of the Flight=Medina], Malik ibn Anas – may God hold him in His favour. Round the whole of the Haram runs a road paved with cut stones.

Such is the brief and unstudied account of the monuments and shrines of Medina the Venerated that the dictates of speed have allowed us to recount. God is the Master of success.

Among the strange affairs that are discussed and listened to by men we witnessed the following. One of the aforementioned khatuns, the daughter of the Emir Mas'ud, whom with her father we have already described, came to the Mosque of the Apostle of God – may God bless and preserve him – on the evening of Thursday the 6th of Muharram, the fourth day after our arrival at Medina, riding in her litter, surrounded by the litters of her ladies and handmaidens and led by Koran-readers, while pages and eunuch-slaves, bearing iron rods, moved around her driving the people from her 'path until she arrived at the venerated Mosque. Wrapped in an ample cloak, she descended and advanced to salute the Prophet – may God bless and preserve him – her servants going before her and the officials of the Mosque raising their voices in prayer for her and extolling her fame. She came to the small rawdah between the venerated tomb and the pulpit, and prayed there wrapped in her cloak while the people who thronged around her were kept back by the rods. She then prayed in the *haud* beside the manbar, and moving thence to the west wall of the venerated rawdah, sat in the place where it is said that the Angel Gabriel – upon whom be eternal happiness – came down. The curtain was then lowered on her, and her pages, slaves, and chamberlains remained without the curtain receiving her commands. She had brought with her to the mosque two loads of provisions as alms for the poor, and stayed in her place until night had fallen.

The announcement then was made of the arrival of Sadr al-Din of Isbahan, chief of the Shafi'ites, who from successive ancestors has inherited renown and regard. He had come to conduct an exhortatory meeting that night, which was the night of Friday the 7th of Muharram, and arrived late, when part of the night had passed and the Haram was filled with people, including the Khatun sitting in her place, awaiting him. The cause of his delay had been the lateness of the Emir of the Pilgrimage, for he himself had been ready to come. At last he arrived and the Emir came too. A throne had been prepared beside the sacred rawdah for this Chief of the 'Ulama [doctors of law and divinity], who is known by this title inherited from father to son, and he ascended it. The Koran-readers took post before him and began[93] to intone with sweet melody and moving and affecting modulation, the while he gazed upon the sacred tomb and wept openly. He then launched upon a khutbah of his own composition that was of bewitching eloquence, and pursued the several paths of homily in the two languages [Arabic and Persian]. He then recited some pleasing verses of his own, among which was the following that, pointing to the rawdah, he repeated at each mention of the Prophet – may God bless and preserve him:

'This is his rawdah, a zephyr diffusing.
    Pray for him now, and send him your greeting.'

He then begged forbearance for his shortcomings in that august place, and exclaimed: 'Ah strange conceit for an ill-speaking foreigner. How dare he speak before the most eloquent of the Arabs? [Muhammad].'

He continued his exhortation until men's spirits were carried away in contrition and emotion. The Persians flung themselves upon him, declaring their repentance, their hearts enravished, and their minds enraptured. They presented their forelocks to him, and, sending for a pair of scissors, he cut them one by one. He would place his turban on the head of one whose forelock had been cut, and straightway another turban would be put on his head, by one of his readers or companions who, knowing his generous habit, hastened to offer their own that they might acquire good repute for their manifest liberality. He continued to remove one turban after another from his head until he had removed a large number and cut many forelocks. He then closed his meeting and said: 'My good friends here assembled, I have spoken to you in the Haram of Great and Glorious God, and to-night I speak to you in the Haram of His Apostle – may God bless and preserve him. A preacher must indulge in some mendicity, and I ask of you a thing I need which, if you grant it me, I shall not blush to tell you of.' All announced their readiness to help, while their sobs rose high. 'My need,' he said, 'is that you bear your heads and stretch forth your arms and beseech this noble Prophet to hold me in his favour and to seek for me the favour of Great and Glorious God'; and then began to enumerate and confess his sins. The people threw off their turbans and stretched forth their arms to the (tomb of) the Prophet – may God bless and preserve him – praying for this man, weeping and imploring. I never saw a night of more tears and contrition than this. When he left the Emir left too, and the Khatun departed from her place. Upon the arrival of Sadr al-Din, the curtain had been raised from her and, wrapped in her cloak, she had remained between her ladies and her servants, while we who regarded her marvelled at her regal mien.

This man Sadr al-Din is remarkable in his nobility, splendour, and majesty, in the magnificence of his circumstance, the elegance of his state, his outward power, his plentiful furnitures, his many slaves and servants, and in the number of his retinue and following, so that kings fall short of his dignity. His pavilion rises into the air like a great crown; it is set with doors

o

fashioned in singular style, and is of remarkable shape and design. From afar you may see it dominating the encampment as it aspires to the skies. The state of this exalted personage is indeed such that a description cannot comprehend it. We attended an audience of his, and observed a man of bright and cheerful countenance who, notwithstanding his great dignity and imposing presence, at once, by his kindness and goodness, put at ease those who had come to visit him. He was pre-eminent both in knowledge and in person. We begged of him, and he granted us, some lines of prose and poetry. He is the greatest of those we have seen in these lands.

On Friday the 7th of Muharram we witnessed such an heretical innovation that Islam should cry out against it (the war-cry), 'O Allah. O Muslims.' It consisted in this. The khatib arrived to deliver the allocution, and ascended the pulpit of the Prophet – may God bless and preserve him. This person, as it was related, followed a path of which men disapproved, unlike the Persian sheik and imam who functioned at the obligatory prayers in the venerated Mosque and whose way was virtuous and godly as befitted the imam of such a noble place. When the muezzins had finished the call to prayers, this preacher rose to deliver the khutbah. The two black banners had been brought in before him and set on either side of the venerated pulpit, and these he stood between. When he had finished the first part of the khutbah he sat for a pause that was contrary to the usual break in the khutbah, which is pro-verbial for its brevity, and an insolent group of Mosque officials then pressed forward, breaking through the ranks of the wor-shippers and trampling on their necks, to beg of the Persians and of those others present on behalf of this unworthy preacher. Some threw off their precious robes, others brought out the costly piece of silk that they had prepared for this purpose and presented it; others took off their turbans and flung them in; and some there were who stripped off their mantles and gave them. Those whose means did not extend to this gave a piece of coarse calico. Some threw in gold parings, and some put forth their hands with one or two dinars, and others gave their moiety. Women cast off their silver anklets, or removed their rings, offering these and other things that would take long to describe. Throughout all this the khatib remained sitting in the pulpit, throwing on those who so sedulously laboured for him among the people looks of avarice and greed that he constantly repeated in his avidity for more. The time for prayers had almost passed, and men of piety and truth were clamouring and openly crying out (their protests), while the khatib, who had no blush of shame upon his face, sat waiting for the drinking up of the last drop of the alms. From this unlawful trade, there was collected before him a large pile, and when he was satisfied he rose and completed the khutbah, and then prayed with the people. Enlightened men left weeping for religion, despairing of the happiness of the world, and assured of the portents of the Day of Judgement. To God belongs the future and the past.

On the evening of that blessed day we bade farewell to the blessed rawdah and holy tomb. Ah what an uncommon parting, perturbing the mind in dismay until it is unsettled, and so commoting the soul from its pangs that it dissolves into fragments. What think you of a site where one must whisper farewell to the Lord [Muhammad] of those that were and those that are to come, the Seal of Prophets, and the Apostle of the Lord of the Universe. In truth it is a place which makes men's hearts to break and sends the heaviest and most sluggish minds to ecstasy. O sorrow, sorrow! Each one reveals his yearning (for the place), and finds no means to leave it or any way to resignation. In the awful grandeur of that sight nothing could be heard save wails and lamentations, and all with the voice of the moment seemed to recite:

> 'My love demands that I should stay,
> But fortune send me on my way.'

May God dispose unto us, through this visit to the noble Prophet, an honoured dwelling in Heaven, making him our intercessor on the Day of Judgement and, by His favour, bringing us beside him in the eternal abode. This by His mercy, for He is the Forgiving, the Compassionate, the Bountiful, the Generous.

We had stayed in Medina the venerated five days, the first being a Monday and the last a Friday, and in the forenoon of Saturday the 8th of Muharram, being the 21st of April, we departed for 'Iraq. May God bring us to our aim, and ease for us our way. At Medina we had furnished ourselves with water for three days, and on the third day of our journey, a Monday, we encamped at Wadi 'l-'Arus. Here men provide themselves with water, digging for it into the ground to a well of sweet spring-water, from which the innumerable persons of this caravan, and the still greater number of camels, quenched their thirst. Power belongs to God. Glory to Him.

From Wadi 'l-'Arus we climbed to the land of Nejd, leaving behind us the Tihamah, and travelling across a level tract of land whose nearer parts the eyes fall short of and whose extremities they cannot reach. We inhaled the breezes of Nejd and the air that has passed into proverb, and our minds and bodies were refreshed by the coolness of those breezes and the salubrity of that air. On Tuesday the fourth day of our journey, we alighted near a watering place called al-'Usaylah, and on Wednesday, the fifth day, we halted at a place called Nuqrah which has wells and tanks like vast cisterns. One of these we found full of rainwater, and it was enough for the whole caravan, showing no diminishment despite the amount of water drawn. This Emir's mode of travel with the pilgrims was to march from midnight to the early part of the forenoon, to rest until midday, and then move forward till the late evening, resuming the march at midnight. Such was his usage.

The night of Thursday the 13th of Muharram, being the sixth day on this journey, we stopped at a water-point called al-Qarurah which has tanks filled with rainwater. This place is in the centre of the land of Nejd. In no inhabited country

have I ever come upon a land more wide-extending or bountiful, of more scented breezes and more healthful air, or more
even-ranging, with clearer skies, more weed-less earth, greater
invigoration for the spirit and the body, and more temperate
weather at all times, than the land of Nejd. But long it would
take to describe its merits, and our talk would cause us to
digress too far.

On the morning of this Thursday we came to al-Hajir where
the water is kept in tanks, although often they dig for it in
shallow pits which they call *ahfar*, or in the singular, *hafar*.
We had feared a dearth of water on this road, especially because
of the great multitude of men and camels, which, if the sea
were brought to it, it would dry up and exhaust. But from
the clouds God in His mercy sent down that which changed
this low-lying plain into a lake, caused the torrents to gush in
their courses, and filled the valleys with the rains of spring.
And so in rapid stream we saw the waters flowing across the
surface of the ground; all by the grace and favour of God, and
from His goodness and mercy to His servants. Praise be to
Him for that.

On the same day, at al-Hajir, we crossed two streams in
torrent; the pools and swamps (we crossed) were numberless.
The next day, Friday, we alighted in the early morning at
Samirah, an inhabited place in whose plain is a kind of fort
surrounded by a large enceinte and dwelt in. It has water in
many wells, that are however brackish, as well as in swamps
and pools. Here the Bedouin barter their products, which are
meat, butter, and milk; and the pilgrims, greedy for meat and
thirsty for milk, rush to buy it, giving pieces of coarse calico
that they bring with them for dealing with the Bedouin, who
will not barter save for this.

Early on the morning of Saturday we halted at Jabal al-
Makhruq [The Hill of the Hole], which is a hill lying in a stretch
of desert and having on its upper sides a tunnel through which
the wind passes. We moved on from this place, and spent part
of the night in Wadi 'l-Kurush where there is no water. We

left it during the night, and on the morning of Sunday came to Fayd.

Fayd is a large fortress with turrets and merlons lying in a level tract of land. Around it stretches a suburb enclosed by a wall of ancient construction. It is inhabited by Bedouin who support themselves by trading and bartering, and doing other useful things with the pilgrims. It is here that the pilgrims leave a part of their provisions (when on their way to Mecca), as a precaution against their running out of them on their return, and in the place they have an acquaintance with whom they leave them. Fayd is halfway, or a little less, from Baghdad to Mecca by way of Medina – may God exalt it. Al-Kufah is twelve days' journey from it by a good and level road furnished, praise be to God, with many tanks.

The Emir of the Pilgrimage entered this place in battle array and under arms, to drive fear into the Bedouin there assembled that they might not be moved by covetousness against the pilgrims. They threw rapacious looks on the pilgrim encampment, but saw no way to approach it. Praise be to God. The water here is plenteous in the wells, which are supplied from underground springs. Among them the pilgrims found one tank in which rainwater had been collected, and it was at once exhausted. From their longing for meat, the hands of the pilgrims were soon filled with sheep they had bartered from the Bedouin, and there was no pavilion, nor tent, nor place of shade but had beside it a ram or two, according to means and wealth. The whole encampment was filled with the sheep of the Bedouin, and the day became a festival. In the same way the Bedouin brought in their camels for those camel-masters and others who wished to buy them for use upon the road. As for butter, honey, and milk, there was none who did not load some or take some for their use according to their needs. All that day, and until noon of the Monday that followed it, the people stayed resting in this place.

We left at midnight, observing the mode of marching we have described, and in the early morning of Tuesday the 18th of Muharram, which was the 1st of May, we halted at a place called al-Ajfur [The Wells] that is celebrated amongst the inhabitants as being the place of (the two lovers) Jamil and Buthaynah of the tribe of 'Udhr. On this Tuesday, we set forward, according to our custom, at noon, and in the late evening encamped in the desert. We moved from it in the night, and after the sun had risen on Wednesday, we alighted at Zarud, which is a depression in a stretch of land covered with sand. It has a large enceinte containing small houses, and resembles a stronghold, being called in these parts, al-Qasr [The Castle]. The water here comes from brackish wells.

In the forenoon of Thursday the 20th of Muharram, which was the 3rd of May, we put down at a place called al-Tha 'labiyah, where there is a ruined construction like a castle of which nothing remains but the enceinte. Beside it is a vast tank of great circumference, being one of the largest and deepest cisterns that exist. Descent is made to it on three sides by many steps, and in it was rainwater enough for all the caravan. To this place came a numerous throng of Bedouin, men and women, who made of it a great and teeming market for camels, rams, butter, milk, and camel fodder. It was a day of brisk commerce. From this point to al-Kufah, there are but three stations that can furnish enough water for the whole caravan: one is Zubalah, another Waqisah, and the third a place that supplies water from the Euphrates and is near to al-Kufah ★ ★ ★ ★. Between these watering points there is water, but not enough, whereas at them there is enough for all the men and camels to draw upon at will. In this watering-place of al-Tha 'labiyah we witnessed a terrifying contention among the people for the water, the like of which has hardly been seen in the struggles for the mastery of cities and fortresses. Enough to tell you that in that place died seven men, crushed by the terrible press and trodden under water by the feet. They hastened to drink water, and succeeded in drinking death. May God pity and pardon them.

On the morning of Friday, we came to a place called Birkat al-Marjum [The Pool of the Stoned One], that is a tank to which water is brought from afar by means of an aqueduct built for it high above the ground and constructed with an excellence that argues great wealth and resources. This person who was stoned to death has a grave on the side of the road that has risen up like a tall hill, for all who pass along must needs throw a stone upon it. Men relate that a king decreed his lapidation for some affair which called for such. God best knows. In this place are many tents belonging to the Bedouin, who at once brought forth what foodstuffs they had to sell them to the pilgrims. The tank was filled with rain and all were able to drink deeply. Praise be to God.

These tanks, pools, wells, and stations on the road from Baghdad to Mecca are monuments to Zubaydah, daughter of Ja'far ibn Abi Ja'far al-Mansur and wife and cousin of (the Caliph) Harun al-Rashid, who applied herself to this throughout her life, leaving on this road facilities and useful works which, from her death until to-day, have been of service to all who every year go on an embassy [pilgrimage] to God Most High.[94] But for her generous acts in this direction this road could not have been traversed. God in His satisfaction will ensure her reward.

On the morning of Saturday, we halted at a place called al-Shuquq, which has two tanks that we found filled with sweet and limpid water. The pilgrims poured out the water that they had and took of this good water, rejoicing at its abundance and renewing their thanks to God. One of these tanks is a huge cistern of great circumference that a swimmer could not cross save with much effort and toil. The water in it was more than two men's statures deep, and the people took joy in swimming and bathing in it, and washing their garments. It was for them a day of rest upon the journey, a gift bestowed by God Most High to those on an embassy to Him, visitors to His Haram. All these tanks were without water at the time the pilgrims moved from Baghdad to Mecca, but God in His mercy sent the clouds to fill them with water in readiness for the coming of the pilgrims. All this from His favour and kindness to the ambassadors [pilgrims] devoted to His service.

We left that place in the evening and spent the night in another called al-Tananir [The Ovens], which also had a tank filled with water. We departed thence on the night of Sunday the 23rd of Muharram, and with the dawn passed by Zubalah, an inhabited village with a tall Bedouin fort and two tanks and wells, being one of the (three) famous watering points on the road. When the sun had well risen on that day we alighted at al-Haythamayn where there are two tanks. Indeed, with God's help, we hardly passed a place in which we did not find water. Thanks be to Him for that.

We passed the night of Monday the 24th of Muharram near a well-filled tank, and the caravan took its fill of water by night. This place as at the foot of the acclivity called 'Aqabat al-Shaytan [Satan's Slope]. With the morning, on Monday, we climbed this slope, which is neither long nor difficult, for the road is without unevenness and is famous on that account; and when the sun was high we halted at an empty tank. We had passed many tanks, and there was not one that had not beside it a Bedouin-built castle. The road is all tanks. May God hold in favour she who bestowed such care on the road of God's embassy.

On the morning of Tuesday we dismounted at Waqisah, which is a wide depression of land with well-filled tanks and a large fort beside which are the ruins of a building. It is inhabited by Bedouin and is the last watering place on the road, there being between it and al-Kufah no watering place of note save the water-courses from the Euphrates. It is three days' journey from al-Kufah, many of whose inhabitants come to meet the pilgrims at Waqisah, bringing with them flour, bread, dates, condiments, and fruits of the season; and the pilgrims felicitate each other on their deliverance. Praise be to Great and Glorious God for the help and succour He has bestowed: praise drawing more bounty, and accompanying His accustomed beneficent works.

We spent the night of Wednesday the 26th in a place called Lawzah, where there is a large tank which the people found full and where they quenched again their thirsts and let the camels drink at will. We marched from it by night and at dawn on Wednesday we passed a place called al-Qar'a', where there are the ruins of buildings. Here also is a tank divided into six compartments that are small cisterns supplying water to the fountains where the people drink. These are so many that volumes could hardly contain and record them. Praise be to God for His goodness and abounding grace.

The night of Thursday we rested at a huge tank full of water, and on the morrow of that day we alighted at a minaret called Manarat al-Qurun [The Minaret of the Horns]. This is a tower rising in a stretch of desert with no buildings around it. It rises from the ground like a column turned by a lathe, and is made of baked bricks between which are inserted octangular and quadrangular panels of terra-cotta ingeniously fashioned. A singular feature of this tower is that it is decorated all over with gazelle horns so set that it appears as the back of a hedgehog. Concerning it men have a legend which, through lack of adequate support, cannot be confirmed.

Near this minaret is a fort with tall towers, and beside this is a great tank which we found filled with water. Praise be to God for what He has bestowed. In the evening of this Thursday we passed al-'Udhayb, which is a fruitful valley that has a building and is surrounded by a fertile plain over which the eye may roam and find relief. We were told that near it (runs the) Bariq. From here we came to al-Ruhbah, (a village) near to (that river) with habitations and cultivations through which runs the water that issues from a spring in the upper part of the village. We encamped a parasang in front of it.

At midnight on Friday the 28th of Muharram we bent our way again and passed al-Qadisiyah, a considerable village with palm-groves, and having water-courses from the Euphrates. In the morning we came to al-Najaf [The Sand-Hill], which stands behind al-Kufah as a kind of boundary between that city and the desert. It is a wide stretch of hard ground over which the eye can roam and find a fullness of satisfaction and heart's content. We arrived at al-Kufah at sunrise on Friday. Praise be to God for the safety He has given us.

A note on the city of al-Kufah
May God Most High protect it

Al-Kufah is a large city of ancient construction. Ruin has secured mastery over the greater part of it, and the deserted is more than the inhabited. One reason for its desolation is the neighbouring tribe of Khafajah that does not cease to do it injury (by raids). But the passage of days and nights is enough to bring to life and to destroy. The buildings of this city are made of bricks entirely, and it is without a wall. At the eastern end stands the ancient mosque, with which no buildings are contiguous east of it. It is an immense mosque with five porticoes on its south side and two on the others. These porticoes are supported by columns made of hard carved stones laid one above the other and bound with molten lead. These columns have no arches over them, after the style we have described in the Mosque of the Apostle of God – may God bless and preserve him. They are of enormous height, reaching to the roof, so that the eyes are bewildered by their surpassing stature. I have never seen on the earth a mosque with taller columns or a higher roof.

In this holy mosque are many sacred monuments, among which is a chamber beside the mihrab, to the right of him who faces the qiblah, that is said to have been the oratory of Abraham the Friend (of God) – may God bless and preserve him. For protection a black curtain is drawn over it, and it is from here that the khatib emerges, dressed in black robes, to deliver the khutbah. People throng around this blessed spot to pray. Hard by it, to the right side of the qiblah, is a mihrab enclosed by a teak balustrade and rising from the paving of the arcade like a small mosque. It is the mihrab of the Prince of the Faithful, 'Ali ibn Abi Talib – may God hold him in His favour – and in that place the accursed wretch 'Abd al-Rahman ibn Muljam struck him with the sword, wherefore the people pray there, weeping and beseeching. In a corner at the end of this south portico, where it adjoins the end of the west portico, is a form of small mosque also enclosed by a teak balustrade. It is here that 'the water welled from the reservoir of the earth'[95] [Koran XI, 40, and XXIII, 27] in the miracle done for Noah – upon whom be (eternal) happiness. Behind this, outside the mosque, is the house wherein he dwelt, and behind this again is another dwelling said to have been the place where Idris (Enoch)[96] worshipped – may God bless and preserve him. Adjacent to these two chambers is an open space that abuts on the south wall of the mosque and is said to be the place where (Noah's) ark was built. At the end of this space is the dwelling of 'Ali ibn Abi Talib – may God hold him in His favour – and the house where his body was bathed. Adjoining this is another said to be the house of Noah's daughter – may God bless and preserve them. These venerable traditions we received from the tongue of a sheikh of the country, and we recorded them as he told them. God best knows the truth of them all.

At the east side of the mosque one climbs to a small chamber containing the tomb of Muslim ibn 'Aqil ibn Abi Talib – may God hold him in His favour. North of the mosque a little way is a large fountain of Euphrates water that has three big basins. A parasang to the west of the city is the famous shrine named after 'Ali ibn Abi Talib – may God hold him in His favour – said to be the place where the camel that bore him in his winding sheet knelt, and to hold his tomb. God best knows the truth of this. The construction of this shrine is most magnificent, according to what we were told, for on account of the shortness of our stay in al-Kufah, whereby we stayed there only the night of Saturday, we did not see it. We removed on the morning of Saturday, and near to midday we halted at a canal

flowing from the Euphrates, which river is half a parasang to
the east of al-Kufah. The eastern part (of al-Kufah) is all groves
of thickly growing palm-trees whose shade is contiguous and
stretches as far as the eye can see. Leaving this place, we passed
the night of Sunday, the last day of Muharram, in the neighbourhood of al-Hillah, which we entered on Sunday.

A note on the city of al-Hillah
May God Most High protect it

Al-Hillah is a large and anciently constructed city of oblong
shape, nothing of whose walls remain except the earth-wall
enclosure that surrounds it. It lies upon the banks of the
Euphrates, which laps and stretches along the length of its
eastern side. It has splendid markets that comprehend all the
urban resources and intrinsic industries. It is solidly built, and
very populous; and both within and without the city are successive palm-groves between which stand the dwellings. In it
we came upon a great bridge secured over a row of large
barges stretching from one bank to the other and having their
sides held together by massive iron chains, huge like twisted
rafters, that were attached to wooden posts fixed on either bank,
revealing great means and power (in those who built it). The
Caliph (al-Nasir li din Ilah) ordered the construction of this
bridge in his solicitude for the pilgrims and his care for their
comfort on the way. They had formerly crossed in boats; and
our pilgrims found (on their return) that this bridge which
had not been there when they were on their way to Mecca –
may God exalt it – had been constructed by the Caliph in their
absence. We crossed the bridge at midday on Sunday, and
encamped on the banks of the Euphrates a parasang away from
the town.

This river is like its name Furat [Prodigality], having the
sweetest and lightest[97] of water. It is a great river, abundant of
water, which ships ascend and descend. The road from al-Hillah
to Baghdad is one of the best and most beautiful, running

between plains and cultivations, with continuous villages right and left. These plains are traversed by canals from the Euphrates that flow through them and irrigate them, and the tillage on them stretches broad and wide without limit. Upon this road the eyes roam happily and the souls are filled with cheer and well-being, while the security upon it is continuous with our praise to God. Glory to Him.

The Month of Safar of the Year 580

[14th of May–11th of June, 1184]
May God let us know His grace and favour

THE new moon of this month appeared on the night of Monday corresponding with the 14th of May. It rose while we were on the banks of the Euphrates outside the city of al-Hillah. We removed on the morning of Monday, and crossed a bridge over a waterway called al-Nil, a branch deriving from the Euphrates. There was a great press, and many men and animals were drowned in the water. We stood aside, resting until the host should disperse, and then crossed in safety and without harm. Praise be to God. From the city of al-Hillah the pilgrims form a chain of men in companies and groups, some going ahead, some keeping in the middle, and some lagging behind. He in haste does not halt for the leisurely, nor do those in the van await the tardy. Wherever they wish along the road they may stop to take breath and to repose, their spirits at rest from the fear of the drum beat that had caused their hearts to tremble as it urged them to rise and depart. Sometimes a sleeper would babble that he had heard the sound of the drum, and rise hastily and fearfully and then, perceiving that it was but an evil dream, return again to slumber.

Among the causes of their dispersion was the many bridges they encountered on their way to Baghdad, for you can hardly walk a mile without finding a bridge over a waterway branching from the Euphrates. This is the road that has most fountains and bridges, and along most of it are the tents of the men who guard the road in the solicitude of the Caliph for the pilgrims, that they might not be accosted for begging or the like. If this throng of men had rushed headlong on to the bridges they could never have crossed them, and would have fallen in heaps upon each other.

The Emir Tashtikin, whom we have mentioned before, tarried three days in al-Hillah until all the pilgrims had passed before him, and then betook himself to His Majesty the Caliph, on whose behalf he governs the province of Hillah. The conduct of this Emir, in his kindness to the pilgrims, his care of them, his watch over their van and rear, and his arrangement of the right and left wings is worthy of praise. He followed a well-directed path of firmness and foresight; and in modesty, urbanity, and cordiality, his course was felicitous. May God advantage him, and through him, the Muslims.

In the afternoon of Monday we halted at a village called al-Qantarah [The Bridge] with broad and fertile lands watered by canals and shaded by the foliage of trees in fruit. It is one of the fairest and most beautiful of villages. Over a branch of the Euphrates at this place, there is a large bridge, arched so that one must climb and descend it, that gives its name to the village, which is also known as Hisn al-Bashir [The Castle of Bashir]. We found that in these regions the barley is reaped at this time, which is the middle of May. We removed from this village at daybreak on Tuesday the 2nd of Safar and stopped for the midday rest at another called al-Farashah that has many inhabitants, is traversed by waters, and is enfolded by a verdant plain that is beautiful to behold. The villages of this road, from al-Hillah to Baghdad, are all of this fashion, being fair and broad. In this village there is a large khan surrounded by a high wall with small merlons.

Leaving this place, we alighted in the evening at a village called Zariran, which is one of the loveliest villages of the earth, the finest to look upon, the broadest in its lands, and the widest in its boundaries, possessing also the most gardens, sweet-scented plants, and palm-groves. It has a market beside which the markets of cities fall short. Concerning the excellence of its site it is enough to tell you that the Tigris laves its eastern side and the Euphrates the west and that it lies like a bride between them. Between these noble and blessed rivers stretch successive plains, villages, and cultivations.

Amongst the merits of this village is that on its eastern side the 'Iwan Kisra [Palace of Chosroes] stands beside it, while before it lies his city (al-Mada'in]. This palace is an edifice of exceeding whitness soaring high into the skies, but of its structures only a part remains. At the distance of a mile we saw it rising, lofty and brilliant. As for al-Mada'in, it is in ruins. We passed it at dawn on Wednesday the 3rd of Safar and marvelled at what we observed of its length and vastness. Another of the virtues of this village of Zariran is that half a parasang to the east of it is the shrine of Salman the Persian – may God hold him in His favour – and its soil would not have been chosen to contain these blessed remains but for its excellence. The village lies on the banks of the Tigris, which flows between it and the noble shrine.

We had heard that the air of Baghdad engenders gladness in the heart and disposes the spirit to joy and conviviality so that you will scarce find in it one who is not cheerful and gay, even though he be a stranger and far from his home. So when we had alighted at this place which is one stage from the city, and had breathed its scented breezes and quenched our burning thirsts from its cool waters, we felt, despite our alien loneliness, the call to happiness, and on our rugged path we sensed joy, the joy of the absent returning. We felt aroused in us the promptings of good cheer, reminding us of the meetings of loved ones in the brightness of youth. If so it is with the stranger absent from his native land, how then shall it be for the pilgrim returning to his kith and home?

'God watered Bab al-Taq with the drenching clouds,
And restored to his native land each stranger.'

At dawn on Wednesday we departed from this village and, as we have described, passed Mada'in Kisra and came to Sarsar which in beauty is a sister of Zariran or near to it. By its southern side flows a large branch of the Euphrates, over which is a bridge built on barges secured from bank to bank by huge iron chains in the fashion we have described concerning the

P

bridge of al-Hillah. We crossed it and, passing the village, halted for our noonday rest when we were about three parasangs from Baghdad. This village of Sarsar has a fine market and a large new congregational mosque; it is one of the villages that charge the soul from their beauty and goodliness.

The fame of these two rivers, the Tigris and the Euphrates, is such that we need not describe them. Their confluence is between Wasit and al-Basrah, where they pour into the sea, and their course runs from north to south. It is enough in their regard to mention the special blessings bestowed by God upon them and their brother the Nile, as is famous and well-known. We removed from this place a little before noon on Wednesday and came to Baghdad before the late afternoon, passing into the city through gardens and meadows of which all description must fall short.

A note on the City of Peace, Baghdad
May God Most High protect it

Baghdad is an ancient city, and although it has never ceased to be the capital of the 'Abbaside Caliphate and the pivot of the Qurayshite, Hashimite Imams' claims,[98] most of its traces have gone, leaving only a famous name. In comparison with its former state, before misfortune struck it and the eyes of adversity turned towards it, it is like an effaced ruin, a remain washed out, or the statue of a ghost. It has no beauty that attracts the eye, or calls him who is restless to depart to neglect his business and to gaze. None but the Tigris which runs between its eastern and its western parts like a mirror shining between two frames, or like a string of pearls between two breasts. The city drinks from it and does not thirst, and looks into a polished mirror that does not tarnish. And the beauty of its women, wrought between its waters and its air, is celebrated and talked of through the lands, so that if God does not give protection, there are the dangers of love's seductions.

As to its people, you scarce can find among them any who

do not affect humility, but who yet are vain and proud. Strangers they despise, and they show scorn and disdain to their inferiors, while the stories and news of other men they belittle. Each conceives, in belief and thought, that the whole world is but trivial in comparison with his land, and over the face of the world they find no noble place of living save their own. It is as if they are persuaded that God has no lands or people save theirs. They trail their skirts trippingly and with insolence, turning not, in deference to God, from that of which He disapproves, deeming that the highest glory consists in trailing one's mantle, and knowing not that the garment, in accordance with tradition, shall go to the flames. Their business they contract with 'borrowed' gold, but none among them 'give any loan to God' [i.e. give alms] [Koran II, 246]. There are no transactions save with 'borrowed' dinars and at the hands of those who give short measure in weighing.* You can hardly gain the better of the leading men of its inhabitants by honest truthfulness, and there is not one of its weighers and measurers to whom does not apply the 'Woe to the (defaulters)' of the Surah of the Defaulters [Koran LXXXIII, where those who give short measure are condemned]. They feel no shame in this, as if they were the remainder of the Midianites, the people of the Prophet Shu'ayb [Koran VII, 85 et seq., where the prophet Shu'ayb exhorts his people of Midian to give full measure and to worship God alone, and is rejected by them with scorn. They are destroyed by an earthquake, as in time are these people of Baghdad in the massacre by the grandson of Jengiz Khan]. The stranger with them is without fellowship, his expenses are doubled, and he will find amongst them none who do not practise hypocrisy with him or make merry with him only for some profit or benefit. It is as if they are forced to this false form of friendship as a condition of gaining peace and agreement in their lives together. The illconduct of the people of this town is stronger than the character

* The author makes play on the word *qard*, which means both 'borrowed' and 'pared'. He means that the Baghdadians gave short measure in their gold.

of its air and water, and detracts from the probity of its traditions and its reports.

I beg the pardon of God for them all save their tradition-bearing faqihs and recollective preachers, for there is no doubt that in the way of preaching and reminding, in persistent admonishment and making to understand, in the assiduous giving of fearful warnings and cautions, they are in a position to claim God's compassion such as will unload these people of many sins, pull the train of pardon over their sinful steps, and prevent the severest disaster from falling upon their houses. But with such men they are beating steel when cold, and seeking to make ice gush water. Hardly a congregational Friday passes but that a preacher addresses them, and the most successful of them remains all his days in recollective assemblies, which is a felicitous and necessary course. The first of these whose discourses we attended was the sheik and imam Radi al-Din al-Qazwini, head of the Shafi'is, and theologian at the Nizamiyah College, and distinguished for his pre-eminence in fundamental studies. We went to the lecture he gave following the afternoon prayer of Friday the 5th of the month of Safar. He ascended the pulpit and the readers, who were on chairs in front of him, began to recite. They filled one with yearning and longing with pleasing voices and sad and moving melodies. The imam then delivered a quiet and grave discourse that dealt with the various branches of learning, including a commentary on the Book of Great and Glorious God and an exposition of the traditions of His Apostle – may God bless and preserve him – with an explanation of their meaning. Like a shower of rain, questions were sprinkled upon him from all sides, and these he did not fall short to answer, and was prompt to do so, delaying not. A number of notes were passed to him and, gathering them together in his hand, he began to answer each one, throwing away each note as he dealt with it, until he had come to the end. When evening fell he descended and the assembly dispersed. His disquisition was learned and homiletic, grave, quiet, and persuasive, revealing God's blessing and his calmness of soul; and the souls of the humble did not grudge the flowing of tears, especially at the end of the convocation when his exhortations dissolved them in contrition and weeping, and caused the repentant to rush into his arms. How many were the forelocks he cut! To how many arguments of the penitent did he apply his theme and cut them! It is by the like of men of the standing of this blessed sheik that the rebellious come to be forgiven and sinners to be absolved, and that protection and salvation are continued. God Most High will reward every man of standing according to his position, and by reason of the blessedness of the learned saints will shield from His displeasure and vengeance those of His servants who are perverse. This from His mercy and bounty for He is the Benefactor, the Generous. There is no Lord but He, and only He may be worshipped.

We went to another of his dissertations, this time after the evening prayers on Friday the 12th of the month. His gathering that day was attended by the chief of the doctors of al-Khurasan, head of the Shafi'i imams. He entered the Nizamiyah College with a great stir and a turning of the eyes of spirits longing for him. The imam we have mentioned above commenced his discourse, delighted at the presence of this learned man and much honoured by it. All the branches of theology came under his review, as in the meeting we have already described. This chief of the learned doctors was Sadr al-Din al-Khujandi, already mentioned in this journal, famous for his beneficent and bounteous acts, and first among the great and illustrious.

On the morning of the Saturday following we attended the sermon of that sheik, faqih, and imam, the only Jamal al-Din Abu 'l-Fada'il ibn 'Ali al-Jawzi, given beside his house on the eastern bank (of the river). Adjoining, with its extremity, the palaces of the Caliph, it is near to the Bab al-Basaliyyah, the last of the gates on the eastern side (of the city), and here he gives a discourse every Saturday. And we were present at the sermon of a man who is no 'Amr or Zayd [i.e. no ordinary man]. 'Under the fur is the prey';[99] he is the wonder of all time,

and the consolation of the faith. He was the head of the
Hanbalis and a specialist in learning of the highest rank, an imam
of the mosque, and a cavalier on the track at that calling,
renowned for his splendid triumphs of eloquence and learning,
controlling the reins of verse and of rhymed prose, and one
who has dived deep into the sea of thought and brought forth
precious pearls. His verse is Radi's in temper but after the
manner of Mihyar; as for his rhymed prose, it reveals the
bewitching eloquence that annuls comparison with Quss and
Sahban. One of his most splendid marvels and greatest miracles
was the following: On his ascending the pulpit, the readers,
who numbered more than twenty, began to recite the Koran.
Two or three of them spoke a verse of the Koran in a moving
and impassioned rhythm, and when they had done, another
group of the same number recited another verse. So they went
on, alternately reciting verses, from various chapters, until they
had ended the reading. The verses they gave were so similar
that even a man of ready mind could scarce tell the number
or name the order; yet when they had finished, this great and
remarkable imam, passing speedily into his disquisition and
pouring into the shells of our ears the pearls of his utterance,
punctuated his discourse at each paragraph with the rhyming
opening words of the verses recited, giving them in the order
of their reading without prematurity or deferment, and ending with the rhyme of the last.

If anyone present at his sermon had thought to name what was
recited verse by verse in the proper order he would have failed.
What then of one who fits them rapidly and extemporarily
to a fine sermon! 'Is not this an enchantment, then, or do you
not see?' [Koran LII, 15]. 'Surely this is manifest favour' [Koran
XXVII, 16]. 'Speak of this sea of knowledge, and be not narrow
in his praise.'[100] Ah, but how far is talk of him from reality!

When he had ended his sermon, he offered some gentle
exhortations and talked of some clear events in his memory,
so that hearts were struck with longing, spirits melted with
ardour, and the sobs of weeping resounded. The penitent raised

loud their voices and fell on him like moths on a lamp. Each
one offered him his forelock, and this he cut, and, touching
each man's head, he prayed for him. Some fainted and he
raised them to him in his arms. We witnessed an awesome
spectacle which filled the soul with repentance and contrition,
reminding it of the dreads of the Day of Resurrection. Had
we ridden over the high seas and strayed through the waterless desert only to attend the sermon of this man, it would
have been a gainful bargain and a successful and prosperous
journey. Praise be to God who granted that we should meet
with him of whose merit inanimate things bear witness and
whose like the worl¹ is too small to contain. Throughout his
audience, questions came rapidly upon him and notes flew to
him and quicker than the twinkling of an eye he answered.
At times most of his sparkling collucution would consist of
answering these questions. But excellence is in the hand of God,
and He grants it to whom He wills. There is no God but He.

We went to another of his addresses on the morning of
Thursday the 11th of the month of Safar at the Bab Badr, in
the square of the palaces of the Caliph, whose belvederes overlook it. This place is part of the harim of the Caliph, and is
set apart for the reception of those who come to preach there,
so that the Caliph, his mother, and the ladies of his harim might
listen from the belvederes. The Gate is opened to the people
who enter the place, which is spread with mats. The imam
holds a meeting there every Thursday, and in the early morning we came to see him, sitting until the learned speaker arrived.
Climbing the pulpit, he loosened the taylasan from his head
in deference to the standing of the place. The Koran readers,
who were arranged in a line before him in chairs, soon began
to recite in order, filling one ·with longing and emotion as they
wished, and the eyes speedily dropped tears. When they had
ended, and we had counted them as doing nine verses from
different chapters (of the Koran), he began a discourse that was
brilliant and superb, and set throughout with the opening words
of the verses. So the sermon went, rhyming with the last verse

of the series until it finished. The verse was: 'God is He who made for you the night that you may rest therein, and the day to see in: God indeed is bountiful to men' [Koran XL, 61], and he continued (rhyming) in *sin* [the last letter of the verse just quoted] and achieving a fine effect. That day was more remarkable than the one before. He began to eulogise the Caliph, and to pray for him and his noble mother, who bore the by-names of al-Sitr al-Ashraf [The Most Noble Veiled One] and of al-Janab al-'Ar'af [Her Most Compassionate Excellency]. He then pursued his exhortation, all extempore and without preparation, and again introducing the verses in the order of their recital. Eyes poured forth their tears, and souls revealed their secret longings. Men threw themselves upon him, confessing their sins and showing their penitence. Hearts and minds were enravished, and there was great commotion. The senses lost their understanding and discernment, and there was no way to restraint.

During his audience he recited erotic poems of great passion, and of remarkable sensibility, firing hearts with emotion and turning from eroticism to asceticism. The last thing he recited, when his audience was already in a state of reverence, stricken by the arrows of his eloquence, was:

'Where is my heart which love hath melted?
Where is my heart not yet restored?
O Sa'd increase my passion with memories of them,
Tell me, by Allah, O Sa'd, hast thou been redeemed (from the miseries of separation)?'

Unceasingly he repeated these verses, his emotion visible upon him, tears almost preventing the issue of words from his mouth, until we feared he would be choked. He hastened to rise and descended from the pulpit speedily, but in a haze. He had inspired hearts with fear and left men on burning coals. They accompanied him with red eyes, openly weeping, and some were rolling in the dust. Oh what a sight! How awesome to look upon! How happy was he who saw it! God by

His grace and favour gave us to profit of this man's blessedness, putting us among those who might through him share
of His mercy.

At the beginning of his meeting, he recited an ode, bright
as fire, 'Iraqi in manner, concerning the Caliph. It opened:

> 'In the embroilment of love, he is as one struck by the
> lightning on the slopes of (Mount) 'Aqil'

and in speaking of the Caliph said, 'O words of God, be an
amulet against the evil eye through the perfect imam.'

When he had finished his recital the assembly was shaken
with emotion. He then began his function, and long displayed
to us the enchantment of his exposition. We had not thought
that a speaker of this world could so possess the soul and operate
on it as did this man. Glory to God who endows exclusively
with perfection those of His servants whom He wills. There
is no God but He.

After this meeting, we went to other preachers in Baghdad,
and we marvelled at their excellence in comparison with the
speakers we knew in the west. In Mecca and Medina – may
God exalt them – we had attended the meetings of those whom
we have mentioned in this journal, but they were poor beside
those of this unrivalled man in their power over our souls,
and we did not find them so good as their repute. 'Where is
the readiness I would like?' What a difference between the
two! How many young men there are, but those like Malik
are few.[101] After this we went to another meeting that was
most good to hear and that roused the attention. A third mejlis
of his we attended on Saturday the 13th of Safar, in the place
we have mentioned, beside his house on the eastern bank (of
the river). His wondrous eloquence took all forms. We witnessed one notable example of his powers: through his exhortation the souls of those present rose as clouds, and from their
tears there poured a heavy shower of rain. Then, at the end of
his meeting, he delivered some erotic verses, ardently mystical
and emotional. At last, weakness overcame him and he sprang

from the pulpit, sad and distressed, but leaving all repenting of themselves, weeping and sadly crying, 'Alas, what a pity!' The weepers moved round like a mill-stone, wailing and all still unrestored from their intoxication. Glory to God who created him to instruct those that have minds, and made him the greatest cause for the penitence of his servants. There is no God but He.

We now return to our description of Baghdad

As we have said, this city has two parts, an eastern and a western, and the Tigris passes between them. Its western part is wholly overcome by ruin. It was the first part to be populated, and the eastern part was but recently inhabited. Nevertheless, despite the ruins, it contains seventeen quarters, each quarter being a separate town. Each has two or three baths, and in eight of them is a congregational mosque where the Friday prayers are said. The largest of these quarters is al-Qurayah, where we lodged in a part called al-Murabba' [the Square] on the banks of the Tigris and near to the bridge. This bridge had been carried away by the river in its flood, and the people had turned to crossing by boats. These boats were beyond count; the people, men and women, who night and day continuously cross in recreation are likewise numberless. Ordinarily, and because of the many people, the river had two bridges, one near the palaces of the Caliph, and the other above it. The crossings in the boats are now ceaseless.

Then (comes the quarter of) al-Karkh, a noted city,[102] then that of Bab al-Basrah [the Basra Gate], which also is a city and has in it the mosque of al-Mansur – may God hold him in His favour. It is a large mosque, anciently built, and embellished. Next is (the quarter) al-Shari', also a city. These are the four largest quarters. Between the al-Shari' and Bab al-Basrah quarters is the Suq al-Maristan [the Market of the Hospital], which itself is a small city and contains the famous Baghdad Hospital. It is on the Tigris, and every Monday and

Thursday physicians visit it to examine the state of the sick, and to prescribe for them what they might need. At their disposal are persons who undertake the preparation of the foods and medicines. The hospital is a large palace, with chambers and closets and all the appurtenances of a royal dwelling. Water comes into it from the Tigris. It would take long to name the other quarters, like al-Wasitah, which lies between the Tigris and a canal which branches off the Euphrates and flows into the Tigris and on which is brought all the produce of the parts watered by the Euphrates. Another canal passes by Bab al-Basrah, whose quarter we have already mentioned, and flows as well into the Tigris.

Another quarter is that called al-'Attabiyah, where are made the clothes from which it takes its name,[103] they being of silk and cotton in various colours. Then comes al-Harbiyyah, which is the highest (on the river bank) and beyond which is nothing but the villages outside Baghdad. Other quarters there are that it would take too long to mention. In one of them is the tomb of Ma'ruf al-Karkhi, a pious man and famed amongst the saints. On the way to the Bab al-Basrah is a splendidly built shrine in which is a tomb with a large convex tombstone bearing the words, 'This is the tomb of 'Awn and Mu'in[104] sons of the Prince of the Faithful 'Ali ibn Abu Talib' – may God hold him in His favour. Also on the west side is the tomb of Musa ibn Ja'far – may God hold them (father and son) in His favour. Many other tombs there are[105] of saints and men of piety and men of noble forebears, whose names I cannot recollect – may God hold them all in His favour.

To the east of the town, on an eminence outside it, is a large quarter beside the quarter of al-Rusafah, where, on the bank, was the famous Bab al-Taq [Gate of the Arch]. In this quarter is a shrine, superbly built, with a white dome rising into the air, containing the tomb of the imam Abu Hanifah – may God hold him in His favour, by which name the quarter is known. Near this quarter is the tomb of the imam Ahmad ibn Hanbal – may God hold him in His favour – and also in this part is the tomb of Abu Bakr al-Shibli – may God's mercy rest upon his soul – and that of al-Husayn ibn Mansur al-Hallaj. In Baghdad many are the tombs of pious men – may God hold them all in His favour.

In the western part of the city are the orchards and walled-in gardens whence are brought fruits to the eastern part. This to-day is the home of the Caliph, and that is honour and circumstance enough for it. The Caliph's palaces lie at its periphery and comprise a quarter or more of it, for all the 'Abbasides [the family of the Caliph] live in sumptuous confinement in those palaces, neither going forth nor being seen, and having a settled stipend. A large part of these palaces is used by the Caliph, and he has taken the high belvederes, the splendid halls, and the delightful gardens. To-day he has no vizier, having only an official called Vice-Vizier who attends the council which deals with the property of the Caliph, and who holds the books and controls affairs. He has an Intendant over all the 'Abbasid palaces, and an amin [a person of confidence] over all the harim [harem] remaining from the time of the Caliph's grandfather and father, and all those included in the Caliph's own harem. He is called al-Sahib Majd al-Din Ustad al-Dar, which is his title, and prayers are said for him after those for the Caliph. He appears little before the public, being busy with his affairs concerning the palaces, their guardianship, the responsibility for their locks, and their inspection night and day.

The lustre of this reign consists only in pages and negro eunuchs, among them being a youth called Khalis who is the commander of the whole army. We saw him one day going forth, preceded and followed by officers of the army, Turkish, Daylami [Persian] and others, and surrounded by about fifty drawn swords in the hands of the men about him. In his regard we saw things strange in our time. He has palaces and belvederes on the Tigris. The Caliph would sometimes be seen in boats on the Tigris, and sometimes he would go into the desert to hunt. He goes forth in modest circumstance in order

to conceal his state from the people, but despite this concealment his fame only increases. Nevertheless, he likes to appear
before the people, and show affection for them. They deem
themselves fortunate in his character, for in his time they have
obtained ease, justice, and good-living, and great and small they
bless him. We saw this Caliph Abu 'l-'Abbas Ahmad al-Nasir
li din Ilah ibn al-Mustadi' bi Nur Ilah Abu Muhammad al-
Hasan ibn al-Mustanjid bi Ilah Abu 'l Muzaffar Yusuf, whose
lineage goes back to Abu 'l-Fadl Ja'far al-Muqtadir billah and
beyond him to his ancestors the Caliphs – may God hold them
in His favour – in the western part in front of his belvedere
there. He had come down from it and went up the river in
a boat to his palace high on the east bank. He is a youth in
years, with a fair beard that is short but full, is of handsome
shape and good to look on, of fair skin, medium stature, and
comely aspect. He is about five and twenty years of age.
He wore a white dress like a qaba' [a full-sleeved gown],
embroidered with gold, and on his head was a gilded cap
encircled with black fur of the costly and precious kind used
for (royal) clothes, such as that of the marten or even better.
His purpose in wearing this Turkish dress was the concealment
of his state, but the sun cannot be hidden even if veiled. This
was on the evening of Saturday the 6th of Safar of the year
580, and we saw him again on the evening of the Sunday following, gazing from his belvedere on the west bank. It was
nearby this that we lodged.

The eastern part of the city has magnificent markets, is
arranged on the grand scale and enfolds a population that none
could count save God Most High, who computes all things.
It has three congregational mosques, in all of which the Friday
prayers are said. The Caliph's mosque, which adjoins the palace,
is vast and has large water containers and many and excellent
conveniences – conveniences, that is, for the ritual ablutions
and cleansing. The Mosque of the Sultan is outside the city,
and adjoins the palaces also named after the Sultan known as
the Shah in Shah. He had been the controller of the affairs of

the ancestors of this Caliph and had lived there, and the mosque
had been built in front of his residence. The (third) mosque,
that of al-Rusafah, is in the eastern part, and between it and
the mosque of the Sultan lies about a mile. In al-Rusafah is
the sepulchre of the 'Abbaside Caliphs – may God's mercy rest
upon their souls. The full number of congregational mosques
in Baghdad, where Friday prayers are said, is eleven.

The baths in the city cannot be counted, but one of the
town's sheiks told us that, in the eastern and western parts
together, there are about two thousand. Most of them are
faced with bitumen, so that the beholder might conceive them
to be of black, polished marble; and almost all the baths of
these parts are of this type because of the large amount of
bitumen they have. The question of this bitumen is strange:
it is brought from a well between Basra and al-Kufah from
which God has caused to ooze the fluid that produces the
bitumen. It comes over the sides of the spring like clay and is
scooped up and, after congealing, carried away. Glory to God
who creates what He wishes. There is no God but He. The
(ordinary) mosques in both the eastern and the western parts
cannot be estimated, much less counted. The colleges are about
thirty, and all in the eastern part; and there is not one of them
that does not outdo the finest palace. The greatest and most
famous of them is the Nizamiyah, which was built by Nizam
al-Mulk and restored in [A.H.] 504. These colleges have large
endowments and tied properties that give sustenance to the
faqihs who teach in them, and are dispensed on the scholars.
A great honour and an everlasting glory to the land are these
colleges and hospitals. God's mercy on him who first erected
them, and on those who followed in that pious path.

The eastern part has four gates: first that on the high part
of the bank, the Bab al-Sultan; then Bab al-Safariyah; then
the Bab al-Halbah; and then Bab al-Basaliyah. These are the
gates in the walls that surround the city from the high to the
low parts of the bank and wind round it in a long semicircle.
Inside, in the markets, are many gates. To be short, the state

of this city is greater than can be described. But ah what is she to what she was! To-day we may apply to her the saying of the lover:

'*You are not you, and the houses are not those I knew.*'[106]

Our departure from Baghdad to Mosul took place after the afternoon prayers of Monday the 15th of Safar, which was the 28th of May. Our stay in Baghdad had been thirteen days. We were in the company of two princesses, the princess daughter of Mas'ud, already mentioned in this journal, and the princess mother of Mu'izz al-Din, Lord of Mosul. With them were the pilgrims of Syria, of Mosul, and of the Persian lands adjoining Darb which are subject to the Emir Mas'ud, father of one of these two princesses. The pilgrims of Khurasan and the lands about it journeyed with a third princess, the daughter of the King al-Daqus [see note 80]. They took the road from the eastern side of Baghdad; ours to Mosul was from the western side. These two princesses were the Emirs and commanders of the troops with whom we went. May God not apply to us the saying:

'The troops perished with their commander.'

These princesses had soldiers in their own pay, and the Caliph had added soldiers to accompany them, in fear of the Bedouin tribe of the Khafajah whose tents were pitched around Baghdad.

The Mas'udi princess, with many youths and much circumstance, came suddenly upon us the evening of our departure from Baghdad. She was withdrawn inside a domed litter placed on two poles that lay between two beasts, one ahead of the other and decked with gilded caparisons. The animals carried her along like a zephyr, speedily and gently. There was an opening both in the front and in the rear of the litter, inside which could be seen the princess, veiled and wearing a golden headband. Before her went a mounted troop of her youths and soldiers. On her right were the nags and excellent hackneys, while behind her was a party of her handmaidens riding both nags and hackneys, on gold-worked saddles. They also wore golden head-bands whose ends fluttered in the breeze. Like a cloud they moved behind their mistress, with banners and timbals and trumpets which they sounded at the mount and dismount. Indeed we saw such pride of feminine sovereignty, such solemn ceremony of rank, as should shake the earth and gloriously trail behind it the robe-trains of the world. And it was fair that glory should serve it, and that this tremor should occur for it.

The kingdom of her father extends over four months' journey. The ruler of Constantinople pays him tribute. He rules his subjects with admirable equity, and (against the Christians) wages holy war unceasingly and in a manner most laudable. One of the pilgrims from our country told us that in this present year of 579 he had conquered about twenty-five Byzantine cities. His by-name is 'Izz al-Din, but his father's name was Mas'ud, and he himself is more commonly known by this name, which is hereditary in that dynasty, going from father to son. One of the glories of this princess, who is named Saljuqah, is that Saladin conquered Amid, the city of her husband Nur al-Din and one of the biggest in the world, but left the city to her in honour of her father and gave her the keys. Because of this, her husband remained king. But enough for you of this affair. The King of Kings, the Giver of Life, the Self-Existent gives power to whom He wills. There is no God but He.

We passed that night in one of the villages of Baghdad. When we arrived, part of the night had gone. Near to it flows the Dujayl, a tributary of the Tigris that waters all those vill-ages. We removed from this place on the morning of Tuesday the 16th of Safar, and the villages on our way were continuous. We prolonged our march until after the midday prayer, when we dismounted and waited the rest of our day that the pil-grims who lagged behind, and the merchants of Syria and Mosul, might overtake us. Then, a little before midnight, we resumed our journey and pursued the march until day had risen when we alighted to rest in shade beside the Dujayl. All that night we journeyed on, and with the morning descended

near a village called al-Harba, one of the most fertile and extensive of villages. Leaving that place, we travelled all night, and
on the morning of Thursday the 18th of Safar we encamped
on the banks of the Tigris near a fort called al-Ma'shuq and
said to have been a lodge of al-Zubaydah, cousin and wife of
al-Rashid – may God hold him in His mercy.

Facing this place, on the eastern bank, lies the city of Surra
man Ra'a [Samarra or 'Pleased is he who looks upon it']¹⁰⁷
which is to-day a lesson to him who looks upon it. Where
is its Mu'tasim, its Wathiq and its Mutawakkil [past Caliphs]?
It is a large city, but in ruins save for a part which is still
inhabited. Al-Mas'udi – may God's mercy rest upon his soul –
dilated on its description, praising its good air and beauty, and
it is as he portrayed it even though only a trace of its splendour
remains. 'God inherits the earth and all upon it' [Koran XIX,
40]. There is no other God but He. All that day we stayed
there resting, a stage distant from Takrit, and on departing
from the place, journeyed all night. At dawn on Friday the
19th of the month (of Safar), which was the 1st of June, we
came to Takrit and halted outside it to rest that day.

An account of the city of Takrit
May God Most High protect it

Takrit is a large city, with a wide countryside and spacious
open places. With fine markets and many mosques, it has a
large population who are of better character and who give
fairer measure than the people of Baghdad. Through it passes
the Tigris, on whose banks it has a strong fortress that is its
impregnable citadel. Around the city are walls which show
signs of weakness. It is one of the ancient towns we have
mentioned.

We left it on the evening of the same day and journeyed
throughout the night; and on the morning of Saturday the
20th of the month, being on the banks of the Tigris, we halted

to repose. From that place a supply of water for a day and night is collected, and this we did and left in the forenoon. Until night we rode and then put down to rest and steal a measure of sleep. We dozed a little, and then removed, marching on through that night and the morning of Sunday, and prolonging our movement until the sun had well risen. We alighted for our midday rest at a village on the banks of the Tigris called al-Jadaydah. Near it is a large village, which we had passed, called al-'Aqr which is topped by a high hill that in the past was the site of a fort and at the bottom of which is a modern khan with towers and merlons, finely and strongly built. The villages and cultivation from this place to Mosul are continuous. It is here that the pilgrim order of march breaks up, each one going his way at his pleasure, speeding ahead or falling back, slowly or speedily, safe, and with mind at rest.

We left it in the late afternoon, and marched until evening, when we halted, and, while the camels ate, snatched a moment of slumber. Before midnight we set forward again and travelled until the morning. In the forenoon of that day, Monday the 22nd of Safar, the 4th of June, we passed a place called al-Qayarah, near the Tigris on its eastern bank. On the right of the road to Mosul is a depression in the ground, dark like a cloud, in which God has caused wells, large and small, to spout forth bitumen. Some of them at times discharge a froth as if it were boiling. Troughs have been made to collect it, and you may see it spread over the ground like clay. It is black, smooth, shiny, and soft, has a sweet smell, and is very viscid, sticking to the finger immediately it is touched. Around these springs is a large black pond thinly overspread with something like a black moss which it casts to the sides, there to precipitate into bitumen.

We saw a remarkable thing which, whenever we heard of it, we wondered at. Near to these springs, on the banks of the Tigris, is another large one whose fumes we could see from a distance. And we were told that when they want to remove the bitumen, they light a fire in it, the fire dries out the moisture, the bitumen congeals, and then they cut it in pieces and carry it away. It is found in all lands as far as Syria, Acre, and all the coastal regions. God indeed creates what He wishes. Glory to Him. Exalted be His greatness, sublime His power. There is no Lord save He. There is no doubt that of this kind is the well which we were told lies between al-Kufah and Basra as we have mentioned in this journal.

It is two stages from this place to Mosul, and we passed by these bituminous wells to stop for our midday rest. We then moved on until evening and alighted at a village called al-Uqaybah, whence, if God wills, one can reach Mosul in the morning. So we left it after midnight and reached Mosul when day had risen on Tuesday the 23rd of Safar, the 5th of June, and dismounted in a suburb in one of the inns near the bank of the river.

An account of the city of Mosul
May God Most High protect it

This city is a large and ancient one, fortified and imposing, and prepared against the strokes of adversity. Its towers are aligned so closely together as almost to touch. Inside them are chambers, one above the other, that run round the walls that encompass the whole city. It was possible to open up these chambers because of the thickness of the structure and the width of the foundations. To warriors these chambers are a safe refuge, and they are a useful appurtenance of war. At the highest point of the town is a great fortress, with stones compactly set, and surrounded with ancient walls with lofty towers. Adjacent to it are the houses of the Sultan. Between them and the town is a broad street that stretches from the top of the town to the bottom. The Tigris flows east of the town, touching its walls whose towers rise from its waters. The town has a large suburb with mosques, baths, khans, and markets.

One of the Emirs of the town, called Mujahid al-Din, constructed on the banks of the Tigris a congregational mosque

than which I have never seen a more splendid. It is impossible
to describe its architectural ornament and its arrangement. It
is covered with reliefs in terra-cotta, and its maqsurah makes
one think of those in Paradise. Round it are iron latticed
windows, adjoined by benches overlooking the Tigris than
which there could be no nobler or more beautiful place to sit in.
The description of this mosque would take long, and for brevity
we have given but a passing glimpse of it. In front of it stands
a finely-built hospital erected by Mujahid al-Din, whom we
have mentioned above. He also built, in the market within the
town, a qaysariyah[108] for the merchants. This is like a large
khan, and is bolted with iron doors and surrounded by shops
and houses one over the other. It is decorated throughout in
a splendid manner, and of an architectural elegance that has
no like, for I have never in any land seen a qaysariyah to
compare with it.

The city has two mosques, one new and the other of the
time of the 'Ummayids. In the courtyard of this latter is a
dome in which rises a marble pillar whose shaft is encircled
by five rings, twisted like bracelets, which are carved from the
body of the marble, and at whose top is an octagonal marble
basin from which projects a pipe. From this water spurts forth
with such energy and strength that it rises into the air, like
a straight glass wand, more than a man's height, and then falls
to the foot of the dome. The Friday prayers are said in both
these mosques, the old and the new, as well as in the mosque
in the suburb. The city has six or more colleges for the pursuit of learning. They are on the Tigris and appear as high
castles. It has as well hospitals besides the one we mentioned in
the suburb. God has specially endowed this town with the holy
earth which holds the tomb of Jirjis [St. George][109] – may God
bless and preserve him. Over it a mosque has been built, and
his tomb is in one of its rooms, on the right of him who enters.
This mosque stands between the new mosque and the Gate
of the Bridge, and will be found on the left of him who goes
towards the (new) mosque from the Gate. We were blessed

by our visit to this holy tomb and by standing at it. God gave us this advantage.

Amongst the benefits God has specially conferred on this town is that about a mile to the east of it, across the Tigris, is the Hill of Penitence. It is the hill on which stood Yunus Jonah – on whom be (eternal) happiness – with his people, and prayed with them until God relieved them of their distress. Near to this hill, also about a mile away, is the blessed spring named after him. It is said that he enjoined his people to purify themselves in it and to take thought of repentance, and that then they ascended the hill praying. On the hill is a large edifice which acts as an asylum for the needy with many chambers, rooms, and ablution and drinking places, all approached by one door. In the middle of this building is a pavilion over which hangs a curtain, and below this is bolted a blessed door, wholly inlaid. It is related that this is the place where Yunus stood – may God bless and preserve him – and that the mihrab of this pavilion was the chamber in which he worshipped. Around the pavilion are candles, thick as the trunks of palm-trees. Men go out to this asylum every Friday night and there devote themselves to God's worship. Around the asylum are many villages. Beside them is a great ruin said to have been the city of Ninawa [Nineveh], which was the city of Yunus – on whom be (eternal) happiness. The remains of the wall that surrounded it are still visible, and evident too are the openings of the gates. The piles of its (ruined) towers are very high.

We slept in the blessed asylum the night of Friday the 26th of Safar. In the morning we went to the blessed spring, drank of its water, purified ourselves in it, and prayed in the mosque beside it. God in His grace and favour will advantage us for our aim in that.

The people of Mosul follow a righteous path, doing pious works. You will meet none of them but has a cheerful countenance and a soft word. They are generous to strangers, receiving them kindly, and using justness in all their dealings with them. Four days we abode in the city.

One of the most glittering of worldly spectacles and awesome to behold we witnessed on Wednesday, the second day
of our arrival at Mosul. (It was the arrival) of the two princesses:
the mother of Mu'izz al-Din, Lord of Mosul, and the daughter
of the Emir Mas'ud whom we have already mentioned. All
the men without exception went forth on horse and on foot;
and the women left too, most of them riding and making a
numerous army. The Emir of the country, with the leaders
of his state, went out to meet his mother. The Mosul pilgrims
entered in the company of their princess with ceremony and
display. They had adorned the necks of their camels with
coloured silks and ornamental collars. The Mas'udi princess
entered at the head of her troop of handmaidens, while before
her was a body of the men who had conducted her. The dome
of her litter was wholly adorned with pieces of gold shaped
like new moons, with dinars the size of the palm of the hand,
and with chains and images of pleasing designs, so that hardly
any part of the dome could be seen. The two beasts that bore
her advanced with jaded steps, and the clatter of their trinkets
filled the ears. The golden ornaments on the necks of her beasts
and the mounts of her maidens formed together a sum of gold
beyond estimation. It was indeed a sight that dazzled the eyes
and provoked reflection. All sovereignty perishes save that of
the One God, the Subduer, who is without partner. More than
one of those persons, worthy of belief, who know of the
princess's affairs, told us that she is known for her piety and
charity and is celebrated for good deeds. Amongst these is her
spending, while on this Hejaz road, a vast sum of money in
alms and in (generous payment) of expenses of the road. She
venerates holy men and women, visiting them in disguise from
a wish to gain their prayers. Her conduct is remarkable, for
all this is with her youthful age and immersion in the pleasures
of the realm. But God guides in the right path those He wishes.

On the evening of the fourth day of our stay in this town,
which was Friday the 26th of Safar, we left it on the beasts
that we had bought in Mosul. We had dispensed with the

offices of the camel-masters, but we should say that the Praised Power had given us the company of only the best of them,[110] and we thank Him for their long and continuous company from Mecca – may God exalt it – to Mosul. We travelled that Saturday night until after midnight, and then halted at a village belonging to Mosul. We removed from it in the forenoon of Saturday, and took our midday rest at a village called 'Ayn al-Rasad under a bridge arched over a stream in which the water hastened by. We enjoyed a blessed repose. In the village is a large new khan. In all the stages of the road there are khans, and it happened that we passed our night in that village. We left it by night and in the morning of Sunday, we came to a village called al-Muwaylihah. From there we went on to spend the night in a large village called Judal, which has an ancient fort. That day we had seen to the right of our road Jabal al-Judi, mentioned in the Book of God Most High [Koran XI, 44] where came to rest the ark of Noah – on whom be (eternal) happiness. The mountain is high and oblong-shaped. We moved on when day had well broken on Monday the 29th of Safar, and stopped for the night in one of the villages of Nasibin [Nisibis] a stage distant from it. The place is called al-K.la.i.

The Month of Rabi' al-Awwal of the Year 580

[12th of June–11th of July, 1184]

May God let us know His favour

THE new moon of this month rose on the night of Tuesday the 12th of June while we were in the aforementioned village. We left it at dawn on that Tuesday and arrived at Nasibin before midday.

An account of the city of Nasibin

May God protect it

Renowned for its age and its past, outwardly fresh, but decrepit within, beautiful to look upon, and of medium size, it stands in a verdant plain which stretches before and behind it as far as the eye can reach. In this plain God has made to run streams of water that irrigate it, and flow in all its parts. The city is begirt with gardens, thick with trees bearing ripe fruits; and round it there bends, like a bracelet, a river with its banks beset with the gardens that cover it with their ample shade. God's mercy upon Abu Nuwas al-Hasan ibn Hani' when he says, 'Nasibin was pleased with me one day and I was pleased with it (to live in). Oh that my lot in this world were Nasibin.' Outside, the city is a natural Paradise, having the trees and plants of Andalusia, radiant with abundance and prosperity, and bright with urban splendour. But inside is the disorder of the desert [i.e. of the Bedouins], so that the gaze does not turn to it, and the eye finds no pleasant place to roam across and no sign of beauty.

The river flows down to it from a spring that issues from a nearby mountain. It divides at its source, one branch taking its way through the plains and cultivations, and the other entering the city and spreading through its streets and penetrating some of its houses. One fork reaches the venerated mosque and, passing through its court, pours into two basins, one in the centre of the court and the other at its eastern gate, and (finally) reaches two fountains at the side of the mosque. Over this river has been built a bridge of hard stone that adjoins the south gate of the city. There are two colleges and one hospital in the place.

The Lord of Nasibin is Mu'in al-Din, brother of Mu'izz al-Din, Lord of Mosul, and both the sons of Babek. Mu'in possesses also the city of Sinjar, which is on the right of the road to Mosul. In one of the northern angles of the venerated mosque lives the sheik Abu 'l-Yaqzan, black of body but white [pure] of heart, and one of the saints whose minds God has illuminated with faith, making them of those whose pious deeds are everlastingly remembered. He is famous for his sermons and renowned for his thaumaturgy. Emaciated by exclusive devotion to God's service, and by asceticism, he is of those whose garments are worn from devotions and is content with what are woven with his own hand, neither does he put aside food for the morrow. God rendered us happy by meeting him, and according us the blessings of his prayers, on the evening of Tuesday, the first of the month of Rabi' al-Awwal. Praise be to Great and Glorious God that He gave us the favour of seeing him, and the honour of shaking his hand. May God profit us from his prayers; for He is the One who hears and who answers. There is no God but He.

We lodged in Nasibin in a khan outside the city, and there passed the night of Wednesday the 2nd of Rabi' al-Awwal. We left in the morning in a large caravan of mules and asses with men from the Hauran and Aleppo and some others from Bilad Bakr and its surroundings, leaving behind the pilgrims of these parts on camels. Our march continued until the beginning of noon. We were ready and on guard against an attack by the Kurds who were the scourge of these parts, from Mosul to Nasibin and the city of Dunaysar, robbing on the highway and 'striving to make mischief in the land' [Koran V, 33 and

64]. They live in inaccessible mountains fast by these lands, whose Sultan has not been helped by God to subdue them and their transgressions. Sometimes they (even) reach the gate of Nasibin, and none can repel or hinder them save Great and Glorious God.

We took our midday rest that Wednesday, on which day we saw to the right of our road, close by the side of the mountain, the ancient city of Dara, large and white, with a towering fort. Nearby, at a distance of half a stage, is the city of Maridin, which sits on the mountain's edge and has at its summit a large castle that is one of the celebrated castles of the world. Both these cities are inhabited.

An account of the city of Dunaysar
May God protect it

This city lies in a wide plain, and is surrounded by gardens of aromatic plants and green vegetables that are irrigated by means of water-wheels. It inclines to the character of the desert and has no walls. Filled with people, it has crowded markets and a wide range of commodities, being the emporium of the people of Syria, Diyar Bakr, Amid, of the Rumi lands that give allegiance to the Emir Mas'ud, and of surrounding countries. It has a wide tillage and many conveniences. With the caravan, we encamped in an open space behind the city, and spent the morning of Thursday the 3rd of Rabi' al-Awwal resting there. Outside the city is a new college – the other buildings being beside it – adjoined by a bath and encompassed by gardens. It is at once a college and a pleasant place of retreat.

The Lord of this city is Qutb al-Din, who is also Lord of the cities of Dara, Maridin, and Ra's al-'Ain. He is a kinsman of the two sons of Babek. These countries are subject to various rulers, after the fashion of the kings of the Arab nations in Spain. All these rulers embellish themselves with titles connected with religion [Din], and you will hear only awesome by-names and appellations that for the wise are without profit.

In this, the subjects and their kings are the same, and the rich share the habit with the poor. Not one of them is known by a cognomen that fits him, or is described by an epithet of which he is worthy. Not one save Salah al-Din [Saladin], Lord of Syria, the Hejaz, and the Yemen, and famous for his virtue and justness. Here the name is in harmony with the subject, and the words fit the meaning. All other titles are but a gust of air, and testimonials made void. The taking on of religious titles: what troubles they involve! 'Kingly titles out of place, like a cat ambitious to mimic the lion's rush.'[111]

We return to the story of our journey – may God bring near its end. We stayed in Dunaysar until we had said the midday prayers of Friday the 4th of Rabi' (al-Awwal). The people in the caravan had lingered there in order to see its market, for every Thursday, Friday, Saturday, and Sunday, there is a much frequented market-day to which come the people of these parts and of the adjacent villages. For continuous along the whole road, right and left, are villages and tall khans. This market, to which the people of these regions throng, is called the Bazar [bazaar]. The market days are all fixed.

We left after the Friday prayers and passed a large village, with a fort, called Tell al-'Uqab [the Hill of the Eagle], which belongs to Christians who pay tribute for Muslim protection [dhimmi]. This village reminded us of the villages of Andalusia in its beauty and freshness, being surrounded by gardens, vineyards, and all kinds of trees. Beside it flows a wide-coursed river on which spreads the shade of the gardens lined along it. There we saw sucking pigs, like sheep in their number and their tameness towards the people there. Then, at the end of the day, we came to another village called al-Jisr [the Bridge], that now belongs to some clients (of the Muslims) who are one of the various sects of the Rum; and there we passed the night of Saturday, the 5th of Rabi'. With the dawn we betook ourselves from it, and, before noon on that day, came to the city of Ra's al-'Ain.

An account of the city of Ra's al-'Ain
May God protect it

This name [the font of water] is a most fitting designation, and in this place are the most excellent properties, for God Most High has given vent to springs in its grounds that pour forth fresh water. They divide into branches and flow in channels spread through the green meadows like strips of silver stretching across a sheet of emerald, beset with trees and gardens, that are disposed along their banks till the end of their cultivated valleys. Of these springs, two are the most copious, and one is situated higher than the other. The higher rises from the ground between hard stones that form something like the hollow of a cave, large and capacious, in which the water rises until it becomes as a vast cistern. The water then pours forth like one of the greatest of rivers until it comes to the other spring, with whose waters it unites. This second spring is one of the most wonderful of the creations of Great and Glorious God. It rises from hard stone at a depth of about four men's statures below the ground, but the spring has opened out a cistern of that depth, and the water, from the force of the spring, rises until it flows over the earth's surface. Sometimes a stout swimmer and strong diver into deep waters tries to reach the bottom, but the water, so strong is the spring, repels him, so that he does not reach half the depth and sometimes even less. This we saw with our own eyes. The water is clearer than pure water and sweeter than the spring of Salsabil, and leaves visible all that is in it. If a dinar be thrown into it on a dark night it will not be hidden. In it they catch a large fish that is as tasty as any that exists. The water from this spring divides into two branches, one going to the right, and the other to the left. That to the right cuts through a convent built beside the spring for the Sufis and for strangers and also called al-Ribat [the Hospice]. That to the left flows beside the convent, and then pours into channels that lead to the places of ablution and other conveniences provided for the needs of man.

Then, below the convent, these two branches meet and join with the river coming from the higher spring. On the bank of the combined rivers hand-mills have been built, that reach along the bank to a place in the middle of the river resembling a dam. At the confluence of the waters of these two springs is the source of the river al-Khabur.

Near this convent, for you can see it, is a college beside which is a bath, and both are about to fall, being decayed and abandoned. I do not think that there is in the world a site like that of this college, for it is a green island, round which the river curves on three sides, with access to it from the one (the fourth). Front and rear it has a garden, and beside it is a water-wheel that sends the water to a garden that is higher than the level of the river. Indeed the whole state of this place is very remarkable. If the villages of eastern Andalusia had such a beautiful site or such sweet springs they would be of the very best. God disposes of all that He creates.

As for the city itself, the interests of its Bedouin are cared for and its urban side neglected. It has no walls to defend it, and no finely built houses to adorn it. It has been sacrificed as a victim to its deserts as if it were but an amulet for its valleys. It has nevertheless all the conveniences of a town, and has two mosques, one new and one old. The old mosque is in the same place as the springs, and in front of it there gushes a fresh spring, other than the two we have mentioned. It is one of the buildings erected by ʿUmar ibn ʿAbd al-ʿAziz – may God hold him in His favour – but the signs of age are about it, and it announces its (coming) dissolution. The other mosque is inside the town, and there the people assemble for the Friday prayers. Our stay in the town that day had been for refreshment, but in all our journey we had not been so cheated.

On Saturday the 5th of Rabiʿ, the 16th of June, we removed from Raʾs al-ʿAin at sunset being wishful of profiting from the darkness and coolness of the night, and evading the choking heat of the middle day; because from that city to Harran was two days' journey, and there were no habitations on the way. On we fared until the morning, and alighted in the desert at a well. We rested a little, and then set forth again when the sun had risen on the morning of Sunday. We marched until the afternoon and then dismounted at a well in a place where there is a high tower with ancient ruins known as Burj Hawa [The Tower of Eve]. There we passed (part of) the night and then, after a short slumber, moved on until the morning, arriving at the city of Harran with the dawn on Monday the 7th of Rabi', the 18th of June. Praise be to God for His smoothing of the way.

A description of the city of Harran
May God protect it

This is a town with no beauty about it. It has no shade to mitigate its feverish heat, and its climate follows from its name [Harran = Hot]. Its water bears no acquaintance with freshness, and its squares and outskirts never cease to burn from the heat of its midday sun. No noontime place of rest will you find there, and you will breathe no air that is not heavy. Thrown into the naked waste, it has been founded in the midst of the wilderness and, without the brightness of a city, its shoulders have been stripped of the clothing of verdure.

But I beg the pardon of God. It is enough honour and merit for this town that it is the ancient city connected with our father Abraham – may God bless and preserve him. South of the city, about three parasangs distant, is a blessed shrine which contains a running spring that was a dwelling-place for him and Sarah – the blessings of God upon them both – and was their place of worship. Because of this blessed connection, God has made the city an abode of ascetic saints and a site for unworldly anchorites. Amongst their most eminent, we met the sheik Abu 'l-Barakat Hayyan ibn 'Abd al-'Aziz, near the mosque named after him. He lives in a *zawiyah* which he has built in the south part of it. Close beside it, at the end of that side, is the *zawiyah* of his son 'Umar, who cleaves to it, and follows the path of his father, doing no wrong. In him I recognised the character of Akhzam.[112] When we came to the sheik, who was above eighty years of age, he shook our hand and prayed for us, and told us to find his son 'Umar. So we turned aside for him and found him, whereupon he prayed for us. We then bade them both farewell and departed, joyous at meeting two men who lived for the life to come. We also met in the old mosque the sheik and ascetic, Salmah, and found him to be a peerless ascetic. He prayed for us, and questioned us, and then we bade him farewell and went our way. There is in the town another Salmah known as al-Makshuf al-Ra's [He of the uncovered Head], who in humility to Great and Glorious God never covers his head and from that takes his name. When we came to the place where he lived, we were told that he had gone forth into the desert on a pilgrimage.

In this town are many men of goodwill who are just, kind to strangers, and generous towards the poor. The people of these cities, from Mosul to Diyar Bakr, Diyar Rabi'ah, and to Syria, are of this way of being kind to strangers and bounteous to the poor. The people of their villages are the same, and the poor and destitute will never need amongst them. In this they display a hereditary inclination to generosity. Indeed the attitude of the people of these parts is remarkable. May God advantage for them for what they are about. As for those devoted to the worship of God, the ascetics, and the anchorites in the hills: they are too many to be counted. May God, by His grace and favour, profit the Muslims by their benedictions and faithful prayers.

This town has markets that are admirably disposed and wonderfully arranged. They are all roofed with wood, and men within them are never out of the long shade. You pass through them as you would pass through a house with large corridors. At every point where four market roads meet a great dome made of plaster has been erected and seems to indicate the branching of these roads. Contiguous with these markets is the venerated cathedral mosque, which is old but has been restored and is of surpassing beauty. It has a great court, with three domes raised on marble columns and under each dome is a well of sweet water. Also in the court is a fourth dome, of great size, raised on ten marble pillars, each nine spans in circumference. In the centre of this dome is a huge marble pillar fifteen spans in circumference. This dome was built by the Rum. Its upper part is hollow as if it were a tall tower, and it is said that it was a store for their furnitures of war. God best knows. The venerated mosque is roofed with wooden rafters and arches. The rafters are massive, and stretch the width of the aisle which measures fifteen paces. There are five aisles, and we have never seen a mosque with wider arches. The wall that is contiguous with the courtyard through which entry is made is full of doors; their number is nineteen, nine to the right and nine to the left, the nineteenth being a huge door that stands in their middle with its arch reaching from the top of the wall to the bottom. It is a splendid sight, and of fine conformation, as if it were the gate of a great city. Its many wooden locks are beautifully worked and it is covered with carving like the doors of the halls of palaces. In the beauty of construction of this mosque and in the fine arrangement of the adjoining markets, we observed a splendid spectacle; and the harmony of design is such as is rarely found in cities.

Harran possesses a college and two hospitals. It is a considerable town, with strong and formidable walls built of hewn stones cemented together in the strongest fashion, as is the case also in the construction of the venerated mosque. It has a strong fortress on its eastern side, divided from it by a wide esplanade; the fortress is also separated from the city walls by a great ditch which, running round it, has its banks strengthened by piled stones, resulting in great security and strength. The walls of the fortress itself are strongly fortified.

Also to the east of the town, a small river runs between its walls and its cemetery. Its source is a spring remote from the town. The town has many inhabitants and is amply supplied; it is clearly prosperous, has many mosques, is filled with conveniences, and is the most splendid of cities. Its ruler is Muzaffar al-Din ibn Zayn al-Din, who acknowledges the suzerainty of Saladin. All this country, from Mosul to Nasibin and the Euphrates is known as Diyar Rabi'ah. Its limit, from Nasibin to the Euphrates, follows the south side of the road. Diyar Bakr is the country which marches with it to the north, with towns like Amid, Mayyafariqin [Martyropolis] and others too numerous to mention. None of their kings resists Saladin, and all are under his subjection, although they had been independent. They remain by his grace, and if he wished, because he walks in the way of God, he could remove them from their possessions.

We had encamped outside the city to the east of it and by the small river we have mentioned. We rested on Monday and on Tuesday; and that day, after the midday prayers, we met with Salmah Makshuf al-Ra's, whom we had failed to find on Monday. We came upon him in his place of worship, and saw a man of saintly aspect and devout manner, of a cheerful and happy countenance, and kind and generous to meet. He treated us sociably and prayed for us, after which we took our leave and went our way, praising Great and Glorious God for granting us the privilege of meeting His true saints and favoured servants.

On the night of Wednesday the 9th of Rabi', after a measure of sleep, we took to our saddles and rode until the morning, when we alighted at an inhabited spot called Tell 'Abdah. This *tell* [mound] is high and broad like a table, and contains ancient ruins. It has running water. We removed from it at sunset, and journeyed throughout the night, passing a village called al-Bayda which has a large new khan and is halfway between Harran and the Euphrates. Facing it, and to the right of the road, as you look over the Euphrates towards Syria, is the city

R

of Saruj, whose story is made famous by al-Hariri in connection with Abu Zayd. It has gardens and running waters as described in his *Maqamat* ['Assemblies' or 'Séances'].

We reached the Euphrates in the morning and, crossing it in well-found boats fitted for the passage, came on the other side to a new-built fortress called Qal' at Najm. Around it are the desert areas (inhabited by the Bedouin), and it has a small market containing necessities like fodder and bread. We stayed there on Thursday the 10th of Rabi' al-Awwal, resting while the caravan finished its crossing. When you cross the Euphrates, you come within the confines of Syria and travel within the dominion of Saladin until Damascus. The Euphrates is the boundary between the regions of Syria and those of Rabi'ah and Bakr. To the left of the road, as you look over the Euphrates to Syria, is the city of al-Raqqah. Bordering it is the town of Malik ibn Tawq known as Rahbat al-Sham and a famous city. We moved on when the first third of the night had passed and rode until we came to the city of Manbij with the morning of Friday the 11th of Rabi', being the 22nd of June.

An account of the city of Manbij [Hierapolis]
May God protect it

It is a town of wide extent, and healthy of air. It is encompassed by ancient walls of great length. Its skies are bright, its aspect handsome, its breezes fragrant and perfumed, and while its day gives generous shade, its night is all enchantment. East and west, gardens thick with trees and divers fruits enfold the town. Water flows freely through it and enters all its parts; and God has favoured it with wells within that are sweeter than honey and delicious to taste. Each house has a well, or even two, and the earth is generous, throwing forth springs of water everywhere. Its markets and streets are broad and spacious, and its shops and booths are like khans and warehouses in size and grandness. The highest of its markets are roofed, and indeed the markets of most of the cities of these regions are of this style. But a lengthy time is on the heels of this town, and ruin has seized it. It had been one of the ancient cities of the Rum, and the remains of their buildings there attest their great attention to it. To the north it has a strong fort, but it is separate from the city and remote. All the towns of these regions have one of the Sultan's forts. The population of Manbij is virtuous and worthy, and they are Sunnis [orthodox] of the Shafi'ite rite, so that through them the town is undefiled by those dissident sects and corrupt beliefs that are found in most of this country. They are upright in their transactions and straightforward in their affairs, and the clear path of their religion is safe from the contradictions of schism. We encamped outside the city in one of its gardens, and stayed there resting a day. We departed from it at midnight, and arrived at Buza'ah in the forenoon of Saturday the 12th of Rabi'.

An account of the town of Buza'ah
May Great and Glorious God watch over it

Standing in a plain of fertile ground and of broad extent, it is smaller than a city, and larger than a village. It has a market where are found both the appurtenances of travel, and the merchandise of a city. At its higher part there is a large and powerful fortress. In ancient times, a king, while seeking to capture it, had become enraged by its stubbornness, and so had ordered the destruction of its walls and had left it, weak and abandoned, in the desert. The town has a surface spring whose waters flow through a broad valley with gardens radiant with verdure and vegetation; and in its elegant splendour, it reveals the beauty of a capital. Facing it, on the side of the valley, is a large village called al-Bab [the Gate] that is the gate between Buza'ah and Aleppo. Eight years ago, it was inhabited by some Isma'iliyah heretics, whose number only God could count. The sparks of their malevolence flew, and their mischief and wrongdoing stopped this road, so that fury possessed the (other) peoples of these regions who, moved by scorn and anger, collected against them from all sides, putting them to the edge of their swords and exterminating them to the last man. Their roots [last remaining people] they made speed to destroy and in this valley they piled high their skulls. God was sufficient defence to the Muslims against their enmity and evil, and caused their deceits to fall upon their own heads. Praise be to God Lord of the Universe. The inhabitants of al-Bab are now Sunnis.

We passed Saturday reposing in the valley of the city, but moved from it at night and, faring until morn, came to the city of Aleppo in the forenoon of Sunday the 13th of Rabi' al-Awwal, being the 24th of June.

An account of the city of Aleppo
May God Most High protect it

Aleppo is a town of eminent consequence, and in all ages its fame has flown high. The kings who have sought its hand in marriage are many, and its place in our souls is dear. How many battles has it provoked, and how many white blades have been drawn against it? Its fortress is renowned for its impregnability and, from far distance seen for its great height, is without like or match among castles. Because of its great strength, an assailant who wills it or feels he can seize it must turn aside. It is a massy pile, like a round table rising from the ground, with sides of hewn stone and erected with true and symmetrical proportions. Glory to Him who planned its design and arrangement, and conceived its shape and outline.

The town is as old as eternity, yet new although it has never ceased to be. Its days and years have been long, and the leaders and the commons have said their last farewell. These are the homes and abodes; but where are their ancient dwellers and those that came to them? Those are the palaces and courts, but where are the Hamdanid[113] princes and their poets? All have passed away, but the time of this city is not yet. Oh city of wonder! It stays but its kings depart; they perish, but its ruin is not yet decreed. Others after them have betrothed her, and to contract her in marriage is not hard. She is desired and it is with ease that she is possessed. This is Aleppo. How often have its kings taken the predicate 'was', and the adverb of time [the time of their rule] been erased while the adverb of place [their capital] (remained). Her name was put in the feminine, and she was decked in the ornaments of a chaste maiden, while (woman-like) upon the treacherous she practised deceit. She was adorned as a bride for the Sword of her State [Sayf al-Dawlah] ibn Hamdan. Alas! Alas! her youth will not endure, suitors she will lack, and after a time ruin will hasten upon her, and the vanguard of misfortune will draw near to her, until 'God has inherited the earth and all upon it' [Koran XIX, 40]. There is no God but He. Glory to Him, splendid is His power. But talk has led us from our purpose: we return now to what we were about.

We say that amongst the honours of this castle is that, as we were told, it was in early days a hill whither Abraham the Friend (of God) – may God's blessings and protection enfold him and our Prophet – was wont to repair with some flocks he had, and there milk them and dispense the milk as alms. The place was therefore called Halab [Ar., 'milk'. Aleppo is, of course, the Western version of Halab]. God best knows concerning this. In the fortress is a venerated shrine, dedicated to him, which men visit to win blessings by praying therein. Amongst its perfect qualities, and a necessity in the defence of fortresses, is that water springs up within it. Two cisterns have been built over the water and they discharge water throughout the year, so never is there fear of thirst. Food also will keep there for all time without impairment. In all the conditions of defence there are no more important and certain than these two attributes. Round the two cisterns, on the side facing the town, is a strong double wall, at the foot of which lies a ditch, whose bottom the eye cannot reach, where water springs. The state of this fortress, both as regards its strength and its beauty, is grander than we can reach in description. Its upper wall is all towers, well-disposed, with dominating high-points and commanding galleries, throughout opened with loopholes. Each tower is garrisoned, and inside the fortress are the suites of the Sultan and apartments for the royal dignitaries.

As for the town, it is massively built and wonderfully disposed, and of rare beauty, with large markets arranged in long adjacent rows so that you pass from a row of shops of one craft into that of another until you have gone through all the urban industries. These markets are all roofed with wood, so that their occupants enjoy an ample shade, and all hold the gaze from their beauty, and halt in wonder those who are hurrying by. Its qaysariyyah is as a walled-in garden in its freshness and beauty, flanked, as it is, by the venerated mosque. He who sits in it yearns for no other sight even were it paradisaical. Most of the shops are in wooden warehouses of excellent workmanship, a row being formed of one warehouse divided by wooden railings richly carved that all open on (separate) shops. The result is most beautiful. Each row is connected with one of the gates of the venerated mosque.

This is one of the finest and most beautiful of mosques. Its great court is surrounded by large and spacious porticoes that are full of doors, beautiful as those of a palace, that open on to the court. Their number is more than fifty, and they hold the gaze from their fine aspect. In the court there are two wells fed by springs. The south portico has no maqsurah, so that its amplitude is manifest and most pleasing to look upon. The art of ornamental carving had exhausted itself in its endeavours on the pulpit, for never in any city have I seen a pulpit like it or of such wondrous workmanship. The woodwork stretches from it to the mihrab, beautifully adorning all its sides in the same marvellous fashion. It rises up, like a great crown, over the mihrab, and then climbs until it reaches the heights of the roof. The upper part of the mosque is in the form of an arch, furnished with wooden merlons, superbly carved and all inlaid with ivory and ebony. This marquetry extends from the pulpit to the mihrab and to that part of the south wall which they adjoin without any interval appearing; and the eyes consider the most beautiful sight in the world. The splendour of this venerated mosque is greater than can be described.

At its west side stands a Hanafite college which resembles the mosque in beauty and perfection of work. Indeed in beauty they are like one mausoleum beside another. This school is one of the most ornamental we have seen, both in construction and in its rare workmanship. One of the most graceful things we saw was the south side, filled with chambers and upper rooms, whose windows touched each other, and having, along its length, a pergola covered with grape-bearing vines. Each window had its moiety of the grapes that hung before it, and each occupant could, by leaning forward, stretch forth his arm and pluck the fruit without pain or trouble.

Besides this college the city has four or five others, and a hospital. Its state of splendour is superb, and it is a city fit to be (the seat of) the Caliph. But its magnificence is all within, and it has nought without save a small river [al-Quwayq] that flows from north to south and passes through the suburb that surrounds the city; for it has a large suburb containing numerable khans. On this river there are mills contiguous with the town, and in the middle of the suburb are gardens that stretch along its length. But whatever may be its state, inside or out, Aleppo is one of the cities of the world that have no like, and that would take long to describe. We lodged in its suburb, in a khan called the Khan of Abu 'l-Shukr, where we stayed four days.

We departed on the morning of Thursday the 17th of Rabi', the 28th of June, and a little before the late afternoon, came to Qinnasrin where we rested awhile. We then moved to a village called Tell Tajir, where we passed the night of Friday the 18th. Qinnasrin is a town famous in time, but it has fallen to ruin, and has become as if it never had a yesterday, nothing enduring but its fading remains and its disappearing traces. But its villages are populated and well arranged, for they stand amongst a large tillage that stretches broad and long before the eyes. One of the towns of Andalusia that resembles it is Jaen, and so it is related that at the time of the conquest of Spain (by the Arabs), the people of Qinnasrin settled in Jaen feeling at home in its resemblance to their native town and addressing themselves to it, as was done in most of that land as is known.

We departed when a third of the night had passed, and rode until after sunrise when we halted to rest at a place called Baqidin in a large khan, strongly fortified, called the Khan of the Turcomans. The khans on this road are like fortresses in their unassailableness and their fortifications. Their doors are of iron, and they present the utmost strength. We left this place and passed the night at a place called Tamanni in a khan strong in the manner already described. We bent our way at dawn on Saturday the 19th of Rabi' al-Awwal, which was the last day of June. On the Friday we had seen, to the right of the road and two parasangs away, the lands of al-Ma'arrah. They are all dark with olive, fig, and pistachio trees, and all kinds of fruits; and their luxuriant gardens and well-ordered villages stretch for a distance of two days' journeying. It is one of the most fertile and productive regions in Islamic lands. Beyond them are the Mountains of Lebanon, of towering height and great length, extending along the sea coast. On their slopes are castles belonging to the heretical Isma'ilites, a sect which swerved from Islam and vested divinity in a man. Their prophet was a devil in man's disguise called Sinan, who deceived them with falsehoods and chimeras embellished for them to act upon. He bewitched them with these black arts, so that they took him as a god and worshipped him. They abased themselves before him, reaching such a state of obedience and subjection that did he order one of them to fall from the mountain top he would do so, and with alacrity that he might be pleased. God in His power allows to stray those whom He wills, and guides whom He wishes. Glory to Him to whom we turn for protection from seducement in religion, asking His protection from the straying of the heretics. There is no Lord but He, and only He should be worshipped. [See note 43. These heretics are the Assassins.]

Mount Lebanon is the frontier between Muslim lands and those of the Franks, for beyond it lie Antioch, Latakia, and others of their cities – may God restore them to the Muslims. On the slopes of this mountain is a fortress called Hisn al-Akrad [the fortress of the Kurds]. It belongs to the Franks, and from it they make raids on Hamah and Hims [Homs or Emessa] whence it can be seen. We arrived at the city of Hamah in the high forenoon of Saturday and lodged in one of the khans in its suburb.

An account of the city of Hamah [Epiphania]
May God Most High defend it

It is a city renowned through the lands, and long a companion of time. It is not of wide extent, nor is it finely built, its quarters are clustered together and its houses piled up, so that the eyes are not cheered in looking down upon it. It is as if she would veil and hide her glory, for you will find her beauty concealed until you have spied out her inmost parts and scrutinised her shades.

To the east of the city I saw a large river [the Orontes] that in its strong course spreads out and branches, and on its banks observed water-wheels that faced each other. Along these banks are disposed gardens that hang their branches over the water, the green leaves appearing like down on its cheeks as it flows through their shade, gliding through the line of their symmetry. On the bank that borders the suburb of the city is a place of ablution, furnished with many rooms and with water coming to all its parts from one of the water-wheels. In it the bather will find no trace of defilement. On the other bank, the one adjoining the lower city, is a small mosque whose eastern wall is pierced with windows from which one looks upon a view that soothes the soul, and holds the gaze enchanted. Beside the river's course, to the north of the city, is a fortress like that of Aleppo in construction, although inferior to it in strength and impregnability. Water comes to it from the river by means of conduits, and rises within it, so there is no fear of thirst, nor need to dread the designs of the enemy.

Hamah lies in a depression, wide and long like a deep trench, with high sides. One is like an o'ertopping mountain, with the upper city touching the slopes of that mountainous side. On the other side the fortress stands on a large, round, and isolated hill. Time undertook its construction, and, from its strength, safety from the enemy has been its lot. The lower city is below the fortress and is conterminous with the side on which the river flows. Both cities are small. The wall of the upper city reaches to the tip of its higher side on the mountain and surrounds it. The lower city has a wall that encompasses it on three sides; for the side contiguous with the river does not need a wall. Over the river is a bridge built of hard stone that extends from the lower city to its suburb. This is a large suburb with khans and houses, and it has shops where the traveller, until such time as he is free to enter the city, may buy the things he stands in need of.

The markets of the upper city are more crowded and handsome than those of the lower, and they include all the products of industry and trade. They are laid out with excellent order, and are surpassingly well organised and divided. Its cathedral mosque is larger than that of the lower city, and it has three colleges and a hospital on the river bank beside the small mosque. Outside this city is a large and extensive plain, mostly composed of vines, but having tilled and sown land, and the sight of it rejoices and enlarges the soul. The gardens are continuous along the banks of the river, which is called al-'Asi [The Rebellious], because it seems to flow from below upwards, its course being from south to north.[114] It passes to the south of Hims [Emessa] and near to it.

We stayed in Hamah until the evening of Saturday, when we left it and fared throughout the night. We crossed the river al-'Asi [Orontes] at midnight by a large bridge built of stone. On this river is the city of Rastan [Arethusa] which was destroyed by 'Umar ibn al-Khattab – may God hold him in His favour. Its ruins are impressive. The Rum of Constantinople say that it contains a great buried treasure, but God best knows of that.

We came to Hims at sunset on Sunday the 20th of Rabi' (al-Awwal), the 1st of July, and lodged outside it in a road-side khan.

An account of the city of Hims [Emessa]
May God Most High protect it

It is of broad extent and of oblong dimensions. Its spectacle is a refreshment to the eyes because of its grace and beauty. It stands in a plain of wide expanse, across which blows no gentle breeze, and whose limits the eye can scarcely reach; a vast, dusty plain without water or trees, or shade or fruit. The city complains of thirst, and brings its water from afar, for it comes by a canal from the river al-'Asi [Orontes] which is about a mile away. On the banks of the river is a strip of gardens, upon whose verdure the eye may dwell, marvelling at its luxuriance. The 'Asi rises in a cave on the slopes of a mountain that overtops the city a stage distant, and faces Ba'la-bakk [Baalbek or Heliopolis] – may God restore it (to the Muslims).

Hims is on the right of the road to Damascus. Its inhabitants are renowned for their courage and their relentless struggles against the enemies who surround them. In this the people of Aleppo come after them. The most praiseful things of this town are its fresh air and its happy breezes which are ethereal but yet make a stout body; for in salubrity it is the brother and partner of the air of Nejd. To the south of the city is a powerful and impregnable castle, stubborn and implacable, and because of its position, separate and detached from it. To its east is a cemetery containing the tomb of Khalid ibn al-Walid – may God hold him in His favour – who was God's drawn sword, and of his son 'Abd al-Rahman and of 'Ubayd Allah son of (the Caliph) 'Umar – may God hold them in His favour. The walls of this city are of the oldest antiquity and the greatest strength, being built of hard black stone compactly laid. Its iron gates are of towering height, awesome to look upon, and fearful in their beetling disdain. It is surrounded by soaring towers, well fortified. But inside you may conceive it to be a disordered wilderness, with shabby environs and patched-up buildings, the sun never shining on its horizons, and having no brightness in its markets, unthriving and without bond.

What think you of a town that is only a few miles from Hisn al-Akrad [the Fortress of the Kurds], the stronghold of the enemy where you can see their fires whose sparks burn you when they fly, and whence each day, should they wish, the enemy may raid you on horseback? We asked one of the sheiks of the town whether there was a hospital in it after the style of the cities of these parts. He first said that there was not, and then added: 'Hims is all a hospital, and proof enough of it is the evidence of its people.' The city has one college.

When you look upon it from a distance you will find in its plain, in its vista, and in the form of its design, some resemblance to the city of Ishbiliyyah [Siviglia] in Andalusia; an image which suddenly falls to your mind. Indeed by this name (of Hims) Siviglia was known of old. It was because of this reason that the Bedouin of Hims settled in Siviglia as is related. And although the resemblance is not complete, there is a suggestion of it from one side.

We tarried in Hims that Sunday and until the early noon of the Monday that followed, which was the 2nd of July, when we removed. Our march we continued until evening, when we alighted at a ruined village called al-Mash'ar, where we fed our beasts. At sunset we set forward and journeyed all night and on until the sun was high on the morning of Tuesday, the 22nd of the month (of Rabi' al-Awwal), when we halted at a large village called al-Qarah, which belongs to Christians who dwell there under treaty and in which there are no Muslims. It has a large khan, like a towering fortress, which has in its centre a big cistern filled with water that comes to it in underground conduits from a distant spring. It is always full. We rested in this khan until noon, when we left it for a village called al-Nabk, where there is running water and a broad tillage, and there we dismounted for the evening meal. After seizing a little slumber, we bent our way and journeyed throughout the night, coming in the morning to the Khan of the Sultan, which was built by Saladin, the Lord of Syria. It is the zenith of strength and handsomeness, with iron doors after their fashion in the building of khans on this road and in accordance with the attention with which they fortify them. Inside the khan is running water which flows through underground conduits to a fountain in the middle. This is like a cistern, with outlets through which the water pours into a small basin that runs around it and then plunges into a conduit below the ground. The road from Hims to Damascus is little populated, except at the three or four places where there are these khans.

Wednesday the 23rd of Rabi' we stayed resting in this khan and overtaking sleep until the beginning of noon, when we departed. We passed through Thaniyyat al-'Uqab [the Eagles' Pass], which overlooks the plain of Damascus and its Ghutah [the name for the surroundings of Damascus]. At this pass the road (from Damascus) divides in two, one branch being that on which we had come, and the other going eastward into the desert by al-Samawah to 'Iraq. This (latter) is the more direct, but it can only be entered upon in wintertime. From this pass, we descended the bed of a valley between the mountains and came to a plain, where we alighted at a place called al-Qusayr. It has a large khan, and the river (Orontes) flows before it. We left it in the morning, and passing between continuous gardens of beauty beyond description, came to Damascus in the forenoon of Thursday the 24th of Rabi' al-Awwal, the 5th of July. Praise be to God, Lord of the Universe.

The Month of Rabi' al-Akhir (580)

[12th of July–9th of August, 1184]

THE new moon rose on Wednesday the 11th [12th] of July when we were in Damascus, lodging in the Dar al-Hadith [House of Religious Tradition] west of the venerated cathedral mosque.

An account of the city of Damascus – may God Most High protect it. She is the paradise of the Orient, the place where dawned her gracious and radiant beauty, the seal of the lands of Islam where we have sought hospitality, and the bride of the cities we have observed. She is garnished with the flowers of sweet-scented herbs, and bedecked in the brocaded vestments of gardens. In the place of beauty she holds a sure position, and on her nuptial chair she is most richly adorned

Damascus was honoured when God Most High gave asylum there to the Messiah and his mother – may God bless and preserve them – 'on a hill having meadows and springs' [Koran XXIII, 50] with deep shade and delicious water. Its rivulets twist like serpents through every way, and the perfumed zephyrs of its flower gardens breathe life to the soul. To those who contemplate her she displays herself in her bridal dress calling to them: 'Come to the halting place of beauty, and take the midday repose.'

Its ground is sickened with the superfluity of water, so that it yearns even for a drought, and the hard stones almost cry out to you. 'Urge on (your horse) with your foot; here is a cool cleansing place and a drink' [Koran XXXVIII, 42]. The gardens encircle it like the halo round the moon and contain it as it were the calyx of a flower. To the east, its green Ghutah

stretches as far as the eye can see, and wherever you look on
its four sides its ripe fruits hold the gaze. By Allah, they spoke
truth who said: 'If Paradise is on the earth then Damascus
without a doubt is in it. If it is in the sky, then it vies with
it and shares its glory.'

A description of her venerated Cathedral Mosque[116]
May God Most High prosper it

For beauty, perfection of construction, marvellous and sumptuous embellishment and decoration, it is one of the most
celebrated mosques of the world. Its general fame in this regard
renders valueless a deep description. One of the strangest things
concerning it is that the spider never spins his web therein,
nor do swallows ever enter it or alight thereon. (The Caliph)
Al-Walid ibn 'Abd al-Malik [A.D. 705–15] – may God's mercy
rest upon his soul – undertook the construction of this mosque,
and sent to the king of the Rum at Constantinople ordering
him to send twelve thousand craftsmen from his country,
offering threats in case he should delay. But he obeyed sub-
missively, after an exchange of letters between them, even as
is recorded in the books of history. Walid commenced the construction and the most exhaustive attention was given to it.
All its walls were inlaid with gold mosaic called fusayfisa [Gr.,
ψρφος]; and mingled with it were all kinds of remarkable
colours in the pattern of plants throwing out branches and
arranged amongst the gold stones with the most wonderful of
exquisite work, that it is impossible to describe, and that dazzles
the eyes with its brightness and lustre. The amount spent on
it, according to Ibn al-Mu'alli 'l-'Asadi in a chapter that he
wrote in description of its building, was four hundred coffers,
each coffer containing twenty-eight thousand dinars, giving a
total of eleven million and two hundred thousand dinars [above
five and a half million sterling].

It was Walid who took that half of the church which
remained in the hands of the Christians and embraced it in

the mosque. For it had been in two parts, the eastern belonging to the Muslims and the western to the Christians. This was
because Abu 'Ubaydah ibn al-Jarrah – may God hold him in
His favour – had entered the town from the west and arrived
at the centre of the church after he had already made peace
with the Christians. But Khalid ibn al-Walid – may God hold
him in His favour – had entered by assault from the east side
of the town, and had arrived to take the eastern half of the
church. So the Muslims took possession of this eastern half and
made of it a mosque, while the half which came under the
treaty of capitulation, that is the western half, remained a church
in the hands of the Christians,[116] until (the Caliph) Walid asked
them for it in return for compensation. They refused, whereupon he seized it from them by force, and himself began its
destruction. The Christians asserted that whosoever should
destroy it would be stricken mad, but Walid replied at once,
'I shall be the first to go mad in the service of God,' and with
his own hands began to tear it down. The Muslims made speed
to complete its destruction. The Christians had sought the protection of 'Umar ibn 'Abd al-'Aziz – may God hold him in
His favour – at the time of his Caliphate [A.D. 634–44] and had
brought forward the pact which they had received from the
Companions (of the Prophet) – may God hold them in His
favour – allowing it to remain to them. He proposed to give
it back to them, but the Muslims were disquieted at this, so
he compensated the Christians with a great sum which satisfied them and which they accepted.

It is related that the first to lay his hand to the foundation
of the qiblah wall was the prophet Hud – upon whom be
(eternal) happiness – and so it is recounted by Ibn al-Mu'alli
in his chronicle. God best knows of this. There is no God
but He. We read in the book *Fada'il Dimashq* [The Merits of
Damascus] that Sufyan al-Thawri – may God hold him in His
favour – declared that one prayer in this mosque is worth thirty
thousand (elsewhere). And in the traditions of the Prophet –
may God bless and preserve him – (it is said) that Great and

Glorious God will continue to be worshipped in it for forty years after the destruction of the world.

A note on the dimensions and size of the Mosque, and the number of its doors and windows

Its measurement in length, from east to west, is two hundred paces, which is equivalent to three hundred cubits; and its measurement in width from south to north is one hundred and thirty-five paces, which is equivalent to two hundred cubits. Its area in the Maghribi marja' [50 square cubits] is twenty-four maraja', which is the same area as that of the mosque of God's Prophet – may God bless and preserve him – (in Medina), except that lengthways the latter extends from south to north. The aisles along the south side are three in number and stretch from east to west, and the breadth of each aisle is eighteen paces, a pace being a cubit and a half.

The aisles are raised on sixty-eight supports: fifty-four of these are pillars, eight are stucco pilasters interspersed between the pillars, two are marble-covered pilasters set with them into the wall that adjoins the court, and four are piers that are covered with marble in a most beautiful fashion, being studded with coloured marble mosaics arranged in rings, and illustrated with mihrabs and rare designs. These latter stand in the central aisle and uphold the Lead Dome together with the dome that is beside the mihrab. The width of each pier is sixteen spans, and the length twenty. Between each pier and the other, lengthwise, lie seventeen paces, and laterally thirteen. The perimeter of each pier is seventy-two spans.

A colonnade ten paces wide runs round the court on three sides, the east, the west, and the north. It has forty-seven supports, fourteen being stucco pilasters, and the remainder pillars. The breadth of the court, exclusive of the covered parts south and north, is one hundred cubits. The whole of the exterior of the mosque's roof is covered with lead slates.

The most impressive thing in this blessed mosque is the Lead

Dome in the centre of the building beside the mihrab. It rises high into the air with a vast circumference, and is supported by the huge erection which is the nave and which extends from the mihrab to the court. Over this nave are three cupolas, one adjoining the wall against the court, one beside the mihrab, and the other beneath (and within) the Lead Dome and between the other two. The Lead Dome chokes the air around it, and when you come before it you look upon an overwhelming sight, an awe-inspiring spectacle which men have likened to an eagle in flight, the Dome being its head, the nave its breast, and the half of the wall of the right aisle together with the half of that on the left, its wings. The width of this nave that leads towards the court, is thirty paces. Men call this part of the mosque al-Nasr [the Eagle] for this resemblance to it. From whatever direction you look upon Damascus, you will see the Dome towering in the air over all other eminences as though it were suspended in space. The blessed mosque is situated towards the north of the city.

The number of gilt and stained-glass windows is seventy-four. In the cupola beneath the Lead Dome are ten; in the cupola adjoining the mihrab and in the adjacent wall, fourteen; along the length of the wall right and left of the mihrab, forty-four; in the cupola adjoining the wall on the court, six; and on the outside of the wall towards the court, forty-seven.

The blessed mosque has three maqsurahs. One is the Maqsurah of the Companions – may God hold them in His favour – which was the first maqsurah ever built in Islam. It was erected by (the Caliph) Mu'awiyah ibn Abi Sufyan – may God hold them in His favour. Beside its mihrab, to the right of him who looks to the qiblah [direction of Mecca], is the Iron Gate by which Mu'awiyah used to enter the maqsurah and come to the mihrab. (Also) beside this mihrab, to the right, is the oratory of Abu 'l-Darda' [the Toothless] – may God hold him in His favour – and behind it was the palace of Mu'awiyah – may God hold him in His favour. To-day it is the great Coppersmiths' Row, and it runs along the south wall of the mosque. There is no more beautiful-looking row of shops than this, nor bigger both in length and breadth. Behind it and close by is the cavalry barrack of Mu'awiyah which to-day is tenanted, and in which the cloth-fullers have a place.

The length of the Maqsurah of the Companions is forty-four spans, and its breadth is half the length. Close by it, to the west and in the centre of the mosque, is the maqsurah that was built at the time that the part used as a church was added to the mosque, as we have already related. It has a pulpit for the khutbah and a mihrab for the prayers. The Maqsurah of the Companions had originally been in the middle of the Muslim part of the church and the wall (of separation) had been in the place where the mihrab was installed in the New Maqsurah. When all the church became a mosque, the Maqsurah of the Companions came to be on one side in the eastern part, and the other maqsurah was built in the middle where had stood the (separating) wall of the mosque before the incorporation (of the Christian half of the church). This New Maqsurah is bigger than that of the Companions. In the west side, by the wall, is another maqsurah belonging to the Hanafites, and here they assemble for study and prayer. Adjoining it is a zawiyah girdled by wooden lattices and forming a sort of small maqsurah. On the east side there is another zawiyah of the same pattern, (also) like a maqsurah. It was installed for praying in by one of the Turkish Emirs of the State, and is joined to the east wall.

In the blessed mosque there are many zawiyahs of this type, used by students for copying (the Koran) and for study and for withdrawal from the press of men; and they are amongst the advantages provided for students. In the wall abutting on the court and enclosed by the south colonnade there are, throughout its length, twenty doors surmounted by stuccoed arches, the whole with hollowed mouldings in the form of windows; and in their unbroken continuity the eyes perceive the most beautiful and graceful spectacle. As to the colonnades that enclose the court from (the other) three sides, they are supported by columns over which are arched embrasures sustained by smaller columns that go round the whole of the court. This court is one of the most beautiful and splendid of sights. Here the population congregate, for it is their place of care-dispelling and recreation, and here every evening you will see them, coming and going from east to west, from Bab Jairun to Bab al-Barid [the Gate of the Mail-post], and others you will see talking to their friends, and some reading. In this manner they will go on, coming and going, until the end of the last evening prayers, and then depart. Some do this in the morning, but the largest assembly is in the evening, and he who surveys it will conceive it to be the night of the 27th of Ramadan the venerated for what he will observe of the multitude of people congregating together. They do not cease from doing this every day. The idle ones among men call them 'ploughmen'.

The mosque has three minarets. One on the west side is like a lofty tower with large apartments and spacious chapels, all leading to large doors and lived in by strangers of pious mode of life. The topmost chamber was where Abu Hamid al-Ghazali – may God hold him in His favour – prayed in seclusion, and to-day it is inhabited by the jurisprudent and ascetic Abu 'Abdallah ibn Sa'id of the family of Qal'at Yahsub, (the name of their native town in Spain) from which they take their name. He is related to the Banu Sa'id who are illustrious for their services to the world. The second minaret is on the west[117] side after the same style, and the third is on the north at the Gate known as the Bab al-Natifiyin [the Gate of the Sweetmeat Sellers].

In the court there are three domes. The largest is on the west side and is supported by eight marble columns, is tall like a tower, ornamented with many coloured mosaics, and like a flower garden in beauty. It is capped by a lead cupola like a large round oven-top. It is said that it was the treasury for the riches of the mosque, which has a large income from its rents and the sale of crops, exceeding, as we were told, eight thousand Tyre dinars [£4,000] a year, which is fifteen thousand mu'mini dinars or thereabouts.[118] Another smaller dome stands in the middle of the court. It is hollow and octagonal and built of marble blocks joined in remarkable fashion, and supported by four small columns of marble. In its lower part it has a round iron grating, in the middle of which is a copper spout which throws out water that rises high and then bends down, so that it is like a silver wand. Men are avid to put their mouths under it to drink, finding it pleasant and good. They call it the Water Cage. The third dome is on the east side raised on eight columns in the manner of the large dome, but smaller.

On the north side of the court is a massive gateway giving on to a large mosque. In the middle of this is a court with a large round marble basin into which water continuously plays from a white, octagonal, marble bowl set in the middle of the basin on the top of a tubed column up which the water rises. This place is called al-Kallasah [the Lime-Kiln],[119] and there to-day prays our companion, the jurisprudent, ascetic, and traditionalist Abu Ja'far al-Fanaki of Cordova. In great numbers men come to follow him in prayers, to receive his benedictions, and to hear his fine voice.

On the east side of the court is a gateway which gives access to one of the most beautiful of mosques, of the most excellent planning and the most elegant construction. The Shi'ites declare that it is the shrine of 'Ali ibn Abi Talib – may God hold him in His favour – which is one of their more remarkable fabrications. A thing of note is that facing this mosque, on the west side of the court, in the corner where the end of the north colonnade meets the beginning of the west colonnade, is a place whose upper part is covered with a veil and in front of which hangs a curtain. Most men say that it is the place where dwelt 'A'ishah – may God hold her in His favour – and that there she related the traditions. The entry into Damascus of 'A'ishah – may God hold her in His favour – like that of 'Ali – may God hold him in His favour – (is disputable), although in the case of 'Ali – may God hold him in His favour – they have in excuse a legend in which they relate that he was seen in a dream praying there The Shi'ites accordingly built a mosque in this place. But as for the place connected with 'A'ishah – may God hold her in His favour – there is no authority attached to it. We but mention this because of its notoriety in the mosque.

The blessed cathedral mosque, both inside and out, is inlaid with gilded mosaics, is embellished with the most superb architectural ornament, and is miraculously executed. Twice it suffered fire and was destroyed and twice rebuilt. Most of its marble went, and its splendour changed. The parts best preserved to-day are the qiblah side and the three cupolas alongside it. Its mihrab is the most wonderful in Islam for its beauty and rare art, and the whole of it gleams with gold. Within it are small mihrabs adjoining its wall and surrounded by small columns, voluted like a bracelet as if done by a turner, than which nothing more beautiful could be seen, some of them being red as coral. The glory of the qiblah of this blessed mosque and the three cupolas adjoining it, irradiated by the gilded and coloured windows whose every colour is reflected on the qiblah wall as the rays of the sun pour through them, is such as to dazzle the eyes. It is all so grand as to beggar description, and words cannot express a part of what the mind can picture. May God by His favour long preserve it for the profession of the faith of Islam and of His word.

In the east corner of the New Maqsurah, inside the mihrab, is a large cupboard containing one of the Korans of (the Caliph) 'Uthman – may God hold him in His favour. It is the copy (of the definitive recension) which he sent to Syria.[120] This cupboard is opened daily after the prayers, and people seek God's blessing by touching and kissing the Book; and the press around it is very great.

The mosque has four portals. The south door is called Bab al-Ziyadah [Door of Increase], and opens on to a large and spacious vestibule, with immense pillars, where the bead-sellers and others have shops. It is an impressive sight. From it the way leads to the cavalry barrack, and to the left as you leave is the Coppersmiths' Row which has been the palace of (the Caliph) Mu'awiyah – may God hold him in His favour – bearing the name al-Khadra' [the Green (Palace)]. The east door is the biggest of them and is called Bab Jayrun. The west door is known as Bab al-Barid [Door of the Mail-post], and the north door is called Bab al-Natifiyyin [Door of the Sweetmeat-sellers]. At the east, west, and north doors there are also huge vestibules all having great doors that were entrances to the (Christian Church) and which remain in their former state. The most imposing to look upon is the vestibule connected with the Bab Jayrun. Going forth from this door, one comes to a long and broad portico at the front of which are five arched doorways with six tall columns. To the left is a large and splendid shrine where the head of Al-Husayn ibn 'Ali – may God hold them both in His favour – was kept until it was moved to Cairo. Beside it is a small mosque called after (the Caliph) 'Umar ibn Abd al-'Aziz – may God hold him in His favour. In the shrine itself is running water.

In front of the portico are steps whereby descent is made to the vestibule, which is like a vast ditch ending in a door of immense height, whose summit the gaze falls short of. Flanking the door are pillars that are like palm-trees in height and mountains in size. Along both sides of this vestibule are columns that sustain circular galleries ranged with perfumers' and other shops; and still above these are other long galleries with rooms and apartments for hire that look down on the vestibule. They are covered by a flat roof where the tenants of these rooms and apartments pass the night. In the centre of the vestibule is a large round marble basin over which is an (open-topped) dome sustained by marble columns and with a deep lead band around its upper part. It is exposed to the elements for no upper vault bends over it. In the centre of the marble basin is a brass spout which throws out water with much force, so that it rises into the air more than a man's height and no * * * *. Around this spout are other smaller ones that hurl high the water which issues from them like silver wands or like branches of that tree of water. The spectacle is more wonderful and delightful to see than can be described.

To the right of him who leaves by the Bab Jayrun, in the wall of the portico in front of him, is a gallery in the form of a large archway set with yellow arches in each of which opens a small door to the number of the hours of the day. An engineering contrivance has been arranged whereby at the end of each hour of the day two brass balls fall each from the mouths of two brazen falcons set above two brass cups, one below each bird. One falcon is beneath the first door, and the other beneath the last (and twelfth). The cups are perforated so that when the balls fall into them, they return through the inside of the wall to the gallery. You may see the two falcons stretching forth their necks with the balls (in their mouths) towards the cups, and throwing them down sharply with splendid precision, so that the imagination might conceive it to be a piece of sorcery. When the balls fall into the cups, a noise is heard from them, and the yellow door corresponding to that hour closes upon the instant. Thus it happens as each hour of the day comes to a close, until all the doors are shut and the (twelve) hours are ended, when the process returns again to the beginning. At night there is another arrangement. In the archway that bends over these (twelve small) arches are twelve perforated brass discs at each of which, inside the wall of the gallery, is set a plate of glass. All this is arranged behind the (hour) arches mentioned above. Behind each glass is a lamp which is turned by water on an hourly system, so that when an hour has passed the light from the lamp illumines the glass and throws its rays upon the disc in front of it, making it appear to the eyes as a red circlet. The lamp then changes on to another disc until the hours of the night are ended and all the discs have been reddened. Inside the gallery is a person trained in its management, who is charged with supervising the movement, reopening the doors and returning the balls to their

places. It is what men call the water-clock [manjanah = Gr.
μαγγανον].

In the vestibule at the west door are the greengrocers' and
perfumers' shops, and it has a row of fruit-shops. At its upper
end is a massive door to which one climbs by a flight of steps.
It has columns soaring into the sky. At the foot of the steps
are two round fountains, one to the right and the other to the
left, which both have five spouts pouring water into a long
marble trough. In the vestibule at the north door are zawiyahs
on platforms and enclosed by wooden balustrades, where
teachers instruct children. To the right of him who leaves,
inside the vestibule, is a convent built for the Sufis, with a
cistern in its middle. It is said that it had been the house of
'Umar ibn 'Abd al-'Aziz – may God hold him in His favour –
and there is a story to it which we shall presently relate. This
cistern has running water in it, and there are ablution places to
whose cubicles the water flows. Also to the right of him who
leaves the Bab al-Barid is a Shafi'ite college which has in its
centre a cistern of running water, and ablution places of the
style described.

In the court (of the Great Mosque) between the domes we
have mentioned, are two columns that stand a little apart from
each other. Their capitals are deep and of brass, fretted and
beautifully engraved, and on the middle night of (the month
of) Sha'ban they are hung with lamps so that they appear as
lighted chandeliers. The people of this town gather together
on this night more than they do on the night of the twenty-
seventh (and last day) of the venerated (fasting-month of)
Ramadan.

In this venerated mosque, after the morning prayers, there
daily assembles a great congregation for the reading of one of
the seven sections of the Koran. This is unfailing, and it is the
same after the evening prayers for the reading of what is called
the Kawthariyah [The Abundance of God], when they read
from the surah al-Kawthar [Koran CVIII] until the end of the
book. To this assembly of the Kawthar come all who do not

well know the Koran by heart; and all such participants receive a daily allowance, more than five hundred persons being able to live from it. This is one of the virtues of this venerated mosque, in which from morn till eve the Koran is read unceasingly. In it lectures are delivered to students, and the teachers receive a liberal stipend. The Malikites have a zawiyah for study in the west side, and there the students from the Maghrib, who receive a fixed allowance, assemble. The conveniences of this venerated mosque for strangers and students are indeed many and wide.

The strangest thing to tell of this mosque concerns the column which stands between the old and the new maqsurahs. It has a fixed *waqf* [endowment] for the benefit of those who lean against it in meditation or study. We saw beside it a jurisprudent from Seville, called al-Muradi. In the morning, at the end of the assembly for the reading of a seventh section of the Koran, each man leans against a column, while in front of him sits a boy who instructs him in the Koran. The boys also have a fixed allowance for their reciting, but those of their fathers who are affluent prohibit their sons from accepting it, although the remainder do so. This is one of the virtues of Islam.

For orphan boys, there is in the town a large school with a generous endowment from which the teachers draw enough to sustain themselves, and disembursements are made from it to support and clothe the children. This also is one of the uncommon things to tell of the virtues of these lands. The instruction of boys in the Koran in all these eastern lands consists only of making them commit to memory; writing they learn through the medium of poetry and other things. The Book of Great and Glorious God is thus kept undefiled from the markings and rubbings out of the boys' efforts. In most (of these) lands the Koran teacher and writing master are separate persons, and from his lesson in Koran reading the student is dismissed to his calligraphy. In this they follow an excellent method, which produces a good hand, for the instructor in that subject is occupied with no other, and while he puts all his efforts into the teaching of it, the pupil does the same in learning it; and finds it easy for he faithfully copies his preceptor.

Round this venerated mosque, one at each side, stand four reservoirs, and each is like a large house. They are enclosed by lavatories to all of which runs water from them. Lengthways through the court runs an oblong basin of stone with many spouts along its length pouring forth water. One of these reservoirs, the largest, is in the vestibule of the Bab al-Jayrun, and it has more than thirty lavatories. In addition to the long reservoir, along its wall, are two large round tanks that are so big as almost to take up the width of the building that contains this reservoir. They are at a distance from each other, and the circumference of both is about forty spans. Water spouts forth in both of them. The second reservoir is in the vestibule of the Bab al-Natifiyyin beside the school. The third is to the left of him who goes forth from the Bab al-Barid, and the fourth to the right of him who emerges from the Bab al-Ziyadah. These reservoirs are among the great advantages afforded to strangers and others.

Damascus is full of fountains, and it is rare for a street or market to be without one. The conveniences in the town are more than can be described. May God in His power preserve it within the lands of Islam.

A note on the venerated shrines of Damascus and its great antiquities

The first of these is the one that contains the head of Yahya ibn Zakariya' [John the Baptist, son of Zacharias] – upon whom be (eternal) peace. This is buried in the south aisle of the venerated mosque in front of the right-hand corner of the Maqsurah of the Companions – may God hold them in His favour. Over it is a wooden chest, that stands out from the column, and on which is a lamp that seems to be of hollow crystal, and like a large drinking vessel. It is not known whether it is the glass of 'Iraq or Tyre, or some other ware.

The birthplace of Abraham – may God bless him and our venerated Prophet – is on the slopes of Mount Qasiyun near a village called Barzah, which is one of the most beautiful of villages. This mountain enjoys an ancient renown for sanctity, for the prophets – the blessings of God upon them – climbed it in order to make their ascent (to heaven). It lies to the north of the city, and is a parasang distant. The blessed birthplace is a long and narrow cave, over which has been erected a large and lofty mosque, divided into many oratories in the form of commanding upper chambers, and surmounted by a tall minaret. From this cave Abraham – may God bless and preserve him – saw first the stars and then the moon and then the sun, as God Most High has described in His glorious and sublime Book [Koran VI, 77–9]. Behind the cave is the place where he would go to pray. All this is related by the *hafiz* [one who has committed the Koran to memory] and Syrian traditionalist, Abu 'l-Qasim ibn Hibat Allah ibn 'Asakir the Damascene in his history, *The Story of Damascus*, which consists of more than a hundred volumes. He also mentions that between Bab Faradis [the Gate of Paradise], which is one of the city's gates north of the blessed mosque and close to it, and Mount Qasiyun are the tombs of seventy thousand prophets. Others say that the seventy thousand were martyrs, and that the prophets buried there were seven hundred. God best knows.

Outside the city is the ancient cemetery where are buried the prophets and men of piety, and its blessedness is renowned. On the side that abuts on the gardens is a low piece of land adjoining the cemetery and said to be the burial place of seventy prophets – may God protect them and prevent any other men from being buried in that place and protect too the tombs around them. It is never without water, and there has formed a pool of it, all because of the wish of God Most High for purity.

Also on Mount Qasiyun, to the west, and a mile or more away from the blessed birthplace (of Abraham), is another cave called The Cave of the Blood, because above it on the mountain is the blood of Habil [Abel] who was killed by his brother

Qabil [Cain] son of Adam – God's blessings upon him. The
blood reaches from about halfway up the mountain to the
cave, and God has preserved red traces of it on stones on the
mountain. The scraping on them has changed them, but they
are like a way on the mountain, and end at the cave. On the
upper half of the mountain[121] there are no traces that resemble
them. It is said that they are the same colour as the stones of
the mountain, but they are only from the place where the
murderer killed his brother and dragged him up to the cave.
It is one of the miracles of God Most High, and His miracles
are beyond computation. We read in the chronicle of Ibn al-
Mu'alli al-Asadi that in this cave prayed Abraham, Moses,
Jesus, Lot, and Job – upon them and upon our noble Prophet
be the choicest blessings and peace. Over it stands a mosque
of perfect construction up to which one climbs by steps. It is
like a round, high tower and is enclosed by a wooden lattice.
Within are apartments and conveniences for residence, and it
is opened (to the public) every Thursday. In the cave (or
grotto), which is broad, there are lighted wax candles and
rush lamps.

At the top of the mountain is a grotto called the Grotto of
Adam – may God bless and preserve him – which has a building over it and is a blessed spot. Below, at the foot of the
mountain, is another called the Cave of Hunger where it is
said that seventy prophets died of hunger. They had possessed
one loaf that they continued to press on each other, passing it
from hand to hand until fate overtook them – God's blessings
upon them. Over this cave too has been built a mosque in
which we saw lamps that are lit (night and)[122] day. To all these
shrines are attached endowments consisting of gardens, arable
lands, and houses, to the extent that all that is in the country
is almost wholly comprised of these pious bequests. For every
mosque, school, or convent newly erected, the Sultan will
assign to it a religious endowment that will support it and
those that dwell therein as well as its officials. These also are
among the generous deeds that are enduring. Amongst the

princesses who possess the means, some order the building of a mosque, or an asylum for the poor, or a school, spending on them large sums, and assigning to them endowments from their properties; and there are Emirs who do the same. In this blessed path they reveal a readiness to do good that will be rewarded by Great and Glorious God.

At the edge of this mountain, where the western plain with its gardens comes to an end, is the blessed hill mentioned in the Book of God Most High [Koran XXIII, 50] as being the dwelling of the Messiah and his mother – God's blessings upon them both. It is one of the most remarkable sights in the world for beauty, elegance, height, and perfection of construction, for the embellished plaster-work, and for the glorious site. It is like a towering castle, and one climbs to it by steps. The blessed dwelling is a small grotto in its middle, like a small chamber, and beside it is another room said to be the oratory of al-Khidr [Elijah] – may God bless and preserve him. Men hasten forward to pray at these two blessed spots, especially in the blessed dwelling. This has an iron door that closes on it. The mosque encloses the hill, where there are circular paths and a fountain than which no more beautiful could be seen. Water is brought to it from the top of the hill, and pours into a conduit in the wall that is connected with a marble basin, into which the water falls. A better sight could not be seen. Behind the fountain are ablution places into every room of which runs water, which flows round the side adjoining the wall that has the conduit.

This blessed hill is the limit of the town's gardens, and the dividing place of its water which here forms seven tributaries, each one taking its own way. The largest of these is called Thawra, and it passes under the hill, through whose base it has cut through the hard stone until it has opened an underground course wide like a cave. Sometimes a boy or man, being a bold swimmer, will plunge from the hill-top into the river and then will be pushed along (by the current) under the water until he passes through the channel beneath the hill and comes out at its foot on the other side. It is indeed a great hazard.

From this hill one may look over all the western gardens of the town, and there is no prospect like it for beauty, comeliness, and spacious vista. And below it flow these seven rivers, passing through divers ways and entrancing the eyes with the beauty of their joinings and separations and their gush and flow. The nobility of the site of this hill, and all its beauties, are greater than a describer can comprehend even in the highest flights of his praise. Amongst the famous places of the world its state is eminent and commanding.

Close to the foot of the hill is a large village called al-Nayrab, which is hidden in the gardens, for only the tops of its buildings are seen. It has a cathedral mosque of unsurpassed beauty whose roof is wholly set with mosaics of many coloured marbles which the beholder would conceive to be a carpet of silk brocade. It has a fountain of exquisite beauty and a place of ablution with ten doors and water running in it and around it. Above this village, to the south, lies a considerable village, and one of the finest, called al-Mizzah, which has a large congregational mosque and a fountain of spring water. Al-Nayrab has a bath, as indeed have most of the villages of Damascus.

To the east of the city, and on the right of the road leading to the birthplace of Abraham – upon whom be (eternal) happiness – is a village called Bayt Lahiyah, by which they mean (the house of) idols. Its church is now a blessed mosque. There Azar [Terah] the father of Abraham carved the idols and gave them shape, but the Friend (of God) Abraham – the blessings of God upon him and our noble Prophet – came and broke them. To-day it is a mosque, and in it the people of the village congregate for their Friday prayers. Its ceiling is overlaid throughout with mosaics of coloured marble, with devices and rare designs making him who looks upon it conceive it to be a carpet of the most perfect embellishment. It is one of the venerated holy sites.

To this hill are attached many pious endowments, comprising

gardens, arable lands, and houses (whose revenues) are assigned to their various uses. Some are allotted under the heading of expenses for the subsistence of visitors who stay there, some for clothing under the heading of covering for the night, and some for food. There are allocations to cover all needs, including those of the resident guardian as imam and the muezzin charged with the service of the place, who draw a fixed monthly stipend from this source. It is a great institution. The present guardian is one of the marabits [marabouts or monks] from Massufi[23] and one of their chief men, called Abu 'l-Rabi' Sulayman ibn Ibrahim ibn Malik, who has standing with the Sultan and the leading personages of the realm. He receives five dinars monthly, exclusive of the revenue of the hill. Kindness is impressed on his features and stamped on him. He is an incumbent of one of those benefices that provide Maghrib strangers lonely in these lands with means of support, such as an imamate in a mosque, lodgement in a school with expenses paid, an appointment to a zawiyah in a cathedral mosque and gaining a livelihood there, assisting in the sectional reading of the seven parts of the Koran, or the curatorship of a blessed shrine and receiving a benefice from its endowments, and such-like ways of living of the same blessed pattern as would take long to describe; and the needy stranger, so long as he has come for righteous purposes, will be cared for without being given cause to blush. The other strangers who are not in this state and who have a trade or craft, are also found divers means of livelihood, such as being a watchman in a garden, supervisor of a bath, or keeper of the clothes of the bathers, manager of a mill, custodian of boys, conducting them to school and returning them to their homes, and many other occupations. In all this they trust only strangers from the Maghrib, for their fame for honesty is high and their repute has spread. The people of the town do not trust their own fellow citizens. This is one of the gifts of God Most High towards strangers. Praise and thanks to Him for what He has granted to His servants.

Should one of the holders of these benefices wish to have

T

audience of the Sultan, the ruler will receive him and treat him liberally, granting him a salary paid according to his ability and office. These virtues are part of the natural character of these people and their king, both of old and now. The discussion has led us successively to another question than that which we were on, but the excursus was needful. God is the guarantor of real help. There is no Lord but He.

To the west of the city is a large cemetery called The Tombs of the Martyrs. Here lie many Companions of the Prophet, followers of the Companions, and saintly imams – may God hold them in His favour. Amongst the famous tombs of the Companions – may God hold them in His favour – is the tomb of Abu 'l-Darda and that of his mother Umm al-Darda – may God hold them in His favour. Another blessed place bears the ancient epitaph, 'In this place are the tombs of many Companions – may God hold them in His favour – amongst whom are Fadalah ibn 'Ubayd and Sahl ibn al-Hanzaliyyah who were of those who swore allegiance to the Apostle of God [Muhammad] – may God bless and preserve him – beneath the tree [Koran XLVIII, 18], and the maternal Uncle of the Believers, Mu'awiyah ibn Abu Sufyan – may God hold him in His favour – whose convex grave is in that place.' I read in *Fada'il Dimishq* [*The Merits of Damascus*] that the Mother of the Believers Umm Habibah, sister of Mu'awiyah – may God hold them in His favour – is buried in Damascus. At this place there is also the tomb of Wathilah ibn al-Aqsa', one of the Choice Ones.[124]

In the place adjoining this blessed spot is an epitaph which says, 'This is the tomb of Aws ibn Aws al-Thaqafi', and in the neighbourhood of this place, close by, is the tomb of Bilal ibn Hamamah, muezzin of the Apostle of God – may God bless and preserve him – and at the top (of the headstone) of the blessed tomb is an epitaph with his name – may God hold him in His favour. Prayers said in this blessed place are answered, as has been experienced by many saints and godly men who have been blessed by their visit to these tombs. There are many

Companions and other saintly men whose names have been effaced and of whom the memory has passed away. Also in this place are the shrines of many of the family of the Prophet, men and women – may God hold them in His favour – whose edifices have been adorned by the Shi'ites and which have large pious endowments.

One of the most embellished of these shrines is that named after 'Ali ibn Abi Talib – may God hold him in His favour – over which has been built a splendid mosque of most elegant construction. Fast by it is a garden filled with oranges with water pouring into it from a spring fountain. All the mosque is draped with curtains, large and small, hanging from its sides. In the mihrab is a huge stone that had been split in half, but has been put together so that there is no sign at all of the cleavage. The Shi'ites say that it split for 'Ali – may God hold him in His favour – either from a blow from his sword or by a divine order done at his hands. It is not recorded that 'Ali – may God hold him in His favour – ever entered this town but, Oh my God, they declare that it was in a dream. Perhaps for them dreams have more validity than the events of consciousness. This stone gave occasion for the erection of this shrine.

In these lands, the Shi'ites have strange manifestations. They are more numerous than the Sunnis, and have filled the land with their doctrines. They have divers sects, among whom are the Rafidites who are blasphemers [see note 58], the Imamites, the Zaydites, who say that the Imamate is exclusive to the house of 'Ali, the Isma'ilites, and the Nusayrites who are infidels for they attribute divinity to 'Ali – may God hold him in His favour. God is above what they say. Then there are the Ghurabites who say that 'Ali – may God hold him in His favour – more resembled the Prophet – may God bless and preserve him – than a raven does a raven and trace this assertion to the Faithful Spirit [the angel Gabriel] – upon whom be (eternal) peace. But God is far above what they say. Other sects there are that it is impossible to enumerate. God has allowed them to go astray, and with them many of His creatures. We beg God to protect us from error in religion, and in Him we take refuge from the schisms of the heretics.

God placed these Rafidites under the power of a Sunni sect called al-Nubuwiyah,[125] who reverence the *futuwah* [manly qualities or mystical heroism of the Prophet] and all virile matters. Whoever is admitted to their order because of a virtue which they recognise in him, they invest with the trousers (of manliness) and admit him to their number. They do not find it fitting that any of them should cry for help when in distress. In this they follow a strange practice. If one of them swears by the manly qualities, he will hold his oath sacred. They kill these Rafidites wheresoever they find them, and in the matter of showing contempt or friendship, their ways are very strange.

One of the venerated shrines is that of Sa'd ibn 'Ubadah, chief of the Khazraj and a Companion of the Apostle of God – may God bless and preserve him. It is in a village called al-Manihah, east of the city and distant four miles. Over his tomb is a small mosque of fine architecture, and the tomb is in its centre with this inscription at the top: 'This is the tomb of Sa'd ibn 'Ubadah, chief of the Khazraj and a Companion of the Apostle of God – may God bless and preserve him.' Among the shrines of those of the family of the Prophet – may God hold them in His favour – are those of Umm Kulthum the daughter of 'Ali ibn Abi Talib – may God hold them both in His favour. She is called 'the little Zaynab', Umm Kulthum being a nickname given her by the Prophet – may God bless and preserve him – because she resembled his daughter Umm Kulthum – may God hold her in His favour. God best knows concerning this. Her venerated tomb is in a village south of Damascus and a parasang distant, called Rawiyah. Over it is a large mosque with houses outside it. It has pious endowments. The people of these parts know it as 'the tomb of the Lady Umm Kulthum'. We went to it and passed the night there, gaining blessings from seeing it. God will profit us in this.

In the cemetery west of the city are many tombs of the relatives of the Prophet – may God hold them in His favour.

Over two of them is a mosque, and it is said that they are the tombs of the sons of al-Hasan and al-Husayn – may God hold them in His favour. There is another mosque containing a tomb said to be that of Sukaynah, daughter of al-Husayn – may God hold them in His favour – but it may be another Sukaynah of the Prophet's family. Amongst the shrines there is also the tomb in the cathedral mosque of al-Nayrab, in a room in the eastern part. It is said to be that of Umm Maryam – may God hold her in His favour. In the village of Darayah is the tomb of Abu Muslim al-Khawlani – may God hold him in His favour – over which is a dome to indicate it. In this village there is also the tomb of Abu Sulayman al-Darani – may God hold them in His favour. This village lies to the west of Damascus and is distant from it four miles. Amongst the tombs that we did not see, but which were described to us, were those of Seth [Gen. v. 3; 1 Chron. i. 1; Luke iii. 38] and Noah [Gen. v. 29] on whom be (eternal) peace. These are in the Baqa', two days' journey from Damascus. Someone who measured the tombs told us that he found that of Seth to be forty arms' lengths [ba'] and Noah's thirty. Beside Noah's tomb is that of a daughter of his. There is an edifice over these tombs, attached to which are many pious bequests, and it has a stipendiary Intendant.

Also among the blessed shrines in the western cemetery, near the Bab al-Jabiyah, is that of Uways al-Qarani – may God hold him in His grace – and those of 'Umayyid Caliphs – God's mercy rest upon their souls. It is said that these are at the Bab al-Saghir [the Little Gate] near the cemetery, and that over them to-day is an inhabited house. The venerated shrines in this city are more than can be recorded, and we have but outlined those that are celebrated and known.

Another of the famous shrines in Damascus is the Masjid al-Aqdam [Mosque of the Footprints], two miles south of the city, on the side of the highway to the Hejaz, the coast, and Egypt. In this mosque is a small chamber containing a stone on which is inscribed: 'A certain pious man in his sleep saw

the Prophet – may God bless and preserve him – who said to
him, "Here is the tomb of the brother of Moses – may God
bless and preserve him." ' The Kathib al-Ahmar [the Hill of
Red Sand] is on this road and near this place, between Ghaliyah
and Ghuwayliyah, as it comes to us in the tradition; these are
two (separate) places. The state of blessedness of this mosque
is very great, and it is said that the light never fades from the
place. The tomb is reported to be where the inscribed stone
lies. It possesses many endowments. As for the footprints, they
are impressed on the stones along the road to the mosque and
you will find a footprint on each stone. The number of footprints is nine and it is said that they are those of Moses – upon
whom be (eternal) peace. God best knows the truth of this.
There is no God but He.

The Month of Jumada 'l-Ula (580)

[10th of August–8th of September, 1184]

May God let us know His favour

THE new moon rose on the night of Friday, the 10th of August according to the foreigners.

A collocation of notes on the conditions of the city (of Damascus)

May God cause it to prosper in Islam

This city has eight Gates: Bab Sharqi [East Gate] is to the east. It has a white minaret, and it is said that Jesus – upon whom be (eternal) peace – will descend there (when He comes in glory), according to the tradition which says that He will descend at the white minaret east of Damascus. Next to this Gate is Bab Tuma [(St.) Thomas' Gate] which also is to the east. Then comes Bab al-Salamah [Gate of Safety], then Bab al-Faradis [Gate of Paradise] which is to the north, then Bab al-Faraj [Gate of Consolation], then Bab al-Nasr [Gate of Victory] which is to the west, then Bab al-Jabiyah [Gate of the Water-Trough] also to the west, then Bab al-Saghir [the Little Gate] to the south-west.

The Great Mosque lies towards the northern side of the city. The city is surrounded by suburbs save on the east side, and a little of the adjacent south. The suburbs are large, but the city itself is not excessively big, and inclines to be long. Its streets are narrow and dark, and its houses are made of mud and reeds, arranged in three storeys one over the other, so that fire speedily takes hold of them. Damascus contains as many people as three cities, for it is the most populous in the world. Its beauty is all outside, not in.

Inside the city is a church held in great consideration by the

Rum. It is called Mary's Church, and after the temple in Jerusalem they have none more esteemed than this. It is an elegant structure with remarkable pictures that amaze the mind and hold the gaze, and its spectacle is wonderful indeed. It is in the hands of the Rum, who are never molested within it.

There are about twenty colleges in the city, and two hospitals, one old and the other new. The new is the finer and bigger, and receives a daily allowance of about fifteen dinars. It has a staff who maintain a register that records the names of the sick and the items they require of medicine, food, and other things. Early each morning the physicians come to the hospital to visit the sick and order the preparation of the proper medicines and food according as suits each person. The other hospital is managed in the same way, but more people use the new. The old one stands west of the venerated mosque. There is also a system of treatment for confined lunatics, and they are bound in chains. We take refuge in God from this trial and sore affliction. Some of them let fall some pleasant witticisms according to what we would hear. One of the drollest I heard was of a man who had taught the Koran. The son of a notable in the town, a youth bearing some traits of beauty called Nasr Allah [the Help of God], was in the habit of reading it to him, and the man became infatuated with this youth. His passion increased until his brain became disordered and he was taken to the hospital, and his sickness and disgrace became notorious. His father used to visit him and once said to him, 'Go, and get back to the part of the Koran you were at,' and the man, jesting with the boldness of the possessed, replied, 'What part of it have I retained? Nothing of the Koran remains in my memory save "when there comes the Help of Allah" ' [Koran CX, 1]. Men laughed at him and at what he said, and we beg of God that he and all Muslims might be forgiven. He remained in this state until he died; may God grant him His forbearance.

These hospitals are among the great glories of Islam, and so are the colleges. One of the finest-looking colleges in the world

is that of Nur al-Din – may God's mercy rest upon his soul –
and in it is his tomb – may God illumine it. It is a sumptuous
palace. Water pours into it through an aqueduct in the middle
of a great canal, filling an oblong fountain and finally falling
into a large cistern in the centre of the building. The eyes are
enchanted by the beauty of the sight, and all who see it renew
their supplications for Nur al-Din – may God's mercy rest upon
his soul.

As for the convents which they call *khawaniq*, they are many
and are used by the Sufis. They are elaborately decorated palaces,
with water flowing to all their parts forming the most agreeable sight one could see. The members of this order of Sufis
are the kings of these parts, for God has sufficed them of the
goods and favours of the world, and freed them from thoughts
of winning their livelihood that they might apply them to His
worship, lodging them in palaces that remind them of the
palaces of heaven. Those happy ones of them who have received
God's help, enjoy, by His grace, the favours of this world and
the next. They follow a noble path, and their social conduct
is admirable. The style of their ritual in worship is remarkable, and excellent is their custom of assembling to listen to
impassioned (dance) music. In these ecstasied and abstracted
states the world forsakes them, such is their rapture and transport. In a word, all their affairs are wonderful, and they hope
for a future life of bliss and felicity.

One of their most splendid convents is a place called al-Qasr,
an enormous structure rising alone into the skies. In its upper
storey are apartments than which I have never seen more beautiful for their lofty site. It is half a mile distant from the city,
and has an extensive garden connected with it. It had once
been the pleasure-lodge of a Turkish king. The story goes that
he was one night taking his ease in it when some Sufis passed
by, and some of the wine which the Turks were accustomed
to drink in the castle was poured out for them. They raised
the matter to Nur al-Din, who immediately demanded it from
its owner as a gift and then gave it in perpetual endowment

to the Sufis. Wonder lasted long at bounty like this, which remained an enduring monument to the merits of Nur al-Din – may God's mercy rest upon his soul.

The virtues of this pious man were great, and he was indeed among the ascetic kings. He died in the month of Shawwal in the year 569 [15th of May, 1174]. After him came Saladin to power, and the virtues of his way are known. His state among kings is great, and a lasting monument to his honour is his raising of the customs tax on the Hejaz road, giving a grant in compensation to its ruler. For long times this accursed tax had lasted before God annulled it at the hand of this just Sultan – may God prosper him. Amongst the merits of Nur al-Din – may God's mercy rest upon his soul – was his assigning to the strangers from the Maghrib who were employed in the Malikite zawiyah of the blessed cathedral mosque many pious endowments including two mills, seven gardens, arable lands, a bath, and two shops in the perfumers' market. I was told by one of the Maghrabis who supervised this, one Abu 'l-Hasan 'Ali ibn Sardal al-Jayyani [from Jaen in Spain], known as al-Aswad [the Black], that if properly controlled these endowments yield five hundred dinars a year. Nur al-Din – may God's mercy rest upon his soul – showed much favour towards these people. May God reward him for the good he did. For the readers of the Book of Great and Glorious God he prepared an endowed house in which they might live.

The conveniences for strangers in this city are beyond computation, more especially for those who commit to memory the Book of Great and Glorious God and those devoted to study, to whom the attitude of this town is most extraordinary. All these eastern cities are of this fashion, but this city is more populous and wealthy. Whoever of the young men of the Maghrib seeks prosperity, let him move to these lands and leave his country in the pursuit of knowledge and he will find many forms of help. The first of these is the release of the mind from the consideration of livelihood, and this is the greatest and most important. For when zeal is present the student will find the way clear to exert his utmost endeavour, and there will be no excuse for lagging behind, save in the case of those addicted to idleness and procrastination, and to them this exhortation is not addressed. We speak only to the zealous, who in their own land find that the search for the means of living comes between them and their aim of seeking knowledge. Well then the door of this East is open, so enter it in peace industrious youth and seize the chance of undistracted (study) and seclusion before a wife and children cling to you and you gnash your teeth in regret at the time you have lost. God is the Helper and the Guide. There is no God but He. I have given counsel to those I found listening, and called to those I heard answering. He who is directed by God is on the right path. Glorious is His power. Exalted is His majesty.

If in all these eastern lands there were nothing but the readiness of its people to show bounty to strangers and generosity to the poor, especially in the case of the inhabitants of the countryside (it would be enough). For you will find admirable their eagerness to show kindness to guests, which is enough to bring them honour. It sometimes comes to pass that one of them offers his piece (of bread) to a poor man, upon whom refusing he will cry and say, 'Had God seen in me any good, this needy man would have eaten my food.' In this they reveal a noble heart. One of their admirable traits is their respect for the pilgrim, despite the shortness of the distance to Mecca and the ease and facility with which they could make the journey. When the pilgrims return, they stroke them with their hands and press upon them to secure their benedictions.

One of the strangest things told us about this is that when the pilgrims from Damascus, together with those from the Maghrib who had joined them, returned to the city in this year of 580, a vast concourse of people, men and women, went forth to meet them, shaking the hands of the pilgrims and touching them, giving dinars to the poor amongst them that they met, and offering them food. One who witnessed it told me that many women met pilgrims and gave them bread which if they bit the women would snatch from their hands and hasten to eat it in order that they might be blessed in the pilgrims' having tasted it. In place of it they gave them dirhams, and did other remarkable things, the opposite of what we were accustomed to in the Maghrib. At the time of the reception of the pilgrims at Baghdad the same thing was done to us, or something near to it. But if we sought to relate this matter exhaustively we should depart from the purpose of our narrative, so we have given a glimpse that offers some indication, and that shall content us in the place of diffuseness.

Any stranger in these parts whom God has rendered fit for solitude may, if he wishes, attach himself to a farm and live there the pleasantest life with the most contented mind. Bread in plenty will be given to him by the people of the farm, and he may engage himself in the duties of an imam or in teaching, or what he will, and when he is wearied of the place, he may remove to another farm, or climb Mount Lebanon or Mount Judi and there find the saintly hermits who nothing seek but to please Great and Glorious God, and remain with them so long as he wishes, and then go where he wills. It is strange how the Christians round Mount Lebanon, when they see any Muslim hermits, bring them food and treat them kindly, saying that these men are dedicated to Great and Glorious God and that they should therefore share with them. This mountain is one of the most fertile in the world, having all kinds of fruits, running waters, and ample shade, and rarely is it without a hermit or an ascetic. And if the Christians treat the opponents of their religion in this fashion, what think you of the treatment that the Muslims give each other?

One of the astonishing things that is talked of is that though the fires of discord burn between the two parties, Muslim and Christian, two armies of them may meet and dispose themselves in battle array, and yet Muslim and Christian travellers will come and go between them without interference. In this connection we saw at this time, that is the month of Jumada 'l-Ula, the departure of Saladin with all the Muslims troops to lay siege to the fortress of Kerak, one of the greatest of the Christian strongholds lying astride the Hejaz road and hindering the overland passage of the Muslims. Between it and Jerusalem lies a day's journey or a little more. It occupies the choicest part of the land in Palestine, and has a very wide dominion with continuous settlements, it being said that the number of villages reaches four hundred. This Sultan invested it, and put it to sore straits, and long the siege lasted, but still the caravans passed successively from Egypt to Damascus, going through the lands of the Franks without impediment from them. In the same way the Muslims continuously journeyed from Damascus to Acre (through Frankish territory), and likewise not one of the Christian merchants was stopped or hindered (in Muslim territories).

The Christians impose a tax on the Muslims in their land which gives them full security; and likewise the Christian merchants pay a tax upon their goods in Muslim lands. Agreement exists between them, and there is equal treatment in all cases. The soldiers engage themselves in their war, while the people are at peace and the world goes to him who conquers. Such is the usage in war of the people of these lands; and in the dispute existing between the Muslim Emirs and their kings it is the same, the subjects and the merchants interfering not. Security never leaves them in any circumstance, neither in peace nor in war. The state of these countries in this regard is truly more astonishing than our story can fully convey. May God by His favour exalt the word of Islam.

Damascus has a castle where the Sultan lives. It stands apart, to the west of the city opposite the Bab al-Faraj [Gate of Consolation], one of the city's gates. The Sultan's cathedral mosque is there, and the Friday service is held in it. Fast by it and outside the city are two horse-courses, so green as to seem to be rolls of silk-brocade. They are enclosed by a wall, with the river running between them, and bordering them is a large wood of poplars forming a very pleasant sight. The Sultan goes

out to them to play sawalajan [a kind of polo],[126] and to race
his horses. There is no place like them for the eye to wander
in. Every evening the Sultan's sons visit them to practise archery,
race horses, and play sawalajan.

In this city and its suburbs there are about a hundred baths,
and it has around forty ablution houses in all of which flows
water. For the stranger, there is no better city in all these lands
than this, for its conveniences are manifold. What we have
mentioned of them is enough. May God by His favour keep
it Muslim territory.

The markets of Damascus are the finest in the world and
the best arranged, and the most handsomely constructed. Especially is this so with the qaysariyahs which are tall as caravanserais
and furnished with iron gates like those of a castle. Each qaysariyah is distinguished by its shape and iron gates. The city
has another market called Al-Suq al-Kabir [the Great Market],
which extends from Bab al-Jabiyah to Bab Sharqi [along the
street called Straight]. In it is a very small chamber used as an
oratory. To the south is a stone on which it is said that Abraham
– may God bless and preserve him – broke the idols which his
father had brought to sell.[127]

The tradition concerning the house named after (the Caliph)
'Umar ibn 'Abd al-'Aziz, which is to-day a Sufi convent and
stands in the vestibule of the Bab al-Natifiyyin and which we
have mentioned before, is a very curious one. It is that the
man who bought and furnished the house and gave it large
endowments, and who instructed that he should be buried in
it and that every Friday all the Koran should be read over his
tomb, assigning to those who attended every Friday a ritl[128]
of white bread, the equivalent of three Maghribi ritls, was a
foreigner called al-Sumaysati [the Samosatian],[129] Sumaysat
[Samosat] being a foreign city (on the Euphrates). This man
was distinguished for his piety and asceticism. The origin of
his prosperity and wealth, as was told to us, (was as follows).

One day, in the vestibule and beside the house of which we
are talking, he came upon a black man, sick and abandoned,

uncared for and neglected; and to merit a heavenly reward and win recompense from Great and Glorious God, he undertook the nursing, serving, and attention of this unfortunate. When his death drew nigh, the sick man called his nurse the Samosatian and said unto him, 'You were kind to me, acted as a servant to me, treated me gently in my sickness, and pitied my condition and my being a stranger in a strange land. I wish therefore to reward you in addition to the reward that Great and Glorious God, if He wills, will grant you on my behalf in the life to come. I was one of the pages of the Caliph al-Mu'tadid the 'Abbaside, and was known as Zimam al-Dar [The Intendant – a eunuch – in charge of the Palace] and possessed esteem and standing. But the Caliph became enangered with me over some affair and I was driven forth and came to this city where, by God's will, I was smitten with this affliction. Then God in His mercy caused you to come to my help. So now I appoint you my trustee and by virtue of that charge you, when I am dead and you have washed me, to go, with the blessings of God Most High, to Baghdad and there enquire with circumspection after the house of the Sahib al-Zimam, the Caliph's page. When you have been directed to it, then use all artifice to rent it, and in this I pray God to give you help. When you are in residence, go to' – and he named a place, giving him indications to it – 'and there dig a certain depth. Then pull away a board that you will find lying crossways under the earth and take what you will find buried beneath. Use this in your own interest, and in the good and charitable works that God may direct you to, and so, if He wills, bring blessings upon yourself.' The testator – God's mercy on his soul – then died and the trustee, with his testament, left for Baghdad. God helped him in the hiring of the house and he came to the place described where he removed a priceless treasure of vast quantity and enormous value. He hid it among bundles of merchandise that he had brought and (with it) left Baghdad for Damascus. There he bought this house named after 'Umar ibn 'Abd al-'Aziz – may God hold him in His favour – and converted it into a convent for the Sufis, embellishing it and buying farms and houses as endowments for it, placing it all to the benefit of the Sufis. He enjoined that he should be buried in it, and that the whole of the Koran should be read over his tomb every Friday, assigning to all those who attended it that which we have described. In this strangers and the poor find much benefit, and the convent is crammed with readers every Friday. When the reading of the Koran is over, they pray for him and then depart, each one being given a ritl of bread as described. To the deceased there remains a fine memorial and the good (that he has done). May God's mercy and approbation rest upon him.

The Kawthar, which we have mentioned, is also read in the cathedral mosque every day following the afternoon prayers, and is especially for those who have not yet learnt the Koran by heart. Its origin is also due to a rich man's dying and enjoining in his will that his tomb should be in the venerated cathedral mosque, and giving endowments that yielded one hundred and fifty dinars a year for the benefit of those who had not memorised the Koran. They read from the surah of the Kawthar to the end of the Koran, and every three months forty dinars is divided among them.[130]

It is related that a king of former times died and also left injunctions that his tomb be in the cathedral mosque, in the qiblah and in a place where it would not be seen. He assigned huge endowments that yielded annually a thousand and four hundred dinars, or even more, for the benefit of the daily readers of a seventh part of the Koran. The place of assembly for the readers of this blessed seventh portion, which happens after the morning prayers each day, is in the eastern part of the Maqsurah of the Companions – may God be pleased with them – and it is declared that in this place is the tomb of the king. The reading of the seventh portion must not be done beyond that area which is contiguous with the south wall towards the east wall. Great and Glorious God will not fail to reward those who do good.

All these noble bequests have remained unchanged with the

passing of days. May God profit the benefactors. Let these requests suffice (to illustrate) a land where men are guided to such acts to gain the approbation of Great and Glorious God. For the poor who are accustomed to sit on the east side of the venerated cathedral mosque, and who have no place of retreat, there is an endowment founded by some of those who seek a heavenly reward and have been guided by God in their bequests. But it would take long to recount the charitable and benevolent acts by which God has protected the stranger in these parts.

It is a custom of the people of Damascus, and of these other virtuous lands, a custom which we hope for them is acceptable to Great and Glorious God, to make it their purpose every year on the day of 'Arafah to stand in their cathedral mosque following the afternoon prayers, their imam with them and their heads uncovered, praying to their Lord and seeking the blessings of the hour in which the deputation to Great and Glorious God and the pilgrims to His Sacred House stand upon (Mount) 'Arafat. They stand praying and beseeching increasingly to Great and Glorious God, entreating His favour for the sake of the pilgrims to His Sacred House, and so continue until the set of the sun's disc. They compute the hour of the return of the pilgrims from 'Arafat, and then themselves disjoin, weeping at their being kept from that sublime standing ground on 'Arafat, and beseeching Great and Glorious God to bring them to it, and not to let them lack the blessings of His acceptance of their (intended) act.

One of the grandest and most remarkable sights in the world, among its imposing edifices of miraculous art and perfection, and admitted to be beyond description even in the most eloquent of tongues, is (achieved by) climbing to the top of the Lead Dome that we have already mentioned in this narrative as rising up in the centre of the venerated cathedral mosque, and entering into its interior, and then turning a reflective gaze on its superb structure, with the cupola poised within it like a hollow sphere inside another larger than itself. We climbed

U

to it with a company of our Maghrib companions in the forenoon of Monday the 18th of Jumada 'l-Ula (first ascending)
a stairway in the western colonnade of the court where had
anciently been a minaret. We walked along the roof of the
venerated mosque, which is all lead slabs arranged in the manner
we have described, each slab being four spans long and three
wide, although it sometimes happened that some were smaller
or bigger, until we came to the dome. This we climbed by
means of a ladder fixed to it, and we were nearly carried away
by giddiness. We therefore crawled round the platform that
encircles it. It is of lead, and is six spans wide. We could not
stand on it because of the fearfulness of our position, and made
speed to enter the inside of the dome through one of the grated
windows that open in the lead-work. Then we observed a spectacle that sends the senses reeling, and that the mind cannot
fully comprehend in the grandeur of its attributes. We walked
around a platform of large wooden planks encircling the small
inner cupola that stands inside the Lead Dome in the fashion
we have described. Here are windows through which one may
look down at the mosque and those within it; and we saw
men as if they were boys in school. This cupola is round like
a sphere, and its exterior is of wood strengthened by stout
wooden ribs bound by iron bands, each rib curving over the
cupola and all meeting at a central wooden disc at the summit.

Inside this cupola as seen from the interior of the venerated
mosque, are wooden panels fitted together and joined in wondrous fashion. They are all gilded in the most beautiful form
of that work, adorned with many colours, exquisitely carved,
dazzling the eyes with the refulgence of the gold. Minds are
baffled at the manner of their assembly and adjustment, so
extreme is the height. One of these wooden panels we saw
lying inside the cupola and it was not less than six spans in
length and four in width, but in their place above they seem
to the eye as if the circumference of each of them were a span
or two spans at most, so great is the height.

The Lead Dome enfolds this cupola. It also is strengthened

by huge ribs of solid wood, bound in the middle by iron bands. These ribs number forty-eight, and the distance between each is four spans. They bend round in remarkable fashion and their ends meet at a central wooden disc at the summit. The circumference of this Leaden Dome is eighty paces, which is two hundred and sixty [forty] spans. Its state is greater than description can attain, and what we have described is but a glimpse from which the remainder can be conceived.

Under the long nave called the 'eagle', which is below these two domes, is a huge canopy which acts as roof to the maqsurah, and between the one and the other is an ornamental stucco ceiling. This is set with countless wooden beams, entwining and arching over each other and so arranged as to present a stupefying spectacle. Engaged in the whole length of the wall are the pilasters supporting the two domes, and in that wall are stones each of which weigh many *qintars* [1 qintar = 100 ritls] and such that an elephant could not move them, much less any other animal. The greatest marvel is how they came to be raised to such a prodigious height, and how human ability achieved it. Glory to God who inspired His servants to such glorious works, enabling them to produce what is not in human nature to do, and revealing His miracles through the hands of those of His creatures whom He wishes. There is no God but He.

The two domes rest on a circular base composed of massive stones. On this stand short, solid pilasters formed of big, hard stones. A window opens between each pilaster, and the windows run all round the circle. The two domes appear to the eye to be one, but we have alluded to their being two, one being inside the other, the uppermost being the Lead Dome. Amongst the wonders that we noticed in these two domes was that we saw in them no spider spinning its web, although for a long time there had been no inspection by anyone, nor any persons engaged to clear their surfaces. In similar places spiders are present in great numbers. We had previously been assured that in the venerated mosque no spider spun its web, nor would the bird called khuttaf [swallow] enter it. We have mentioned this before in our narrative.

We left and went down, consumed with wonder at this stupendous spectacle, so miraculously constructed and beyond description's reach. Men say that on the face of the world there is no more wonderful structure to look upon, none loftier or more marvellously built, than this dome, save what is reported of the Dome (of the Rock) in Jerusalem, which is said to be still higher in the skies than this. In a word, the spectacle and consideration of the superb aspect of its form, and its vast proportions when observing it both by climbing and by entering it, is more astounding than what is told of the wonders of the world. Power belongs to the One God, the Conqueror, there is no God but He.

The people of Damascus and other peoples of these lands observe a curious ceremonial in their funerals. They walk in front of the bier with reciters who chant the Koran with moving voices and tearful notes that tear the heart for grief and compassion. They lift up their voices which strike the ears and move the eyes to tears. They pray over the bier in the cathedral mosque, in front of the maqsurah, and every bier must go to this mosque. When they come to the door they cease their intoning and enter to the place where prayers will be said over the bier. But if the departed be one of the imams of the mosque or one of its keepers, then a distinction is made for him, and they come into the place of prayer still chanting the Koran.

They sometimes assemble for the ceremony of condolence in the west cloister of the court, beside the Bab al-Barid, and recite the prayers one by one and then sit down. In front of them are copies of the Koran which they read while the managers of the obsequies raise their voices to announce the venerated and leading men of the city as they arrive at the ceremony, vesting them with imposing appellations of distinction, which they confer on all alike, and all referring to din [religion]. You will hear whatever you wish: Sadr al-Din,

Shams al-Din, Badr al-Din, Najm al-Din, Zayn al-Din, Baha
'l-Din, Jamal al-Din, Majd al-Din, Fakhr al-Din, Sharaf al-Din,
Mu'in al-Din, Muhyi 'l-Din, Zaki 'l-Din, Najib al-Din, without a limit to similar false titles. Particularly in the case of
jurisprudents you may have such designations as Sayyid al-
'Ulama, Jamal al-'Immah, Hujjat al-Islam, Fakhr al-Shari'ah,
Sharaf al-Millah; Mufti 'l-Fariqayn and such-like pretentious
epithets without end. Each will then repair to his shari'ah,[131]
haughtily sweeping his train, with aloofness and disdain. When
they have finished, and have ceased reciting the Koran and that
part of the ceremony is ended, their preachers rise one by one
according to their degree and exhort, invoke pious memories,
warn of the deceits of the world, put men upon their guard,
recite some fitting lines of poetry, and then end with words of
consolation for the bereaved, and prayers for him and the
deceased. The speaker will then sit and be followed by another
in the same style until they have all ended and gone their ways.
Ofttimes there is such an assembly that is profitable to whoever attends it.

The people of these parts address each other as Mulai [Lord]
and Sayyid [Sir], and use the expressions 'Your servant' and
'Your Excellency'. When one meets another, instead of giving
the ordinary greeting he says respectfully, 'Here is your slave,'
or 'Here is your servant at your service.' They make presents
of honorifics to each other. Gravity with them is a fabulous
affair.

Their style of salutation is either a deep bow or a prostration, and you will see their necks in play, lifting and lowering,
stretching and contracting. Sometimes they will go on like this
for a long time, one going down as the other rises, their turbans tumbling between them. This style of greeting, inclining
as in prayer, we have observed in female slaves, or when hand-
maids make some request. How strange are these men. How
can they assume the titles of anklet-wearers [women]. They
apply themselves with assiduity to things that proud souls disdain, and practise abuses of the capitation, which Muslim law

forbids. In this direction they have many vain customs. What odd people! If they treat each other in this way, reaching such an extravagance of epithets in their common intercourse, how do they address their Sultans and comport themselves with such? The tail is equal to the head with them, and they do not distinguish between the governor and the governed. Glory to God who created men of all kinds. He has no partner. There is no God but He.

A singular habit in all these lands is their walking, great and small, with their hands behind their backs, one hand holding the other. They make their deep inclinations of greeting in this fashion, which has an air of obedience, in token of humbleness and modesty, as if they had been treated with violence, and had had their hands bound behind their backs. They deem this posture to set them apart as persons of distinction and honour, as well as giving liveliness to their limbs and relief from fatigue. The venerable among them is he who draws his train a span along the ground, or puts his hands behind his back the one over the other. They have adopted this manner of walking as obligatory, and every one of them has embellished himself with this bad practice and seen it to be good. I beg the pardon of God for them.

But in the etiquette of shaking hands they have usages which renew their security (with God) and invite God's pardon (for their other faults), according to the preaching of the tradition transmitted from the Prophet of God – may God bless and preserve him – on the matter of hand-shaking. They employ them after the prayers, more especially after the morning and afternoon prayers. When the imam salutes (the congregation) and has ended the prayers, the people go to him and shake his hand and then advance on each other, shaking hands with those to right and left of them. They then leave this pardon-bringing service with the grace of Great and Glorious God. We have already mentioned in this narrative how they employ this habit of shaking each other's hands when they observe the new moon, and how they pray for each other the blessings and happiness of the new month, and that they might be accompanied by felicity and well-being during that month and those that will follow. That also is a beneficial practice, for which God will advantage them because of the prayers for each other, the renewal of affection, and the shaking of each other's hands by the Faithful. (All this is from) the mercy and favour of God Most High.

We have also spoken, in another place in this journal, of the righteous path of the Sultan of these lands, Salah al-Din [Saladin] Abu 'l-Muzaffar Yusuf ibn Ayyub, of his memorable deeds in affairs of the world and of religion, and of his zeal in waging holy war against the enemies of God. Because north of this land there is none belonging to Islam, most of Syria being in the hands of the Franks, God in His mercy gave to the Muslims here this Sultan, who never retires to a place of rest, nor long abides at ease, nor ceases to make his saddle his council-chamber. We have been staying in this city for two months, yet when we alighted at it he had already gone forth to the siege of the fortress of Kerak, of which also we have made mention, and he still invests it – may God Most High assist him to conquer it.

We listened to one of the jurisprudents and leading men of Damascus, who acknowledged the righteousness of this Sultan and who attended his audiences. He spoke of him in the presence of a gathering of learned men and jurisprudents, describing three acts of virtue in three stories, and we have seen fit to record them here. One concerns the magnanimity of his disposition. He had just forgiven the crime of someone who had offended against him and said, 'For my part, I would rather miss the mark in being merciful than strike home in (deserved) punishment.' Here is the forbearance that was the aim of Ahnaf. Again at a symposium of poetry held in his presence, where the bounty and excellencies of ancient kings were talked of, he declared: 'By Allah, did I give the world to him who came to me in hope, I would not deem it too much; and if I emptied to him all that is in my treasury, it would not console him for the hot blush on his cheek as he asked of me.' Here indeed was the way of al-Rashid or of Ja'far in generosity. In another instance, a favourite and much-liked slave appealed to him against a cameleer, complaining that the man had sold him an unsound camel, or had restored to him a camel with an unsoundness that had not been there before. The Sultan answered, 'What can I do for you? The Muslims have a qadi who decides between them; over both the chief men and the people the justice of our laws extends, and its injunctions and its interdicts we must alike obey. I am but the servant of the law and its Shihnah', which is the word for chief of police, 'and justice will decide for you or against you.' In this settlement we see the manner that was 'Umar's. These stories are enough to shed glory on the Sultan. May God, by His favour, grant that Islam and the Muslims may long enjoy his preservation to them.

The Month of Jumada 'l-Akhirah (580)

[9th of September–7th of October, 1184]

May God grant us His blessings

THE new moon rose on the night of Sunday the 9th of
September according to the foreigners, while we were in
Damascus – may God protect it – on the point of departure to
Acre – may God restore it to us – to seek a passage by sea with
some Christian merchants in the ships they had got ready for
the autumn sailing which they called 'al-salibiyah'.[132] May God
let us know His avouched grace, giving us of His care and
protection, in His power and strength. Glory be to God, the
All-Merciful, the Benefactor, the Giver of wealth and benefits.
There is no God but He.

We left Damascus on the evening of Thursday the 5th of
the said month, which was the 13th of September, in a large
caravan of merchants travelling with their merchandise to Acre.
One of the strangest things in the world is that Muslim caravans go forth to Frankish lands, while Frankish captives enter
Muslim lands. In this regard, as we were leaving, we observed
a singular event. When Saladin was laying siege to the fortress
of Kerak, already mentioned in this diary [p. 311], the Franks,
having been summoned from all sides, had marched upon him
in great strength and sought to arrive before he did at the place
of water, and also to intercept his supplies from Muslim
country. But the Sultan, leaving the fortress, led his whole
force against them and arrived before them at the watering
place. The Franks shunned his path, and, following a rough
road on which most of their animals perished, directed themselves towards the fortress of Kerak. The Sultan had closed
to them all other roads leading to their own country, and
there was left to them no other but the road by the fortress
through the desert. Thus, because of the circuitous route that

must be followed, their supplies were distant from them. Seizing the opportunity, and taking advantage of the opening that fell to him, Saladin schemed an incursion on their country. Unexpectedly he arrived at the city of Nablus and attacked it with his soldiers and took it. He took prisoner all within it, and seized with it fortified places and villages. The hands of the Muslims were filled with prisoners beyond number, both Franks and a sect of the Jews known as al-Samarah [Samaritans] descended from al-Samiri [Koran XX, 87]. Large numbers were put to a speedy death, and the Muslims acquired plunder it is not possible to estimate, with all the goods, provisions, baggage, furnitures, cattle and horses, and such-like. The victorious Sultan allowed the Muslims to take what they could, and conceded it to them. Each hand held what it gained, and became rich and prosperous. The army erased all traces of the Frankish lands through which it passed, returning victorious, with booty and in safety. Many Muslim prisoners they had also freed. It was a raid the like of which had not been heard of in the land.[133] We left Damascus when the foremost Muslims had already come, each bearing the booty he had laid his hands on. The prisoners tallied thousands, and their number we could not ascertain. The Sultan reached Damascus the first Saturday after our departure, and we learnt that he will rest his soldiers a little and then return to the fortress of Kerak. May God assist him, and in His power and glory, cause it to fall to him. We ourselves went forth to Frankish lands at a time when Frankish prisoners were entering Muslim lands. Let this be evidence enough to you of the temperateness of the policy of Saladin.

We passed the night of Friday in Darayah, a village belonging to Damascus, and a parasang and a half from it. We removed from there at daybreak on Friday to a village called Bait Jann, which lies amongst the hills. Thence we left, on the morning of Saturday, for the city of Banyas. Halfway on the road, we came upon an oak-tree of great proportions and with wide-spreading branches. We learnt that it is called 'The Tree of Measure', and when we enquired concerning it, we were told that it was the boundary on this road between security and danger, by reason of some Frankish brigands who prowl and rob thereon. He whom they seize on the Muslim side, be it by the length of the arms or a span, they capture; but he whom they seize on the Frankish side at a like distance, they release. This is a pact they faithfully observe and is one of the most pleasing and singular conventions of the Franks.

A note on the city of Banyas [Belinas]

God Most High defend it

This city is on the frontier of the Muslim territories. It is small, but has a fortress below the walls of which winds a river that flows out from one of the gates of the city. A canal leading from it turns the mills. The city had been in the hands of the Franks, but Nur al-Din – may God's mercy rest upon his soul – recovered it [in 1165]. It has a wide tillage in a contiguous vale. It is commanded by a fortress of the Franks called Hunin* three parasangs distant from Banyas. The cultivation of the vale is divided between the Franks and the Muslims, and in it there is a boundary known as 'The Boundary of Dividing'. They apportion the crops equally, and their animals are mingled together, yet no wrong takes place between them because of it.

We departed from Banyas on the evening of the same Saturday for a village called al-Masiyah, near to the Frankish fort we have mentioned. We passed the night in it, and removed on Sunday at daybreak. Between Hunin and Tibnin we passed a valley thick with trees, most of which were bay. The valley was of great depth, like a deep ravine whose sides come together and whose heights reach to the skies. It is known as al-Astil. Should soldiers penetrate it, they would be lost, there being no refuge or escape for them from the hand of those that lay in wait for them. Its descent and ascent, on both sides, is toilsome. Marvelling at the place, we passed it, travelling close beside, and came to one of the biggest fortresses of the Franks,

* Chastian Neuf.

called Tibnin. At this place customs dues are levied on the caravans. It belongs to the sow known as Queen[134] who is the mother of the pig who is the Lord of Acre – may God destroy it We camped at the foot of this fortress. The fullest tax was not exacted from us, the payment being a Tyrian dinar and a qirat [one-twentieth part] of a dinar [about eleven shillings] for each head. No toll was laid upon the merchants, since they were bound for the place of the accursed King [Acre], where the tithe is gathered.[135] The tax there is a qirat in every dinar (worth of merchandise), the dinar having twenty-four qirat.[136] The greater part of those taxed were Maghribis, those from all other Muslim lands being unmolested. This was because some earlier Maghribis had annoyed the Franks. A gallant company of them had attacked one of their strongholds with Nur al-Din – may God have mercy upon him – and by its taking they had become manifestly rich and famous. The Franks punished them by this tax, and their chiefs enforced it. Every Maghribi therefore paid this dinar for his hostility to their country. The Franks declared: 'These Maghribis came and went in our country and we treated them well and took nothing from them. But when they interfered in the war, joining with their brother Muslims against us, we were compelled to place this tax upon them.' In the payment of this tax, the Maghribis are pleasingly reminded of their vexing of the enemy, and thus the payment of it is lightened and its harshness made tolerable.

We moved from Tibnin – may God destroy it – at daybreak on Monday. Our way lay through continuous farms and ordered settlements, whose inhabitants were all Muslims, living comfortably with the Franks. God protect us from such temptation. They surrender half their crops to the Franks at harvest time, and pay as well a poll-tax of one dinar and five qirat for each person. Other than that, they are not interfered with, save for a light tax on the fruits of trees. Their houses and all their effects are left to their full possession. All the coastal cities occupied by the Franks are managed in this fashion, their rural districts, the villages and farms, belonging to the Muslims. But

their hearts have been seduced, for they observe how unlike
them in ease and comfort are their brethren in the Muslim
regions under their (Muslim) governors. This is one of the misfortunes afflicting the Muslims. The Muslim community bewails
the injustice of a landlord of its own faith, and applauds the
conduct of its opponent and enemy, the Frankish landlord, and
is accustomed to justice from him.[137] He who laments this state
must turn to God. There is comfort and consolation enough
for us in the exalted Book: 'It is nothing but a trial; Thou
makest to err with it whom Thou pleasest, and guidest whom
Thou pleasest' [Koran VII, 155].

On the same Monday, we alighted at a farmstead a parasang
distant from Acre. Its headman is a Muslim, appointed by the
Franks to oversee the Muslim workers in it. He gave generous
hospitality to all members of the caravan, assembling them,
great and small, in a large room in his house, and giving them
a variety of foods and treating all with liberality. We were
amongst those who attended this party, and passed the night
there. On the morning of Tuesday the 10th of the month,
which was the 18th of September, we came to the city of Acre
– may God destroy it. We were taken to the custom-house,
which is a khan prepared to accommodate the caravan. Before
the door are stone benches, spread with carpets, where are the
Christian clerks of the Customs with their ebony ink-stands
ornamented with gold. They write Arabic, which they also
speak. Their chief is the Sahib al-Diwan [Chief of the Customs],
who holds the contract to farm the customs. He is known as
al-Sahib [the Director or Master], a title bestowed on him by
reason of his office, and which they apply to all respected persons, save the soldiery, who hold office with them. All the dues
collected go to the contractor for the customs, who pays a vast
sum (to the Government). The merchants deposited their baggage there and lodged in the upper storey. The baggage of
any who had no merchandise was also examined in case it contained concealed (and dutiable) merchandise, after which the
owner was permitted to go his way and seek lodging where

he would. All this was done with civility and respect, and without harshness and unfairness. We lodged beside the sea in a house which we rented from a Christian woman, and prayed God Most High to save us from all dangers and help us to security.

A note on the city of Acre

May God exterminate (the Christians in) it and restore it (to the Muslims)

Acre is the capital of the Frankish cities in Syria, the unloading place of 'ships reared aloft in the seas like mountains' [Koran LV, 24], and a port of call for all ships. In its greatness it resembles Constantinople. It is the focus of ships and caravans, and the meeting-place of Muslim and Christian merchants from all regions. Its roads and streets are choked by the press of men, so that it is hard to put foot to ground. Unbelief and unpiousness there burn fiercely, and pigs [Christians] and crosses abound. It stinks and is filthy, being full of refuse and excrement. The Franks ravished it from Muslim hands in the first [last] decade of the sixth [fifth] century,[138] and the eyes of Islam were swollen with weeping for it; it was one of its griefs. Mosques became churches and minarets bell-towers, but God kept undefiled one part of the principal mosque, which remained in the hands of the Muslims as a small mosque where strangers could congregate to offer the obligatory prayers. Near its mihrab is the tomb of the prophet Salih – God bless and preserve him and all the prophets. God protected this part (of the mosque) from desecration by the unbelievers for the benign influence of this holy tomb.

To the east of the town is the spring called 'Ayn al-Baqar [the Spring of the Cattle], from which God brought forth the cattle for Adam[139] – may God bless and preserve him. The descent to this spring is by a deep stairway. Over it is a mosque of which there remains in its former state only the mihrab, to the east of which the Franks have built their own mihrab; and Muslim and infidel assemble there, the one turning to his place of worship, the other to his. In the hands of the Christians its venerableness is maintained, and God has preserved in it a place of prayer for the Muslims.

Two days we tarried at this place, and then, on Thursday the 12th of Jumada, corresponding with the 20th of September, we set forth across country to Sur [Tyre]. On our way we passed by a great fortress called al-Zab [al-Zib or Casal Imbert] which dominates the continuous villages and farms, and by a walled town called Iskandarunah [Iscandelion]. We sought a ship which we had learnt was bound for Bijayah [Bougie] and on which we wished to embark. And so we alighted at this town on the evening of that same Thursday, for the distance between the two cities (of Acre and Tyre) is thirty miles. We lodged in a khan in the town prepared for the reception of pilgrims.

A note on the city of Sur [Tyre]
May God Most High destroy it

This city has come proverbial for its impregnability, and he who seeks to conquer it will meet with no surrender or humility. The Franks prepared it as a refuge in case of unforeseen emergency, making it a strong point for their safety. Its roads and streets are cleaner than those of Acre. Its people are by disposition less stubborn in their unbelief, and by nature and habit they are kinder to the Muslim stranger. Their manners, in other words, are gentler. Their dwellings are larger and more spacious. The state of the Muslims in this city is easier and more peaceful. Acre is a town at once bigger, more impious, and more unbelieving. But the strength and impregnability of Tyre is more marvellous than is told of. It has only two gates, one landwards, and the other on the sea, which encompasses the city save on one side. The landward gate is reached only after passing through three or four posterns in the strongly-fortified outer walls that enclose it. The seaward gate is flanked by two strong towers and leads into a harbour whose remarkable situation is unique among maritime cities. The walls of the city enclose it on three sides, and the fourth is confined by a mole bound with cement. Ships enter below the walls and there anchor. Between the two towers stretches a great chain which, when raised, prevents any coming in or going forth, and no ships may pass save when it is lowered. At the gate stand guards and trusted watchers, and none can enter or go forth save under their eyes. The beauty of the site of this port is truly wonderful. Acre resembles it in situation and description, but cannot take the large ships, which must anchor outside, small ships only being able to enter. The port of Tyre is more complete, more beautiful, and more animated. Eleven days we tarried in the city, entering it on Thursday, and leaving it on Sunday the 22nd of Jumada, which was the last day of September; this was because the ship in which we had hoped to sail we found to be too small, so that we were unwilling to set forth in it.

An alluring worldly spectacle deserving of record was a nuptial procession which we witnessed one day near the port in Tyre. All the Christians, men and women, had assembled, and were formed in two lines at the bride's door. Trumpets, flutes, and all the musical instruments,[140] were played until she proudly emerged between two men who held her right and left as though they were her kindred. She was most elegantly garbed in a beautiful dress from which trailed, according to their traditional style, a long train of golden silk. On her head she wore a golden diadem covered by a net of woven gold, and on her breast was a like arrangement. Proud she was in her ornaments and dress, walking with little steps of half a span, like a dove, or in the manner of a wisp of cloud. God protect us from the seduction of the sight. Before her went Christian notables in their finest and most splendid clothing, their trains falling behind them. Behind her were her peers and equals of the Christian women, parading in their richest apparel and proud of bearing in their superb ornaments. Leading them all were the musical instruments. The Muslims and other Christian onlookers formed two ranks along the route, and gazed on them without reproof. So they passed along until they brought her to the house of the groom; and all that day they feasted. We thus were given the chance of seeing this alluring sight, from the seducement of which God preserve us.

We then returned by sea to Acre and landed 'there on the morning of Monday the 23rd of Jumada, being the first day in October. We hired passages on a large ship, about to sail to Messina on the island of Sicily. My God Most High, in His power and strength, assure the easing and lightening (of our way).

During our stay in Tyre we rested in one of the mosques that remained in Muslim hands. One of the Muslim elders of Tyre told us that it had been wrested from them in the year 518 [27th of June, 1124], and that Acre had been taken twelve [actually twenty] years earlier [24th of March, 1104], after a long siege and after hunger had overcome them. We were told that it had brought them to such a pass – we take refuge in God from it – that shame had driven them to propose a course from which God had preserved them. They had determined to gather their wives and children into the Great Mosque and there put them to the sword, rather than that the Christians should possess them. They themselves would then sally forth determinedly, and in a violent assault on the enemy, die together. But God made His irreversible decree, and their jurisprudents and some of their godly men prevented them. They thereupon decided to abandon the town, and to make good their escape. So it happened, and they dispersed among the Muslim lands. But there were some whose love of native land impelled them to return and, under the conditions of a safeguard which was written for them, to live amongst the infidels, 'God is the master of His affair' [Koran XII, 21]. Glorious is God, and great is His power. His will overcomes all impediments.

There can be no excuse in the eyes of God for a Muslim to stay in any infidel country, save when passing through it, while

w

the way lies clear in Muslim lands. They will face pains and terrors such as the abasement and destitution of the capitation and more especially, amongst their base and lower orders, the hearing of what will distress the heart in the reviling of him [Muhammad] whose memory God has sanctified, and whose rank He has exalted; there is also the absence of cleanliness, the mixing with the pigs, and all the other prohibited matters too numerous to be related or enumerated. Beware, beware of entering their lands. May God Most High grant His beneficent indulgence for this sin into which (our) feet have slipped, but His forgiveness is not given save after accepting our penitence. Glory to God, the Master. There is no Lord but He.

Among the misfortunes that one who visits their land will see are the Muslim prisoners walking in shackles and put to painful labour like slaves. In like condition are the Muslim women prisoners, their legs in iron rings. Hearts are rent for them, but compassion avails them nothing.

One of the beneficent works of God Most High towards the Maghrib prisoners in these lands of Frankish Syria is that every Muslim of these parts of Syria or elsewhere who makes a will in respect of his property devotes it to the liberation of the Maghribis in particular because of their remoteness from their native land and because, after Great and Glorious God, they have no other to deliver them. They are strangers, cut off from their native land, and the Muslim kings of these parts, the royal ladies, and the persons of ease and wealth, spend their money only in this cause. Nur al-Din – God have mercy on him – during an illness which had struck him, swore to distribute twelve thousand dinars for the ransoming of Maghribi prisoners. When he was cured of his sickness, he sent their ransom, but with them were despatched a group who were not Maghribis, but who were from Hamah, one of his provinces. He ordered their return and the release of Maghribis in their place, saying, 'These men can be ransomed by their kindred and their neighbours; but the Maghribis are strangers and have no kindred (here).'

Consider now the beneficent work of God Most High towards these Maghrib people. He decreed that they should have in Damascus two of the most considerable and wealthy merchants, who were deep in riches. One was named Nasr ibn Qawam and the other Abu 'l-Durr Yaqut, lord of al-'Attafi. Their business is all along this Frankish coast, and there is mention of no one else but them. They have agents who take a share in the profits. Their caravans come and go with their merchandise and stores, bringing great riches; and their influence over the Muslim and Frankish princes is great. Great and Glorious God assigned to them the part of ransoming the Maghribi prisoners with their wealth and that of the bequeathments; for these are made in their name on account of the fame of their probity and integrity and the vast sums of their own wealth that they have spent in this cause. No Maghribi can secure release from captivity save at their hands, and for a long time they have been prodigal of their wealth and efforts in releasing God's servants the Muslims from the hands of His enemies the infidels. May God Most High not fail to reward those who perform these righteous deeds.

By an unhappy chance, from the evils of which we take refuge in God, we were accompanied on our road to Acre from Damascus by a Maghribi from Buna in the district of Bougie who had been a prisoner and had been released by the agency of Abu 'l-Durr and become one of his young men. In one of his patron's caravans he had come to Acre, where he had mixed with the Christians, and taken on much of their character. The devil increasingly seduced and incited him until he renounced the faith of Islam, turned unbeliever, and became a Christian in the time of our stay in Tyre. We left to Acre, but received news of him. He had been baptised and become unclean, and had put on the girdle of a monk, thereby hastening for himself the flames of hell, verifying the threats of torture, and exposing himself to a grievous account and a long-distant return (from hell). We beg Great and Glorious God to confirm us in the true word in this world and the next, allowing us not to deviate from the pure faith and letting us, in His grace and mercy, die Muslims. This pig, the lord of Acre whom they call king, lives secluded and is not seen, for God has afflicted him with leprosy.[141] God was not slow to vengeance, for the affliction seized him in his youth, depriving him of the joys of his world. He is wretched here, 'but the chastisement of the hereafter is severer and more lasting' [Koran XX, 127]. His chamberlain and regent is his maternal uncle, the Count, the controller of the Treasury to whom the revenues are paid, and who supervises all with firmness and authority. The most considerable amongst the accursed Franks is the accursed Count, the lord of Tripoli and Tiberias.[142] He has authority and position among them. He is qualified to be king, and indeed is a candidate for the office. He is described as being shrewd and crafty. He was a prisoner of Nur al-Din's for twelve years or more, and then ransomed himself by the payment of a great sum in the time of the first governorship of Saladin, to whom he admits his vassalage and emancipation.

The caravans from Damascus branch away through the territory of Tiberias because its road is smooth, but mule caravans go through Tibnin, which road although rough is direct. The lake of Tiberias is sweet. Its breadth is four or five parasangs, and although statements about its length vary, the nearest to the truth is that it is about six parasangs, albeit we did not see it. There is a dispute as well about the width. In Tiberias there are the tombs of many prophets – God's blessings upon them – such as those of Shu'ayb, Sulayman, Yahuda, Rubil, Shu'ayb's daughter the wife of Moses the Interlocutor, and others – God's blessings upon them all. Nearby is Jabal al-Tur [Tabor]. Between Acre and Bait al-Maqdis [Jerusalem] lies three days' journey, and between Damascus and Jerusalem eight. Jerusalem is to the south-west[143] of Acre in the direction of Alexandria. May God restore it to the Muslims, and cleanse it, by His strength and power, from the hands of the polytheists [the believers in the Trinity].

The cities of Acre and Tyre have no gardens around them, and stand in a wide plain that reaches to the shores of the sea. Fruits are brought to them from the orchards that are in the neighbourhood. They possess broad lands and the nearby mountains are furnished with farmsteads from which fruits are brought to them. They are very rich cities. At the eastern extremity of Acre is a torrent course, along the banks of which extending to the sea is a sandy plain, than which I have seen no more beautiful sight. As a course for horses there is none to compare with it. Every morning and evening the Lord of the town rides over it, and there the soldiers parade – destroy them, God. Beside Tyre's landward gate is a fresh spring down to which a stairway leads. The wells and cisterns of the town are many, and there is no house without one. May God Most High, in His grace and favour, restore to it and to its sister (cities) the word of Islam.

On Saturday the 28th of Jumada, being the 6th of October, with the favour of God towards the Muslims, we embarked on a large ship, taking water and provisions. The Muslims secured places apart from the Franks. Some Christians called 'bilghriyin' [from the Italian *pellegrini* = pilgrims] came aboard. They had been on the pilgrimage to Jerusalem, and were too numerous to count, but were more than two thousand. May God in His grace and favour soon relieve us of their company and bring us to safety with His hoped-for assistance and beneficent works; none but He should be worshipped. So, under the will of Great and Glorious God, we awaited a favouring wind and the completion of the ship's stowing.

The Month of Rajab the Unique (580)

[8th of October–6th of November, 1184]

May God let us know His grace and favour

THE new moon rose on the night of Tuesday, corresponding with the 9th of October, while we were aboard the ship in the port of Acre, awaiting the completion of the stowing and our sailing in the name of God Most High with His favour and beneficent indulgence and by His generous will. Our stay there was prolonged twelve days, through the failure of the wind to rise. The blowing of the winds in these parts has a singular secret. It is that the east wind does not blow except in spring and autumn, and, save at those seasons, no voyages can be made and merchants will not bring their goods to Acre. The spring voyages begin in the middle of April, when the east wind blows until the end of May. It may last longer or less according to what God Most High decrees. The autumn voyages are from the middle of October, when the east wind (again) sets in motion. It lasts a shorter time than in the spring, and is for them a fleeting opportunity, for it blows for (only) fifteen days, more or less. There is no other suitable time, for the winds then vary, that from the west prevailing. Voyagers to the Maghrib, to Sicily, or to the lands of the Rum, await this east wind in these two seasons as they would await (the fulfilment of) an honest pledge. Glory to God, creating in His wisdom, and miraculous in His power. There is no God but He.

During all this time that we were on the ship, we passed the nights ashore and sometimes had to search for our vessel. When therefore at daybreak of Thursday the 10th of Rajab, the 18th of October, the ship set sail, we, according to our habit, were ashore passing the night. The day was not fair for the Rum to prepare for the sea, and we had lost our prudence

and forgotten the proverb concerning the preparation of water
and provisions, 'A man should not leave his saddle'. So when
we came to morning we could not see the ship, nor was there
any trace of it. At once we hired a large boat with four oars
and put off to follow the ship. It was most perilous, but God
preserved us, and we overtook the ship at eventide, praising
Great and Glorious God for His benefits. The beginning of
that day was the distressful part of this long voyage, but its
end, God be praised, brought comfort. In all circumstances,
let us praise and render gratitude to God. Steadily we sailed
on, under a propitious wind of varying force, for five days.
Then the west wind came out of ambuscade and blew into
the ship's bows. The captain and ruler of the ship, a Genoese
Rumi, who was perspicacious in his art and skilled in the duties
of a sea-captain, made shift to elude this wind by tacking right
and left, and sought to return not on his tracks. The sea was
calm and gentle. At midnight, or near to it, on the night of
Saturday the 19th of Rajab, being the 27th of October, the
west wind fell on us and broke a spar of the mast known as
the 'ardimun' [Italian, *artimone*],[144] throwing half of it, with
the attaching sails, into the sea. God saved us from its falling
on the ship, for in size and bulk it resembled a mast. The
mariners hastened forward and lowered the sail on the main-
mast, stopping the ship's progress. The sailors needed for the
long-boat tied to the ship were called, and they pulled to the
half-spar and its sails that had fallen into the sea and brought
them out. We were delivered from a state which only God
Most High can know of. They began to raise the main-sail,
and on the artimone set a sail called the 'dallun' [Gr., δολων].[145]
We spent a grey night until the dawn gleamed. Great and
Glorious God had granted us security. The mariners began to
fashion another spar from some wood which they had ready.
But the west wind was at the beginning of its perversity, and
we wavered between hope and despair; yet there triumphed
our faith in the beneficent offices of God Most High and in
His hidden favour and known grace. Glory to Him for He is

worthy of it; great is His power and exalted is His majesty. There is no God but He.

On Wednesday the 23rd of the month the east wind blew: gently, languidly, and mildly; and our spirits rejoiced, for we hoped it would increase and grow stronger; but it was a dying breath. A thin mist then veiled the sea, whose waves were calmed so that it became like a 'palace made smooth with glass' [Koran XXVII, 44]. In all four quarters there scarce was air to breathe. So we remained, playing on the surface of the water, which seemed to the eye to be a sheet of molten silver; or we might be wandering between two skies. This is the wind the sailors call the 'ghalini' [Gr., γαληνη = calmness].

The night of Thursday the 24th of Rajab, the 1st of November according to the non-Arabs, was a festival for the Christians, and they celebrated it with lighted candles. Hardly one of them, big or little, male or female, but carried a candle in his hand. Their priests led them in prayers on the ship, then one by one rose to preach a sermon and recall the articles of their faith. The whole ship, from top to bottom, was luminous with kindled lamps. In this manner we passed most of that night, and when we came to the morn, the same still wind was with us, and remained until the night of Sunday the 27th of the month. A north wind then rose, the ship resumed its course, and our spirits were cheered. Praise be to God.

The Month of Sha'ban the Honoured (580)

[7th of November–5th of December, 1184]
May God let us know His benignity

THE new moon was obscured to us, and we reckoned that the days of Rajab were completed on the night of Thursday the 8th of November. From the time of our sailing from Acre, we had been twenty-two days on the sea, and therefore were wanting in felicity and felt only wretchedness and despair. But we hoped for the benign offices of Great and Glorious God, and for His unrevealed bounty, which by His grace and favour, is vouched unto us. The provisions of the travellers were becoming scarce, but by the charity of God in this ship they were as if in a city filled with all commodities. All they might wish to buy could be found: bread, water, and all kinds of fruit and victuals, such as pomegranate, quince, water-melon, pear, chestnut, walnut, chick-pea, broad-bean raw and cooked, onion, garlic, fig, cheese, fish and many other things it would be too long to describe. All this we saw being sold. Throughout all these days we had seen no land – may God soon dispel our cares – and two Muslims died – God have mercy on them. They were thrown into the sea. Of the (Christian) pilgrims two died also, and then were followed by many. One of them fell alive into the sea, and the waves carried him off more quickly than a flash of lightning. The captain of the ship inherited the effects of the departed Muslims and Christian pilgrims, for such is their usage for all who die at sea. There is no way for the (true) heir of the dead to gain his inheritance, and at this we were much astonished.

At daybreak on Tuesday the 6th of the month, the 13th of November, mountains appeared to us out of the sea. The west wind had mounted and blew fiercely and without intermission; then the wind blew changingly from east and west, and drove us to one of those mountains, and we anchored beside it. We asked concerning the place, and learnt that it was one of the (Eastern) Roman islands [of the Greek archipelago]. There are more than three hundred and fifty of these islands and they are under the governance of the ruler of Constantinople. The Rum are as wary of the inhabitants of these islands as they are of the Muslims, for no amity exists between them. We remained in the anchorage all that Tuesday, and the beginning of Wednesday. Some people from the island, after obtaining a safe-conduct, came to the ship, and for a few hours sold bread and meat to those upon it.

On Wednesday we put to sea, having been on board the ship for eight and twenty days. The following Thursday there appeared to us the island of Crete. This island is also under the sovereignty of the ruler of Constantinople. It is more than three hundred miles long, and we have previously mentioned it on our sea-journey to Alexandria. Along its length we journeyed, having it to our right. All the way the sea was agitated and the wind unfavourable, while with proper resignation we awaited relief from Great and Glorious God, and expected – exalted is His majesty – that by His grace and favour, we should receive His covenanted aid and easement.

On Saturday the 10th of Sha'ban, which was the 17th of November, we parted from the coast of Crete, and made speed under a favourable north wind. It roared and blew so that the ship flew on its wings the sails. The sea became possessed of the devil and was greatly commoted. Its waves surged and foamed, so that their raging crests we conceived to be snowy mountains. Our spirits were yet gladdened, and hope triumphed over despair.

During the twenty-six days in which we had not seen land, we had made conjectures, and talked soothingly of death for fear that we should exhaust our provisions and water, and come upon the twin disasters, hunger and thirst. Some said that we had strayed on our course towards the Gharb coast of Africa and others thought that we had diverged to the mainland of

the territory of Constantinople and its vicinity; still others said
Lattakiyah in Syria, and others Damietta on the coast of Alexandria. We were fearful that the wind would drive us to one
of the desert islands of (Eastern) Rome and there we would
have to winter, or even be forced by the situation to live in
one of its houses. In none of the prospects was there any happy
choice until God should bring us relief and remove our sadness and despair, fortifying our spirits after the hardships we
had suffered and the afflictions we had endured. His abundance
comes from God, who says: _

> 'The sea is bitter of taste, intractable:
> No need of it have I.
> Is it not water and we earth?
> Why then do we endure it?'[146]

Now, by the grace of God Most High, we may bend our
looks for the happy sight, if God wills, of the coast of Sicily.
At midnight on Sunday the 11th, the wind changed to the
west and brought on us the tempest from that side. Strongly
the wind blew and took us northward. On the morning of
Sunday the storm had increased, and the sea was raging, throwing up waves like mountains. They struck the ship such blows
that, with all its size, it tossed like a tender twig. It was as
high as the walls of a city, yet the waves reared up and flung
into its midst a shower of water like drenching rain. With the
darkening night the buffeting increased and our ears were
smitten by the bellowing. The fury of the wind became a
grave affair; the sails were lowered and only the small dallun
were left, at half-mast. Despair of this world fell upon us, and
we bade life farewell in peace. Waves came upon us from all
sides and we thought we were destroyed. O night on which
sable locks would go grey, recorded amongst the grey nights
and first in the number of our adventures and misfortunes.
Long for us was that night, long like the night of Sul.[147]

Morning had scarcely come when to our misfortune we saw
the coast of Crete on our left. Its mountains had (earlier) been

before us, and we had left them behind to our right. But the wind had taken us from our course, and we who had thought to have passed it were mistaken. We had gone astray from the known and auspicious way whereby the coast of Crete should have been on our right when facing Sicily. We submitted ourselves to fate, and swallowing our chokings at this vexation, said:

'He whose wants are satisfied, will either curse or repine.'

Meanwhile the sun had brightened, and the sea had somewhat settled, and we stood constant to our aim of anchoring on that coast until God should fulfil His decrees and execute His judgement. All (modes of) travel have their (proper) season, and travel by sea should be at the propitious time and the recognised period. There should not be a reckless venturing forth in the months of winter as we did. First and last the matter is in the hands of God; but beware, beware of embarking on such hazards; although caution is useless in the face of destiny. God is sufficient unto us and the best protector.

When we were off the coast, the wind helped us a little so that we drew away from it and left it on our right. We returned near to our intended course, and made progress part of the night of Tuesday the 13th. We had been on the ship thirty-four days. The sails were set 'musallabah' [square-rigged], which the Rum deem to be the best method of sailing, since they cannot but catch the wind which comes aft of the ship on its course [see note 132]. On the morning of Tuesday we found the same conditions, with the wind helping us, wherefore we rejoiced and were glad. There then appeared ships sailing in our direction, and we were enlivened to know that we were on the course intended. Praise and thanks to God in all conjunctures. The wind then changed, and blew from the west with violence. After taking us along part of Wednesday night and Wednesday itself, it drove us despite ourselves to a harbour at the tip of one of the Rumani [Greek] islands [Zante?]. A strait of twelve miles separates it from the mainland. We arrived at this place on the morning of Thursday the 15th of Sha'ban the Honoured, being the 22nd of November. Praise be to Great and Glorious God for the safety He has granted us. There followed us to the harbour five ships, two of which had sailed from the coast of Alexandria about fifty days before but had been taken astray by the wind. Four days we tarried in that harbour, and our people renewed their water and provisions, for the habitations were at hand. The islanders came and to people on the ship sold bread, meat, oil, and whatever victuals they had. Their bread was not of wheat entirely, but was mixed with barley and baked to blackness. People rushed for it, despite its dearness – and indeed there was nothing cheap for sale – and thanked God for what He had granted. When in this harbour, we had been forty days on board. Praise be to God in all conjunctures. During our stay in it the west wind abated not at all, but blew as violently as possible. Praise be to God Most High that it did not find us moving on the high seas. Praise be to God for His benign offices.

We sailed from this harbour on Tuesday the 19th of Sha'ban, the 26th of November, under a good and favourable wind, rejoicing at it, and perceiving the beneficent work of Great and Glorious God, and the benevolence of His decrees. There is no God but He. We continued on our way until Thursday the 22nd of Sha'ban, the 29th of November, when the wind changed and blew from the west. A cloud rose with crashing thunder, driven by a furious wind and preceded by dazzling lightning. On to us in the ship it poured a continuous shower of hail that dismayed our spirits; but soon it was over and our disquiet was relieved. But the night of Friday we passed in desolation; and despair in its lurking hole was revealed to us. Then when dawn shone and daylight came, we saw the coast of Sicily before us. Oh joyous news; may if be that adversity return not again.

By night-time on Saturday the 1st day of December, we were less than a third or half the way from the coast. But every ending is already recorded and settled (by destiny). How many hopes does misfortune pass by? There was not a moment before a wind struck in our faces and drove us back. It stopped our eyes from seeing and continued to rage so that it nearly broke and shattered the (ship's) wood. The sails were lowered from the mast, and placing our souls in the care of their Creator, we stopped on our course. Rain clouds chased after us; and they and the night and the sea threw us into a threefold obscurity. The swollen waves beat incessantly upon us, their shocks making the heart to leap. Our souls threw away all desires and prepared to meet Fate. That tenebrous night we passed under the blows of the tempest, suffering terror, and enduring vicissitudes, oh what vicissitudes! On the morning of Saturday we came upon a violent day which multiplied the miseries of the night. The wind and the waves threw us where they willed, and we resigned ourselves to fate, grasping tenaciously at our hopes (of the life to come). Then at eventide we were overtaken by the favour of God Most High, when the wind softened, the sea calmed, and the face of the sky blazed bright. By the morning of Sunday the 2nd of December, the 25th of Sha'ban, our despair had changed to confidence, and men's faces stared about as if they had but risen from the shroud. The wind helped us a little, and we looked again for any trace of land in sight, and made conjectures as to where and when. Great and Glorious God is truly good to those who worship Him, and secures us with His known gracious favour and habit. There is no God but He.

The Month of Ramadan the Venerated (580)

[6th of December, 1184–4th of January, 1185]
May God in His grace and favour let us share His blessings and during
it accept our prayers. There is no Lord but He

THE new moon rose on the night of Friday the 7th of
December while we were going back and forth off the
mainland [Italy]. God granted us a light east wind by which
we travelled gently on until we came to this place opposite
the mainland. Here we observed many farms and habitations,
and learnt that it was part of Calabria and belongs to the Lord
of Sicily, for his territories on the mainland extend two months'
(journey) from this place. Many of the (Christian) pilgrims
went ashore to escape the hunger that had smitten those on
the ship, our provisions being exhausted. It is enough to tell
you that we made do with a ritl [5 lb.] of dried biscuit which
we divided amongst four of us and moistened with a little
water. With this we were content. Every pilgrim who landed
sold what remained of his provisions, and the Muslims, in sympathy with fellow travellers, bought what they could, despite
the dearness which reached a dirham of pure (silver) for a biscuit. What think you of a voyage of two months on board
a ship over a distance we had thought to cross in ten or fifteen
days at most. The prudent was he who brought victuals for
thirty days, but the rest brought enough for only twenty or
fifteen. A singular circumstance of our sea journey was that
while on board we had seen the new moon of three months:
Rajab, Sha'ban, and Ramadan the present month.

On the morning of the 1st day of this month we observed
before us the Mountain of Fire, the famous volcano of Sicily,
and rejoiced thereat. May God Most High reward us for what
we have endured, and end (our days) with the best and most

magnificent of His favours. May He animate us in all circumstances to gratitude for what He has bestowed on us. A favourable wind then moved us from that place, but on the evening of Saturday the 2nd of the month its force increased and drove the ship with such speed that in but an instant it had brought us to the mouth of the strait. Night had fallen. In this strait the sea is confined to a width of six miles and in the narrowest place to three. The sea in this strait, which runs between the mainland and the island of Sicily, pours through like the 'bursting of the dam'[148] and, from the intensity of the contraction and the pressure, boils like a cauldron. Difficult indeed is its passage for ships. Our ship continued on its course, driven by a strong wind from the south, the mainland on our right and the coast of Sicily on our left.

When it came to midnight on Sunday the 3rd of the blessed month (of Ramadan), and we were overlooking the city of Messina, the sudden cries of the sailors gave us the grievous knowledge that the ship had been driven by the force of the wind towards one of the shore lines and had struck it. At once the captain ordered that the sails be lowered, but the sail on the mast called the 'ardimun' [artimone] would not come down. All their efforts they exerted on it, but they could do naught with it, because of the strain of the wind. When they had laboured in vain, the captain cut it with a knife piece by piece, hoping to arrest the ship. During this attempt the ship stuck by its keel to the ground, touching it with its two rudders, the two shafts by which it steers.[149] Dreadful cries were raised on the ship, and the Last Judgement had come; the break that has no mending and the great calamity which allows us no fortitude. The Christians gave themselves over to grief, and the Muslims submitted themselves to the decree of their Lord, finding only and clinging and holding fast to the rope of hopefulness in the life to come. In turn the wind and the waves buffeted the ship until one of its rudders broke. The captain then threw out one of the anchors, hoping to take hold with it, but to no purpose. He cut its rope and left it in the sea.

When we sure that (our time) had come, we braced ourselves to meet death, and, summoning our resolution to show goodly patience, awaited the morn or the time of destiny. Cries and shrieks arose from the women and the infants of the Rum. All with humbleness submitted themselves (to the will of God), and 'men were despoiled of their manhood'.[160]

We, meanwhile, were gazing at the nearby shore in hesitance between throwing outselves in to swim and awaiting, it might be, relief with the dawn from God. We formed the resolve to remain. The sailors lowered the long-boat into the sea to remove the most important of their men, women, and effects. They took it one journey to the shore, but were unable to return, and the waves threw it in pieces on the beach. Despair then seized our spirits; but while we were suffering these vicissitudes, dawn shone and aid and succour came from God. We made certain of our eyes, and there before us was the city of Messina less than half a mile away.

We marvelled at the power of Great and Glorious God in the management of His designs, and said:

'Many are taken off in death upon the threshold of their house.'

The sun then rose and small boats came out to us. Our cries had fallen on the city, and the King of Sicily, William himself, came out with some of his retinue to survey the affair. We made speed to go down to the boats, but the violence of the waves would not allow them to reach the ship. We at last descended into them at the end of the terrible storm. Our deliverance on to the shore was like that of Abu Nasr from destiny.[161] Some of the chattels belonging to men had been destroyed, but 'they took comfort that although without plunder, they had returned in safety'.[162] The strangest thing that we were told was that this Rumi King, when he perceived some needy Muslims staring from the ship, having not the means to pay for their landing because the owners of the boats were asking so high a price for their rescue, enquired, this King, concerning them and, learning their story, ordered that they be given one hundred

x

ruba'i of his coinage in order that they might alight. All the
Muslims thus were saved and cried, 'Praise be to God, Lord
of the Universe.'

The Christians took from the ship all that they had had
therein. The next day the waves had shattered it and thrown
it in pieces on the shore: a lesson to those who saw, and 'a sign
to those who pondered' [Koran XV, 75]. Wonder fell upon
us for our deliverance; and to Great and Glorious God we
renewed our thanks for His beneficent offices and gracious
decrees, and for preserving us from the falling of this fate upon
us on the mainland, or on one of the islands inhabited by the
Rum where, even had we been saved, we should have been
for ever slaves. Help us, Great and Glorious God, to render
thanks for these gifts and favours, and for this merciful solicitude and compassion. All this is in His power, and it is His
faculty to be kind and beneficent. There is no God but He.
Another sign of the loving-kindness and benevolence of Great
and Glorious God towards us in this disaster was the presence
of this Rumi king. But for that, all within the ship would
have been robbed of everything, or all the Muslims might have
been placed in servitude, for such was their custom. The arrival
of the King at this city was on account of his fleet, which was
being built and which proved a saving mercy to us. Praise be
to God for His avouched and beneficent care. There is no
God but He.

Recollections of the city of Messina in the island of Sicily

May God restore it (to the Muslims)

This city is the mart of the merchant infidels, the focus of
ships from the world over, and thronging always with companies of travellers by reason of the lowness of prices. But it
is cheerless because of the unbelief, no Muslim being settled
there. Teeming with worshippers of the Cross, it chokes its
inhabitants, and constricts them almost to strangling. It is full
of smells and filth; and churlish too, for the stranger will find

there no courtesy. Its markets are animated and teeming, and it has ample commodities to ensure a luxurious life. Your days and nights in this town you will pass in full security, even though your countenance, your manners [lit. 'hand'] and your tongue are strange.

Messina leans against the mountains, the lower slopes of which adjoin the intrenchments of the town. To its south is the sea, and its harbour is the most remarkable of maritime ports, since large ships can come into it from the seas until they almost touch it. Between them and the shore is thrown a plank over which men come and go and porters take up the baggage; thus no boats are needed for loading and unloading save for ships anchored far out.

You will observe ships ranged along the quay like horses lined at their pickets or in their stables. This is all because of the great depth here of the sea which forms the strait, some three miles wide, that separates the island from the continent. On the coast opposite to Messina, is the town known as Rayah [Reggio], the capital of a large province.

This town of Messina is at the extremity of Sicily, an island having many towns, cultivated places, and hamlets that it would take long to name. Its length is seven days' journey, and its width five. On it is the aforementioned volcano, draped in clouds so high it is, and for ever, summer and winter, covered by snow.

The prosperity of the island surpasses description. It is enough to say that it is a daughter of Spain in the extent of its cultivation, in the luxuriance of its harvests, and in its well-being, having an abundance of varied produce, and fruits of every kind and species.

But it is filled with the worshippers of the Cross, who promenade in its upper districts and live at ease in its sheltered parts. The Muslims live beside them with their property and farms. The Christians treat these Muslims well and 'have taken them to themselves as friends' [Koran XX, 41], but impose on them a tax to be paid twice yearly, thus taking from them the amplitude of living they had been wont to earn from that land. May Almighty and Glorious God mend their lot, and in His goodness, make a happy recompense their heritage.

The mountains are covered with plantations bearing apples, chestnuts and hazel-nuts, pears, and other kinds of fruits. There are, in Messina, no Muslims save a small number of craftsmen, so the Muslim stranger there will feel lonely.

The finest town in Sicily and the seat of its sovereign, is known to the Muslims as al-Madinah, and to the Christians as Palermo. It has Muslim citizens who possess mosques, and their own markets, in the many suburbs. The rest of the Muslims live in the farms (of the island) and in all its villages and towns, such as Syracuse and others. Al-Madinah al-Kabirah ['the great City' – Palermo], the residence of their King, William, is however the biggest and most populous, and Messina is next. In al-Madinah, God willing, we shall make our stay; and thence we hope to go to whichever of the western countries that Great and Glorious God shall at His will determine.

Their King, William, is admirable for his just conduct, and the use he makes of the industry of the Muslims, and for choosing eunuch pages who all, or nearly all, concealing their faith, yet hold firm to the Muslim divine law. He has much confidence in Muslims, relying on them for his affairs, and the most important matters, even the supervisor of his kitchen being a Muslim; and he keeps a band of black Muslim slaves commanded by a leader chosen from amongst them. His ministers and chamberlains he appoints from his pages, of whom he has a great number and who are his public officials and are described as his courtiers. In them shines the splendour of his realm for the magnificent clothing and fiery horses they display; and there is none of them but has his retinue, his servants, and his followers.

This King possesses splendid palaces and elegant gardens, particularly in the capital of his kingdom, al-Madinah. In Messina he has a palace, white like a dove, which overlooks the shore. He has about him a great number of youths and

handmaidens, and no Christian King is more given up to the
delights of the realm, or more comfort and luxury-loving.
William is engrossed in the pleasures of his land, the arrangement of its laws, the laying down of procedure, the allocation
of the functions of his chief officials, the enlargement of the
splendour of the realm, and the display of his pomp, in a
manner that resembles the Muslim Kings. His kingdom is very
large. He pays much attention to his (Muslim) physicians and
astrologers, and also takes great care of them. He will even,
when told that a physician or astrologer is passing through his
land, order his detainment, and then provide him with means
of living so that he will forget his native land. May God in
His favour preserve the Muslims from this seduction. The
King's age is about thirty years. May God protect the Muslims
from his hostility and the extension of his power.

One of the remarkable things told of him is that he reads
and writes Arabic.[153] We also learnt from one of his personal
servants that his 'alamah[154] is: 'Praise be to God. It is proper
to praise Him.' His father's 'alamah was: 'Praise be to God in
thanks for His beneficence.' The handmaidens and concubines
in his palace are all Muslims. One of the strangest things told
us by this servant, Yahya ibn Fityan, the Embroiderer,[155] who
embroidered in gold the King's clothes, was that the Frankish
Christian women who came to his palace became Muslims,
converted by these handmaidens. All this they kept secret from
their King.[156] Of the good works of these handmaidens there
are astonishing stories.

It was told to us that when a terrifying earthquake[157] shook
the island this polytheist [a Muslim would deem William to
be so, since he accepted the dogma of the Trinity] in alarm
ranged round his palace, and heard nothing but cries to God
and His Prophet from his women and pages. At sight of him,
they were overcome with confusion, but he said to them: 'Let
each invoke the God he worships, and those that have faith
shall be comforted.'

The pages, who are the leaders of his state and the managers of his affairs, are Muslims, there being none who do not, voluntarily and for a heavenly reward, fast in the holy month [of Ramadan], and give alms that they might be nearer to God. They redeem prisoners and bring up their young ones, arranging for their marriage and giving them assistance, and doing all the good they can. All this is done by Great and Almighty God for the Muslims of this island and is one of the mysteries of His care for them.

In Messina we met one of their leading and most distinguished pages called 'Abd al-Massih, whose wish (to see us) had been conveyed to us. He entertained us with regard and generosity, and then spoke openly to us, revealing his close-guarded secrets. He had first looked about his audience-room, and then, in self-protection, dismissed those servants about him whom he suspected. He then questioned us about Mecca – may God hallow it – and about its venerable shrines, and those of Holy Medina and of Syria. As we told him he melted with longing and fervour, and asked if we would give him some blessed token we had brought from Mecca and Medina – may God hallow them – and begged us not to be sparing of what we could give him. 'You can boldly display your faith in Islam,' he said, 'and are successful in your enterprises and thrive, by God's will, in your commerce. But we must conceal our faith, and, fearful of our lives, must adhere to the worsnip of God and the discharge of our religious duties in secret. We are bound in the possession of an infidel who has placed on our necks the noose of bondage. Our whole purpose therefore is to be blessed by meeting pilgrims such as you, to ask for their prayers and be happy in what precious objects from the holy shrines they can give us to serve us as instruments of faith, and as treasures on our bier (in token of the life to come).' Our hearts melted in compassion for him, and we prayed that his end might be happy, and gave him some of our treasures as he wished. Profusely he expressed his thanks and gratitude, and told us in confidence of his colleagues the other pages, who have a notable repute for good works. In the release of prisoners they most acquire merit in God's eyes, and all their servants are of a like temper.

Another singular circumstance concerning these pages is that when in the presence of their Lord and the hour for prayer is at hand they will leave the chamber one by one that they might make their prayers. They sometimes do so in a place where the eye of their King might follow them, but Almighty and Glorious God conceals them. They thus continue to labour in their purpose, covertly advising the Muslims in their unending struggle for the faith. May God, in His grace, advantage them and bring them to a happy end.

In Messina, the King has a shipyard containing fleets of uncountable numbers of ships. He has a similar yard at al-Madinah [Palermo].

We lodged (in Messina) at an inn, and stayed there nine days. Then, on the night of Tuesday the 12th of the holy month (Ramadan) and the 18th of December, we embarked on a small ship sailing to al-Madinah. We steered close to the shore, so that we might keep it within sight. God sent us a light breeze from the east that most pleasantly urged us on our way. So we sailed along, bending our gaze on the continuous cultivations and villages, and on the fortresses and strongholds at the tops of the lofty mountains. To our right we saw nine islands [Aeolian or Lipari], rising up like lofty mountains in the sea, close to the shores of Sicily. From two of them [Vulcano and Stromboli] fire issues unendingly, and we could see the smoke ascending from them. At the close of night a red flame appeared, throwing up tongues into the air. It was the celebrated volcano. We were told that a fiery blast of great violence bursts out from air-holes in the two mountains and makes the fire. Often a great stone is cast up and thrown into the air by the force of the blast and prevented thereby from falling and settling at the bottom. This is one of the most remarkable of stories, and it is true.

As for the great mountain in the island, known as the Jabal al-Nar [Mountain of Fire=Etna], it also presents a singular feature in that some years a fire pours from it in the manner of the 'bursting of the dam' [see note 148]. It passes nothing it does not burn until, coming to the sea, it rides out on its surface and then subsides beneath it. Let us praise the Author of all things for His marvellous creations. There is no God but He.

On the evening of Wednesday following the Tuesday we have chronicled, we came to the port of Shafludi [Cefalu], between which and Messina lies a day and a half's sailing.

Recollections of the town of Shafludi [Cefalu] in the island of Sicily

May God restore it (to the Muslims)

Cefalu is a coastal town, with an ample produce from its soil and with many commodities, beset with vine and other trees, and having well-ordered markets. A community of Muslims lives there. Set over the town is a mountain, on whose large circular summit is a fortress, than which I have never seen any more formidable. They hold it in readiness for any sea attack that a fleet from the lands of the Muslims – may God render them victorious – might make upon them unawares.

We sailed from Cefalu at midnight, and came to the town of Thirmah [Termini] in the early forenoon of Thursday, after an easy voyage. The two towns are five and twenty miles from each other. At Termini we changed from that ship to another which we chartered, that the sailors accompanying us might be of the country (through which we should travel).

Recollections of the town of Thirmah [Termini] in the island of Sicily

May God deliver it (to the Muslims)

Better situated than the place we have just described, this town is strongly fortified, and surmounts and towers above the sea. The Muslims have a large suburb, in which are their mosques. The town has a high and impregnable fort, and in its lower part is a thermal spring which serves the citizens as baths. It enjoys an extreme fertility and abundance of victuals; indeed, the whole island in this regard is one of the most remarkable in God's creation. We passed Thursday the 14th anchored in a river below the town into which the tide from the sea flowed and ebbed,[158] and there we stayed the night of Friday. The wind then changed to the west, and we had no way to sail.

Between us and our destination, al-Madinah, the town known to the Christians as Palermo, lay five and twenty miles, and we feared that we would be held long at Termini. But we thanked God Most High for His gracious favour in having (already) brought us in two days across a passage that stayed other ships, as we were told, twenty or thirty days and more; and on the morning of Friday in the middle of the holy month, we rose determined to journey overland by foot. We discharged our design, and, carrying some of our effects, and having left some of our companions to guard the chattels remaining in the ship, we set forth.

We travelled along a road like a market so populous it was, with men coming and going. Groups of Christians that met us themselves uttered the first greetings, and treated us with courtesy. We observed in their attitude and insinuating address towards the Muslims that which would offer temptation to ignorant souls. May God, in His power and bounty, preserve from seducement the people of Muhammad – God's blessings upon him.

We came at last to Qasr Saʿd [Solanto Castle], which lies a parasang from Palermo, and being seized with fatigue, turned aside and passed the night in it. The castle is on the seashore, and is lofty and ancient, for it was built in the time of the Muslim occupation of the island. It always was, and still is, by the grace of God, inhabited by pious (Muslims). Around it are numerous tombs of ascetic and pious Muslims, and it is known for its grace and blessedness, being visited by men from all countries. Opposite it is a spring known as ʿAyn al-Majnunah [the Spring of the Mad Woman]. The castle has a strong iron door. Inside are the living quarters, and commanding belvederes, and well-planned suites; the place indeed has all the conveniences of living. At its summit, is one of the finest mosques in the world. It is an oblong building with long arcades spread with spotless mats of a workmanship such as I have never seen better; and within it are hung forty lamps of brass and crystal. In front of the mosque is the broad road which girdles the upper part of the castle. In the lower part is a well containing sweet water.

We passed the most pleasing and agreeable night in that mosque, and listened to the call to prayer, which long we had not heard. We were shown high regard by the residents of the mosque, amongst whom was an imam who led them in the obligatory prayers and, in this holy month, the tarawih [special and additional prayers of twenty prostrations, performed in the month of Ramadan].

Near this castle, about a mile away in the direction of Palermo, is a similar castle known as Qasr Ja'far, which contains a spring of sweet water.

We noticed on this road churches prepared for the Christian sick.[159] In their cities they have them after the model of the Muslim hospitals, and we have seen their like at Acre and Tyre. We marvelled at such solicitude.

After the morning prayers, we bent our way to al-Madinah. On arrival we made to enter, but were stopped and directed to a gate near the palace of the Frankish King – may God relieve the Muslims of his dominance. We were then conducted to his Commissioner that he might question us as to our intentions, as they do in the case of all strangers. Over esplanades, through doors, and across royal courts they led us, gazing at the towering palaces, well-set piazzas and gardens, and the ante-chambers given to the officials. All this amazed our eyes and dazzled our minds, and we remembered the words of Almighty and Glorious God: 'But that all mankind would become one people (i.e. infidels), we would have given those who denied merciful God silver roofs for their houses, and stairways to mount to them' [Koran XLIII, 33, gold and silver having no value in the sight of God].

Amongst the things we observed was a hall set in a large court enclosed by a garden and flanked by colonnades. The hall occupied the whole length of that court, and we marvelled at its length and the height of its belvederes. We understood that it was the dining-hall of the King and his companions, and that the colonnades and the ante-chambers are where his magistrates, his officials, and his stewards sit in presence.

The Commissioner came out to us, walking majestically between the servants who surrounded him and carried the train of his robes. We looked upon a stately old man with long white moustaches, who questioned us in supple Arabic as to our design and our country. We told him, and he showed pity for us, and, with repeated salutations and invocations, ordered that we be allowed to depart. He gave us much cause to wonder. His first question to us had been for news of Constantinople and what we knew of it, but alas we had nothing we could tell him. We shall give news of it later.

One of the strangest examples of seducement into waywardness that we witnessed happened as we left the castle, when one of the Christians seated at the gate said to us: 'Look to what you have with you, pilgrims, lest the officials of the Customs descend on you.' He thought, of course, that we carried merchandise liable to customs duty. But another Christian replied to him saying, 'How strange you are. Can they enter into the King's protection and yet fear? I should hope for them (to receive) nothing but thousands of *rubayyat*. Go in peace, you have nothing to fear.' Overwhelmed with surprise at what we had seen and heard, we departed to an inn where we took lodgings on Saturday the 16th of the holy month and the 22nd of December. On leaving the castle, we had gone through a long and covered portico down which we walked a long way until we came to a great church. We learnt that this portico was the King's way to the church.

Recollections of al-Madinah [Palermo], the capital of Sicily

May God restore it (to the Muslims)

It is the metropolis of these islands, combining the benefits of wealth and splendour, and having all that you could wish of beauty, real or apparent, and all the needs of subsistence, mature and fresh. It is an ancient and elegant city, magnificent and gracious, and seductive to look upon. Proudly set between its open spaces and plains filled with gardens, with broad roads and avenues, it dazzles the eyes with its perfection. It is a wonderful place, built in the Cordova style, entirely from cut stone known as *kadhan* [a soft limestone]. A river splits the town, and four springs gush in its suburbs. The King, to whom it is his world, has embellished it to perfection and taken it as the capital of his Frankish Kingdom – may God destroy it.

The King's palaces are disposed around the higher parts, like pearls encircling a woman's full throat. The King roams through the gardens and courts for amusement and pleasure. How many – may they not long be his – palaces, constructions, watchtowers, and belvederes[160] he has, how many fine monasteries whose monks he has put in comfort by grants of large fiefs, and how many churches with crosses of gold and silver! May it be that God will soon repair the times for this island, making it again a home of the faith, and by His power delivering it from fear to security. For He can perform what He desires.

The Muslims of this city preserve the remaining evidence of the faith.[161] They keep in repair the greater number of their mosques, and come to prayers at the call of the muezzin. In their own suburbs they live apart from the Christians. The markets are full of them, and they are the merchants of the place.[162] They do not congregate for the Friday service, since the *khutbah* is forbidden. On feast-days (only may) they recite it with intercessions for the 'Abbasid Caliphs.[163] They have a qadi to whom they refer their law-suits, and a cathedral mosque where, in this holy month, they assemble under its lamps. The ordinary mosques are countless, and most of them are used as schools for Koran teachers. But in general these Muslims do not mix with their brethren under infidel patronage, and enjoy no security for their goods, their women, or their children. May God, by His favour, amend their lot with His beneficence.

One point of resemblance between this town and Cordova – for one thing always resembles another in some direction – is its having in the middle of the new city an old one known as the Qasr al-Qadim [the old Castle], just as there is in Cordova – God protect it. In this old castle are mansions like lofty castles with towers hidden in the skies, bewildering the sight with their splendour.

One of the most remarkable works of the infidels that we saw was the church known as the Church of the Antiochian.[164] We examined it on the Day of the Nativity [Christmas Day], which with them is a great festival; and a multitude of men and women had come to it. Of the buildings we saw, the spectacle of one must fail of description, for it is beyond dispute the most wonderful edifice in the world. The inner walls are all embellished with gold. There are slabs of coloured marble, the like of which we had never seen, inlaid throughout with gold mosaic and surrounded by branches (formed from) green mosaic. In its upper parts are well-placed windows of gilded glass which steal all looks by the brilliance of their rays, and bewitch the soul. God protect us (from their allurement). We learnt that its founder, after whom it was named, spent hundredweights of gold on it. He had been vizier to the grandfather of this polytheist King. This church has a belfry supported by columns of coloured marble. It was raised cupola over cupola, each with its separate columns, and is therefore known as the Columned Belfry, and is one of the most wonderful constructions to be seen. May God, in His kindness and benevolence, soon exalt it with the adhan ['call to prayers', i.e. make it a Muslim mosque].

The Christian women of this city follow the fashion of

Muslim women, are fluent of speech, wrap their cloaks about them, and are veiled. They go forth on this Feast Day dressed in robes of gold-embroidered silk, wrapped in elegant cloaks, concealed by coloured veils, and shod with gilt slippers. Thus they parade to their churches, or (rather) their dens [a play on the words kana'is, 'churches', and kunus, 'dens'], bearing all the adornments of Muslim women, including jewellery, henna on the fingers, and perfumes. We called to mind – in the way of a literary witticism – the words of the poet: 'Going into the church one day, he came upon antelope and gazelle.'

We invoke God's protection for this description which enters the gates of absurdity and leads to the vanities of indulgence, and seek protection also from the bewitchment that leads to dotage. In truth He is the Lord of power and forgiveness.

Seven days we spent in this city, living in a hostel used by Muslims. We left it on the morning of Friday the 22nd of this holy month and the 28th of December, bound for Trapani, where there are two ships, one waiting to sail to Andalusia and the other to Ceuta. We had sailed to Alexandria in this, and both were carrying pilgrims and Muslim merchants.

Through a line of continuous villages and farms we trended, observing land, both tilled and sown, such as we had never seen before for goodness, fertility, and amplitude. We compared it to the 'qanbaniyah' [Latin, campania, 'countryside', a relic of the Roman occupation] of Cordova, but this soil is choicer and more fertile.

We passed one night only on the road at a place called 'Alqamah [Alcamo], a large and spacious town with markets and mosques. Its inhabitants, and those of the farms we had passed on our way, were Muslims all. Leaving 'Alqamah at daybreak on Saturday the 23rd of the holy month and the 29th of December, we passed, not far from it, a castle called Hisn al-Hammah [the Castle of the Baths]. It is a large place with many thermal springs which God throws up from the ground charged with special elements, and so hot that the body can hardly bear them. We passed one on our road and, dismounting from our animals, refreshed our bodies by bathing in it. We arrived at last at Trapani in the late afternoon of that day and lodged in a house that we hired for the purpose.

Recollections of the town of Atrabanish [Trapani] in the island of Sicily

May God restore it (to the Muslims)

Trapani is a small city enclosed by walls, and white as a dove. It possesses an excellent harbour, most suited for shipping, and is therefore much used by the Rum, particularly those who sail to the Barr al-'Adwah [the coast of Africa].[165] Between it and Tunis is only a day and a night's journey, and the voyage is never stayed, winter or summer, save when the wind is unfavourable. Otherwise, the crossing by that course is very short.

Trapani is furnished with markets and baths and all the commodities needed in a town. But it lies in the throat of the sea, which encompasses it on three sides. It is joined to the land by only a narrow strip, and the yawning sea waits to engulf the rest. Its people indeed say that the sea will assuredly swallow it. May the end of its days be remitted. But the future is veiled from all save God Most High.

The low prices, resulting from the wide cultivation, make life easy and comfortable in this town, where the Muslims and the Christians have each their mosques and their churches. Near to its eastern corner and inclining to the north, is a great mountain of immense height. At its summit is an isolated crag, on which is a Rumi stronghold connected to the mountain by a bridge. Near to it on the mountain the Rum have a large town, the women of which are said to be the fairest of all the island. God grant that they be made captives of the Muslims. On the mountain are vineyards and cornfields, and we learnt that it has some four hundred springs. It is called Jabal Hamid [Mount St. Julian],[166] and its ascent is quite easy on one side, its people saying that through it Sicily may be conquered. God grant that it be. But in no case will they allow a Muslim to ascend to it, and for this reason they have prepared this strong fortress. Should they apprehend aught, they would collect their women inside it and cut the bridge, leaving a great ditch between them and those on the heights of the adjacent mountain.

It is a strange fact that this town should have all these springs, as described, while Trapani, lying in the plain, should have no water save in a well at some distance from it, and in the not deeply sunk wells of its houses where it is brackish and cannot be swallowed.

At Trapani we found the two ships waiting to sail to the west. We hope, if God wills, to embark on the one bound for Spain. May God with His favour vouch unto us His accustomed beneficent offices.

To the west of Trapani, and about two parasangs from it, are three small close-lying islands called Malitimah [Maritimo], Yabisah [Levanzo], and al-Rahib [Favignana], which was named after a monk who lived on its summit in a fortress-like building that serves as a place of ambush for the enemy. The other two islands are uninhabited, and in this lives no one but the monk we have mentioned.

The Month of Shawwāl (580)

[5th of January–2nd of February, 1185]
May God grant us His grace and favour

THE new moon commenced on the night of Saturday the 5th of January, according to testimony given to the Hakim of Trapani to the effect that the new moon of the month of Ramadan had been seen on the night of Thursday and that the people of the capital of Sicily, already described, had begun the fast on that Thursday.[167] The people therefore began their festival of the ending (of the month of fasting) after taking count from that Thursday. We prayed, on this holy feast-day, in a mosque in Trapani with a group of its inhabitants who had refrained, for a proper reason, from going to the *musalla* [place of prayer, where the khutbah was recited. See note [163]. We offered up the traveller's prayer.[168] May God restore every stranger to his homeland. The remainder of the people, with timbal and horn, went to the *musalla* with their magistrate. We marvelled at this, and at the Christian's tolerance of it.

Having agreed on the price of our passage in the ship going, within the will of God, to Spain, we turned our minds to provisions for the journey. But God alone can assure our help and easement, for there arrived an order from the King of Sicily stopping all ships from sailing from the shores of his island. It seems that he is preparing a fleet, and no ships may sail until the fleet has left. May God frustrate his designs, and may he not achieve his ends. The Genoese owners of the two ships hurried aboard to protect themselves from the Wali, but he relaxed as the result of a bribe the Genoese gave him, so that they remained in their ship and awaited a wind on which to sail.

At this time there came from the west the sad news that the Lord of Majorca had seized Bajāyah [Bougie].[169] May God

Y

grant that it be not so, and give, in His grace and favour, success and quiet to the Muslims.

The people of Trapani are making conjectures as to the destination of the fleet this tyrant is preparing. As to its numbers, some say there are three hundred sail, between galleys and dromonds, while others say there are more, and that a hundred ships carrying victuals are to accompany it. May God frustrate it, and turn fortune against it. Some men say its destination is Alexandria – may God guard and defend it – and others Majorca – God defend it[170] – while yet others say Africa – God defend it – in defiance of the Treaty, being urged thereto by the bad news from the west; but this conjecture is the most unlikely, for the King appears to respect the Treaty.[171] May God lend His aid against him, and not for him.

There are others who see the levy as intended solely for Constantinople the Great, because of the momentous news which has come concerning it; news which inspires the soul with bodings of strange events, proving incontestably the truth of the traditions transmitted from the Chosen One [Muhammad][172] – God's blessings upon him. The report had it that the sovereign of Constantinople [Manuel Comnenos] had died and left the kingdom to his wife, who had a young son. But his cousin had usurped the throne, killed the widow, and seized the boy. A son of the rebel had been enjoined to kill the boy, but, his heart being moved to compassion, he had released the youth, who after many hazards, had been brought by destiny to this island.[173] He arrived in wretched state as a menial, being servant to a monk, and concealing his royal figure in a lackey's cloak. But the secret came out and the affair was disclosed, for the cloak was of no avail. When by order of William King of Sicily the youth was brought before him and questioned, he declared that he was the serf and servant of the monk. But a party of Genoese on their way to Constantinople confirmed his identity and proved that it was he. There were besides, the signs and indications of royalty that shone from him, amongst which, as it was related to us, was the following:

It happening that King William went forth on one of his feast-days, the people had disposed themselves to greet him, and the youth in question was placed amongst the personal suite. All bowed deeply in humility and deference to the King that his looks might fall upon them: all save the youth, who did not incline deeply in salutation. Then was it known that his royal dignity had held him from giving the reverence of a subject. King William took great care of him, bestowing on him a dwelling-place and keeping him under most careful protection for fear that his cousin the rebel might do him mischief unawares.

He had a sister famed for her beauty with whom the usurping cousin had become enamoured. Yet he could not marry her, for the Rum do not take their kinswomen in marriage. But impetuous love, blind and deafening desire, and the transports that lead their possessor to bliss and then desert him, impelled him to take her and go with her to the Emir Mas'ud, Prince of Darub [Cilician Gates] and of Quniyah [Iconium, or modern Konia] and the lands of the foreigners adjoining Constantinople. Of the zeal of this Emir for Islam we have already spoken in these writings. It is enough to tell you that the Prince of Constantinople still pays tribute to him, and propitiates him by ceding some neighbouring territories.

In the presence of the Emir, he embraced, together with his (beloved) cousin, the creed of Islam; and a golden crucifix which had been heated by fire, he trampled beneath his feet. This, according to their fashion, is the surest way of renouncing the Christian religion and giving allegiance to the faith of Islam. He then married his cousin and achieved the object of his desire. Finally, he took the Muslim armies to Constantinople and entered it with them, slaying of its inhabitants some fifty thousand of the Rum. He was aided in his enterprise by the Aghr . . . . . n, who are a sect of the people of the Book. They speak Arabic, and for all other sects of their race they bear a concealed enmity. They do not allow the eating of pork. The citizens weakened themselves by their dissensions, and God struck the spring of strife between them so that the Muslims seized Constantinople.[174]

Its countless riches were taken to the Emir Mas'ud, who placed over forty thousand Muslim horsemen in the city, which now adjoined the Muslim lands. This conquest if it be true, is one of the greatest portents of the Day of Judgement. God best knows of hidden things.

We found this story to be spread about the island on the tongues of the Muslims and Christians alike, who believe it, and have no doubts about it. News of it had been brought by some Rum ships which had arrived from Constantinople, and the first question of the King's Commissioner when we were brought before him on our entry into Palermo had been whether we had news of Constantinople. We knew nothing, and did not understand the meaning of the question until later.

They then enquired concerning the question of the King of Constantinople, this youth, and the rebel's pursuit of him, for he has spies who seek to kill him; indeed, because of this the youth is kept near to the Prince of Sicily, so closely guarded that an eye-glance can hardly fall on him. We were told that he is a tender shoot of youth with the rosy hue of a stripling, slender and with a royal splendour about him. He studies with diligence the Arabic and other tongues, is distinguished for his kingly bearing, and is sagacious, despite his youthful age and inexperience.

Now, as it is reported, the Sicilian King intends to despatch the fleet to Constantinople,[175] in shame for this youth and what befell him. But however these designs may fare, Almighty and Glorious God will drive him back with losses, showing him the unblessed nature of his way, and raising tempests to confound him. For as He desires so can He accomplish. This news from Constantinople – God grant that it be true – is one of the greatest miracles and awaited manifestations of the world. God indeed is all-powerful in His decrees and in what He predetermines.

The Month of Dhu 'l-Qaʿdah (A.H. 580)

May God accord us His grace and favour

THE new moon rose on the night of Monday the 4th of February, while we awaited in Trapani the end of winter and the sailing of the Genoese ship in which we hoped to travel to Andalusia. Pray God – Mighty and Glorious is He, and to be praised – may bless our aim, and help us with His grace and favour in our designs.

During the time of our stay in this town, we learnt painful things about the grievous state of the Muslims in this island concerning their relations with the worshippers of the Cross – may God destroy them – their humiliation and abasement, their state of vassalage under the Christians, and the duress of the king, bringing the calamities and misfortunes of apostasy on those of their women and children for whom God had ordained such suffering.

The King sometimes used force as a means of making some of their sheiks renounce their faith. There is the story of recent years concerning one of the learned doctors in Muslim law in the capital of their tyrant king. He is known as Ibn Zurʿah, and was so pressed by the demands of the officials that he declared his renunciation of Islam and plunged into the Christian religion. He diligently memorised the New Testament, studied the usages of the Rum, and learnt their canon law, until he was accepted into the body of priests who give judgement on law-suits between Christians. When a Muslim case arose, he would give judgement on that too, based on his previous knowledge of the Muslim religious law; and thus recourse was made to his decisions under both codes. He owned a mosque opposite his house which he converted into a church. God protect us from the results of apostasy and false ways. With all this, we heard that he but concealed what was really his true faith; and it may be that he took advantage of the exception allowed for in God's words, 'Save he who, being under compulsion, yet in his heart believes' [Koran XVI, 106].

During the last few days there has come to this town the leader and Lord of the Muslim community in this island, the Qa'id Abu 'l-Qasim ibn Hammud,[176] commonly known as Ibn al-Hajar. This man belongs to that noble house on the island of which the eldest son successively assumes the Lordship (of the Muslims). We were further told that he is an upright man, liking good, loving his kind, full of acts of charity such as ransoming prisoners, and distributing alms to travellers and stranded pilgrims, together with many noble deeds and generous acts.

The town became greatly disturbed on his arrival. He had recently been out of favour with this tyrant, who had confined him to his house, on charges preferred against him by his enemies, who traduced him with untrue stories, including that of corresponding with the Almohades – whom God support. He would have been destroyed, but for the Guardian Angel, and even then suffered a series of divestments which exacted from him more than thirty thousand mu'mini dinars. He was parted from all the houses and properties which he had inherited from his forebears, and at last was without wealth. More recently the tyrant had taken him back in his favour, and had granted him a post in his government. But he discharged his duties like a slave, his person and his property impounded.

When he arrived at Trapani, he expressed a wish to meet us. We met and he revealed to us such matters concerning his and his people's relations with their enemies as to draw tears of blood from the eyes and melt the heart in suffering. For instance, he said to me, 'I have wished to be sold (as a slave), I and my family, that perhaps the sale would free us from the state we are in and lead to our dwelling in Muslim lands.' Reflect on a state of affairs which could lead this man, notwithstanding his great authority and exalted rank, his large household, his sons and his daughters, to make such a choice. For him and for all the Muslims of this island, we begged of Almighty and Glorious God a happy deliverance; and upon every Muslim standing in worship before Great and Glorious God lies the duty of offering prayers on their behalf. In tears ourselves, we left him crying. But our spirits had been enriched by the nobleness of his actions, his rare qualities, the soundness of his judgement, his limitless beneficence and generosity, and the goodness of his character and nature.

When in Palermo we had seen houses belonging to him, his brothers, and members of his house, which were like lofty and superb castles. The condition of these men, in a word, was exalted, and his wa. so in particular. During his time here he has performed many good deeds towards those pilgrims who are poor or distressed, mending their affairs, and giving them the money for the cost of their journey, as well as provisions. May God prosper him for it, and give him by His grace, his just reward.

The (Muslim) people of this island suffer, amongst other tribulations, one that is very sore. Should a man show anger to his son or his wife, or a woman to her daughter, the one who is the object of displeasure may perversely throw himself into a church, and there be baptised and turn Christian. Then there will be for the father no way of approaching his son, or the mother her daughter. Conceive now the state of one so afflicted in his family or even in his son. The dread of their falling to this temptation would alone shorten his life. The Muslims of Sicily therefore are most watchful of the management of their family, and their children, in case this should happen. The most clear-sighted of them fear that it shall chance to them all as it did in earlier times to the Muslim inhabitants of Crete. There a Christian despotism so long visited them with one (painful) circumstance after the other that they were all constrained to turn Christian, only those escaping whom God so decreed. But the word of chastisement shall fall upon these infidels. God's will shall prevail: there is indeed no God but He.

So great is the standing of this al-Hamudi [Abu Kassim] amongst the Christians – may God destroy them – that they declare that if he turned Christian, not a Muslim in the island but would follow him and imitate his act. May God protect them all, and deliver them, in His grace and favour, from their plight.

We came upon another striking example of their state, such as breaks the spirit in pity and melts the heart in compassion. One of the notables of this town of Trapani sent his son to one of our pilgrim companions, desiring of him that he would accept from him a daughter, a young virgin who was nearing the age of puberty. Should he be pleased with her, he could marry her; if not, he could marry her to any one of his country-men who liked her. She would go with them, content to leave her father and her brothers, desiring only to escape from the temptation (of apostasy), and to live in the lands of the Mus-lims. Her father and brothers were disposed to this proposal, since they themselves might find escape to Muslim lands when the embargo that impeded them should be suspended. The man sought after, in order to earn a heavenly reward, accepted the offer, and we helped him to seize an opportunity which would lead him to the felicities both of this world and the next.

We ourselves were filled with wonder at a situation which would lead a man to give up so readily this trust tied to his heart, and to surrender her to one strange to her, to bear in patience the want of her, and to suffer longings for her and loneliness without her. We were likewise amazed at the girl – may God protect her – and at her willingness to leave her kin for her love of Islam, and her wish 'to seize a solid handle' [Koran II, 256; XXXI, 22]. May Almighty and Glorious God protect and guard her and console her by uniting her to her own and, by His grace, confer on her His favours. When her father had consulted her as to the project she had said, 'If you hold me back, the responsibility (before God) will be yours.' The girl was motherless, but had two brothers and a little sister from the same father.

The Month of Dhu 'l-Hijjah (A.H. 580)

[5th of March–3rd of April, 1185]

May God accord us His favour and blessings

THE new moon was concealed from us by the continuing storm, so we completed the days of the month of Dhu 'l-Qa'dah, by computation, on the night of Wednesday the 6th of March. We were still in this city [Trapani], eagerly awaiting an early departure, and the good news of a favouring wind. May God in His power promote our purposes and ensure our safety. It happened that we saw the new moon on the night of Wednesday. It had waxed, so it was known that it had risen on the night of Tuesday, and the computation of the month was changed thereto. At midday of Wednesday the 9th of the month, the 13th of March – which was the Day of 'Arafah, may God give us of His blessings, and the blessings of the holy station on 'Arafat – we embarked on the ship. May God prosper it, and grant us safety in it.

We passed the night ready for travelling – God grant that our journey be expeditious – and on the morning of the Feast of Sacrifice we were on the deck of the ship. May God help us to endure tribulation in it. We are more than fifty Muslims. May God protect all, and in His grace and favour, unite them to their native lands. Praise be to Him who can ensure this. We were eager to sail, but the wind was not propitious, and for twelve days we came and went between the ship and the shore, being each night disposed to sail. At last God allowed us to put to sea on the morning of Tuesday the 21st of Dhu 'l-Hijjah, the 25th of March.

We sailed, by the blessings of God Most High, in three Rumi ships which had agreed to keep course together, the foremost keeping contact with the last. We came to the island of al-Rahib [Favignana], which we have already mentioned in this narrative, and which lies about eighteen miles from Trapani. The wind having changed, we turned aside to its port. There by a singular coincidence we found the ship of Marco the Genoese, which had come from Alexandria with more than two hundred of our companions, the Maghrabi pilgrims. We had parted with them at Mecca – may God sanctify it – in the month of Dhu 'l-Hijjah of the year 9 [A.H. 579], and had heard no news of them since leaving them, nor had they of us. Amongst them was a party of our company from Granada, including the jurisprudent Abu Ja'far ibn Sa'id, our companion and guest in Mecca at the time of our sojourn there. When they learnt of us, they gazed upon us from the ship, clinging to its sides and edges, raising their voices to announce the good news of our safety and our meeting, joyful at our reunion, weeping for happiness, lost in amazement, and marvelling at the good cheer which had befallen them. We felt the same for them, and the day was indeed felicitous, and following the great Feast, we took it as a new feast. Friends visited each other, and we and they passed the happiest and pleasantest of nights. This meeting we took to be a happy augury of our hopes of reunion, if Almighty and Powerful God pleases, with our native lands.

At dawn of the night of Tuesday the 22nd of the month, God gave us a favouring wind, and we sailed in four ships, heading, under the providence of God Most High, for the island of Andalusia [Spain]. All that day we sailed along, our ships urged by an easy wind, but our longings for Andalusia almost took the place of the wind, for their excitement and commotion. May God help and speed us. But after a day and two nights under way, the wind changed and blew from the west into our faces, turning us back along our tracks so that we returned to our start at the port of the island of Favignana. We arrived there on the night of Thursday, the 24th of the month. We sailed from it on the evening of Friday following, alone and without the other ships, and were alarmed by a vehement wind which drove the ship on at speed, so that by the morning of Sunday the 27th of the month we had come to the tip of the island of Sardinia, which we speedily passed. Its length is more than two hundred miles. Joyfully we announced the good news to each other, and in a day and two nights our ship was able to cross more than five hundred miles, a remarkable thing. The favouring wind then stilled, and another blew and took us, on the night of Monday the 28th of the month, the 1st of April, towards the coast of Africa. On Monday we anchored at an island known as Khalitah [Galita]. It is uninhabited, but it is said that it was inhabited of old, and is now the mark of the enemy. About thirty miles lie between it and the mainland, which is visible to the eye. In the entrance to the port we endured rough seas, from which God protected us, and, since the storm continued, we remained in it awaiting relief from God Most High. Four days we stayed there, the last being Thursday, the beginning of Muharram.

The Month of Muharram of the Year 81 *(581)*

[4th of April–3rd of May, 1185]

God grant us His grace and favour

THE new moon was obscured from us, and we computed
it as beginning on the night of Thursday the 4th of April.
May God grant us the blessings of this year, and its favours,
giving us of its benefits and preserving us from its evils, and
vouchsafing our reunion with our native land. He is indeed
the Listener and the Answerer. On the night of Friday following, God sent us an east wind and on it we put to sea. It was
a soft and gentle wind, but it then became turbulent, and a
strong wind drove along the ship at the greatest speed and
smoothness. From the time of our embarking (at Trapani) we
had been unceasingly snuffing at the east in our anxiety for
a wind, but there came not a breeze, so that from its absence
we deemed it to be a thing of fable, till God overtook us with
His benevolence and benign works and sent it to us now in
the month of April. May God in His grace and favour grant
us safety. This wind accompanied us for about two days, during
which we progressed with celerity. We passed the island of
Sardinia on our right. Varying winds then played with us, and
there we stayed, going the length and breadth of the sea and
perceiving no land until our thoughts were agitated and we
conceived that the winds would bring us to the coast of Barshlunah [Barcelona]. May God destroy it. But God brought us
relief, and we descried the coast of the island of Yabisah [Iviza]
on the night of Saturday the 10th of the month, although we
could hardly see it from the cloud-enveloped distance. But on
Saturday it appeared clearly to us, and after undergoing difficulties from the varying winds at its ingress, we entered the
port and anchored. The city was four miles away. Our place of
anchorage was opposite the island of Faramantirah [Formentera],

which is separated four or five miles from Iviza and has many inhabited villages. We stayed in its port near two rugged mountains which confront each other and which are called al-Sheikh and al-'Ajuz ['The Old Man' and 'The Old Woman'].

That night, at eventide, we descried the mountains of Andalusia, the nearest being the mountain of Daniyah [Denia] known as Qa'un [Mongo]. We gazed upon this land, joyful to see it, and rejoicing in approaching it. On the morning of Sunday, the 11th of the month, we came to the port of Denia, but the wind being from the west, we awaited Almighty and Glorious God's fulfilment of His beneficent works, if He so willed, by sending a favourable wind by which to spread our sails under His mercy. And on the morning of Tuesday the 13th, with the favour and blessings (of God) we sailed with a light east wind we hardly felt, begging Almighty and Glorious God to animate its life and strengthen its force. The mountains of Denia were now visible before us. May God complete His favour to us, and in His power perfect His work on our behalf. By His goodness, the wind continued and spread so that we came to Qartagannah [Cartagena] (and landed) on the evening of Thursday the 15th, thanking God for the safety and health He had granted. Praise be to Him, Lord of the Universe, His blessings upon Muhammad, Seal of the Prophets, and Leader of the Messengers (of God).

We left after the Friday prayers on the 16th of the month, and passed the night in the territory of Cartagena, in the tower known as the Tower of the Three Cisterns; from it on Saturday we fared to Murcia, thence the same day to Libralah [Lebrilla], thence on Sunday to Lurqah [Lorca], on Monday to al-Mansurah, on Tuesday to the plain of Qanalish [Caniles di Baza], on Wednesday to Wadi Ash [Guadix]. On Thursday the 22nd of Muharram [581], the 25th of April [1185], we came to our home in Granada.

'She threw away her staff and there she stayed,
As does the traveller at his journey's end.'

Praise be to God for His beneficent works, and for the ease-ment and relief He gave us. His blessings upon the Lord of the Messengers and of others, Muhammad, his noble Messenger and Chosen One, and upon his family, and his Companions who followed the true course by his guidance. May he be preserved, exalted, and honoured.

The span of our journey, from the time of our leaving Granada, to that of our return, was two full years and three months and a half.

Praise be to God, Lord of the Universe.

Notes

1. A.H. = Anno Hijrah, or the 'Year of the Migration' of the prophet Muhammad to Medina from Mecca in A.D. 622, from which date the Muhammadan era begins. In their calendar the months are computed by the time elapsing between consecutive new moons, and the resulting lunar years of 354 days do not coincide with our solar years with their fixed almanac months. The lunar year is eleven days shorter than the solar, and so each cycle of a hundred Muhammadan years gains three years on a western cycle. The formula

$$\text{A.H.} - \frac{3 \text{ A.H.}}{100} + 621 = \text{A.D.}$$

gives a rough correspondence. The lunar months occupy a different place in the calendar each year, so that, for example, the sacred months in which the pilgrimage must be performed will some years fall in the winter and in others in the summer, spring or autumn. The date of the lunar month, like that of the Jewish, gives the age of the moon.

2. The legal Muslim day begins at sunset. When therefore Ibn Jubayr says that he left at 'the first hour of Thursday the 3rd of February' he left after sunset on Thursday, which was the first hour of the 8th of Shawwal, which extended to sunset of Friday the 4th of February. This adjustment must be made throughout the book in such cases. By the same token, 'the night of Thursday' must be rendered 'Wednesday night' in our style.

3. The text says 'al-Ghaydaq'. I have accepted Schiaparelli's emendation.

4. I have accepted Schiaparelli's substitution of 'Qashmah' for 'Nashmah'. There is a burgh named Casma that was part of the lands of Medina Sidonia and that is near to the sea and on Ibn Jubayr's road to Tarifa. Moreover, the Arabic 'N' is very easily confounded with the 'Q'.

5. Rum is the term the Arabs use to describe the Christians of the Orient, in distinction to those of the West, whom they called Franks. The Genoese and other Italians, although sometimes included amongst the Franks, were more generally confounded with the Greeks as 'Rum'.

6. An Arabic mile measured 1,921 metres as compared with 1,609 in an English mile.

7. Qusmarkah. Schiaparelli refers to *Carta Catalana*, 1375 (see Nordenskiöld, *Periplus*), which says 'Cauo sa March', and to Benincasa, 1476 (see Lelewel, *Portulan général*), 'Caou sa March', both of which are close to the Arabic transcription.

8. Although the Barr all-Gharb (Land of the West) of the North African coast usually refers to the western sector extending from the Gulf of Qabes westward, in this case the author comprehends as well the shores of Egypt.

9. Wright edited this 'The Islands of the Bath', but I am with Schiaparelli, who quotes Idrissi, I, c, p. 101, and Bakri, *Description de l'Afrique septentrionale*, ed. de Slane, p. 85. The Carta Catalana has 'Illa de colomi'.

10. Ar. *funduk*, probably derived from the Greek πανδοκειον. Up to modern times, according to Amari, *Voyage en Sicile de Muhammad ebn Djubair*, the Sicilian dialect employs the word 'funducu' to describe the simpler inn on main roads or in villages. Many of these inns are found in the Attarin (Ar., *perfume*) quarters.

11. *Zakat* in its primitive sense denotes 'purification', whence it is used to describe that portion of property bestowed in alms as a sanctification of the remainder to its owner. It is a religious duty incumbent on every Muslim who is free, adult, and possessed of property upon which *zakat* is due. This must have been in his possession for a whole year. *Zakat* is not due on the necessaries of life like houses, or implements of work, such as books or tools. The *zakat* varies according to the type of property. Camels, cattle, horses, sheep and goats, silver, gold, mines, and the fruits of the earth have each their particular assessment. Articles of merchandise are appraised and, if the value exceed two hundred dirhams, a *zakat* of $2\frac{1}{2}$ per cent. is paid on it. When collected, *zakat* may be given to paupers, the needy, debtors, slaves for the purchase of their freedom, travellers, the collectors of *zakat*, or be disbursed in the service of God or for religious warfare.

12. These *mudaris* or colleges were theological seminaries founded in Cairo by Saladin to promote the orthodox Shafi doctrine of the Sunni persuasion against the Shi'ite heresy and the speculative philosophy of the Dar al-'Ilm (House of Learning) established by the Fatimids. The students boarded in these collegiate-mosques, whose administration seems in part to have been copied by the early universities of Europe (see Reuben Levi, *A Baghdad Chronicle*, Cambridge, 1929, p. 193). For descriptions of these celebrated academies, which were almost as famous for their architectural beauties as for their educational merits, cf. Hitti, *History of the Arabs*, pp. 410–12 and 659–61, and Stanley Lane-Poole, *A History of Egypt in the Middle Ages*, p. 204.

13. *Ibn al-Sabil* (son of the road) is the legal term for the traveller to whom, at need, help may be given from the Bayt al-Mal (Treasury) from funds provided by the *zakat*.

14. These mu'mini dinars were struck by the first Almohade Caliph, 'Abd al-Mu'min (1130–63). As Ibn Jubayr says, they were worth half the Egyptian dinar. Amari, *ibid.*, note 78, says that he examined some of these coins in the French Cabinet des Medailles together with the French numismatist M. A. de

Longperrier, and found that their weight was 4.75 grammes, and that the gold was very pure. The Tyrian dinar was not quite equivalent to the Egyptian. Dinars and dirhams were respectively the standard gold and silver coins that were instituted by the 'Umayyad Caliph 'Abd al-Malik about the year A.D. 691. The names derived from the Roman denarius and the Greek drachma. In transition to the Arabic, the silver denarius of the Romans became the gold coin of the Arabs. It weighed almost sixty grains Troy and was worth intrinsically something under ten shillings. It is to-day the name of the equivalent of the pound sterling in Jordan and Iraq. The drachma or dirham remained the name of the silver coin, weighed about $47\frac{1}{2}$ grains Troy, was rated at about fifteen dirhams to the gold dinar and, at the ratio of gold and silver of those days, was worth about eightpence. It should not be forgotten, however, that gold and silver had a considerably higher purchasing power before the discovery of the New World in the fifteenth century, and an ounce of gold could command an amount of food and labour that at the beginning of the twentieth century would have been paid by three ounces. The dirham was also the unit of the system of weight.

15. The Festival of the Sacrifice has various names: 'Id al-Adha, 'Id al-Baqr, 'Id al-Kabir in Arab lands, while in Persia it is called 'Id Qurban, and in Turkey and Egypt 'Id Bayram. It commemorates Abraham's preparedness to sacrifice his son Ishmael, and is part of the ceremonies connected with the Hajj or pilgrimage. It falls on the 10th day of the Muslim month of Dhu 'l-Hijjah, the twelfth month of their calendar, and the month in which the pilgrimage to Mecca must be made. Ibn Jubayr will perform his pilgrim rites a year later.

16. Misr is the name applied to Fustat, now old Cairo. Al-Qahira, 'the Victorious', or modern Cairo, was founded in A.D. 969 by the Fatimid Dynasty.

17. The editor of the text quotes Maqrizi, vol. II, p. 436, as saying that it was the head of Zayd ibn Ali 'l-Husayn.

18. The Tabi'un, or followers of the Companions of the Prophet, are important in the Sunni law for the traditions of the prophet which they related.

19. Abraham is extolled as the 'Friend of God' both in the Koran (IV, 125), and in the Bible (Isa. xli. 8 and 2 Chron. xx. 7).

20. 'Sharifah' (pl. Sharifat) is the feminine of 'Sharif', a title bestowed on the descendants of Muhammad through al-Hasan, the eldest son of his daughter Fatimah. His Majesty the late King Abdulla of Jordan was the head of the line.

21. A congregational mosque (jami') is the large mosque in the city, where Muslims gather for the midday prayers and the allocution called the khutbah. The smaller mosque is called masjid.

22. The prophet's fifteen to twenty wives are called 'Mothers of the Muslims' because by Koranic injunction (XXXIII, 53) their widowhood became perpetual, and no Arab could marry a woman he had called 'Mother'.

z

23. The 'Abbaside Caliphs and their dependents wore black clothing in mourning for the many persons of the Prophet's family who were martyred by the previous dynasty of 'Umayyid Caliphs.

24. The *taylasan* is a scarf thrown over the turban, with one end drawn under the chin and dropped over the left shoulder.

25. It is the prerogative of the Caliph to be prayed for in these Friday *khutbahs*. When Saladin removed the Fatimid Caliph of Egypt, he replaced the name of the Fatimid in the prayers with that of the 'Abbaside Caliph of Baghdad, whose name is here given in full. Saladin's own name then follows as the reigning sovereign.

26. The Almohades (*Muwahhadis*, 'Unitarians') arose from a revolt, led by a Berber, against the anthropomorphic tendencies then prevalent in Islam. Believing themselves to be the only true believers, they carried fire and sword from Morocco northward through Spain, and westward to the frontiers of Egypt, to form a vast new empire. The grandson of the first caliph of the dynasty, 'Abd al-Mu'min, was Ya'qub I or al-Mansur (The Victorious), who gained this sobriquet by his defeat of Alphonso VIII of Castile, and who was ruling at the time of these travels. The expectations here reported of the enlargement of his empire to include Egypt and the Hejaz were never fulfilled, for his successor was utterly defeated by the allied Christian princes of Spain, and the dynasty was soon extinguished.

27. This Nilometer was constructed in A.D. 716 by order of the 'Umayyad Caliph Sulayman. The octagonal column stands in a square well sixteen feet in diameter. The waters of the Nile at their lowest cover seven cubits of the column, and when they cover sixteen, the *Wafa'a 'l-Nil* (Full Nile Water) is announced by the Nile-crier, whereupon the embankments of the irrigation canals are cut (about the 24th of August), and the occasion is made one of popular merrymaking. The rate of taxation was determined by the height of inundation from ancient times, as testified by Strabo when describing the Nilometer at Assuan.

28. In Koran IV, 164, it has 'and God spake directly unto Moses', whence he is called Kalim Ilah, or 'God's Interlocutor'.

29. The Arabs probably obtained the word *barid*, 'a post-stage', by corrupting the Latin word *veredus*, 'a post-horse'. The Muslim Empire had a network of post-roads, with post-houses where horses were kept at government expense. The length of the stage varied according to the nature of the country covered, but in Syria it was generally six miles (see Mukaddasi, 181–2).

30. Schiaparelli, p. 354, note 22, says that among the many works that bear the title *Al-Masalik wa'l Mamalik* or *Routes and Countries*, which Ibn Jubayr cites, there has been preserved that of Abu 'Ubayd al-Bakri, whose text relative to Egypt is unedited. Cf. Quatremère in *Notices et Extraites*, ecc XII, pp. 437 *seq.* Regarding the Wall of the Old Women, see *Al-Khitat* of al-Maqrizi, vol. I, pp. 38 *seq.* and 199 *seq.* Another work of this title, and perhaps the earliest of

Arabic geographical treatises, is that of Ibn Khurdadbih, a Persian of the ninth century of our era who, as Chief of the Post in the province of Jibal, the Medea of the ancients, compiled this official handbook.

31. The redoubtable Reginald de Chatillon equipped five galleys and a large number of smaller vessels and ravaged the Muslim territories on the Red Sea. His armament was totally destroyed in the early months of 1183 by a fleet prepared by Saladin and commanded by the chamberlain Husam al-Din Lu'lu. See Ibn Athir, *Tarikh al-Kamil*, ed. Tornberg, vol. XI, p. 323; Abu Shamah, *Kitab al-Raudatain*, Cairo, 1287-8, vol. II, p. 35 (in *Historiens des Croisades, Auteurs Arabes*, vol. IV, p. 230), and Al-Maqrizi, *Kitab al-Suluk* (in Burckhardt, *Travels in Nubia*, London, 1822, p. 497). It was from his castle of Kerak that Reginald later made his swoop on the Muslim caravan that included the sister of Saladin and so, violating the truce, precipitated the fall of Jerusalem.

32. 'Sea of Na'm' seems to be corrupt, and the editor of the text suggests 'Sea of Yemen'.

33. Schiaparelli points out (p. 354, note 24) that the dimensions of the temple (*birba*) at Ikhmim given by al-Maqrizi, *Khitat*, vol. I, pp. 239-40, are the same as those of Ibn Jubayr except for the length, which he gives as a hundred and seventy spans. Idrissi in *Description de l'Afrique et de l'Espagne*, pp. 46-7, talks of the *birba*, but places it in the centre of the city, while Ibn Jubayr has it 'east of the city and below the walls'. This is the one, it would seem, mentioned by Herodotus, vol. II, p. 91, as being surrounded by palm-trees. It was dedicated to Perseus, whom the inhabitants claimed as being of their city by descent. They told Herodotus that the gymnastic games they regularly held were celebrated on instructions received from him when he visited them at the time of his bringing away the Gorgon's head from Libya. Idrissi, it seems, speaks of the one founded by Trajan (A.D. 53-117), which is the one mentioned by Abu 'l-Fida that Reinaud, *Geographie d'Aboulféda*, vol. II, p. 152 (1848), declared to have been in ruins for some years. Al-Maqrizi says that the temple of Ikhmim was destroyed in the year A.H. 780 (A.D. 1378-9), and Ibn Battuta, vol. I, p. 111, says in A.D. 1326 that the destruction had begun then.

34. Quss ibn Sa'idah al-Iyadi, Bishop of Najran, to whose persuasive eloquence the youthful Muhammad had listened as spellbound, and Sahban Wa'il were two great preachers, one Christian, the other Muslim, whose eloquence in the early days of Islam has passed into proverb.

35. 'Aydhab was the port on the Red Sea where the pilgrims, after the desert journey from Qus or from Aswan on the Nile, took ship to Jiddah, the port of Mecca. It was then an important terminal port for the Yemen, Abyssinian, and Indian trade, but it was destroyed in 1422 by the Sultan of Egypt, and Suakin took its place. Its site has been identified at 22'20" N., 36'32" E., twelve miles north of Halayb.

36. For the lacuna in the text the editor has supplied Qina, and Schiaparelli Uswan (Aswan), which latter I prefer. By that route the pilgrim would continue up the Nile from Qus until Aswan, where he would leave the river and turn east across the desert to 'Aydhab. Al-Maqrizi, *Khitat*, vol. I, p. 197, mentions this route, as does Aub 'l-Fida, *Geographie*, vol. II, p. 144: 'Ibn Sayd fait remarquer qu'à Asouan, dans la direction de l'orient, commence la route des pèlerins qui vont s'embarquer à Aydab et dans les autres ports de la mer Rouge pour se rendre à la Mekke. En partant d'Asouan les pèlerins suivent la route Alouadhah; cette route se joint avec celle qui part de la ville de Cous [Qus]. Elle porte le nom d'Ouadhah (Ouverte), parce qui à la différence de celle de Cous elle suit un sol uni.'

37. *Qara'*, lit. 'upper part of the road', and so, I presume, the side of the road, the main path being beaten hollow by the countless treadings of the passing camels.

38. Writing in A.D. 943, Mas'udi, vol. II, p. 438, declares that the round citron (al-utruj al-mudawwar) and the orange-tree (shajar al-naranj) had been brought from India since A.H. 300 (A.D. 912) and were first planted in Oman, whence they were carried by caravan from al-Basrah into 'Iraq and Syria. He observes that the trees were becoming numerous in Syria and Palestine, but that the fruit had lost its original flavour, perfume, and colour because of the change from the peculiar soil, climate, and water of its native land.

39. *Hisbah* is the punishment applied by the *Muhtasib*, an official who, by Koranic precept, 'arranges the affairs of the good and restrains the wrongdoer'. It consists of flagellation with a *dirrah* (scourge), although in this case our author would like the sword to be used.

40. *Daqal*, according to Mas'udi, vol. IV, p. 27, is the 'Iraqi name for the mast of a ship (see Glossary, Wright, p. 31).

41. The date was in fact the 1st of Rabi' al-Akhir, the 24th of July, and, as Schiaparelli indicates, Ibn Jubayr seems to have followed the appearance of the moon rather than the calendar.

42. Although the text says 'the above-mentioned Emir of Mecca', that prince has not hitherto been mentioned, so we may assume some earlier lacuna in the MS.

43. The Great Divide of Islam is between Sunni and Shi'ah. The Sunnis, who represent by far the greater part of Islam, acknowledge the first four caliphs who succeeded Muhammad, and belong to one of the four orthodox schools of jurisprudence: Hanbali, Hanafi, Maliki, and Shaf'i. They follow the path or *sunnah* of Muhammad as described in the 'six authentic' books of *hadith* (traditions), and from this they derive their title, to which assumption the rest of Islam, although itself having traditions, has acquiesced. The Shi'ites, or 'followers' of 'Ali, the fourth caliph and son-in-law of Muhammad, reject the first three caliphs, Abu Bakr, 'Umar, and 'Uthman, and regard them as usurpers who prevented 'Ali

from succeeding directly to the Prophet. The caliphate, or imamate, which latter title they prefer to use, they hold to be hereditary in the house of 'Ali, and while the rest of Islam gave allegiance to the first four caliphs in Mecca, and then successively to the 'Umayyad caliphs of Damascus and the 'Abbaside caliphs of Baghdad, they themselves dissembled, and sometimes even proclaimed, their sole devotion to the descendants of 'Ali. Yet even as to these, the inveterate schismatics disputed. The majority, the Twelvers, deem the succession to have ended at the twelfth Imam, who, disappearing without issue into a cave about the year 878, still guides his people through his theologians and, in a state of temporary occultation, awaits the time when he shall return as the Mahdi, or 'The Rightly-Guided One', to restore the true Islam, to conquer the world, and then to fill it with righteousness before the end of all things. This to-day is the religion of the masses of 'Iraq and the State religion of Persia, where the Shah is but the surrogate of this hidden imam. It is a doctrine which has lent itself to much imposture, and the Mahdi of the Sudan, Muhammad Ahmad, the destroyer of Gordon, disdaining the occupation of boatbuilding, at which his family had achieved some merit, preferred to be one of the many pretenders to this title, and thereby brought much tribulation to his countrymen. The doctrine is the more dangerous because the divinely appointed Shi'ite imam, unlike the elected Sunni caliph, not only inherits the temporal sovereignty of Muhammad, but is impeccable and infallible beyond even, it may be, the pontiff of Rome. It is notable that King Abdulla of Jordan, himself the senior living member of the House of 'Ali, rejects this theory of their great prerogative, and, a sincere Sunni, subscribes to the elective principle for the caliphate.

Another group is the Severners, which regard Isma'il as the seventh Imam, rather than his brother Musa. These Severners, or Isma'ilis, include the Carmathians (see p. 85), the Nusayris (p. 291), the Fatimids, the Druzes, and the Assassins, all dangerous fanatics. The Assassins, happily, are led to-day by the Agha Khan, who, claiming descent from this seventh Imam, receives a tenth of the revenue of his followers, and, like his grandfather, the friend and helper of Napier, has, by the counsel and precept he has given to his often turbulent adherents in India and elsewhere, given signal service to the cause of peace and order. Their 'prophet', Sinan (p. 264), was the infamous Old Man of the Mountain.

Shi'ism has many other sects, and for this has earned our Sunni traveller's strictures (p. 291).

44. *Ihram*, lit. 'prohibition', denotes the doffing of laical dress and the assuming of the pilgrim garb, the *rida* and the *izar* (see Glossary, p. 396), and the abstention from certain actions until, at the proper time, this garb is laid aside. In this state, the pilgrim is prohibited, *inter alia*, from deviating from absolute chastity, from covering the head, wearing anything sewn or having seams, cutting the beard, hair, or nails, anointing the head, plucking a blade of grass or cutting a green tree, and from hunting or slaying animals save the five 'noxious creatures' – a biting

dog, a kite, a crow, a rat, and a snake or scorpion. For any transgressions of the rules of *ihram*, special expiatory sacrifices are ordained, and it is said that none but the Prophet could be perfect in the intricacies of the matter.

45. The *'Umrah* (Lesser Pilgrimage) consists of a visit to the sacred mosque at Mecca, with the sevenfold circumambulation of the Ka'bah and the ritual running between al-Marwah and al-Safa, at any time of the year except during the eighth, ninth, and tenth days of the month of Dhu 'l-Hijjah, those being the days of the *Hajj* or Greater Pilgrimage. It is a meritorious act to perform the *'Umrah*, but the sacrifices, etc., are omitted and it has not the merit of the *Hajj*.

46. The Talbiyat or 'Waiting for Orders' is the cry which the pilgrim, on assuming the pilgrim garb, must constantly cry out as he approaches Mecca. In full it is:

'Here am I, oh God, here am I. (Labbayka, Labbayka.)
No partner hast Thou, here am I.
Verily praise and grace are Thine, and dominion.
No partner hast Thou, here am I.'

47. This is part of the ancient practice of associating the church visible with a bride. Doubtless it was this that led to the covering and veiling of the Ka'bah and its early guardianship by eunuchs.

48. The *tawaf* is the rite of the sevenfold circumambulation, three times at a quick pace and four at normal speed, of the Ka'bah. It is an ancient and pagan practice, preserved by Muhammad to conciliate his idolatrous opponents.

49. This building, the Maqam, which Ibn Jubayr later describes, once housed the sacred standing stone of Abraham on which he stood when, with the help of his son Ishmael, he built the Ka'bah. For both the building and the stone itself, which in the time of Ibn Jubayr was lodged inside the Ka'bah, the author uses the term *maqam* indiscriminately. When the building is intended, I have employed a capital M.

50. In the index to the Sunna, *Kitab al-Kawkab al-Durri*, MS., Leiden, 607, the tradition is given as follows: 'The water of (the well of) Zamzam is for the end for which it is drunk. If you drink it for a cure, it will cure you; if to fill your stomach, it will satisfy it; and if to ease a burning thirst, it will quench it. This well is the hollow (made by the feet) of Gabriel, and with its waters God quenched the thirst of Ishmael.'

51. The ceremony of al-Sa'i consists in running seven times between the hills of al-Safa and al-Marwah in commemoration of Hagar, who, seeing her son Ishmael dying of thirst, ran seven times in great perturbation along the torrent bed until the Angel Gabriel brought forth water from the well of Zamzam.

52. *Halal*, lit. 'that which is loosed or untied', or, in other words, that which is lawful as distinguished from *haram* or that which is unlawful. In this case it means release from the state of *ihram* described at note 42.

53. When the Ka'bah was rebuilt for the eighth time by the Quraysh, they were compelled, through lack of funds, to curtail the plan followed since the time of Abraham and to reduce its proportions by nearly seven cubits in the direction of al-Hatim.

54. Burton, *Pilgrimage to al-Madinah and Meccah*, vol. II, p. 310, note 2, explains that the tradition, as told to him, is that a Jew, having refused to sell his house which was on that spot, was allowed to keep it *in loco* as a lasting testimony to the Prophet's regard for justice.

55. The Carmathians were an Isma'ilite sect of the Shi'ite Muslims whose eponymous founder was Hamdan Qarmat. Towards the close of the ninth century they became a public force, and dominated the peninsula for a hundred years. In A.D. 930 they horrified the Muslim world by capturing Mecca and carrying off the sacred black stone to Bahrayn. It was restored in 951 by order of the Fatimate Caliph al-Mansur.

56. Two words in the text are uncertain, being without diacritical points. I have accepted De Goeje's suggestion, *yaftakha yadaihi bihi*.

57. The comparison is irreverent, it would seem, because the author is alluding to pigeon-towers (*abraj hamam*).

58. The Zaydis are the Yemen Shi'ites, who to-day number a million. Of all the Shi'ites they are the most akin to the orthodox Sunnis and the least fanatical. They are the followers of Zayd, the grandson of al-Husayn son of 'Ali the fourth caliph and son-in-law of Muhammad. The Rafidites are so styled because they are 'rejectors' of the three caliphs who preceded their hero 'Ali. The adjective *sabbabun* I have translated as 'blaspheming', but Mr. 'Ali Sami 'l-Nashar of Alexandria University suggests that perhaps the text should have been edited as *saba'iyun*, meaning the followers of 'Abdullah ibn Saba', a Jewish convert to Islam who first expounded the concept of the divinity of 'Ali.

59. In Muslim countries a small oratory with a niche (*mihrqb*) to indicate the direction of Mecca is often found near a spring or well, or at one of the receptacles that are daily filled with water for the use of travellers (note by Schiaparelli).

60. Instead of Jiyad, Ibn Batuta, vol. I, pp. 321, 323, Ibn Rosteh, *Bibl. Geog. Arab*, vol. VII, p. 44, and al-Fakihi, *Chron. Stadt Mecca*, vol. I, p. 479, vol. II, p. 14, have Ajyad. Al-Muqaddasi gives the reading of Ibn Jubayr. Ajyad al-Akbar and Ajyad al-Asghar (Ajyad the Greater and Ajyad the Lesser) are two mountain passes near Mount Abu Qubays (Ibn Batuta, vol. I, p. 303) and Mount al-Khandamah behind it (*ibid.*, p. 336).

61. Ibn Batuta, vol. I, p. 323, calls this Bab al-Sidrah (The Lotus Tree Gate).

62. These words must be spurious.

63. A kinsman persecutor of the Prophet, and his wife who strewed thorn bushes in the sand where Muhammad would walk barefooted. In flames they expiate their want of grace, or perhaps of tact (Koran CXI).

64. Accepting the variation of al-Balawi, which the editor of the text prefers. The text itself says, 'all traces of which have to-day been destroyed'.

65. So called, according to the tradition of Muhammad, because of the two wings Ja'far received instead of the arms he lost at the Battle of Mutah.

66. Regarding the sighting of the new moon and its official recognition, see al-Battani, edit. Nallino, vol. I, pp. 265–6, and the addition at p. lxxv.

67. Here a posture in the daily prayers in which the head and waist are inclined and the palms of the hands rest upon the knees. Usually a section of the daily prayers.

68. The Shaf' and watar prayers are those with respectively an even and an odd number of rak'ahs of prayers, and that are said after the last night prayers and before the dawn prayers. Prayers with an odd number of rak'ahs, three, five, or seven, are especially meritorious, and indeed odd numbers are generally favoured by Muslims, and by many it would be considered unlucky to begin a work or embark upon a journey on a date of even number.

69. The one prescribed by law for the communal prayers.

70. The 'Chapter of Power', Koran XCVIII, which relates how 'on the night of Power' Muhammad received his first revelations. The word al-Qadr can also mean 'divine decree'. The night thus received its name either from its excellence above all other nights, or because of the divine determinations sent down that night in the form of the Koran. Some Muslims believe that the divine decrees or predeterminations for the forthcoming year are annually fixed on this night. Muslim doctors are not unanimous as to what night exactly it falls, but it is one of the last ten nights of the month of Ramadan.

71. See Concordance et Indices de la Tradition Musalmane, A. J. Wensinck, Tome I, p. 406, for reference to the book and chapter, together with the author, of those collections of traditions òf Muhammad where this quotation occurs.

72. Tashriq, lit. 'drying flesh in the sun'. It is the name given to the three days that follow the Sacrifice, and during them the flesh of the victims is dried.

73. These cairns mark the places where the devil, in the guise of an old man, came before Adam, Abraham, and Ishmael, and was repelled by stoning. To this mode of attack they were prompted by the resource of the Archangel Gabriel.

74. The Arabs believed that each new moon's crescent took thirty nights to form before it appeared to sight.

75. Tarwiyah, or 'giving attention', refers to Abraham's giving attention to the vision in which he was on this day commanded to sacrifice Ishmael his son. Alternatively, it may have the connotation 'carrying water', referring to the provisions made by the pilgrims on this day.

76. This Qarun is the Korah of the Bible who led the rebellion against Moses (Num. xvi and Jude 11). Mention of him and of his riches is made in three chapters

of the Koran: XXVIII, 76–82, XXIX, 39, and XL, 24–5. In the Talmud it is said that three hundred white mules were needed to carry the keys of his treasure (note from Schiaparelli).

77. 'Lawful magic' is the technical expression in Arabic rhetoric for the art of oratory, as opposed to 'unlawful magic', which comprehends the arts of divination, sorcery, and the like.

78. The Psalms of David, with the Torah (Pentateuch) and the Evangel (not quite the Gospel of the New Testament), are, with the Koran, the books that are deemed by Muslims to be divinely inspired.

79. The editor of the text says: 'This date is erroneous; it is clear from those that precede and follow that Ibn Jubayr left Mecca on Tuesday the 20th of Dhu 'l-Hijjah, or the 3rd of April.

80. Isbahan (Isfahan) is more correctly in 'Iraq 'Ajami, which, with Khurasan, formed part of the great Empire of Khwarizm ruled by the Seljuk Turk princes of Khiva. 'Imad al-Din ('Ala al-Din) Tukush Shah ruled from A.D. 1172–99. Schiaparelli points our (note 74) that the use of the definite article *al* before *Daqus* indicates that Ibn Jubayr considered it to be an epithet meaning 'The Brave' rather than a Turkish surname.

81. The word 'Bdellium' (Gr. βδελλιον) is used by Pliny as the name of a plant exuding a fragrant gum. It is similar to true myrrh. (See Gen. ii. 12 and Num xi. 7.)

82. Doughty, *Arabia Deserta*, vol. I, p. 19, thus describes this sudden departure on the signal that is 'eloquent in the desert night, the great caravan rising at the instant, with sudden untimely hubbub of the pilgrim thousands; there is a short struggle of making ready, a calling and running with lanterns, confused roaring and ruckling of camels, and the tents are taken up over our heads. In this haste aught left behind will be lost, all is but a short moment, and the pilgrim army is remounted.'

83. *Rawdah* (garden) after the saying of Muhammad's: 'Between my tomb and my pulpit is a garden of the gardens of Paradise.' By synecdoctic extension, the author sometimes uses it to refer to the whole south portico, in which the *rawdah* proper is situated. This is the adytum or inner sanctuary of the Mosque at Medina. The term is also used to indicate the tomb itself.

84. Sir Richard Burton, in *Pilgrimage to al-Madinah*, vol. I, p. 305, states that in order to distinguish the superior merit of the Ka'bah in Mecca, 'men should not kiss the tomb as at the Ka'bah'.

85. Al-Sharishi, vol. II, p. 142, gives this measurement as forty-four spans, which perhaps is the correct one. The editor of the text wrongly offers this alternative to the thirty spans of the east side.

86. Burton is sadly astray in a translation of this passage (*ibid.*, vol. I, p. 323), even quoting this chest, which is only five spans long, as being the prophet's coffin.

87. *Baki' al-Gharqad*, lit. 'the place full of the roots of the buckthorn'. Burton, *Pilgrimage, etc.*, vol. I, p. 405, describes this tree, and declares it to bε the *Rhamnus Nabeca* or *Zizyphus Spina Christi* that is supposed to have crowned the Saviour's head. It is a form of lotus, but Burton says that disappointed 'lotus-eaters' have successively compared it with a bad plum, an unripe cherry, and an insipid apple. Burton refers to Forskal's *Descriptiones animalium, avium, . . . et flora Aegyptiaco-Arabica*, but gives no reference, and since an exhaustive search made therein for me by the late Librarian of the Cambridge University Library, Mr. A. Scholfield, Fellow of King's College, revealed no trace of the plant, I must conclude that Burton did not check his reference.

88. The two lights referred to are his two wives, Ruqayah and Umm Kulthum, daughters of the Prophet.

89. The Fugitives (*Muhajirun*) were those converts to Islam who fled with the Prophet from the persecution of Mecca to the protection of Medina. The Helpers (*Ansar*) were the early converts in Medina.

90. In the sixth year of his caliphate, according to Abulfeda and Yaqut, 'Uthman inadvertently dropped into this well the prophetic ring, which had come to him through the first two caliphs, he being the third. It had been used as a seal for letters to neighbouring kings. This well therefore also bears the name Bir al-Khatim (The Well of the Seal-ring), for the ring was never found, despite a thorough search. It obtained its name 'Aris from a Jew in Madina, and it is also called Bir al-Taflat (The Well of Saliva), from the Prophet's having spat in it. The sweetening effect of this operation was no longer apparent in 1853 when Sir Richard Burton found it to have 'a pronounced medicinal taste' (*ibid.*, vol. I, p. 413).

91. The Confederates were some leaders of the Jewish tribe of the Banu 'l-Nadir who had been driven out from Madina by Muhammad, and the Quraysh and other tribes of Mecca who had rejected the Prophet. By means of this ditch, the forces of Muhammad were able to hold Mecca from them (Koran XXXIII).

92. According to Ibn Batuta, vol. I, p. 265, the name of this spring is 'Ain al-Zarqa'.

93. I have accepted Schiaparelli's alternative of 'began' from al-Sharishi, vol. II, p. 141. The text has *abtadaru*, 'they made haste to'.

94. So great were the conveniences, together with endowments to maintain them, provided on this desert pilgrim route by the piety of Zubayda that it was called Darb Zubayda (Zubayda's Way) and has been trodden by pilgrim feet for above a thousand years. The crossing, from Madina to al-Kufa, is about six hundred miles, and since our traveller's caravan took twenty days, they covered an average of thirty miles a day: eloquent testimony of the efficiency of the march discipline of the motley host and of the facilities of the road.

95. Sale's translation of *far al-tannur* is 'the oven poured forth water', Palmer's 'the oven boiled', and Rodwell's 'the earth's surface boiled up'. But *tannur* can mean 'reservoir' or 'a place where waters collect', and *far*, in reference to water, means 'welled from the earth'. These are the significances which surely attach to the words when talking of the Deluge.

96. The Enoch who, in Gen. iv. 17 and 18, is given as the eldest son of Cain, and in Gen. v. 21-4 as the sixth in descent from Cain's brother Seth. The juxtaposition of his name with that of Noah reminds us that the apocryphal Book of Enoch is the conglomerate of literary fragments that once circulated under the names of Noah, Enoch, and possibly Enoch's half-as-long living son Methuselah.

97. The abstemious Arabs are great connoisseurs of water, and one of their tests is to weigh it. Lightness is a sign of wholesomeness and digestibility.

98. The 'Abbaside Caliphs were descended from al-'Abbas, the paternal uncle of the Prophet. This dynasty, like the present ruling houses of Jordan and 'Iraq, was Hashemite and Qurayshite. That is, it derived from Hashim, great-grandfather of the Prophet Muhammad, of the tribe of Quraysh. The full title of the ruler of Jordan is 'His Hashemite Majesty King Abdullah I'.

99. See Freytag, *Arabum Proverbia*, vol. II, p. 316, note 30. The significance of the proverb here is that all you desire is under the skin of this brilliant faqih. The proverb was one of the reasons for the arrest and execution of the assassin of Sir Lee Stack, the Sirdar of the Egyptian Army, in 1924, for he had been heard to mutter it before the commission of the crime. In that case, of course, the murderer used it in its hunting sense.

100. See Freytag, *ibid.*, vol. I, p. 370, note 88. The original words referred to Ma'an ibn Sajidah ibn 'Abdullah Shaybanita, whose 'liberalitate' had passed into proverb.

101. The expression 'Where is the readiness . . . etc.' refers to words spoken by 'Ali, the fourth caliph, to his lukewarm followers after the taking of al-Anbar in northern 'Iraq by his rival, Mu'awiyah. Malik ibn al-Ashtar was 'Ali's fighting general.

102. Preferring the *mashurah* (noted) of al-Sharishi to the *musawwarah* (walled) of the text. It is unlikely that this quarter of the city would be walled.

103. Tabby. The thick watered silk or moreen of this name is so called from the quarter in Baghdad where it was made.

104. Schiaparelli omits the name of Mu'in, instead of which he reads *min* (of). He supports this by quoting Ibn Batuta, vol. II, p. 108, and recalls that neither in Ibn Sa'd, III, I, 11-12, nor in Tabari, I, 3,470 *seq.*, is there any mention of Mu'in among the sons of 'Ali.

105. This cemetery is now called al-Kazimayn.

106. This misra' (hemistich) occurs among some verses attributed by Ibn Bassam to the poet Ibn Khafajah, and published by Dozy in his *Récherches*, p. 340. Note by the textual editor.

107. Samarra is the town on the Tigris to which the Caliph al-Mu'tasim, fearful of a rising in Baghdad against his oppressive Turkish guards, removed his seat of government in A.D. 836. It was a fatal move, for it placed the caliphs at the mercy of their praetorians. Ibn Jubayr indulges a grim conceit in a play on its name.

108. The word *qaysariyah*, deriving from the Greek καισάρεια, denotes here a large square building containing store-rooms and shops for merchants. The name was confined to those Arab countries that were subject to the Byzantines, e.g. Egypt, Syria, and Morocco, and was not employed in 'Iraq. It would seem to indicate a market building that was specially licensed by the Caesar in return for a settled fee.

109. St. George is a noted martyr in the Orient, even among Muslims, who include him among their prophets, and confound him with Elijah. Tabari, vol. I, pp. 795-812, has a note on him.

110. Of the men of this trade, Doughty, in *Arabia Deserta*, vol. I, p. 3, says: 'The camel-masters are sturdy, weathered men of the road, that can hold mastery over their often mutinous crews; it is written in their hard faces that they are overcomers of the evil by the evil, and able to deal in the long desert way with the perfidy of the elvish Beduins.'

111. Verse attributed to Ibn Rashiq al-Qayrawani (c. A.D. 1070).

112. Proverbial among the Arabs for his taking after his father. See Freytag, *Arabum Proverbia*, vol. I, p. 658.

113. The Hamdanids were a nomadic dynasty in northern Syria whose capital was Aleppo. The founder, Sayf al-Dawlah (The Sword of the State), was a scourge in the side of the Byzantines, but also a munificent patron of learning. Himself a poet, his court was filled with poets, philosophers, and musicians. To the historian Abu 'l Faraj of Isfahan, who produced one of the most celebrated works of Arabic literature, the *Kitab al-Aghani* (The Book of Songs), he gave one thousand pieces of gold, with his regrets that he could only so inadequately reward him. His martial exploits, together with his promotion of the arts of peace, reviving for a space the dying flame of Arab nationalism, has made him ever dear to Arab minds.

114. The Orontes was called by the Greeks Αξιος Ποταμός from the old Syrian name, Atzoio, meaning 'The Rapid', and this the Arabs corrupted to al-'Asi, 'The Rebel', because, unlike the other rivers of the country, it flowed from south to north. Its one hundred and seventy miles' course is mainly unnavigable and is little used for irrigation, but its valley was a high-road for armies and trade between Egypt and Palestine and Asia Minor.

115. This is the Great or 'Umayyad Mosque that, until the Muslim conquest of Damascus in A.D. 635, had been the Cathedral Church of St. John the Baptist. For eighty years it sheltered under one roof the practice of the Christian and the Muslim faiths, until the tolerance of the Caliph 'Umar was exchanged for the bigotry of Walid. The building begun by the Emperor Theodosius I in A.D. 375 was largely destroyed, and re-erected as a mosque. Retaining much of the materials and form of the church, it is not of the usual pattern of mosque, and has the nave and aisle design of the Christian basilica, with, of course, the added *mihrab*, colonnades, etc. The Byzantine decorative manner is also evident.

116. The Muslims in their conquests distinguished between territory taken by assault and that acquired as a result of capitulation. The former became an integral part of the Muslim Empire; the latter remained in the possession of the vanquished, who paid tribute. This privilege was offered only to Christians and Jews, who are not idolators, but *Ahl al-Kitab* (People of the Scriptures). Hitti, *History of the Arabs*, p. 150, quotes the terms of capitulation for Damascus:

'In the name of Allah, the Compassionate, the Merciful. This is what Khalid ibn Walid would grant to the inhabitants of Damascus if he should enter therein: he promises to give them security for their lives, their property, and their churches. Their city wall shall not be demolished, neither shall any Muslim be quartered in their houses. Thereunto we give to them the pact of Allah and the protection of His Prophet, the Caliphs, and the Believers. So long as they pay the poll-tax, nothing but good shall befall them.' The poll-tax was one dinar and one jarib or measure of wheat on every head; women and children, the aged and the destitute, as well as monks and those sorely distressed, were exempt.

117. Guy Le Strange, in *Palestine Under the Muslims*, p. 246, corrects this to 'east'.

118. Ibn Batuta, vol. I, p. 201, has twenty-five thousand gold dinars.

119. *Kallasah* meaning 'lime-kiln', and referring here to the kiln north of the mosque which provided lime for its building. Saladin, who rebuilt it after a fire that burnt it down, is buried in a mausoleum that still exists in the north of the building.

120. When, in the time of the thrid Caliph, 'Uthman, disputes arose as to the true form of the revelations made to Muhammad, the Caliph appointed a committee to prepare a definitive version. Copies of it were then sent to all the chief cities, and this recension of 'Uthman has remained to this day the standard text.

121. The sense of this passage required the substitution of 'mountain' for 'cave' which is in the text.

122. The words 'and night' have been introduced from Ibn Batuta, vol. I, p. 232.

123. The text gives only *masu . . .*, and Dozy conjectures *massufiyin*, from Massuf, a North African town. King Abdulla of Jordan suggested to me that *masuwamin*, 'specially garbed', might be intended.

124. The 'Choice Ones' were those poor Companions of the Prophet who lived without labour in the mosque at Madina. They are believed to be the early mystics of Islam.

125. This Sunni sect, al-Nubuwiyah, revered a quality of the Prophet Muhammad, *futuwah*, or 'manliness', which gave its name to another and wider organisation. Starting in the twelfth century as a Darwish order, the Futuwah bestowed on its members the patched robe of a Sufi mystic which they called *libas al-futuwah*, or 'the trousers of manliness'. They defined *futuwah* as 'abstaining from injury, giving unreservedly, and being without complaint'. Having been invested with the trousers of a Sufi, the Caliph Nasir, probably as part of his plan to restore the power of the caliphate, reorganised the order on the model of the Christian knightly orders. Its members, *fityan*, were initiated in a special ceremony, took an oath, and assumed the distinctive garments. The Futuwah had a particular attachment to 'Ali, and many of the brotherhood were descendants of the son-in-law of the Prophet. They availed the Caliph nothing in his design, and although the order survived him, it languished and disappeared without achievement. The Nubuwiyah sect which Ibn Jubayr found in Syria had adopted the same motto and dress, but it is interesting that, despite the excessive devotion of the Futuwah to 'Ali, the Nubuwiyah were the scourge of the fanatical Shi'ite sects of Syria, who almost made a god of him.

126. 'Ball on horseback' was the sole distraction allowed himself by Nurredin, Saladin's great predecessor. 'Yet,' he declared, 'I do not play to amuse myself, but rather for needful recreation, since a soldier cannot always be in battle. And at this game we are a-horse and ready for sudden attack by the enemy.'

127. This sentence is misplaced, and should have come in the description of the Bayt Lahiyah (The House of Idols) on p. 288.

128. The *ritl* is a measure of weight that in those days averaged six hundred dirhams (a dirham being 47½ grains Troy) and was equivalent to six pounds. By inversion of the 'l' and the 'r', it is the Greek λιτρα, or litre. It is, however, not only a standard of weight, but also a measure of capacity, for, like the Romans, the Arabs calculated cubic measure by the weight of a specific quantity of oil or wine. See Guy Le Strange's *Palestine Under the Muslims*, pp. 48–51, for a careful description of mediaeval Syrian weights and measures.

129. The name of this Samosatian was Abu 'l-Qassim 'Ali ibn Muhammad. See al-Dhahabi in *Al-Mushtabih fi Asma'i 'l-Rijal*, ed. de Jong, Lugd. Bat., 1881, pp. 276 and 303.

130. The editor of the text notes that there must be some mistake here, since the sums are utterly disproportionate to each other.

131. *Shari'ah*, according to Dozy, Supplément I, p. 748, *a*, is 'a chamber where the fakihs read the Koran and preach'.

132. *Salibiyah*, 'cross-like', means that the sails were set cross-ways to the mast, or, in other words, were square-rigged. The expression is used again on p. 332, where the comment is made that this is the favourite rig among the Rum, since it caught the wind coming aft of the ship.

133. This unsuccessful expedition against Kerak, and the burning of Nablus on his way back, was Saladin's last engagement in Palestine for some years. His next campaign led, in A.D. 1187, to the capture of Jerusalem.

134. Agnes of Courtenay, mother of Baldwin IV.

135. The Assizes of Jerusalem, a collection of usages compiled by John of Ibelin, a Cypriot lawyer, specify one hundred and eleven articles on which duty was paid at Acre.

136. A *qirat* was the twenty-fourth part of anything, in this case of a dinar. It is an Arab corruption of the Greek word κερατιον, the fruit of the keratea, carob, or lotus tree, also known as St. John's bread. From it derives our word 'carat'. Many names of Arab weights and measures came from the Greek and Latin, being those in use in the Syrian provinces of the Byzantine Empire at the time of the Muslim invasion. Mukaddasi, writing at the close of the tenth century A.D., says that the qirat is equivalent to three and a half barleycorns. A barleycorn, or *habb*, weighs about seven-tenths of a grain, English.

137. The manorial system in the Latin Kingdom of Jerusalem maintained the village system of the Arabs. Tenants paid from a quarter to a half of the crop, with the addition of poll-tax and labour dues. As is to be expected, the bulk of the village inhabitants were native Syrians, and it is interesting to observe that our author finds that they deem themselves to be in better case under their Frankish lords than their brother Muslims under Muslim lords.

138. Acre was taken by the crusaders on the 24th of March, A.D. 1104, which was the 24th of Jumada al-Akhirah, A.H. 497, which, of course, is in the last decade of the fifth century A.H. (note by Schiaparelli).

139. 'Adam was sent a red bull, which he used to plough the ground; and he dried the sweat on his brow.' Tabari, vol. I, p. 129; al-Kashaf (Cairo, 1281), vol. II, p. 33; Ibn Athir, vol. I, p. 29; cf. Koran XX, 115, and Gen. iii. 17–19 (note by Schiaparelli).

140. In Syria the Franks adopted from the Arabs the tabor (Ar., *tunbur*, a lute or drum) and the naker (Ar., *naqqarah*, a kettledrum) for their military bands, which hitherto had been served only by trumpets and horns. See P. K. Hitti, *History of the Arabs*, p. 664.

141. Ibn Jubayr refers to King Baldwin IV, who had been a leper since childhood. The King of the Latin Kingdom of Jerusalem would also be Lord of Acre. At the time of Ibn Jubayr's visit, Baldwin's sickness was so advanced that he had already, in 1183, caused his little nephew, the son of his sister Sybilla, to be

anointed King, although Baldwin IV continued active for a time. In 1184 he handed over the regency to Count Raymond of Tripoli, and died in 1185.

142. Count Raymond of Tripoli continued to be regent for the infant Baldwin V. The King's maternal uncle was Joscelin of Courtenay, Seneschal of the Kingdom and notoriously interested in its finances. The prudence of Raymond secured a truce with Saladin soon after Ibn Jubayr left the country, but it was broken by the perfidy and rashness of Raymond de Chatillon, and in 1187 Jerusalem was lost to the Christians. The county of Tiberias had come to Raymond through his wife.

143. Ibn Jubayr should have said 'south-east', but the westward trend of the coast as the voyager sails south might have deceived him.

144. Although the artimone mast means mizzen or after-mast, it was not always so, and, according to M. Jal's *Glossaire Nautique*, art. 2, 'Artimon', it meant, in the thirteenth century, the foremast of a three-masted ship.

145. Jal, *ibid.*, states that the dolon sail was smaller than the artimone, and was square-rigged, whereas the artimone was fore-and-aft.

146. Verses of Ibn Rashiq al-Qayrawani. See *Diwan ibn Hamdis*, ed. Schiaparelli, p. 476; *Tiraz al-Mughalis*, Cairo, 1284, p. 220; al-Maqqari, vol. I, p. 23 *seq.*

147. Sul is the pass in Derbend in the Caucasus whose nights were proverbial for their length. As the editor of the text indicates, the expression derives from a poem by Hunduj ibn Hunduj al-Murri, *Lisan*, XIII, 412.

148. The 'bursting of the dam' of Ma'rib, brought about by a flood, is a memorable event in Arab history and much quoted in Islamic literature. It occurred in the middle of the sixth century, but the ruins of the dam are visible to this day. The event was a great catastrophe to the Arabs, and is referred to in the Koran (XXXIV, 16).

149. To explain the fact of two rudders being mentioned, the editor of the text quotes Jal, *Glossaire Nautique*, where, in the article on 'Timo', he cites several passages from documents of the years 1246 and 1268 showing that ships had two rudders, one on each side.

150. Lit. 'The male-camels were deprived of their sexual powers', meaning, metaphorically, that the men were robbed of their strength. The editor of the text refers to Freytag, *Arabum Proverbia*, vol. II, p. 251, which translates the passage as 'the wild ass was stopped in its onslaught', but this is clearly inappropriate.

151. Like the editor of the text, I am unable to find the origin of this proverb.

152. See Freytag, *Arabum Proverbia*, vol. I, p. 537, note 41. The significance is that if, after wide travels, a man returns home without booty, he yet may be content with being unhurt.

153. Although Norman French was the language of war, society, and the chase, the languages of inscriptions and documents were Greek, Arabic, and Latin.

154. 'Alamah, or 'sign', was the technical term for a kind of motto with which Muslim princes headed their rescripts after the formula Bismillah, 'In the name of God', etc. This is a further indication of the degree to which the Norman kings of Sicily adopted Muslim practice. The 'alamah of King William I, indeed, was only syntactically different from that of the Fatimid Caliph of Egypt, Dhahir (1020–35). See Novairi, Manuscript arabe de le Bibliothèque royal, ancien fonds, n° 702, A, fol. 56, r° (note from Amari).

155. Silk and gold embroidering was introduced into Sicily by its Arab conquerors, and when the Normans arrived in the island in the year 1060, the industry went on much as before, though with greater magnificence. The famous imperial mantle at Vienna, perhaps the most sumptuous of mediaeval embroideries, bears round its edge an Arabic inscription recording that it was made at Palermo in Sicily in the year 1134. Beset with pearls and gems, and worked with gold thread on red silk, it displays a lion leaping on a camel. This design probably represents the capture of the island by the Normans from the Arabs. A fragment of the brocade in pink silk, with a pattern of gazelles, birds, and trees, in gold, in which the Emperor Henry VI (d. 1197) was buried in Palermo, can still be seen in the British Museum. According to the usage of those days, the industry was practised within the precincts of the royal palace, and the intendant of the manufactory was one of the most important servants at the court. (Sacy, Chrest. ar., vol. II, pp. 287 and 305). In addition to providing splendid vestments for the sovereign and other personages, it served as a respectable screen for a seraglio.

156. Conversion to Islam was, of course, forbidden in this Christian kingdom. On the other hand, conversion to Christianity was not encouraged, and indeed the Arab troops which composed so large a part of the Sicilian infantry were deemed to be more trustworthy when unconverted.

157. This earthquake took place in 1163, destroying Catane and other towns in Sicily, while the sea invaded part of Messina. King William was then only seventeen years of age.

158. As is commonly known, there is barely any tide in the Mediterranean, but Amari (p. 72) suggests that in this case the rise and fall was caused by the winds of the north, north-east, and north-west.

159. Amari, p. 76, says that Ibn Jubayr no doubt refers to the leper hospital which William II made in the Church of St.-Jean, founded by Robert Guiscard on the road to Qasr Ja'far.

160. 'Watch-towers and belvederes.' Such synonyms are employed, here and elsewhere, to make rhymed prose, which is the reason for the otherwise unnecessary repetition.

161. At Palermo the terms of the capitulation secured to the Muslims the full enjoyment of their own laws.

AI

162. For the greater part of this century, the trade of the island was largely controlled by the Muslim merchants.

163. The *khutbah* should be delivered not only on Fridays, but on the two great festivals of 'Id al-Fitr and Id al-Adha. Since it includes intercessions, by name, for the Caliph and the reigning sovereign (who should be a Muslim), the prudence of the Norman King could scarcely allow the weekly assembly of thousands of Muslims to profess a faith at once religious and political. But the wisdom of William or his government is attested by the solution of permitting the observance of the *khutbah*, as Ibn Jubayr relates, on the two great feast days. The religious fervour of the Muslims at the time of these festivals would not be embittered by the denial of a sacred duty, and the precautionary police and administrative arrangements that must always attend so large and potentially dangerous an assembly would not be too inconvenient if limited to two occasions in the year. At the same time, the Norman King could smile with indulgence at the intercessions for the 'Abbassid caliphs, who at that time had declined to the position of pawns or even prisoners of the Seljuk sultans.

164. The Church of the Antiochian was named after its Greek founder, the celebrated George of Antioch, Admiral of the Sicilian fleet, who had warred against the Eastern Empire and carried off the silk-workers of Thebes and Peloponnesus to Sicily. He had formerly been an officer in the service of a Muslim prince in al-Mahdiyah, Africa. See Hitti, *History of the Arabs*, p. 609. This church is now called La Martorana, after the name of the founder of a convent attached to the church. The belfry and mosaics remain. See Amari, p. 81.

165. Barr al-'Adwah, 'Land of Passage', means that part of the North African coast which is opposite to Spain, and to which direct passage can be made from that country. By extension, Ibn Jubayr includes Tunisia and the intervening country.

166. The mountain was renamed St. Julian by the Normans in gratitude to the saint, who had given valuable assistance in its capture by setting a pack of hounds at the infidels. See Amari, p. 83. The well-known beauty of the women is attested by our traveller's wish (for awareness of womanly charms is congruous with Muslim piety) that they should one day fall prisoner to the Muslims.

167. An important occasion, since the sight of the new moon is the signal for the end of the fast of the month of Ramadan, and the beginning of the joyful 'Id al-Fitr.

168. The traveller may dispense with a certain number of prostrations as well as the attendance at the congregational prayers on Fridays.

169. The news was indeed true. Abu Ya'qub Yusuf ibn 'Abd al-Mu'min, the Almohade sovereign of Morocco, Algiers, Tunis, and part of Spain, had just died, and his Almoravid rival, 'Ali ibn 'Isa, who held only Majorca, had by surprise taken Bougie from the Almohades. Ibn Jubayr, as his chagrin shows, was

an Almohade supporter. Consult Condé, *Hist. de la dom. des Arabes en Espâna,* part III, cap. 50.

170. Ibn Jubayr's allegiance to the Almohades did not cause him to wish success to a Christian assault on the rival but nevertheless Muslim Almoravids of Majorca.

171. William II had concluded a treaty of peace with Abu Ya'qub (see note 169, p. 386) in 1180. In consideration of the religious fanaticism of their subjects, which on both sides dictated the extermination of the infidel, the treaty was for ten years only, and styled a truce. William's grandfather, Roger, had indeed conquered territories in Tripoli and Tunis which had been lost by William I, but William II, despite his powerful navy, was too much preoccupied with his designs against the Byzantine Empire, then led by the redoubtable Manuel Comnenos, to embroil himself with the Almohade ruler. Neither would he be unmindful of the large market in Tunis for the wheat of Sicily, and, equally or more important, he could not forget that his army was half composed of Moors, and that his Muslim subjects were numerous and inimical.

172. Muhammad had promised the Muslims that they should conquer Constantinople (see, as noted by Amari, the collection of traditions of Muhammad translated into English by Matthews under the title *Mishcat ul musabih,* lib. xxiii, cap. II, vol. II, p. 550, Calcutta, 1809). Ibn Jubayr's confidence that the promise would be fulfilled was confirmed after the passage of three centuries, when the Turks seized the capital of the Eastern Roman Empire in A.D. 1453.

173. Ibn Jubayr seems to have shared the general misapprehension in the island on this matter. The youth who had arrived in Sicily was not the son and heir of Manuel, the deceased Emperor of the Byzantine Empire, but a grandnephew named, like the heir, Alexis. The boy-heir had in fact succeeded, as Alexis II, in 1180 under the unpopular guardianship of his mother, the Empress Maria. But, as Ibn Jubayr says, the throne was usurped by a cousin of Manuel, Andronicus Comnenos, who, gaining the support of the Army, had marched on Constantinople. Maria was strangled, and the youthful wearer of the purple soon followed his mother, throttled by a bow-string, the callous tyrant observing with a kick: 'Thy father was a knave, thy mother a whore, and thyself art a fool.'

Before his usurpation, Andronicus, as Ibn Jubayr relates, had found asylum with the Muslim Sultan of Iconium, whence he had made frequent incursions on his cousin the Emperor Manuel's province of Trebizond, earning for these impious acts against Christian lands the penalty of excommunication. But Andronicus himself never renounced his faith, and it was his brother John who was converted to Islam and received the hand of the Sultan's daughter. 'The sister famed for her beauty' who, as Ibn Jubayr declares, had gone with Andronicus to the protection of the Sultan, was in fact the niece of Manuel, Theodora, the widow of Baldwin III of Jerusalem. She became not the wife but the mistress of the future Emperor, and in the luminous pages of Gibbon we may read that 'the queen of

Jerusalem was exposed to the East his obsequious concubine; and two illegitimate children were the living monuments of her weakness'. Of Andronicus himself the master says: 'in every deed of mischief he had a heart to resolve, a head to contrive, and a hand to execute'. During the civil war that followed the Emperor Manuel's death and Andronicus's usurpation, the Sultan (it was Qilij Arslan II, son of Mas'ud I, but sometimes addressed by his father's name, p. 240) profited by the upset to seize some border villages, and it was this which was magnified by Ibn Jubayr's informants into a Muslim conquest of Constantinople. Andronicus was himself not long after overthrown, and, abandoned to the fury of his numerous sufferers, endured for three days the most painful agonies that their resentment could suggest. The sword of a pitying or a bitter Latin at last released him from his purgatory.

174. No Muslims entered Constantinople, and it was not the Rum (Byzantine Greeks) who were slaughtered. Rather, the Greeks themselves celebrated the advent of Andronicus to Constantinople with a barbarous massacre of the Latin citizens of the town. The text goes on to say that the 'Aghr . . . . . n helped Andronicus in his enterprise. The editor of the text has supplied 'Aghriqiyun (Ar., 'Greeks') from Maqrizi, cod. Leid. 372, vol. III, near the end, but since the previous sentence says that the Greeks were the victims, and the next goes on to say that these Aghr . . . . . n spoke Arabic and did not permit the eating of pork, it does not seem that the author here intends Greeks, although, of course, it was the Greeks who performed the main carnage. I was utterly baffled by this word until Dr. Erwin I. J. Rosenthal of the University of Cambridge suggested that the Qaraites might have been intended. He referred me to Benjamin of Tudela's Itinerary, tr. and ed. by A. Asher, London and Berlin, 1840, pp. 15–25. Benjamin visited Constantinople in the sixties of the twelfth century, and found it to be the spiritual centre of a Jewish sect of that name. There were five hundred Qaraites then in the city, and they were distinct from the two thousand Rabbinite or orthodox Jews, from whom they lived separated by a wall. This division might easily be improved by an outsider into 'a concealed enmity'; the Qaraites might easily have spoken Arabic (or it might be 'Hebrew' was intended, for an error in two letters could change 'Hebrew' into 'Arabic'); and the name Qara'iyun (Ar., Qaraites) is not, in Arabic characters, unlike Aghriqiyun. On the other hand, the Qaraites, from all reports, were peaceful souls who were characterised by widespread literary activity (see Encycl. Judaica, vol. IX, pp. 943 f.). But Ibn Jubayr, speaking second-hand and at a remote distance of alien races and creeds, so far departs from his customary exactitude throughout this whole matter that we can but conjecture his meaning, if indeed he knew himself. He is, of course, in this case not speaking from personal experience, but we are astonished that his informants, who would have been the leading Muslims of Sicily, themselves en rapport with the reliable Christian sources, should be so ignorant of great events some two years after their occurrence.

175. This fleet was indeed despatched to Constantinople, in accordance with William II's thesis that the best way of dealing with the schismatic Greeks was to capture Constantinople, to remove the ruling house of Comnenos, and to place the Greek Empire under Latin rule. His ancestors had driven them from southern Italy, and their revenge he must constantly apprehend. The whole Latin world joined him in this hatred, which, compounded with religious animosity, finally led to the diversion of the Fourth Crusade (A.D. 1204) to the conquest of Constantinople. William's fleet left Sicily on the 11th of June, 1185, with more than two hundred sail, but the expedition, although gaining a naval victory and sending a land force as far as Thessalonica, finally miscarried with the loss of many men.

176. The Qa'id Abu 'l-Qassim ibn Hammud was no doubt a scion of the illustrious family which had usurped, for a few years, the caliphate of Cordova. Amari, p. 95, suggests that he might have been in correspondence with Qa'id Pièrre, late first chamberlain of William, who some years earlier had sought refuge at the court of the Almohades.

Glossary

'abat, sing. *'aba',* a Bedouin type cloak.

Abu, father.

adhan, the call of the muezzin to prayer.

akamah, a hill.

'alamah, a motto placed by Muslim princes at the top of their rescripts.

amin, a person of trust.

'aqabah, a declivity

'Arafah, the vigil of the Feast of Sacrifice, when the pilgrims proceed to Mt. 'Arafat.

ardimone, Italian, a sail.

ashakin, sing. *ishkan,* travelling-seats.

'asr, the time of the afternoon prayer.

'atamah, the time of the night-fall prayer.

awbah, a measure of capacity, equalling five bushels.

awqaf, sing. *waqf,* pious endowments.

ba', a measure of the two arms extended.

barid, a post-stage, in Syria usually six miles.

billighriyin, from It. 'pilgrims'.

birba, from Pers., an ancient Egyptian temple.

Bismillah, the invocation 'in the name of God'.

burdah, a long under-mantle.

cubit, a measure of length from the elbow to the tip of the middle finger, here being about 22 inches.

dallun, from Gr. δολων, a small sail.

daqal, a mast.

dawraq, pl. *dawariq,* an earthenware jar.

dhimmi, protection and religious tolerance enjoyed by Christians and Jews in return for tribute paid to the Muslim rulers.

dhu 'l-Hijjah, the twelfth month of the Muslim calendar, and the third of the sacred months.

dhu 'l-Qa'dah, the eleventh Muslim month.

dinar, a gold coin weighing 59½ grains troy and worth something less than 10s.

dirham, a silver coin weighing 47½ grains Troy and at the ratio of gold and silver then obtaining worth about eightpence.

duha, the early part of the forenoon with the sun well up.

dum, the Palma Thebaica. See *muql*.

Emir, a prince or leader.

fanak, a small fox, or martin.

faqih, a Muslim jurisprudent or theologian.

farqa'ah, a whip of office carried by a preacher.

fusayfisa, from Gr. ψηφος, mosaic.

futuwwah, the mystical heroism of the prophet or his son-in-law 'Ali. A sort of order of chivalry based on that quality.

ghalini, from Gr. γαλήνη, calmness of the sea.

gharib, the central nave of the mosque at Damascus.

ghashawah, pl. *ghashawat*, from Pers. *kajawah*, a litter.

hafar, pl. *ahfar*, wells.

hafiz, one who has learnt the Koran by heart.

halal, lit. 'that which is lawful'. Specifically, release from the state of *ihram*.

haram, the sacred territory of Mecca.

haram, 'that which is unlawful'. It can also have a good sense, e.g. *Bait 'l Haram*, 'the sacred House'.

haramiyah, highway robbers.

harariq, a kind of war-ship, properly 'fire-ships'.

harim, the women of the household; womenfolk, or the part of the house devoted to the women.

harrabah, spearmen.

harwalah, to move or run briskly.

hatim, a semicircular wall on the north side of the Ka'bah enclosing the area known as the Hijr. Also an illuminated wooden erection put up in the Haram by the various persuasions.

hawdaj, a camel litter.

Hijr, a sacred enclosure adjoining the Ka'bah and confined by the Hatim.

hill, territory at Mecca outside the boundaries of the sacred territory.

hinna, *Lawsonia inermis*, a red dye used on the person.

hisbah, a scourging, usually with whips.

Hubal, an idol of the Quraysh.

Ibn, pl. *Banu*, a son.

ifadah, the ritual return of the pilgrims from 'Arafat and Mina.

'ifrit, demons mentioned in the Koran XXVII, 39.

ihram, lit. 'prohibition', applies to the clothing, the ceremony of the toilette, and the ritual state of preparedness for the pilgrimage.

imam, a leader, model, or examplar. There are three kinds: (1) the Imam or Caliph of the whole Muslim people; (2) the leaders of the four systems of orthodox theology; (3) the leader of prayers in any masjid or place of prayer.

iqamah, introductory words delivered before the prayers.

irdabb, a measure of capacity, being 43½ gallons.

izar. See *rida*.

jama', a congregational mosque.

jabbanah, a cemetery.

jahiliyah, the pre-Islamic days of paganism.

jilabah, pl. *jilab*, a small ship built without nails and used on the Red Sea.

jinn, genii.

Jumada 'l-ula, the fifth month of the Muslim calendar.

Jumada 'l-thaniyah, the sixth Muslim month.

jumrah, a cairn of stones.

Ka'bah, lit. 'cube', the sacred shrine of Islam in the middle of the great mosque at Mecca that contains the 'black stone' or *Hajar al-aswad*.

kadhan, a kind of limestone.

kawthariyah, the recital of the 108th surah of the Koran, entitled *Al-Kawthar* or The Abundance of Good.

khan, an inn or caravanserai.

khaniqah, a convent.

kharaj, land tax.

khatib, a preacher.

khatun, voce Persiana, a princess or lady of rank.

khidab, dyeing of the hair and hands with henna.

khutbah, the sermon delivered on Fridays at the time of the midday prayer, and on the two great festivals ('Id al-Fitr and 'Id al-Adha) after sunrise.

kiswah, the covering of the Ka'bah.

Koran, the sacred scriptures of Islam that were revealed to Muhammad through the archangel Gabriel and then delivered orally by the prophet. They were collected into literary form after his death.

kuhl, collyrium, an eye-paint.

kurjiyah, a kind of turban.

kus, a drum used in the pilgrim caravan.

Labbayka, lit. 'Here am I', the opening words of the cry of the pilgrim approaching Mecca. See p. 374, n. 46.

madhi, a species of honey.

madrasah, a college, in this work usually theological.

maghrib, sunset, or prayers said at that time.

maharah, a species of litter.

majra, pl. *majari*, a sea journey equivalent to 100 miles.

manjanah, a water-clock.

maqam, the stone on which Abraham stood when building the Ka'bah.

maqsurah, a closed-off place in a mosque where devout men recite their supererogatory prayers.

maraj', pl. *maraja'*, a measurement of surface, representing 50 square cubits.

masjid, a mosque or place of prayer.

mastabah, a stone bench.

mas'udi, a kind of honey imported to Mecca.

Mawla, lord, seigneur.

mihrab, a niche in a mosque wall indicating the direction of Mecca.

mil, the Arab mile, deriving from the Byzantines and containing 4,000 cubits and so being something over 2,000 yards.

milhaf, a kind of cloak.

minbar, a pulpit.

mirkan, pl. *mirakin*, small shells.

Mizab, the famous water-spout on the north side of the Ka'bah.

muezzin, one who makes the call to prayers.

Muharram, first month of the Muslim calendar.

mujawir, pilgrims who have taken up residence in Mecca.

mu'mini, a gold mu'mini dinar. See p. 368, n. 14.

muql, the Theban palm. Sails were made from its leaves.

murabit, hermits, marabouts.

musalla, an oratory.

Mustakhlaf, Al-, the Commissioner at the royal court at Palermo.

nab', a hard wood used for making arches.

Nahr, 'Id al-, the Day of Sacrifice.

nakhl, the date palm.

natif, a kind of confectionery.

pace, a measure of length equalling three spans.

parasang, an ancient Persian measure of length; about three and a quarter miles. Cf. Gr. παρασαγγης.

qaba', a long-sleeved gown.

qadi, a judge.

Qadr, Laylat al-, the Night of Qadr, being the night in the month of Ramadan on which the first revelation of the Koran was made to Muhammad. Surah XCVII. See p. 376, n. 70.

qafiz, a measure of grain, equalling three bushels.

qamah, a man's height.

qariyah, a ship's yard or spar to. supporting a sail.

qasidah, a poem.

qiblah, the direction of Mecca.

qinbar, cocoa-nut fibre used for caulking ships.

qintar, a measure of weight, being 100 ritls (*q.v.*).

qirat, the twenty-fourth part of a dinar. See p. 383, n. 136.

qirsh, a shark with whose oil ships were greased.

Rabi' al-awwal, the third month of the Muslim calendar.

Rabi' al-thani, the fourth month of the Muslim calendar.

Rajab, the seventh month of the Muslim calendar.

rahbah, an open place surrounded by houses.

rak'ah, a section of the daily prayers, or an attitude adopted in prayer whereby the worshipper inclines his head and body, while placing the hands on the knees with the fingers separated a little, and repeats the prayer appropriate to that attitude.

Ramadan, the ninth and fasting month of the Muslim calendar.

rawdah, lit. 'garden', the area round a tomb and often the tomb itself.

ribat, an asylum or hospice for the needy.

rida and *izar*, the two white cotton cloths, each 6 feet long by $3\frac{1}{2}$ broad, that form the pilgrim garb. The rida is thrown over the back and exposes the arm and shoulder and is knotted on the right side. The izar is wrapped round the loins from waist to knee and is knotted and tucked in at the middle.

ritl, a standard weight, being 5 lb., and, by inversion of the 'l' and 'r', the Greek λιτρα, or litre, for it is also a measure of capacity. See p. 382, n. 128.

ruba'i, a quarter dinar, Sicilian money.

sa', a measure of capacity, being a corn measure of the days of the Prophet the equivalent of 'four times the quantity of corn that fills the two hands, that are neither small nor large, of a man'.

Safar, the second month of the Muslim calendar.

saj, teak.

sahur, food taken at the hour of sahar, the first hour of dawn, in the month of Ramadan.

salat, the liturgical prayers that are recited five times a day.

salabiyah, lit. 'crossways', and referring here to sails set square to catch a wind aft or on the quarter.

samun, a hot wind.

sawlajan, a form of early polo.

sa'i, the ritual march between al-Safa and al-Marwah.

Sayyid, lord, sir, and, not here, certain descendants of Muhammad.

Sha'ban, the eighth month of the Muslim calendar.

shaqadif, a species of litter.

sharif, a descendant of the Prophet through his grandson Hasan.

shaut, one circuit of the Ka'bah.

Shawwal, the tenth month of the Muslim calendar.

shihnah, chief of police.

shimal, sing. *shamlah*, a large kind of cloak.

sirwal, the Arab cotton bloomers.

span, the measure from the end of the thumb to the end of the little finger when extended.

surah, a chapter in the Koran.

sunnah, traditions of the deeds and sayings of Muhammad.

tahlil, the ejaculation, 'There is no deity but God'.

tahmid, the ejaculation, 'God be praised'.

takbir, the ejaculation, 'God is great'.

talbiyat, the cry of the pilgrim approaching Mecca.

tarwih, pl. *tarawih*, lit. 'rest', prayers, usually of twenty rak'ahs, recited at night during the month of Ramadan, and so called because the congregation sit down and *rest* after every fourth rak'ah and every second 'salam'.

tarwiyah, Yaum al-, the eighth day of the month of Dhu 'l-Hijjah, when the pilgrims start from Mecca to Mount 'Arafat and 'provide themselves with water'.

tasbih, the ejaculation, 'I extol the holiness of God'.

tashahhud, the declaration of faith, 'I testify that there is no deity but God and Muhammad is the Messenger of God'. It is recited during the stated prayers as well as when a person becomes a Muslim.

tashir, the muezzin's announcement of the hour of the dawn repast in Ramadan called sahur.

tashriq, the three days, 'the days of the Drying Flesh' that follow the Feast of Sacrifice.

taslim, the benediction said at the close of the usual form of prayer: 'The peace and mercy of God be upon you.'

tawaf, the seven ritual circumambulations round the Ka'bah.

taylasan, a scarf thrown over the turban with one end brought under the chin and thrown across the left shoulder. It is worn almost exclusively by judges and theologians.

'Umrah, al-, the Lesser Pilgrimage that can be done at any time of the year except during the days of the Hajj or Greater Pilgrimage. It consists of a visit to the sacred mosque in Mecca, performing the tawaf, running between al-Safa and al-Marwah, and the ceremony of ihram, but omits the sacrifices.

'ushar, Asclepias gigantea.

ustadar, from *ustadh al-dar*, Prefect of the Palace or Intendant of the Eunuchs.

utrujj, Citrus cedra.

wali, governor.
wazir, vizier.

zakat, alms bestowed as a sanctification of the property remaining to the owner. See p. 368, n. 11.
zawraq, pl. *zawariq*, *voce Persiana*, small boats.
zawiyah, an angle or small chapel in a mosque where men may withdraw to pray, study, or meditate.
zuhr, midday, and prayers at that time.

Index of Persons

Names compounded with 'al' are indexed under the first letter of the second word, e.g. 'al-Husayn' will be found under 'H'.

Al-'Abbas ibn al-Muttalib, uncle of Muhammad, 42, 92; concludes covenant with the Ansar, 160; his tomb at Medina, 204. *See also* Dome of al-'Abbas.

'Abbasids, 226, 236

'Abdullah ibn 'Abd al-Hakam, his tomb in al-Qarafah, 41

'Abdullah ibn 'Abd al-Muttalib, father of Muhammad, his house, 167

'Abdullah ibn Ja'far al-Tayyar, his tomb at Medina, 204

'Abdullah ibn Hudhafah al-Sahmi, Companion of the Prophet, his tomb in al-Qarafah, 40

'Abdullah ibn al-Qasim, kinsman of Muhammad, his tomb in al-Qarafah, 38

'Abdullah ibn 'Umai ibn al-Khattab, descends into the valley of Dhu Tawa, 108; esteems the prayer habits of the Yemenite Saru, 134; his house at Medina, 201, 268

'Abdullah ibn al-Zubayr, place where his body was crucified, 106; initiates the 'umrah of the hill after re-building the Ka'bah, 136

'Abd al-'Aziz ibn Ahmad ibn 'Ali ibn al-Hasan al-Khuwarizmi, his tomb in al-Qarafah, 42

'Abd al-Masih ("Servant of the Messiah"), page at the court of King William II at Palermo, his meeting with Ibn Jubayr, 342

'Abd al-Rahman al-Awsat, called Abu Sahmah, son of the Caliph 'Umar ibn al Khattab, his tomb at Medina, 204

'Abd al-Rahman, son of the general Khalid ibn al-Walid, his tomb at Hims, 268

'Abd al-Rahman ibn Muljam, slayer of the Caliph 'Ali, 220

'Abd al-Rahman ibn al-Qasim, friend of Malik, his tomb in al-Qarafah, 41

'Abd al-Wahhab, qadi, his tomb in al-Qarafah, 41

Abel (Habil), scene of his murder, 285

Abraham, "the Friend of God" (see note 19), 38; his mosque at Munyat ibn al-Khasib, 51, 105; his well at Mecca, 102; receives the Black Stone, 104; his words in the Koran, 105; mountains on which he placed the pieces of birds (Koran II, 260), 108; his mosque in al-Zahir, 108; his prayers for Mecca (Koran II, 126, and XIV, 37), 110, 116; ancient mosque wall near the Mount of Mercy, 'Arafat, attributed to him, 179; his oratory in the mosque at al-Kufah, 219; city of Harran connected with him, 254; milked his flocks at Aleppo, 261; birthplace on Mount Qasiyun, 285, 286, 288; breaks the idols of his father Terah, 302

Abu 'l-'Abbas Ahmad al-Nasir li din Ilah ibn al-Iman Abu Muhammad al-Hasan al Mustadi' billah ibn al-Imam Abu 'l-Muzaffar Yusuf al-Mustan-jid billah, thirty-fourth 'Abbasid Caliph, A.D. 1180-1225, invocations made for him in the *khutbah* at the Cairo mosque, 43; embellishments done by his order

Abu 'l-'Abbas Ahmad al-Nasir—cont.
in the Hijr in the Haram at Mecca,
83, 92, 99; constructs a bridge at
al-Hillah for the benefit of pilgrims
going to Mecca, 221, 224, 231, 232,
236; his appearance and character,
237, 239

Abu 'l-'Abbas Ahmad ibn Tulun
(founder of the Tulunid dynasty
in Egypt) A.D. 868-884, his mosque
between Misr and Cairo, 441

Abu 'Abdullah Muhammad al-Muqtafi
li Amri Ilah, thirty-first 'Abbasid
Caliph, A.D. 1136-60, his inscription on the door of the Ka'bah, 87

Abu 'Abdullah ibn Sa'id, Spanish
jurisprudent, his chamber in the
mosque at Damascus, 277

Abu Ayyub the Ansarite, his house in
Quba, 205

Abu Bakr Sayf al-Din (Safadin) ibn
Ayyub, brother of Saladin, invo-
cations for him in the khutbah at
Cairo, 43; prayers for him at
Mecca, 92

Abu Bakr al-Shibli, Sufi imam, his
tomb at Baghdad, 236

Abu Bakr the Faithful, first Caliph of
Islam, ascends Mount Hira, 109;
his house and mosque at Mecca,
111, 112; seeks refuge with
Muhammad on Mount Abu
Thawr, 112, 164; his place in
Bilal's house at Mecca, 171; his
tomb at Medina, 197, 199; his
house in Medina, 201; his house in
Quba, 205

Abu 'l-Barakat Hayyan ibn 'Abd
al-'Aziz, holy man of Harran, 254

Abu 'l-Darda, Companion of the
Prophet, his oratory in the mosque
at Damascus, 275; his tomb at
Damascus, 290

Abu 'l-Durr Yaqut, Syrian merchant,
ransomes Maghrib prisoners, 323

Abu 'l-Fadl Ja'far al-Muqtadir billah,
eighteenth 'Abbassid Caliph, A.D.
907-932, 237

Abu Ja'far ibn ('Ali) al-Fanaki al-
Qurtubi, jurist and traditionalist,
86, 100, 146, 278

Abu Ja'far ibn Sa'id, Granada jurisprudent, 362

Abu Hamid al-Ghazali, imam, 115, 277

Abu Hanifah, founder of the Hanafi
sect of Sunni Muslims, his tomb
at Baghdad, 235

Abu 'l-Hasan, jeweller of Muhammad,
his tomb in al-Qarafah, 40

Abu 'l-Hasan 'Ali ibn Sardal al-Jayyani
(of Jaen in Spain), known as
al-Aswad, 'The Black', adminis-
trator of the endowments of
Nur al-Din, given to the Great
Mosque at Damascus, 298

Abu 'l-Hasan al-Dinawari, jurisprudent,
his tomb in al-Qarafah, 41

Abu Ibrahim Ishaq ibn Ibrahim,
Tunisian jurisprudent, 198

Abu Lahab (Koran CXI), his tomb near
Mecca, 107

Abu 'l-Makarim Tashtikin. See Emir
of the Iraq pilgrimage.

Abu Muhammad al-Mustadi' bi Amri
Ilah, thirty-third 'Abbasid Caliph,
causes the two mil at Mecca to be
erected, 103

Abu Muslim al-Khawlani, his tomb in
al-Qarafah, 41; another tomb
reported in Darayyah, 293

Abu 'l-Muzaffar Yusuf ibn Ayyub
Salah al-Din=Saladin, q.v.

Abu Nasr, proverb concerning, 337

Abu Nuwas al-Hasan ibn Hani, poet,
his lines on Nasibin, 248

Abu 'l-Qasim 'Ali ibn Muhammad the
Samosatian, 302. See Note 129.

Abu 'l-Qasim ibn Hammud, called Ibn
al-Hajar, Muslim leader in Sicily,
358-9, 360

Abu 'l-Qasim ibn Hibat Allah ibn Asakir the Damascene, Syrian traditionalist and author of a history of Damascus, 285

Abu 'l-Rabi' Sulayman ibn Ibrahim ibn Malik, 289

Abu Shahmah, by-name of 'Abd al-Rahman al-Awsat, the son of the Caliph 'Umar, q.v., 204

Abu Sulayman al-Darani, his tomb at Darayyah, 293

Abu Talib, uncle and guardian of Muhammad, 167; his house where Muhammad was reared, 167

Abu 'Ubaydah ibn al-Jarrah, his entry into the Cathedral of St. John, Damascus, 273

Abu 'l-Walid al-Azraqi, author of Notes on Mecca, 104, 113

Abu 'l-Yaqzan, holy man at Nasibin, 249

Abu Zayd, character in the Maqamat, or 'Assemblies' of al-Hariri, 258

'Ad, founder of an extinct South Arabian tribe (Koran VII, 65 et seq.), pyramids suggested as tomb of him and his sons, 46

Adam, his tomb on Mount Abu Qubays, 104; chamber in house at the foot of the Mount of Mercy attributed to him, 178; Grotto of on Mount Qasiyun, 286; his oxen, 318. See note 139.

Agnes of Courtenay, mother of King Baldwin IV of Jerusalem, 316

Ahl al-Suffah, 'The Choice Ones', 205. See note 124.

Ahmad, son of Abu Bakr, his tomb in al-Qarafah, 40

Ahmad ibn Hanbal, founder of the fourth orthodox sect of the Sunnis, his tomb at Baghdad, 235

Ahmad ibn Hassan, a physician of Granada and companion of the author on his journey, 25; is taken before Saladin in Alexandria, 31; sees strange incident at the Well of Zamzam, 143-4

Ahnaf, forbearance of, 311

Al-Ahzab, 'The Confederates' (Koran XXXIII), 207

Akhzam, 255. (See note 112).

'A'ishah, daughter of Abu Bakr and wife of Muhammad, her mosque near Mecca, 109, 128, 136; her tradition concerning the reconstruction of the Ka'bah, 137; her path to the mosque at Medina, 201; her house at Quba, 205; her place in the Damascus Mosque where she would relate her traditions, 278; legend concerning her entry into Damascus, 278-9

'Ali ibn 'Abdullah ibn al-Qasim, kinsman of Muhammad, his tomb in al Qarafah, 38

'Ali ibn Abi Talib, fourth Caliph and nephew and son-in-law of Muhammad, his mosque near Mecca, 109, 136; his mosque near Medina, 207; place of birth, now a mosque, 167, 171; place where he fought the jinn, 196; site of his murder in the mosque at al-Kufah, 220; his house in al-Kufah, 220; his shrine in al-Kufah, 220; his shrine near the Damascus Mosque, 278, 279; another shrine in the cemetery west of Damascus, 291; legend concerning his entry into Damascus, 278-9

'Ali ibn al-Husayn ibn 'Ali, called Zayn al-'Abidin, his tomb in al-Qarafah, 38

'Ali ibn Muwaffaq, governor of Jiddah, 70, 74

'Alids, supporters of 'Ali and his house, 71; their rule regarding the commencement of the fast of Ramadan, 145

Almohades (al-Muwahhidun), 'The Unitarians', Moorish dynasty which ruled Spain A.D. 1130-1212 and Morocco A.D. 1130-1269; augury of their dominion over Egypt, 45; author's wish that they would liberate the Hejaz, 73; sole true supporters of Islam, 73; propagation of their faith in Egypt and the Hejaz, 73, 74, 358

'Ammar, one of the Ahl al-Suffah, 'Choice Ones', 205

'Amr ibn al-'As, his mosque in Misr, 36, 42, 46; another in Alexandria, 46

Al-Anbari, qadi, speaks in his tomb at al-Qarafah, 41

Ansar, 'Auxiliaries', early converts of Medina to Islam, 160

Antiochan, The, the Admiral George of Antioch who commanded the fleet of Roger II of Sicily, 349. See note 164.

'Aqil ibn Abi Talib, his tomb at Medina, 204

Al-Aqta', Maghrib holy man his tomb, in al-Qarafah, 42

'Asafiri, his tomb in al-Qarafah, 41

Asbagh, follower of Malik, his tomb in al-Qarafah, 41

Ashab, follower of Malik, his tomb in al-Qarafah, 41

Asiyah, wife of Far'aun, her tomb in al-Qarafah, 38

Asma', daughter of Abu Bakr, her tomb in al-Qarafah, 40

'Awn, son of 'Ali ibn Abi Talib, his tomb in Baghdad, 235. See note 104.

Aws ibn Aws al-Thaqafi, his tomb at Damascus, 290

Al-'Ayna', saint, her tomb in al-Qarafah, 41

Azar (Terah), father of Abraham, makes idols at Bait Lahiyah, 288

Babek, brother of Nur al-Din, 190, 249, 250

Bajilah, sub-tribe of the Yemenite Saru, 131

Baldwin IV, King of Jerusalem, 316, 324. See note 141.

Bali, sub-tribe of the Yemenite Quda'ah, 60

Banu'l-Najjar, their house at Quba the dwelling of Abu Ayyub the Ansarite, 205

Banu Sa'id, tribe of, 277

Banu Shu'bah, a bedouin tribe, robbers on the road to 'Arafat, 123, 163, 176, 177, 184

Bilal ibn Hamamah, muezzin of Muhammad, his house at Mecca, 171; his tomb at Damascus, 290; muezzin at Medina his descendant, 201

Bujat, a Sudanese tribe, their ill treatment of the pilgrims, 64; their sultan, 66; their corrupt practices, 66

Bunan the Pious, his tomb in al-Qarafah, 41

Buthaynah, lover of Jamil, 215

Cain (Qabil), scene of his killing Abel, 286

Carmathians, carry off the Black Stone, 85

Chosroes (Kisra), king of Persia, his mirror and drinking-cup in the mosque of Medina, 202; palace of, 225

Christians of Syria, ravage the Muslim territories of the Red Sea with a fleet under Reginald de Châtillon, seize pilgrim ships, and threaten to remove the body of Muhammad from his tomb in Medina, 52; Christian and Muslim travellers and merchants come and go through each others' territories in

Christians of Syria—*cont.*
time of war, 300, 301, 313; a wedding ceremony, 320; a festival at sea, 328. *See* Franks.

Christians of Sicily, their relations with the Muslims, 339, 345; their women dress like Muslim women, 349-50

Companions of the Prophet (Al-Sahabah), *passim*; their tombs in al-Qarafah, 39 *et seq.*; the same at Medina, 204; the same at Damascus, 290-1; their Maqsurah in the Damascus Mosque, 275-6, 284, 304

Copts, their churches and monuments at Ikhmim, 53

Al-Daqus (Tukush Shah), Lord of Isfahan, 190; his daughter the *khatun*, 190, 239. *See* note 80.

Al-Da'udi, The Sharif, accompanies a pilgrim caravan to Medina, 135

David, psalms of, 187

Daud, a saint, his mosque at Ikhmim, 53

Dhu 'l-Nun ibn Ibrahim (Thawban), the Egyptian, a saint, his tomb in al-Qarafah, 41; his mosque at Ikhmim, 53

Elijah (al-Khidr), his oratory on Mount Qasiyun, 287

Emir of the 'Iraq Pilgrimage, Abu 'l-Makarim Tashtikin, 66, 170, 174, 177, 179, 180; his splendid encampment on 'Arafat, 181, 184; 185, 188, 189, 190; vastness of his caravan, 191-2; his system of march, 193; 208, 209, 212; enters Fayd with military precautions, 214; his efficiency and exemplary character, 224

Enoch (Idris), his oratory at al-Kufah, 220

Eve (Hawwa'), stopping place at Jiddah, 70; tower named after her between Ra's al-'Ayn and Harran, 254

Fadalah ibn 'Ubayd, Companion of the Prophet, his tomb near Damascus, 290

Fatimah, daughter of Asad and mother of 'Ali, her tomb at Medina, 204

Fatimah, daughter of Muhammad and wife of 'Ali, 92; house where born, 111, 167; chamber or tomb at Medina, 199; her house at Medina called Bayt al-Huzn, 204; her house at Quba, 205

Fatimids ('Ubaydin), 46; customs tax imposed by them on pilgrims, 48; omen of their end, 74

Franks have a fort near Mount Sinai, 67; in Syria, 72; their cities and fort on Mount Lebanon, 265; hold most of Syria, 311; march on al-Karak, 313; many captured at Nablus by Saladin, 314; some Frankish brigands, 315; their customs regulations, 316-17; manorial system, 316; good landlords, 317; pray beside Muslims, 318-19; seize Acre, 318. *See* Christians of Syria.

Gabriel, the Archangel, passes on God's revelation to Muhammad, 77, 110; his cupola on Mount Abu Thawr, 114; site at Medina where he descended, 199, 207, 291

Genoese sea-captain, his skill in commanding the ship that took the author from Acre to Sicily, 327

Genoese ship, conveys author from Ceuta to Alexandria, 26 *et seq.*; brings author home from Sicily, 357 *et seq.*; owners bribe the Governor of Trapani for permission to sail, 353

George, St. (Jirjis), his tomb at Mosul, 244. See note 109.

Ghurabiti, heretical Shi'ites, 291

Ghuzz, a tribe of Turks, a quarrel, 60; their Governor at 'Aydhab, 66; the omen of their invasion of Egypt, 74, 148, 149, 150

Hagar (Ajar), mother of Ishmael, her tomb near the Ka'bah, 83

Al-Hajjaj ibn Yusuf, 'Umayyad general, crucifies the body of 'Abdullah ibn al-Zubayr, 106; demolishes and rebuilds the Ka'bah, 137

Hamdanid princes of Aleppo, 260

Hamzah, uncle of Muhammad, 42, 92; his tomb and mosque on Mount, Uhud, 197, 203

Hanafite rite, 98; in Ramadan, 145; on 'Arafat, 183; their hatim, 187; their school in Aleppo, 263; their maqsurah in the Damascus Mosque, 276

Hanbalite rite, 98; in Ramadan, 145

Al-Hariri, author of the Maqamat, 258

Al-Harith ibn Mudad, verses of, 106

Harun al-Rashid, his mosque at Jiddah, 70, 179, 216; his generosity, 311

Al-Hasan ibn 'Ali ibn Abi Talib, 37; his birth-place, 111, 167; his play-thing in the Medina Mosque, 200; his tomb there, 204; tomb of his sons at Damascus, 293

Al-Hasan ibn al-Qasim, kinsman of Muhammad, his tomb in al-Qarafah, 38

Hasanites, 71

Hassan ibn Thabit, his verse about Kada', 106

Hashimites, 226

Hubal, idol of the Quraysh, 109

Hud, the prophet (Koran VII, 65), begins building of the Damascus Mosque, 273

Hunduj ibn Hunduj al-Murri, his verses, 331. See note 147.

Al-Husayn ibn 'Ali ibn Abi Talib, his head in Cairo, 36, 38; his birth-place, 111, 167, his play-thing in the Medina Mosque, 200; head first buried in Damascus, 280; tomb of his sons in Damascus, 293;

Al-Husayn ibn Mansur, al-Hallaj, his tomb in Baghdad, 236

Al-Husayn ibn al-Qasim, kinsman of Muhammad, his tomb in al-Qarafah, 38

Husaynites, 71

Ibn Abi'l Sayf, Yemenite jurisprudent, 131

Ibn Awf, Malikite imam and jurisprudent of Alexandria, 99

Ibn Halimah, foster-brother of Muhammad, his tomb in al-Qarafah, 40

Ibn Jubayr, Abu 'l-Husayn Muhammad ibn Ahmad, author of these Travels, secretary to the Governor of Granada, 15; incident that prompted the pilgrimage, 15; his style, 20; his character, 20; departs from Granada, 25; embarks at Ceuta, 26; disembarks at Alexandria, 29; visits Cairo, 36-49; ascends the Nile, 50-8; crosses the Red Sea to Jiddah, 66-9; at Mecca, 75-188; at Medina, 197-212; crosses the desert to al-Kufah, al-Hillah, 212-22, Baghdad, 226-239; ascends the Tigris and enters Syria, 239-70, Damascus, 271-312; in northern part of the Latin Kingdom of Jerusalem, 313-25; sails from Acre, 326; in Sicily, 338-61; home to Granada, 365

Ibn al-Mu'alli 'l-'Asadi, historian, 272 273, 286

Ibn Rashiq al-Qayrawani, his verses, 331. See note 146.

Ibn Tulun, *see* Abu l-'Abbas Ahmad ibn Tulun.

Ibn al-Zubayr ibn al-'Awwam, his tomb in al-Qarafah, 40

Ibn Zur'ah, Palermo jurisprudent, compelled to abjure Islam, 357

Ibrahim, son of Muhammad, his tomb at Medina, 203, 204

Ibrahim ibn Salih, builder of the two columns on the way to al-Safa', 87

Imamites, heretical Shi'ites, 291

'Isa Abu Mukthir, 104

'Isa ibn 'Abdullah, kinsman of Muhammad, his tomb in al-Qarafah, 38

Ishmael (Isma'il), his tomb near the Ka'bah, 83; the place of his intended sacrifice, 16; stone with the imprints of his feet, 162

Isma'ilites, heretical Shi'ites, village of exterminated by other Muslims, 259; their leader, Rashid al-Din Sinan, the "Old Man of the Mountains", 264, 291

Ja'far, his generosity, 311

Ja'far ibn Abi Ja'far al-Mansur, father of al-Zubaydah, 216

Ja'far ibn Abi Talib, his house in Mecca, 112. *See* note 65.

Ja'far ibn Muhammad al-Sadiq, kinsman of Muhammad, his tomb in al-Qarafah, 39; that of his two sons there, 38

Ja'farites, 71

Jamal al-Din, qadi, of Mecca, 173

Jamal al-Din Abu 'l-Fada 'il ibn 'Ali al-Jawzi, imam and head of the Hanbalite rite, two eloquent sermons 229

Jamal al-Din, vizier of the Lord of Mosul, his baths and monuments at Mecca and Medina, 122-5; sinks wells on highroads, 123; brings water to 'Arafat, 123; builds two strong walls round Medina, 123; restores the doors of the Haram, 123; is carried dead, in his coffin, through all the rites of the pilgrimage in Mecca, 123; his mausoleum near the prophet's at Medina, 124, 202; repairs roads and builds hostels for the benefit of poor travellers, 124; gives generous board to the poor, 125; restores the house of Bilal, 171; provides steps for laden beasts on the Mount of Mercy, 178

Jamil, lover of Buthaynah, 215

Al Jawhari, jurisprudent, his tomb in al-Qarafah, 42

Jesus, prays on Mount Qasiyun near Damascus, 286; site at Damascus where he will descend in glory, 295. *See* Messiah.

Job, prays on Mount Qasiyun near Damascus, 286

St. John the Baptist (Yahya ibn Zakariya'), his head in the Damascus Mosque, 284

Jonah (Yunus), the prophet, the hill near Nineveh where he prayed, 245; his city, Nineveh, 245

Joseph, his city on the Nile (Memphis, *q.v.*), 50

Jumanah bint Fulaytah, aunt of the Emir Mukthir, 128

Ka'b al-Ahbar, jurisprudent, his tomb in al-Jizah, 47

Khadijah, wife of Muhammad, 92; her house in Mecca, 110, 112, 167

Al-Khafajah, Bedouin tribe, raid al-Kufah, 219; threat to travellers, 239

Al-Khafajah, verses by, 239. *See* note 106.

Khalid ibn al-Walid, early Islamic general, gate by which he entered Mecca the day of its conquest by Muhammad's forces, 107; his tomb at Emessa, 268; enters Damascus by assault, 273

Khalis, eunuch commander of the Caliph's army in Baghdad, 236

Al-Khazraj, a Bedouin tribe, their chief, 292

Kurds, robbers around Mosul, 249

Lot, 286

Lu'lu', chamberlain and admiral of Saladin, destroys the Christian fleet on the Red Sea, 52

Al-Mahdi, Muhammad ibn Abi Ja'far al-Mansur al-'Abbasi, third 'Abbasid Caliph, enlarges the Mosque at Mecca, 86-7, 104; orders construction of the two columns at al-Safa', 87; extends the Haram, 104-5; restores the torrent at al-Safa' to its ancient course, 105

Majd al-Din, Ustad al-Dar, vice-vizier of the Caliph, 236

Maghribis or Moors, Saladin's care for them, 34; only true Muslims, 73; cultivators near Mecca, 119; their testimony of the new moon rejected, 172; endowments for in Damascus, 283, 289, 298; their honesty, 289; fight the Franks, 316; penal customs dues on them in Latin Syria, 316; endowments for them there, 322-3; an apostate, 323; returning pilgrims, 362

Malik (ibn Ashtar), Ali's general, 233. See note 101.

Malik ibn Anas, founder of the Maliki sect of Sunni Muslims, and author of al-Muwatta', 'The Levelled Path', 137; his rules concerning the 'return' at 'Arafat, 180; his tomb at Medina, 203; his house at Medina, 207

Malik, uncle of Ja'far ibn Muhammad, kinsman of Muhammad, 41.

Malik ibn Tawq, his town, 258

Malikites, sect of Sunni Muslims, their mosque in Alexandria, 46, 98-9; place where pilgrim garb assumed, 109; 142; their rites during Ramadan at Mecca, 145, 156-7; a Malikite guide on 'Arafat, 180; their zawiyah in the Damascus Mosque, 283, 298

Al-Mansur, second 'Abbasid Caliph, his mosque at Baghdad, 234

Marco, the Genoese, his ship, 363

Mary, church of, in Damascus, 296

Mary, daughter of 'Ali ibn Abi Talib, her tomb in al-Qarafah, 39

Ma'ruf al-Karkhi, his tomb in Baghdad, 235

Mas'ud, 'Izz al-Din Qilij Arslan II, Sultan of Iconium, 189, his power, 190, 239; Emperor of Byzantium pays him the jizyah, 240, 250, 355; gives refuge to Andronicus Comnenus, 355; extends his territories as far as Constantinople, 355-6

Mas'ud, Saljuqah bint, daughter of above, princess, or khatun, in the pilgrim caravan, 189; her good works, 190, 246; at the Mosque in Medina, 207-9; author travels under escort of her troops from Baghdad to Mosul, 239; her ceremonious entry into Mosul, 246

Mas'ud I, father of Mas'ud 'Izz al-Din Qilij Arslan II, 240

Al-Mas'udi, historian, 241

Al-Mayanishi, jurisprudent, his bath at Mecca, 122

Messiah finds shelter with his mother on a hill near Damascus, 271, 287 (Koran XXIII, 50). See Jesus.

Midianites, 227

Mihyar, poet, 230

Al-Miknasi, jurisprudent, Malikite imam at Mecca, 101

Moses, the Interlocutor, born in Askun, and there cast into the Nile, 50,

Moses, the Interlocutor—*cont.*
286; his footprints in the Mosque of al-Aqdam near Damascus, 294; tomb of his wife, daughter of the prophet Shu'ayb, at Tiberias, 324

Mu'adh ibn Jabal, Companion of the Prophet, his tomb in al-Qarafah, 40

Mu'awiyah ibn Abi Sufyan, Companion of the Prophet and founder of the 'Umayyad dynasty, constructs the Maqsurah of the Companions in the Damascus Mosque, 275; his house called al-Khadra near the mosque, 280; his tomb at Damascus, 290

Mujahid al-Din, Emir of Mosul, constructs a mosque, a hospital, and a bazaar there, 243-4

Muhajirun, (fugitives) who fled with Muhammad from Mecca to Medina, their tombs at Medina, 204. *See* note 89.

Muhammad, the prophet of Islam, passion, destroys idols, 109; his birth-place, 111, 166; first verse of the Koran revealed to him on Mount Hira, 110; day and month of his birth, 111; receives the prophetic inspiration in same house, 110, 167; hides in a cave on Mount Abu Thawr from his persecutors, 113; stone at al-Khayf bearing his head imprint, 163; brought up by Abi Talib, 167; stone on which he leant in Bilal's house, 171; his decree regarding the 'standing' on 'Arafah, 178; rock on the Mount of Mercy beside which he had his 'standing', 179; orders combining of sunset and early night prayers at Muzdalifah, 182; his sepulchre at Medina, 198 *et seq.;* palm tree which leaned towards him, 197, 200; cave on Mount Uhud his retreat, 203;

tombs of his wife and son, 204; place where his camel knelt, 205; recites the first *rak'ah* at Quba, 205; his fountain near Medina, 206

Muhammad, son of Abu Bakr, his tomb in al-Qarafah, 40; tombs of his sons there, 40

Muhammad ibn 'Abdullah ibn Abd al-Hakam, his tomb in al-Qarafah, 41

Muhammad ibn 'Abdullah ibn Muhammad al-Bakir ibn 'Ali Zayn al-'Abidin ibn al-Husayn ibn 'Ali, kinsman of Muhammad, his tomb in al-Qarafah, 38

Muhammad ibn Jubayr. *See* Ibn Jubayr.

Muhammad ibn Isma 'il ibn 'Abd al-Rahman, Chief of the Shayba guardians of the Mecca Mosque, descendant of 'Uthman ibn Talhah ibn Shaybah ibn Talhah ibn 'Abd al-Dar, 77; is arrested and his house sacked by order of the Emir Mukthir, 168; is reinstated, 170; deposed by the Caliph, 185

Muhammad ibn Mas'ud ibn Muhammad ibn Harun al-Rashid, called al-Sabti (the Ceutan), his tomb in al-Qarafah, 41

Mu'in, son of 'Ali ibn Abi Talib, his tomb in Baghdad, 235. *See* note 104.

Mu'in al-Din, Lord of Nasibin, brother of Mu'izz al-Din (below), 249

Mu'izz al-Din, son of Babek, Lord of Mosul, his mother in the pilgrim caravan with the author, 190, 239; her entry into Mosul, 246; 249

Mukthir ibn 'Isa ibn Fulaytah ibn Qasim ibn Muhammad ibn Ja'far ibn Abi Hashim al-Hasani, Emir of Mecca, A.D. 1176-1203, 70; practises extortions on the pilgrims to Mecca, 72; of the stock of Hasan ibn Ali, 74; 92, 93, 94, 99; his house, 103, 120, 122, 125, 130,

Mukthir ibn 'Isa ibn Fulaytah—*cont.*
135, 140, 145; leaves Mecca to meet Sayf al-Islam (Tughtagin), the brother of Saladin, 147-8; 150, 159; orders the arrest of the Chief of the Shayba, 168; 173-4; anger of the Caliph for him, 176

Munih, leading Abyssinian in 'Aydhab, 64

Al-Muqaddam, vizier, constructs a hatim in the Haram at Mecca, 98

Muqbil the Ethiopean, saint, his tomb in al-Qarafah, 41

Al-Muradi, jurisprudent of Seville, lectures in Damascus, 283

Musa ibn Ja'far, his tomb at Baghdad, 235

Muslim ibn 'Aqil ibn Abi Talib, his tomb at al-Kufah, 220

Muslims of Syria, Frankish and Muslim travellers move unmolested through each other's territories in time of war, 300, 313; pray beside the Franks, 318-19; as tenants of the Franks, 317; pay customs to the Franks, 316-17

Muslims on the sea, pious resignation amidst the dangers of the sea, 336; rescued by King William II of Sicily from the shipwreck, 337-8

Muslims of Sicily, their relations with the Christians of Messina, 339; favoured by the King, 340; members of the court and administration, 340; court physicians, 341; court handmaidens, 341; court pages, 340; in Cefalu, 344; in Termini, 344; enjoy special privileges at Palermo, 348; their *khutbah* forbidden, 348; access to fort on Mount Hamid forbidden, 352; forced to apostasy, 357; tempted to apostasy, 359-60

Al-Mu'tadid, sixteenth 'Abbasid Caliph, A.D. 892-902, 303

Al-Mu'tasim, eighth 'Abbasid Caliph, A.D. 833-42, 241

Al-Mutawakkil, tenth 'Abbasid Caliph, A.D. 847-61, 241

Muzaffar al-Din ibn Zayn al-Din, Lord of Harran, vassal of Saladin, 257

Al-Muzani, follower of the Imam Muhammad ibn Idris al-Shafi', 41

Al-Nubuwiyah, Sunnite organisation in Syria, fight fanatical Shi'ites, 292

Najm al-Din al-Khabushani, administrator-imam of the school in al-Qarafah, 40; his house in Cairo, 41

Al-Nasir, thirty-fourth 'Abbasid Caliph. See Abu 'l 'Abbas Ahmad al-Nasir, etc.

Nasr ibn Qawam, Syrian merchant, ransoms Muslim prisoners, 323

Nizam al-Mulk, Persian vizier of Malikshah, founds Nizamiyah College in Baghdad (A.D. 1065-7), 238

Noah, place where 'the water welled up from the earth' (Koran, XI, 40, XIII, 27), 220; place where the ark was built at al-Kufah, 220; house of his daughter at al-Kufah, 220; Mount where his ark rested, 247; his tomb and that of one of his daughters near Damascus, 293

Nur al-Din, Lord of Amid, 190, 240

Nur al-Din Mahmud ibn Zangi, suzerain of Syria, his college in Damascus, 296; his generosity to the Sufis, 296; his merits, 298; leaves endowments for Maghrabis, 298; takes Banyas from the Franks, 315; ransomes Maghrib prisoners, 322

Nusayris, heretical Shi'ites, 291

Persians, their abandon in worship, 208-9; a Persian sheikh, 210; as guards, 236

Qarun (Korah), 175. *See* note 76.

Al-Qasim ibn Muhammad ibn Ja'far al-Sadiq ibn Muhammad ibn 'Ali Zayn al-'Abidin, kinsman of Muhammad, his tomb in al-Qarafah, 38

Qilij Arslan II. *See* Mas'ud 'Izz al-Din Q.A.

Quda 'ah, Yemenite tribe, 60

Quraysh, 104; their idols, 109; re-build' the Ka'bah, 82, 137, 226. *See* note 53.

Quss ibn Sa'idah, eloquent Bishop of Najran, 55, 230. *See* note 34.

Qutb al-Din, Lord of Dunaysar, 250

Radi al-Din al-Qazwini, chief of the Shafi'ites and faqih in the Nizamiyah College, Baghdad, his *khutbah*, 228

Rafidites, heretical Shi'ites, 97, 291, 292

Ramasht, a Persian, his gifts to the Haram at Mecca, 98

Al-Rashid. *See* Harun al-Rashid.

Raymond, Count of Toulouse, 324. *See* note 142.

Rubil ibn Ya'qub ibn Ishaq ibn Ibrahim, his reported tomb at al-Qarafah, 38; at Tiberias, 324

Al Rudhabari, his tomb in al-Qarafah, 41

Rum, Greek or eastern living Christians (*see* note 5), 27, sea-captains 28, 327; prisoners work on the citadel in Cairo, 43; in Alexandria, 52, 256; 259; 267; King of Byzantium sends artificers to re-build the Damascus Mosque, 272; their Cathedral of St. Mary in Damascus, 296; 326, 330, 332, 338, 351, 355-7

Sa'd ibn 'Ubadah, chief of the Khazraj, Companion of the Prophet, his tomb in al-Manihah, 292

Sadr al-Din al-Khujandi, head of the Shafi'ite imams and chief of the doctors of Khurasan, 208-10, 229

Safiyyah, aunt of Muhammad, her tomb at Medina, 203

Sahban Wa'il, noted early Muslim preacher of great eloquence, 55, 230. *See* note 34.

Sahib al-Ibriq, thaumaturgic saint, his tomb in al-Qarafah, 41

Sahib al-Zimam, chief of the Caliph's eunuchs at Baghdad, 303

Sahl ibn al-Hanzaliyyah, Companion of the Prophet, 290

Saladin (Abu 'l-Muzaffar Yusuf ibn Ayyub), Sultan of Egypt, Syria, etc., 31, 32, founds colleges and hostels at Alexandria, 33; his care for strangers in his land, 33, 34; his revenues, 34, 35; supports school in al-Qarafah, 40; his name in the *khutbah* in Egypt, 43; builds the citadel in Cairo, 43; founds a hospital in Cairo, 43; his bounty to a variety of institutions, 40, 42; builds bridges near Cairo against invasion, 45; receives land-tax when Nile at certain level, 47; security in his dominions, 49; destroys Ansina and conveys its materials to Cairo for building, 51; 56; abolishes customs dues imposed on pilgrims, 48, 63, 71, 72, 73, 92, 298; prayers for him at Mecca, 92, 99; instructs Emir of Mecca to treat the pilgrims well, 92; dispute with the ruler of Aden, 175; cedes Amid to the daughter of the Sultan Mas'ud, 240; alone worthy of his high titles, 251; his subject kings, 257; confines of his jurisdiction in Syria, 258; constructs khan on the road between Emessa and Damascus, 269; lays siege to Kerak, 300-1, 311, 313-14; his energy, 311; three stories

Saladin (Abu'l Muzaffar Yusuf—cont. illustrating his merits, 311-12; seizes Nablus, 314, 324

Salih, prophet (Koran VII, 73), tomb of his son in al-Qarafah, 38; his tomb at Acre, 318

Saljuqah, princess, daughter of the Sultan Mas'ud. See Mas'ud.

Salmah, ascetic of Harran, 255

Salmah al-Makshuf al-Ra's, another ascetic of Harran, 257

Salman, one of the Ahl al-Suffah ('The Choice Ones'), 205; his mosque on the road to Uhud, 207

Salman the Persian, his tomb in al-Mada'in, 225

Samaritans made prisoners by the troops of Saladin, 314

The Samosatian, Abu'l Qasim 'Ali ibn Muhammad, 302. See note 129.

Sarah, her place of retreat at Harran, 254

Sariyat al-Jabal, Companion of the Prophet, his tomb in al-Qarafah, 40

Saru, Yemenite tribe in the al-Sarah mountains, bring produce to Mecca, 118, 131, 165, 168; derivation of their name, 131; their system of bartering, 132; their character and country, 132; their mode of prayer, 133; their dress, 133; Muhammad's remark about them, 134; a story to show their intelligence, 134; their headlong manner of entering the Ka'bah, 133, 137, 149, 168-9, 170, 174, 186; their 'standing' place on 'Arafat, 180

Sayf al-Dawlah ibn Hamdan, founder of the Hamdanid dynasty in north Syria (A.D. 944-67), 261

Sayf al-Islam ibn Ayyub (Tughtagin), brother of Saladin, visits Mecca on his way to the Yemen, 147-51; seizes the ships of 'Uthman ibn 'Ali of Aden, 176

Seth or Sheth (Gen. v. 3.), his tomb near Damascus, 293

Al-Shaf'i, imam, his tomb in al-Qarafah, 40

Shafi'ites, 97, 98, 99; place where pilgrim garb assumed, 109; their rites during Ramadan at Mecca, 146; their chief, 208; 259; their college in Damascus, 281

Shahinshah, title of the Turkish sultan at Baghdad, 237

Sharifs of Mecca, 71, 127

Shayban al-Ra'i, his tomb in al-Qarafah, 42

Shayba, Banu, hereditary custodians of the Ka'bah, 77, 88, 89, 137, 149, 158-9, 163, 169, 170

Shi'ites, their mosque in Damascus, 279; their sects, 291

Shu'ayb, prophet (Koran VII, 85), his tomb and that of his daughter the wife of Moses at Tiberias, 324

Shu'bah. See Banu S.

Shuqran, sheikh of Dhu 'l-Nun, his tomb in al-Qarafah, 42

Sinan, Rashid al-Din, the Old Man of the Mountain and leader of the Assassins, a sect of Isma'ilis, 264

Solomon (Sulayman), son of David, imprisons the 'ifrit in Aydhab, 67; his tomb in Tiberias, 324

Sufis, their ribat at Mecca, 101; their convent at Ra's al-'Ayn, 252; their convent in the Damascus Mosque, 282, 302-4; their convents and privileged position in the east, 297; their rectitude and discipline, 297

Sufyan al-Thawri, 273

Sukaynah, daughter of al-Husayn, her tomb in Damascus, 293

Sunnis, 97, 162, 259, 291, 292

Taj al-Din, preacher, 184

Tashtikin. See Emir of 'Iraq pilgrimage.

Tughtagin. See Sayf al-Islam.

Tukush Shah. See al-Daqus.

Turks of 'Iraq, 184, 236
Turks in Syria, 297

'Ubayd Allah, son of the Caliph 'Umar, his tomb at Hims, 268
'Ubaydites (Fatimids), extinction of in Egypt, 46; their heavy customs dues on pilgrims, 48; omen of their end, 74
'Udhr, Bedouin tribe, 215
'Umar, son of Abu 'l-Barakat, saint of Harran, 255
'Umar ibn 'Abd al-'Aziz, 'Umayyad Caliph 'Umar II, his cupola and his house at Mecca, 112; orientates the prophet's mosque in Medina, 198; constructs mosque at Ra's al-'Ayn, 253; indemnifies the Christians for their church at Damascus, 273; his oratory in the Damascus Mosque, 280; his house at Damascus, 281, 302-3
'Umar ibn al-Khattab, the second Caliph, his mosque in Jiddah, 70; ascends Mount Hira, 109, 111; cupola between al-Safa and al-Marwah attributed to him, 112; his conversion in the house of Bilal, 171; his tomb at Medina, 197, 199; his house at Medina, 201; his house at Quba, 205; constructs the Castle of the Celibates near Medina, 206; destroys Rastan (Arethusa), 267; his way of resolving disputes, 311
'Umayyads, 244, tombs of their caliphs at Damascus, 293
Umm 'Abdullah ibn al-Qasim ibn Muhammad of the house of 'Ali, her tomb in al-Qarafah, 39
Umm al-Darda, her tomb at Damascus, 290
Umm Habibah, sister of the Caliph Mu'awiyah, her tomb at Damascus, 290

Umm Kulthum, daughter of 'Ali ibn Abi Talib, called 'the little Zaynab', her tomb near Damascus, 292
Umm Kulthum, daughter of the prophet, 292
Umm Kulthum, daughter of Muhammad ibn Ja'far al-Sadiq, her tomb in al-Qarafah, 39
Umm Kulthum, daughter of al-Qasim ibn Muhammad ibn Ja'far, her tomb in al-Qarafah, 39
Umm Maryam, her tomb in the mosque at al-Nayrab, 293
Umm Salimah, her mosque on the Mount of Mercy, 178
'Uqbah ibn 'Amir al-Juhani, standard-bearer of Muhammad, his tomb in al-Qarafah, 40
'Uthman ibn 'Affan, the third Caliph, ascends Mount Hira, 110; his Koran at Mecca, 163; wells named after him at 'Usfan, 190; his recension of the Koran at Medina, 201; house at Medina where he was martyred, 202; his tomb at Medina, 204; buys the well of Rumah near Medina, 206; drops the prophet's ring into the well of Aris, 205; his Koran in the Damascus Mosque, 279. See note 90.
'Uthman ibn 'Ali, Emir, Governor of Aden, driven from Aden by Sayf al-Islam, 175; combats the Banu Shu'bah who rob on the road to 'Arafat, 176
Uways al-Qarani, his tomb at Damascus, 293

Al-Walid ibn 'Abd al-Malik, sixth 'Umayyad caliph, A.D. 705-15, turns the Cathedral of St. John at Damascus into a mosque, 272, 273
Warsh, Koran reader, his tomb in al-Qarafah, 42

Wathilah ibn al-Asqa', one of the Ahl al-Suffah ('The Choice Ones'), his tomb at Damascus, 290

Al-Wathiq, ninth 'Abbasid Caliph, A.D. 842-7, 241

William II, King of Sicily, called 'The Good', his dominions in southern Italy, 335; watches the author's shipwreck at Messina, 337-8; his shipyard there, 343; his confidence in the Muslims, 340; resides at Palermo, 340; his palaces there, 340, 346, 348; his ministers and pages Muslims, 340-1; his physicians and astrologers, 341; his age, 341; his attention to government, 341; writes Arabic, 341; uses a Muslim device, 341; stops ships from sailing from Sicily, 353; conjectures as to destination of his fleet, 354; respects treaty with the Almohade sovereign of North Africa, 354; protects youth alleged to be fugitive King Alexis of Byzantium, 354; intends to invade Constantinople, 354; compels certain Muslims to apostasy, 357

Yahuda, prophet, his tomb at Tiberias, 324

Yahya ibn Fityan, embroiderer at the court at Palermo, 341

Yahya ibn al-Hasan ibn Zayd ibn al-Hasan, kinsman of Muhammad, his tomb at al-Qarafah, 38

Yahya ibn al-Qasim, kinsman of Muhammad, his tomb at al-Qarafah, 38

Yaqtin ibn Musa builds the two columns at the Gate of al-Safa, 87

Yemenite camel-masters on the Qus-'Aydhab road, 60

Zayd ibn Thabit, Koran written by him still in Mecca, 99

Zaydis, heretical Shi'ites, manner of prayer, 97; their rites during Ramadan, 145; 291

Zaynab, daughter of Yahya ibn Zayd ibn al-Husayn ibn 'Ali, her tomb in al-Qarafah, 39

Zimam al-Dar, or Sahib al-Zimam, q.v.

Al-Zubaydah, daughter of Ja'far ibn Abi Ja'far al-Mansur, wife and cousin of the Caliph Harun al-Rashid, her house near the Haram at Mecca, 100; wells and cisterns made by her at Muzdalifah, 177; the same on the pilgrim road between Baghdad and Mecca, 216; her lodge on the Tigris opposite Samarra, 241

Al-Zubayr ibn al-'Awwam, tomb of his son in al-Qarafah, 40; tomb of his mother on Mount Uhud, 203

Index of Places

Names compounded with 'al' are indexed under the first letter of the second word, e.g. 'al-Hillah' will be found under 'H'.

'Abdayn, Ma'al, the Water-point of The Two Slaves, between Qus and 'Aydhab, 59

Abu Qubays, mountain near Mecca, its site, 103; the Black Stone on it during the Flood, 104; the tomb of Adam on it, 104; 109, 127, 158, 167

Abu Thawr, mountain beside Mecca, its site, 112; a cave on it gives refuge to Muhammad, 112, 113; proverb concerning it, 114, 164

Abu Tij, city of Upper Egypt, 53

Acre, city in Latin Syria, 66, 243, 313; trade with Damascus, 301, 316; its customs-post, 317; its port, 318; captured by the Franks, 318, 321; its mosque, 318, 319, 320; its farmsteads, 325; its hippodrome, 325; its plentiful wells, 325; Ibn Jubayr embarks for home here, 325; season for sailing from, 326

Aden, 175

Africa, 29, 330, 354, 363

Al-Ajfur, wells at, 215

Alcamo ('Alqamah), Sicily, 350

Alcaudete (al-Qabdhaq), 25. See note 3

Alcazar (Qasr Masmudah), 26

Aleppo, 249, 259; its description, 260-3; 266; its impregnable fortress, 260, 261, 266; origin of its name, 261; frequented by Abraham, 261; its markets, 262; its cathedral mosque, 262; its Hanafite college, 263; relentless courage of its citizens in fighting the Latins, 267

Alexandria, 26, 29; its lighthouse, 29, 32-3; its customs department, 31, 32; its underground constructions, 32; colleges, students' hostels, baths, and hospitals, 33; provision for poor strangers, 33; taxes and revenues, 34; great number of its mosques, 35; Mosque of 'Amr ibn al-'As, 46, 49, 51; Rum prisoners marched through the city, 52; 55, 56, 58, 66, 74, 324, 350, 354, 362

Amid, 190, 240, 257

Amtan, a well between Qus and 'Aydhab, 61

Andalusia, 26; its jurisprudents waive the duty of pilgrimage in certain circumstances, 72; its fertility, 248; its beauty, 251; 253, 264, 268, 350, 362, 365

Ansina, city on the Nile, destroyed by Saladin and its materials removed to Cairo, 51

Antioch, 265

'Aqabah of Aylah (Elim), 67

'Aqabat al-Shaytan (The Devil's Slope), place on the pilgrim route from Medina to Baghdad, 217

'Aqil, Mount, 233

Al-'Aqiq, valley on the road between Mecca and Medina, 196

Al-'Aqr, village on the Tigris, 242

'Arafat, the 'Mount of Recognition', twelve miles from Mecca, 123, 172, 173, 174, 177, 178, 179, 180, 182, 185; pilgrims 'stand' on it on the ninth day of Dhu 'l-Hijjah, 176-83; 192, 206, 305, 361

'Arafat, hill near Quba, 205

Arcos, Arkush, Spain, 25

Arethusa (Rastan), 267

Al-'Arim, torrent that burst the dam of Ma'rib and destroyed Saba', 336, 344

Aris, well at Quba near Medina where 'Uthman dropped the prophet's ring, 205

Armenia, 189

Askun, village on the Nile and possible birth-place of Moses, 50

Aswan (Uswan), 51, 60. See note 36.

Al-'Asi. See Orontes.

Assiut (Usyut), Upper Egypt, 53

Al-Astil, valley between Hunin and Tibnin in Syria, 315

Al-'Attabiyah, a quarter in Baghdad, 235

'Aydhab, city on the west coast of the Red Sea, customs exactions, at, 48; Christian corsairs at, 52; 58, 59, 60, 61, 62; its port, 63; its pearl fishing, 64; its inhabitants like wild beasts, 64; ill-treatment of the pilgrims here, 64-5; its special craft called jilbah, 65; best avoided by pilgrims, 66; Solomon imprisons the afrites here, 67, 182

'Ayn al-Baqar, spring near Acre, mosque and church there, 318

'Ayn al-Majnunah, spring near Palermo, 345

'Ayn al-Rasad, village near Mosul, 247

'Ayn Sulayman, valley near Mecca, 119

Ayqat al-Sufun, islands off the coast of the Red Sea, 68

al-Bab, village between Buza'ah and Aleppo, 259-60

Bab al-'Abbas, in the Haram at Mecca, 101

Bab 'Ali in the Haram at Mecca, 101, 103

Bab Badr at Baghdad, 231

Bab Banu 'Abd al-Shams. See Bab Banu Shayba.

Bab Banu Makhzum. See Bab al-Safa.

Bab Banu Shayba, also called Bab Banu 'Abd al-Shams, in the Haram at Mecca, 101, 102, 103, 109, 144, 148, 151, 188

Bab al-Baqi' (Gate of the Cemetery) at Medina, 203, 204, 206

Bab al-Barid (Gate of the Mail-post), in the Damascus Mosque, 277, 280, 281; Shafi'ite college there, 282; 284, 308

Bab al-Basaliyyah at Baghdad, 229, 238

Bab Basrah at Baghdad, 234, 235

Bab Dar al-'Ajalah in the Haram at Mecca, 101

Bab Dar al-Nadwah in the Haram at Mecca, 101

Bab al-Faradis (Gate of the Gardens) at Damascus, 285, 295

Bab al-Faraj (Gate of Consolation) at Damascus, 294, 301

Bab al-Hadid (The Iron Gate) at Medina, 206, 207

Bab al-Halbah at Baghdad, 238

Bab al-Hazwarah in the Haram at Mecca, 101

Bab Ibrahim (Abraham's Gate) in the Haram at Mecca, 86, 101, 102, 105

Bab al-Jabiyah (Gate of the Water-carrier) in the Damascus Mosque, 293, 295, 302

Bab Jayrun, in the Damascus Mosque, 277, 280; the water-clock there, 281-2, 284

Bab Jibril, in the Medina Mosque, 202

Bab Jiyad in the Haram at Mecca, the Greater and the Lesser, 101; the Lesser also called Bab al-Khalaqiyyin, 101

Bab al-Khalaquiyyin. See Bab Jiyad the Lesser.

Bab al-Khashyah (Gate of Fear) in the Medina Mosque, 202

Bab al-Ma'la (Gate of the Upper Part), Mecca, 106

Bab al-Masfal (Gate of the Lower Part), Mecca, 107

Bab al-Nabi in the Haram at Mecca, 91, 93, 101

Bab al-Nasr (The Victory Gate), Damascus, 295

Bab al-Natifiyyin (Gate of the Sweet-meat Sellers) in the Damascus Mosque, 277, 280; Sufi convent there, once the house of 'Umar ibn 'Abd al-Aziz, 282, 284, 302

Bab al-Qiblah, Medina, 206

Bab al-Rahmah in the Ka'bah, 79, 90

Bab al-Rahmah (Gate of Mercy), in the Medina Mosque, 202

Bab al-Rakha (Gate of Abundance) in the Medina Mosque, 202

Bab al-Ribat in the Haram at Mecca, 101

Bab al-Safa in the Haram at Mecca, once called Bab Banu Makhzum, 77, 86, 87, 97, 99, 101, 102, 104, 105, 130, 149, 151

Bab al-Safariyyah, Baghdad, 238

Al-Bab al-Saghir, Damascus, 293, 295

Bab Salamah (Gate of Security), Damascus, 295

Bab al-Shari'ah (The Watering Gate), Medina, 206

Bab al-Sharqi (The East Gate), Damascus, 294, 302

Bab al-Suddah in the Haram at Mecca, 76, 101

Bab al-Sultan, Baghdad, 238

Bab al-Taq (Gate of the Arch), Baghdad, 225, 235

Bab Tumah (St. Thomas's Gate), Damascus, 295

Bab al-'Umrah in the Haram at Mecca, see Bab al-Zahir.

Bab al-Zahir, also called Bab al-'Umrah, at Mecca, 101, 107

Bab al-Ziyadah (Gate of Increase) in the Damascus Mosque, 279, 284

Badr, site of the Battle of, its palm-trees, fort, spring, 194, 196; roll of drums still heard there, 194

Baghdad, 66, 188, 214, 225; its description, 226 et seq.; its character, 226; its vain and usurious citizens, 227; its eloquent preachers, 228-34; its quarters, 234-5; its hospital, 234; the Caliph's palace, 236; its fine markets, 237; its mosques, 237-8; sepulchre of the 'Abbasid caliphs, 238; its baths, 238; its colleges, 238; its gates, 238, 241, 303

Bahr al-Na'am, part of the Red Sea, 52. See note 32.

Ba'albek (Ba'labakk), ancient Heliopolis in Syria, 267

Banyas, Muslim city of, 314, 315

Baqidin, place between Aleppo and Hamah, 264

Baqi' al-Gharqad, cemetery at Medina, 203. See note 87.

Barcelona, 364

Bariq, river near al-Kufah, 218

Barr al-'Adwah (Land of Passage), 351. See note 165.

Barzah, village near Damascus, 285

Al-Basrah, 226; bitumen on road from it to Kufah, 238, 243

Batn Marr, fertile valley near Mecca, 119, 188, 189

Al-Bayda, place between Mecca and Medina, 196

Al-Bayda, village between Harran and the Euphrates, 257

Bayt Jann, village near Damascus, 314

Bayt al-Huzn (House of Grief), Fatimah's house at Medina, 204

Bayt Lahiyah, village near Damascus, 288

Bayt al Maqdis. See Jerusalem.

Bilad Bakr. See Diyar Bakr.

Birkat al Marjum, water-point on the Medina—Baghdad road, 216

Birmah, village in the Nile delta, 35

Black Stone, in the Ka'bah, passim; its position, 76, 78, 79, 81; description of, 85; 91, 93, 94, 97, 98; deposited on Mount Abu Qubays during the Flood, 104; 132, 138

Al-Buda-'ah, well near Medina, 206
Bougie (Bijayah), port in Algiers, 319, 323; seized by the Almoravide ruler of Majorca, 353
Al-Bulyanah, village of Upper Egypt, 57
Buza'ah, Syrian town, 259-60
Byzantine empire (Bilad al-Rum), 189, 250

Cabra (Qabrah), Spain, 25
Cairo, mausoleum of al-Husayn ibn 'Ali, 36 et seq.; cemetery of al-Qarafah; see al-Qarafah; its mosques and colleges, 42; its citadel, 43; its hospital, 43; Mosque of Ibn Tulun, 44; 50, 74, 280
Calabria, 334
Canalis di Baza (Qanalis) in Spain, 365
Cape St. Mark (Qawsamarkah), promontory and anchorage on the west coast of Sardinia, ancient Jewish habitation there, 27; Muslim prisoners sold in market there, 27; ruler of the island visits harbour, 27
Cartagena (Qartajannah), 26, 365
Casma(Qashmah), Spain, 25. See note 4.
Cefalu (Shafludi), Sicily, 344
Ceuta (Sabtah), Morocco, 26, 66, 350
Chemmis or Panopolis. See Ikhmim.
Cilician Gates (Darb; pl. Durub), 189, 355
Cordova, resembles Palermo, 348-9, 350
Constantinople, its Greek ruler pays the jizyah to the Sultan of Iconium, 240, 318; Greek archipelago subject to it, 330; also Crete, 330, 331; Sicilian fleet destined for it, 354; its throne usurped by Andronicus Comnenos, 354 et seq. See note 174.
Crete, dependency of Constantinople, 29, 330, 331, 332; its Mulsim inhabitants constrained to turn Christian, 359

Dabiq, cloth made there, 150
Dajwah, in the Nile delta, 36
Damanhur, city in the Nile delta, 35
Damascus, 269, 270; description of, 271 et seq.; the Messiah and His Mother there, 271, 287; its Ghutah, 269-71; the Great or 'Umayyad Mosque, 272-83, 305-8; an orphan school, 283; venerated shrines, 284 et seq.; head of John the Baptist, 284; birthplace of Abraham, 285; a history of, 285; traces of Abel's murder, 285; cemeteries, 290, 292; its gardens and rivers, 288; pious endowments, 289-90; its gates, 295; its suburbs, houses and streets, 295; Mary's Church, 296; colleges and hospitals, 296; college and tomb of Nur al-Din, 296; Sufi convents, 297; facilities for stranger students, 298; generosity of its citizens, 298-9; commerce with Egypt and Acre, 301, 324; its castle, 301; the Sultan's Mosque, 301; its hippodromes, baths, and markets, 301-2; ascent of the Lead Dome of the Great Mosque, 305-8; funeral customs, 308; manner of greeting of the citizens, 309; their manner of walking, 310. See also Mosque of Damascus.
Damietta, 331
Dandarah, city of Upper Egypt, its temple, 57
Dara, ancient city near Nisibis, 250
Darayah, town near Damascus, 293, 314
Dar al-Nadwah (House of Counsel) in the Haram at Mecca, 86, 87, 188
Dashnah, city of Upper Egypt, 57
Denia, Spain, 26, 365
Dhat al-'Alam, well between Mecca and Medina, also called al-Rawha, 196
Dhu 'l-Hulayfah, mosque at, 196; limit of the sacred territory of Medina, 197

Dhu Tawa, valley near Mecca by which the prophet entered Mecca, 108

Dinqash, water-point in the desert between Qus and 'Aydhab, 60; camel-litters used across this desert, 60; a quarrel at the water-hole, 60

Diyar Bakr, 249, 250, 255, 257, 258

Diyar Rabi'ah, 255, 257, 258

Dujayl, a canal running from the Tigris, 240

Dunaysar, town of north Syria, 249

Ecija (Istijah), Spain, 25

Egypt (Misr or Diyar Misr), 48; omen of its invasion, 45; 74, 99, 118, 120, 150; commerce with Damascus, 301

Emessa (Hims), attacked by the Franks of Hisn al-Akrad, 265, 266; description of, 267-8; courageous struggle with the Franks, 267-8; its strong fort, 267-8; tomb of Khalid ibn al-Walid and his son 268; fine walls, but desolate interior, 268; resembles Seville, 268, 269

Eolie Islands, Sicily, 343

Ethiopia, its merchants in Egypt, 57; its exports to Mecca, 117

Etna, Mount, 343

Euphrates, 215, 218, 220, 221, 222, 223, 224, 226, 235, 257, 258

Al-Farashah, village between al-Hillah and Baghdad, 224

Favignana, Island of, Sicily, 352, 361-2

Fayd, walled desert city midway between Medina and Baghdad, 214

Formentera, Balearic Islands, 364-5

Galita, island of, 363

Ghaliyah, 294

Gharb, Barr al- (Land of the West) or North Africa, 29, 330. See note 8.

Gharqad, Baqi' al-, cemetery at Medina, 203

Ghutah of Damascus, 269, 271

Ghuwayliyah, 294

Gizeh (al-Jizah), town beside Cairo, 47

Granada, 25, 362, 366

Guadix, Spain, 365

Al-Hajir, water-point between Qus and 'Aydhab, 59

Al-Hajir, water-point in the Nejd, 213

Al-Hajun, mountain pass near Mecca, 106, 110, 136

Hamah, north Syrian city, description of, 265-7, 322

Al-Haram, the Great Mosque of Mecca, passim; abode of Abraham, 75; its description, 77 et seq.; spread with white sand, 82; its arcades and columns, 85-6; its dimensions, 85; additions to it by the Caliph al-Mahdi, 86, 87; its minarets, 87, 96; its imams, 97; its gates, 101 et seq.; improvements wrought in it by Jamal al-Din, 122-3; its aspect and ceremonies during Ramadan, 144 et seq.; becomes a market during the pilgrimage, 188; Dome of 'Abbas, 84, 96, 97; Jewish Dome, 84, 96, 97, 99, 151. See also Ka'bah.

Harba, village near the Tigris, 241

Al-Harbiyyah, quarter in Baghdad, 235

Harran, north Syrian city, 253; description of, 254 et seq.; 257

Al-Hasaniyyah, fortress of al-Hasan near al-Safra', Medina, 195

Hatim, an illuminated wooden structure put up by the various sects in the Haram at Mecca, 98, 125, 153, 154, 183; description of, 98

Al-Hatim, wall enclosing the Hijr at the Ka'bah, 82

Hauran, 249

Al-Haythamayn, water-point on the Medina—Baghdad road, 217

Hejaz (Al-Hijaz), 25, 68; sectarianism of its population, 71; ill-treatment of pilgrims there, 71, 72; Saladin its lord, 250

Al-Hijr, sacred enclosure beside the Ka'bah, 81, 82, 83, 84, 98, 114, 115, 134, 135, 137, 142, 146, 148, 150, 155

Al-Hillah, city on the Euphrates, description of, 221-2, 213, 214

Hims. See Emessa.

Hira, Mount, near Mecca, 109; first verse of the Koran revealed on it to Muhammad, 110; cave at its summit whither Muhammad retired, 163, 165

Hisn al-Akrad (Castle of the Kurds), Frankish fortress in Syria, 265, 268

Hisn Bashir (al-Qantarah), 224

Hisn al-Jadid (The New Castle), near Medina, 195

Hisn al-Hammah (The Castle of the Thermal Water), Sicily, 350

Hisn al-'Uzzab (Castle of the Celibates), built by the caliph 'Umar near Medina, 206

Hunin (Chastiau Neuf), crusader fortress, 315

Iconium, city in Asia Minor, 355

Ikhmim (ancient Chemmis or Panopolis) on the Nile, description of its temple, 53-5, 56, 57. See note 33.

India, its merchants at Qus on the Nile, 57; its caravans in Egypt, 61; its ships at 'Aydhab, 63; its wood used to build the ships of 'Aydhab, 65; its products brought to Mecca, 117, 175

'Iraq, 66; its products in Mecca, 117-18; rough manners of its pilgrims in Mecca, 170, 186; 'Iraqis bring candles to Mecca, 183; its pilgrims form a large multitude, 81, 191; its glass, 284

Isfahan, Persian city, 190. See note 80.

Iskandarunah (Escandelion), crusader town between Acre and Tyre, 319

Islands of the Doves (Jaza'ir al-Hamam), 29. See note 9.

Iviza, Balearic Islands, 26, 364-5

al-Jadaydah, village on the Tigris, 242

Jaen, Spain, 25; resembles Qinnasrin, 264

Jaghjagh, river at Nisibis, 248

Al-Jam'. See Muzdalifah.

Jeliver (Shallabar), Spain, 25

Jerusalem (Bayt al-Maqdis), its mosque, 100; its temple, 296; distance from al-Karak, 301; its Dome of the Rock, 308; distance from Acre and Damascus, 324; Christian pilgrims to, 325

Jiddah, port for Mecca, customs exactions there, 48, 52, 62, 63, 64, 66, 68; navigational hazards of its approach, 69-70; its description, 70 et seq.; its ancient ruins, 70; place where Eve stayed, 70; mosque of 'Umar ibn al-Khattab, 70; mosque of Harun al-Rashid, 70; its inhabitants, 71; their harsh existence, 71; adjacent ancient city, reputedly Persian, with many cisterns, 71; Saladin abolishes the customs dues, 71, 74, 75

Al-Jisr, village in north Syria, 251

Al-Jizah. See Gizeh.

Judal, village between Mosul and Nisibis, 247

Al-Judi, mountain on which the Ark rested, 247; resort of hermits, 300

Julian, Mount St., in Sicily, 351-2

Ka'bah, the sacred shrine of Islam, called passim the Ancient or the Venerated House, 75; description of, 77 et seq.; its custodian, 77; its height, 77; its angles, 78; its

Kah'Bah,—*cont.*
door, 78, 87; its *Kiswah* or veil, 87-8, 185; its interior, 78-80, 89-90; its windows, 79; its Bab al-Rahmah, 79, 90; its dimensions, 81; the ceremony of opening its door, 88-9; its stones and construction, 94; birds never alight on it, 94; re-built by 'Abdullah ibn al-Zubayr, 136; washed with the water of Zamzam, 138; in the state of *ihram*, 169. *See also* Black Stone, Hatim, Hijr, Mizab, Multazam, Zamzam.

Kada', mountain pass near Mecca, 106

al-Kallasah, lime-kiln near the Damascus Mosque, 278

al-Karak (Kerak), crusader fortress in Transjordan, description of, 301; besieged by Saladin, 301, 311, 313-14; one of the principal Christian fortresses, 301

al-Karkh, quarter in Baghdad, 234. *See* note 102.

al-Kathib al-Ahmar (The Hill of the Red Sand), stands on the great road from Damascus to the Hejaz, 294

al-K.la.i (?), village belonging to Nisibis, 247

al-Khabur, river in north Syria, 253

al-Khadra (The Green), name of the Caliph Mu'awiyah's house in Damascus, 280

al-Khayf, at the edge of Mina, 162; its mosque, 162, 183, 184

al-Khubayb, a water-point near 'Aydhab, 63

Khulays, pilgrim caravan station north of Mecca, 191, 193

Khurasan, pilgrims from, 81, 181, 186, 191, 239; its products brought to Mecca, 117; its pilgrims bring candles to Mecca, 183; of the Hanafite rite, 183; a preacher from, 186; its ruler, 190

al-Kufah, city south of Baghdad, 214, 215, 217; its description, 219 *et seq.*; its mosque, 219; chief of its doctors, 229; bitumen on road from it to Basra, 238, 243

Latakia (al-Ladhiqiyah, Laodicea), Frankish city in northern Syria, 265, 331

Lawzah, water-point on the Medina—Baghdad pilgrim road, 218

Lebanon, Mountains of, 264, 265; resort of hermits, 300

Lebrilla, Spain, 365

Levanzo, island off west coast of Sicily, 352

Lorca, Spain, 365

al-Ma'arrah, Syrian city, 264

Mabraz, caravan rally-point at Qus, 59

al-Mada'in, city of Chosroes near Baghdad, 225

al-Maghrib, Mauretania, or North-West Africa, its pilgrims, 58; its *marja'*, or measure of surface, 274; its merchandise at Mecca, 117; its measure of weight, 120; season for sailing to, 326

Mahatt al-Laqitah, place between Qus and 'Aydhab, 59

al-Ma'jan, holy basin in the Ka'bah, 80

al-Makhruq, hill in the desert between Medina and Baghdad, 213

Majorca, island of, 26; its Almoravid ruler takes Bougie, 353, 354

al-Ma'la, Upper Mecca, 106, 136, 160

Malij, region in the Nile delta, 36

Manarat al-Qurun, minaret south of al-Kufah, 218

Manbij, north Syrian city (Hierapolis), 258-9

Manfalut, city on the Nile, its fine corn, 53

al-Manihah, village belonging to Damascus, 292

Manshat al-Sudan, city on the Nile, 56

al-Mansurah, Spain, 365

Maqam Ibrahim, the stone on which Abraham stood to build the Ka'bah, 77, 79; description of, 80; 81, 100, 130, 155, 163, 170; footprints of Abraham, 80; the sanctuary so called in the Haram, 75, 81, 82, 84, 86, 91, 94, 97, 98, 146, 151, 154, 155, 156, 159, 164, 186. See note 49.

al-Maqlah, hill between Misr and Qus, 51, 53

Maritimo, island west of Sicily, 352

Maridin, north Syrian city, 250

al-Marwah, elevated platform of ritual significance at Mecca, 76, 102; description of, 102-3, 105, 112, 118, 128, 149

al-Mas'a, ritual course between al-Marwah and al-Safa, traversed by the Emir of Mecca, 130; traversed by Saladin's brother, Sayf al-Islam, 149

al-Mash'ar, village near Hims (Emessa). 269

al-Masfalah, the lower part of Mecca, 105, 112

al-Masiyah, village near Banyas, 315

al-Ma'shuq, castle on the Tigris, former residence of al-Zubaydah, 241

Massuf, north African town, 289

Mayyafariqin, city of Diyar Bakr, 257

Mecca (Makkah or Bakkah), passim, 48, 52, 53, 66, 70, 75; its Haram and Ka'bah, 77 et seq.; its monuments and history, 105 et seq.; its gates, 106; its cemetery, 106; its sacred or inviolable territory, 108; its walls, 110; its illustrious shrines, 110 et seq.; special favours conferred on it by God, 116 et seq.; its abundant produce brought from many lands during the pilgrimage, 116 et seq.; infested by thieves, 119; prices, 120; baths, 123; its faculty of expanding to include the pilgrims, 174; 175, 184, 185; fruits brought to it from Batn Marr, 119; 189, 233, 342. See also Haram.

Medina (al-Madinah or Madinat al-Nabi, 'The City of the Apostle of God'), 48, 52, 53, 67; wall built by Jamal al-Din, 123; 147; also called Taybah, 168; 196, 197; its sacred territory, 197; its haram and the tomb of Muhammad, 198 et seq.; its cemetery, Baqi' al-Gharqad, 203; its gates, 206; the Prophet's fountain, 206; 212, 214, 233, 342. See Mosque of Medina.

Medina Sidonia (Madinat Ibn al-Salim), Spain, 25

Memphis, Egypt, Joseph imprisoned there, 50; store where he laid up the grain (Gen. xli. 35), 50

Messina, Sicily, 321, 336, 337; description of, 338 et seq.; Straits of, 336

Mil, the green milestones on the Mas'a at Mecca, 102-3

Mina, valley on the road from Mecca to 'Arafah where the pilgrims perform certain ceremonies, 109; description of, 160; its ceremonies, 160-2, 176, 177, 183; its markets, 184-5

Minorca, island of, 26

Misr (Old Cairo), 35, 36; its colleges, 42; its walls, 43; its hospital, 44; bridges to its west constructed by Saladin, 45; traces of the fire of, 46; antiquities, 46; 47, 49, 50, 51, 52, 53, 58, 67, 74

al-Mizzah, village belonging to Damascus, 288

Mizab, the Water-Spout of the Ka'bah, 82, 83, 115, 116

Mongo (Jabal Qu'un), mountain near Denia, Spain, 365

Mercy, Mount of. See Rahmah, Jabal al-.

Mercy, Mount of (Jabal al-Rahmah), near Badr, 194
Mosque:
of Abraham at Munyat Ibn al-Khasib, Egypt, 51
of Abraham at al-Zahir near Mecca, 108
of Abraham on Mount of Mercy, 179
of Abu Bakr at Mecca, 112
of 'A'ishah near Mecca, 109, 128, 136
al Aqdam near Damascus, 293
of Aleppo, 262
of 'Ali near Mecca, 136
of 'Ali near Medina, 207
of the Blessed Covenant near Mina, 160
of 'Amr ibn al-'As in Misr, 36, 42, 46
of 'Amr ibn al-'As in Alexandria, 46
near the Cairn of al-'Aqabah, 161
of the Caliph, Baghdad, 237
'Umayyad of Damascus, 272 et seq. See Mosque of Damascus, below.
of Daud at Ikhmim, Egypt, 53
of Dhu 'l-Hulayfah near Medina, 196-7
Dhu 'l-Nun at Ikhmim, 53
of al-Fath (of Victory) near Medina, 207
of Jerusalem, 100
of Hamzah on Mount Uhud, 203
of Harran, 256
of Harun al-Rashid at Jiddah, 70
of al-Khayf at Mina, 162, 183, 184
of Ibn Tulun between Misr and Cairo, 44, 74
of al-Kufah, 219; oratory of Abraham, 219; site of 'Ali's assassination, 220; site of the earth's boiling for Noah, 220; Enoch's oratory, 220; place where Noah's Ark was built, 220; 'Ali's house, 220; house of Noah's daughter, 220
of al-Mansur at Baghdad, 234
Great, of Mecca. See under Haram.
or Haram of Medina, its dimensions, 100, 198; improvements effected

by Jamal al-Din, 123; the Prophet's pulpit there, 197, 210; description of, and of the Prophet's tomb, 198 et seq., 274
of Mount Abu Qubays, 103
of al-Qu' a, 205
al-Rusafah, Baghdad, 238
of Salman near Medina, 207
of the Sultan at Baghdad, 237
of 'Umar ibn al-Khattab at Jiddah, 70
Mosque of Damascus, the Great or 'Umayyad Mosque, its description, 272-83, 305-8; re-built by the Caliph al-Walid ibn 'Abd al-Malik, 272; its cost, 272; once a Christian church, 273; captured by the Muslims, 273; a tradition of the Prophet about it, 273; its dimensions and the number of doors and windows, 274 et seq.; 'Umar ibn 'Abd al 'Aziz (Omar II) indemnifies the Christians for it, 273; the Lead Dome, 274, 275, 305-8; the Gharib (central nave), 274, 275, 307; Maqsurah of the Companions, 276; the New Maqsurah, 276; court and arcades, 276-7; minarets, 277; revenues, 277-8; 'A'ishah, a tradition concerning, 278; the Water Cage, 278; 'Ali ibn Abi Talib, his nearby shrine, 278; twice burnt, 279; the Mihrab, 279; the Koran of 'Uthman, 279; the doors, 279-80; al-Husayn ibn 'Ali, his head preserved here, 280; the water clock, 281; endowments, 283; John the Baptist, his head preserved here, 284; ascent of the Lead Dome and a description of the interior, 305-8
Mosul, 188, 239; its ruler Mu'izz al-Din, 190; its pilgrims, 191; its merchants, 240; its bitumen, 242; description of, 243 et seq.; tomb of St. George, 244; 249, 255, 257
Mujaj, water-point between Qus and 'Aydhab, 61

Muhassir, valley between Muzdalifah and Mina, 177, 183

al-Multazam, place of prayer in the Ka'bah, 76; its situation, 78, 94, 130, 138, 146

al-Munyah, suburb of Qus, 58

al-Munyah, near Cairo, 36

Munyat ibn al-Khasib, Nile City, 50, 51, 55

Murcia, Spain, 26, 365

al-Mustajar (Place of Refuge), wall in the Ka'bah, 83

al-Muwaylihah, village between Mosul and Nisibis, 247

Muzdalifah (The Approacher), plain and mosque between Mina and 'Arafat, also called al-Ma'shar al-Haram and al-Jam', 173, 177, 182, 183

al-Na'am. See Bahr al-Na'am.

al-Nabk, village between Hims (Emessa) and Damascus, 269

Nablus, Palestine, captured by Saladin, 314

al-Najaf, a hill near al-Kufah, 219

Najd, or Nejd, Arabia, salubrious climate, 212, 213, 267

Nakhlah, valley near Mecca, 119

Nasibin. See Nisibis.

al-Nayrab, village near Damascus, 288, 293

al-Nil, canal of the Euphrates near al-Hillah, 223

Nile, River, 32, 35; bridges built by Saladin near Misr, 45, 46; the Nilometer, 47; 48, 50, 51, 53, 56; dam near Manshat al-Sudan, 57, 226

Niniveh (Ninawa), Jonah's city, 245

Nisibis (Nasibin), 247; description of, 248-50, 257

al-Nizamiyah, college at Baghdad, 228, 229; description of, 238

Nuqrah, water-point in the Najd, 212

Orient (i.e. Damascus), facilities for students, 298-9; resort of ascetics and anchorites, 300; generosity of Orientals to strangers, 299; enthusiastic welcome of returning pilgrims, 299-300

Orontes (al-'Asi), River, 265-7, 270

Osuna (Oshunah), Spain, 25

Palermo (al-Madinah), capital of Sicily, main centre of the Muslims, 340, 348; its shipyard, 343; palaces of the king, 340, 346, 348; its description, 348 et seq.; Muslims practise their faith, 348; ladies' fashions, 349-50; its Church of the Antiochian, 349

Persia, of the Hanafite rite, 98; language of, 186, 208

Pharaonic Sea, its famous storms, 67-8

al-Qadisiyah, village near al-Kufah, 218

Qal 'at Najm, ancient castle on the upper Euphrates, 258

Qal 'at Yahsub (Alcala la Real), Spanish town, 277

Qalyub, on the Nile delta, 36

al-Qantarah, village between al-Hillah and Baghdad, also called Hisn Bashir, 224

al-Qar'a', water-point on the Medina-al-Kufah road, 218

al-Qarafah, the Cairo cemetery, tombs of the kinsmen of the Prophet, 38-9; tombs of the ladies of the house of 'Ali, 39; tombs of some Companions of the Prophet, of their followers, and of imams, ascetics, etc., 39, 40-2; its school, 40; Sepulchre of the Martyrs, 42; monthly financial allocation from the Sultan, 40, 42

al-Qarah, village between Hims and Damascus, 269

al-Qarin (al-Qurayn), pilgrim station near Mecca, 75

al-Qarurah, water-point in the Nejd, 212

Qasiyun, Mount, near Damascus, cave where Abraham was born, 285; scene of Abel's killing, 285; cave where Jesus and various prophets 'prayed, 286; place where the Messiah and His mother took shelter, 271, 287; oratory of Elijah, 287

al-Qasr, Sufi convent near Damascus, 297

al-Qasr, castle at Zarud in the Nejd, 215

Qasr Ja'far (Ja'far's Castle), near Palermo, 346

Qasr Masmudah or Qasr al-Kabir (Alcazar) on the Moroccan coast, 26

al-Qasr al-Qadim (The Old Castle) at Palermo, 349

Qasr Sa'd, castle with a mosque near Palermo, the resort of Muslims, 345

al-Qayarah, place near the Tigris, 242

Qift, city of Upper Egypt, 57

Qila' al-Diya', place between Qus and 'Aydhab, 59

Qina, city of Upper Egypt, ways of its women, 57

Qinnasrin, town of north Syria, resembles Jaen, 263

al-Qu'ayqi'an, Mount, near Mecca, 127

Quba', town close to Medina, 197, 205

al-Qurayn, staging post for pilgrims near Mecca, 75

al-Qurayah, quarter of Baghdad, 234

Qus, city of Upper Egypt, 50, 51, 52, 53, 55; its fine markets 57; 58, 59, 60

al-Qusayr, near the Orontes, has a large khan, 270

al-Quwayq, river at Aleppo, 263

Rahbat al-Sham, north Syrian city, 258

Rahmah, Jabal al-(Mount of Mercy), isolated hill on 'Arafat, its composition, 178; Dome of Umm Salimah, 178; 179, 182; wall attributed to Abraham, 179

Rahmah, Jabal al-, near Badr, 194

al-Raqqah, city on the Euphrates, 258

Ra's al-'Ayn, north Syrian city, 250; its description, 252-3

Rastan (Arethusa), Syria, destroyed by 'Umar ibn al-Khattab, 267

al-Rawha. See Dhat al-'Alam.

Rawiyah, village near Damascus, 292

Red Sea (Bahr al-Qulzum or Pharaonic Sea), crusader fleet there, 52; see also note 31; ships that ply on it, 65; its famous storms, 67-8; its reefs, 68

Reggio (Rayah), Calabria, 339

Roda (al-Rawdah), island on the Nile between Misr and Gizah, 47

al-Ruhbah, village near al-Kufah, 218

Rumah, well at Medina, 206

al-Rusafah, quarter of Baghdad, 235; cathedral mosque and tombs of the 'Abbasid caliphs there, 238

Sa on the Nile delta, 35

al-Safa (hard rock), an eminence of ritual, 76, 102; significance at Mecca, 105, 106, 112; description of, 102-3; 104, 118, 128, 149, 171

al-Safra, valley near Medina, 147, 194, 196

Sa'id (Upper Egypt), 51, 53, 55, 57, 72

Samarra (Surra man ra'a), city on the Tigris, 241

al-Samawah, in the Syrian desert, 269

Samirah, on the Medina – Baghdad pilgrim road, 213

Samosata (Sumaysat) on the Euphrates, 302

al-Sarah, mountains in the Yemen, 131

Sardinia, 26; its dangerous sea, 27, 28, 363, 364

Sarsar, village south of Baghdad, 225, 226

Saruj, city of south Turkey, 258

Satan's Mount, Medina, 206

Seville, resembles Hims (Emessa), 268, 283

Shaghib, water-point between Qus and 'Aydhab, 60, 61

al-Shari', quarter of Baghdad, 234

al-Shaykh wa 'l-'Ajuz (The Old Man and the Old Woman), mountains in the island of Iviza, 365

Shi'b 'Ali ('Ali's Pass), on the road from Mecca to Medina, 196

al-Shubaykah, well near al-Zahir, 107, 108

al-Shuquq, water-point on the Medina – Baghdad road, 216

Sicily, 26, 28, 29, 66, 331, 332, 335, 336; its ruler's dominions in Italy, 335; its fertility, 339; condition of the Muslims amongst the Christians, 339; earthquake on, 341. See William, King of, and the towns under their names.

Sierra Nevada Mountains, Spain, 25

Sinai, Mount (Jabal Abu Tur), 67

Sinjar, city north of the Euphrates, 249

Spain, 117, 264, 339, 352, 353

Sphinx (Abu 'l-Ahwal), of Egypt, 46

Subk, on the Nile delta, 36

Sul, in the Caucasus, 331. See note 147.

Syracuse, 340

Syria, 66, 72, 190, 239; merchants of, 240, 243, 250, 255, 258, 279; custom dues levied by the Franks, 316, 317, 322

Tabor, Mount (Jabal al-Tur) near Nazareth, 324

al-Ta 'if, city near Mecca, 106; provides fruits to Mecca, 119

Takrit, city on the Tigris, 241

Tamanni, a khan between Aleppo and Hamah, 264

al-Tananir, water-point on the Medina – Baghdad road, 217

Tandatah, village of the Nile delta, 36

al-Tan 'im, near Mecca, 107, 128

Tarifa, Island of, 25

Taybah, name for Medina, 168

Tell 'Abdah, near Harran, 257

Tell Tajir, near Aleppo, 263

Tell al-'Uqab, village near Ra's al-'Ayn belonging to Christians paying tribute, 251

Termini (Tharmah), Sicily, 344-5

Thabir, Mount, near Mecca, 162

al-Tha 'labiyah, fort and water-point on the Mecca – Baghdad pilgrim road, 215

Thaniyyat al-'Uqab (The Eagle's Pass), near Damascus, 269

Thawra, water course near Mount Qasiyun, Damascus, 287

Tiberias, its Count, 324; on easy caravan route to Damascus, 324; its lake, 324; its tombs of prophets, 324

Tibnin (Thoron), Frankish fortress, 315, 316; on rough mule route to Damascus, 324

Tigris, River, 224, 225, 226, 234, 235, 236, 240, 241, 242, 243, 244, 245

Tihamah, on the Hejaz coast, 212

Trapani (Itrabanish), 350; description of, 351 et seq.

Tripoli, Syria, Count of, 324

al-Tu 'aman (The Twins), two forts at al-Safra, 195

Tubul, Jabal al- (Mount of the Drums), its legend, 194

Tunis, 351

Turban, place between Mecca and Medina, 196

Tyre (Sur), its glass, 284; description of, 319 et seq.; its impregnability, 319; better rapport of its citizens with the Muslims, 319; its Gates, 319; its port, 320; a wedding, 320; captured by the Franks, 321; surrounded by gardens, 325; abundance of water, 325

Ubhur, port on the Red Sea near Jiddah, 69

al-'Udhayb, fertile valley near al-Kufah, 218

Uhud, Mount, near Medina, tombs on its slopes, 203 et seq.; cave where the Prophet sheltered, 203; Battle of, 206

al-'Uqaybah, village on the Tigris, 243

'Uranah, valley near 'Arafat, 178

al-'Ushara', water-point between Qus and 'Aydhab, 61, 63

'Usfan, place north of Mecca, 190

Uswan, Assuan or Aswan. See Aswan.

Usyut. See Assiut.

'Usaylah, Ma' al-, water-point in the Najd, 212

al-Wadah, sandy stretch between Qus and 'Aydhab, 62, 63

Wadi 'l-Arak at 'Arafat, 179

Wadi 'l-'Arus, water-point on the Medina – Baghdad pilgrim road, 212

Wadi 'l-Kurush, valley on the Medina – Baghdad road, 213

Wadi 'l-Samk, valley between Mecca and Medina, 193

Waqisah, water-point on the Medina – Baghdad pilgrim road, 215, 217

al-Wasitah, quarter of Baghdad, 235

Wasit, swamp on the old course of the Tigris, 226

Yemen (al-Yaman), its merchandise, 52, 57; best camel-litters made there, 60; merchandise of India goes through it, 61; its ships at 'Aydhab, 63; its timber used for ships, 65; 72, 99; its products in Mecca, 117-8; Sayf al-Islam goes there, 147, 175; Saladin its Lord, 251

Yanbu', on the Red Sea, 147

al-Zahir, village north of Mecca, 107; its wells, 108; Mosque of Abraham, 108; 148, 188; its palm-trees and spring, 189

Zamzam, Well of, in the Haram at Mecca, 76, 80, 97; the dawariq or earthen jars for cooling its water, 84; its depth, 84; its Dome, 76, 81, 84, 86, 93, 96, 97, 99, 135, 142; properties of the water, 121; a story, 125-6; its water used to wash the Ka'bah, 138; its alleged rising, 140-3; 152, 157, 158-9

Zante, 332

Zariran, village south of Baghdad, 224, 225

Zarud, station on the Medina – Baghdad pilgrim road, 215

al-Zib (Casal Imbert), Frankish fortress on the Syrian coast, 319

Zubalah, water-point on the Medina – Baghdad pilgrim road, 215, 217

Western Forms of Names occurring in the Text

Abel – Habil
Abraham – Ibrahim
Acre – 'Akka
Africa, North – Barr al-Gharb
Alcamo – Alqamah
Alcaudete – Al Qabdaq
Alcazar – Qasr Masmudah
Aleppo – Halab
Alexandria – Iskandariyah
Arcos – Arkash
Arethusa – Rastan
Assiut – Usyut
Assuan – Uswan

Baalbak – Ba'labakk
Barcelona – Barshlunah
Belinas – Banyas
Bougie – Bijayah

Cabra – Qabrah
Cain – Qabil
Canalis di Baza – Qanalis
Cape St. Mark – Qawsamarkah
Cartagena – Qartajannah
Casal Imbert – Al-Zib
Casma – Qashmah
Cefalu – Shafludi
Ceuta – Sabtah
Chastiau Neuf – Hunin
Chemmis – Ikhmim
Chosroes – Kisra
Cilician Gates – Darb; pl. Darub
Cordova – Qurtabah
Crete – Iqritish
Constantinople – Al-Qustantiniyah

Damascus – Dimishq
Denia – Daniyah

Ecija – Istijah
Egypt – Diyar Misr

Elijah – Khidr
Elim – 'Aqabah of Aylah
Emessa – Hims
Enoch – Idris
Escandelion – Iskandarunah
Ethiopia – Ard al-Habash
Euphrates – Al-Furat
Eve – Hawwa

Fatimids – 'Ubaydin
Favignana – Al-Rahib
Formentera – Faramantirah

Gabriel, Angel – Jibra'il
Galita – Khalita
Genoa – Janua
George, St. – Jirjis
Gizeh – Al-Jizah
Granada – Ghranatah
Guadix – Wadi Ash

Hajar – Ajar

Iconium – Qunyah
Iviza – Yabisah

Jaen – Jayyan
Jeliver – Shallabar
Jerusalem – Bayt al-Maqdis
Jesus – 'Isa
Job – Ayyub
John the Baptist – Yahya ibn Zakariya'
Jonah – Yunus
Joseph – Yusuf

Kerak – Al-Karak

Latakia – Al-Ladhiqiyah
Lebrilla – Libralah
Levanzo – Yabisah
Lorca – Lurqah
Lot – Lut

Marettimo– Malitimah
Marra – Ma'arrat al-Nu'man
Mary – Maryam
Mauretania – Al-Maghrib
Mecca – Makkah or Bakkah
Medina – Al-Madinah
Medina Sidonia – Madinat Ibn al-Salim
Messiah, the – Al-Masih
Moses – Musa

Niniveh – Ninawa
Nisibis – Nasibin
Noah – Nuh
Nureddin – Nur al-Din

Orontes – Al 'Asi
Osunah – Ushunah

Palermo – Al-Madinah

Koran – Qarun

Red Sea – Bahr al-Qulzum
Reggio – Rayah
Roda – Al-Rawdah

Saladin – Salah al-Din
Samosata – Sumaysat
Seth – Shayth
Seville – Ishbiliyah
Sinai, Mount – Jabal Abu Tur
Soloman – Sulayman
Syracuse – Sarqusah
Syria – Suriyah

Tabor, Mount – Jabal al-Tur
Termini – Tharmah
Thomas – Tuma
Thoron – Tibnin
Tigris – Al-Dajlah
Trapani – Itrabanish
Tripoli (North Africa) – Tarabalis al-Gharb
Tripoli (Syria) – Tarabalis al-Sham
Tyre – Sur
Tukush Shah – Al-Daqus
Tuldequinas – Tughtagin
(Sayf al-Islam)

Yenbo – Yanbu'
Yemen – Al-Yaman

ISBN 81-87570-26-1

ISBN 81-87570-71-7

ISBN 81-87570-45-8

ISBN 81-87570-53-9

ISBN 81-87570-67-9

ISBN 81-87570-52-0

ISBN 81-87570-61-X

ISBN 81-87570-16-4

ISBN 81-87570-90-7

ISBN 81-87570-14-8

ISBN 0-7195-5143-9

ISBN 81-85063-38-9

ISBN 81-85063-68-0

ISBN 81-85063-73-7

ISBN 81-87570-03-2

ISBN 81-85063-84-2

Man Know Thyself

Maulana Wahiduddin Khan

Search for Truth

Maulana Wahiduddin Khan

The Concept of God

Maulana Wahiduddin Khan

The Creation Plan of God

Maulana Wahiduddin Khan

The Man Islam Builds

Maulana Wahiduddin Khan

Non-Violence and Islam

Maulana Wahiduddin Khan

Islamic Fundamentalism

Maulana Wahiduddin Khan

The Shariah and Its Application

Maulana Wahiduddin Khan

Muhammad: The Ideal Character

Maulana Wahiduddin Khan

Polygamy and Islam

Maulana Wahiduddin Khan

Uniform Civil Code
A CRITICAL STUDY

Maulana Wahiduddin Khan

The Way to Find God

Maulana Wahiduddin Khan

The Teachings of Islam

Maulana Wahiduddin Khan

The Good Life

Maulana Wahiduddin Khan

The Garden of Paradise

Maulana Wahiduddin Khan

The Fire of Hell

Maulana Wahiduddin Khan